The Organization of Higher Education

The Organization of Higher Education

Managing Colleges for a New Era

Edited by
MICHAEL N. BASTEDO

The Johns Hopkins University Press
Baltimore

© 2012 The Johns Hopkins University Press
All rights reserved. Published 2012
Printed in the United States of America on acid-free paper
2 4 6 8 9 7 5 3 1

The Johns Hopkins University Press
2715 North Charles Street
Baltimore, Maryland 21218-4363
www.press.jhu.edu

Library of Congress Cataloging-in-Publication Data

The organization of higher education : managing colleges for a new era / edited
by Michael N. Bastedo.
p. cm.
Includes bibliographical references and index.
ISBN-13: 978-1-4214-0447-9 (hardcover : alk. paper)
ISBN-13: 978-1-4214-0448-6 (pbk. : alk. paper)
ISBN-10: 1-4214-0447-8 (hardcover : alk. paper)
ISBN-10: 1-4214-0448-6 (pbk. : alk. paper)
1. Universities and colleges—Administration.   2. Organizational
change.   I. Bastedo, Michael N.
LB2341.O819 2012
378.1'01—dc23   2011023111

A catalog record for this book is available from the British Library.

*Special discounts are available for bulk purchases of this book. For more information,
please contact Special Sales at 410-516-6936 or specialsales@press.jhu.edu.*

The Johns Hopkins University Press uses environmentally friendly book
materials, including recycled text paper that is composed of at least 30 percent
post-consumer waste, whenever possible.

To Marvin W. Peterson
Esteemed scholar of higher education organizations,
patient mentor to hundreds of students,
colleague and friend to administrators and faculty from around the world

CONTENTS

PART ONE

REVIEWING THE FIELD

CHAPTER ONE

Organizing Higher Education

A Manifesto

MICHAEL N. BASTEDO

Modern organization theory is built upon the study of colleges and universities. Resource dependence theory resulted from studies of power and the budgetary process at the University of Illinois (Pfeffer, 2005; Pfeffer & Salancik, 1974, 1978). "Old" institutional theory was built upon studies of adult education and community colleges (Clark, 1956, 1960) and "new" institutional theory on studies of college "chartering" effects (Kamens, 1971, 1974, 1977; Meyer, 1970) prior to extensive work in K–12 schools (Meyer & Rowan, 1978; Meyer & Scott, 1983). Organizational culture was built in the 1980s upon studies of distinctive liberal arts colleges conducted over a decade earlier (Clark, 1970, 1972, 2008). "Garbage can" theory was constructed entirely from a study of college presidential leadership (Cohen & March, 1986), and "loose coupling" was based on observations of schools and universities (Weick, 1976). The major frameworks not founded on studies of colleges—primarily organizational ecology and transaction-cost economics—are few and far between.

In turn, higher education as an organizational form has never been more powerful. Colleges and universities, through their research, disciplines, and academic programs, increasingly define the legitimacy of knowledge in modern society (Clark, 1983; Frank & Meyer, 2007). Even as the university comes under attack for its high costs and lack of attention to student learning, the university's role in defining what is known, how it should be known, and what should be pursued as knowledge in the future is largely taken for granted. This is a phenomenon that translates to higher education not simply in the developed world but also, through the massive expansion of higher education, in nearly every developing country (Schofer & Meyer, 2005), leading to pervasive efforts to establish "world class" universities in countries both large and small (Salmi, 2009).

The nature of academic work—autonomous, driven by knowledge generation,

insisting on precision and originality, embedded in cutting-edge technology, conducted 24/7, and supported by a wide range of personal services—has become a
model for how to organize elite, professional life in modern society. Higher education has thus defined not just what it means to be a student but what it means
to be an employee after college. College-educated people increasingly expect to
have autonomy in their work and expect that work to contribute to their own
learning. They expect the work they do to add value to *themselves* in addition to
value for their company. And like higher education, they increasingly want their
work to add value to the world beyond their business and to be engaged in nonprofit and philanthropic efforts on a routine basis.

People like to talk about how "higher education is becoming more like a business," but the reverse is more provably true: business is becoming more like
higher education. Consulting firms, law firms, and hospitals have long operated
as quasi universities at the top of the professional prestige hierarchy (Abbott,
1988). But now companies like Microsoft, Google, and Xerox are organized as
campuses rather than as traditional firms. Employees are recruited using rigorous exams, certifications, and auditions and have far more autonomy than in
traditional firms. Research and development functions have become greatly expanded in the quest for innovation, and "firms as campuses" have become total
institutions (Goffman, 1961) that provide transportation, personal services,
gyms, and entertainment to facilitate 24/7 work schedules.

Even sabbaticals are migrating to firms. In 2008, 38% of large to mid-sized
companies allowed some form of paid or unpaid leave to employees (Galinsky,
Sakai, & Wigton, 2010). General Mills, Goldman Sachs, Timberland, American
Express, Hallmark, and Procter & Gamble all offer three months or more of fully
paid sabbatical leave to some employees, and many more offer one to three
months of paid leave. A consulting firm, yourSABBATICAL.com, seeks to advise
corporate human resource departments on how to design their sabbatical leave
policies. Tim Ferriss (2009), a best-selling author and self-styled lifestyle design
expert, promotes the idea of "mini-retirements" from work. "Though it can be
relaxing, the mini-retirement is not an escape from your life but a reexamination
of it—the creation of a blank slate . . . where meetings, e-mail, and phone calls
don't exist for a set period of time" (p. 256).

A whole new subset of organizations now exist in the space between for-profit
firms and nonprofit organizations. These are sometimes called B corporations,
for-benefit corporations, or low-profit limited liability corporations (L3Cs). In
2006, a group of Stanford graduates formed B Lab, which certifies companies
that fulfill a pledge to consider social responsibility beyond simply the needs of

shareholders. Each year, 10% of B corporations are audited by B Lab to ensure their continued commitment to socially responsible behavior. In early 2011, there were nearly four hundred certified B corporations earning almost $2 billion in corporate revenue, and B corporations can now be legally chartered in the state of Maryland. According to his official biography, B Lab cofounder Jay Coen Gilbert has enjoyed two sabbaticals in Australia and Costa Rica.

Understanding higher education has an immense amount to contribute to our comprehension of organizations, knowledge generation, and our society writ large. Yet the study of organizational topics within higher education is in sharp decline, owing largely to a lack of perceived connection between organization theory and major contemporary concerns in higher education, such as student access, cost escalation, and social justice. Questions related to governance, elite leaders, and field dynamics have been emphasized disproportionately, and major questions—who will attend college, who stays in college, how much do students learn, how much should college cost, how the equity and stratification in our higher education system can be improved—have, with notable exceptions, been largely ignored or marginalized.

As a result, scholars of higher education interested in access, equity, and social justice often fail to see the usefulness of organization theory, and scholars of organization theory see themselves as disconnected from the rest of the field. This disconnect is intellectually unnecessary and unproductive and limits the impact of organizational scholarship on the field of higher education. I would argue that if this trend continues, it threatens the very survival of organizational studies in the field.

This book seeks to reinvigorate the study of higher education as an organization. The book's authors seek to address these criticisms by reevaluating and reconsidering the state of the field of higher education organizations and proposing lines of inquiry for the future. In the first half of the book, we reconsider our existing theories of higher education organizations, most of which have been taught and used since at least the 1970s. In the second half of the book, we address new theories of organizations that have particular applicability in the modern context. As a result, we are seeking to become both a primer on the contemporary study of higher education organizations and a message to the field about the potential of pursuing new avenues of research.

This chapter lays out an argument about the state of organization theory in higher education. In particular, I argue that the great achievements of organization theory have left a disproportionate mark on the field, causing us to overemphasize issues in the organizational environment, which focuses attention almost exclusively on the organizational elites who interact with that environment: presidents, trustees, and other public policymakers. This chapter examines how this evolved historically and provides an agenda for using organization theory to study the most pressing issues facing higher education today.

But first: How did we get here?

What Is the State of Organization Theory in Higher Education?

THE RISE OF OPEN SYSTEMS MODELS

The state of organization theory in higher education was reviewed many times by Marvin Peterson, to whom this book is warmly dedicated. By 1974, open systems models were already sharply in ascendancy, viewing higher education as embedded in an environment that drives resources (Peterson, 1974). The relationship between government and higher education was rapidly gaining in importance, and field-level collaborations were emerging to adapt to environmental pressures, such as regional accreditation agencies and consortia. Studies of governance and decision making were prevalent, but studies of organizational practice below the top leaders were sparse—a concern that has been echoed again and again over the decades.

By the 1980s, open systems models had firmly taken hold over organizational scholarship and were elaborated to address issues of organizational culture, university strategy, and adaptation in turbulent environments (Peterson, 1985, 1986). The major theoretical traditions developed during the 1970s—resource dependence, institutional theory, anarchical models, organizational culture and climate, strategy and organizational change—yielded a rich variety of studies in higher education, leading to a fertile period of research into the 1990s that is still widely read and cited today. Indeed, these studies provide the foundation for courses in higher education, and these traditions are reconsidered and reinterpreted throughout this book.

Over the course of the 1990s, there was a shift in emphasis toward studying more field-level phenomena, including globalization, for-profit models of higher education, and virtual universities. Peterson (2007) sees this as a shift in higher education toward a postsecondary knowledge industry characterized by high levels of interdependence, innovation, and entrepreneurship. As is often the case, our theorizing itself has modeled the emerging shifts in higher education toward business practices and revenue-driven decision making, instead of looking at higher education as a traditional institution and conservator of knowledge (Gumport, 2000).

As a result, our organizational thinking has moved increasingly toward strategic models (Gumport, chap. 2; Toma, chap. 5). We also see this in the rise of impression management through marketing, branding, and development (Hartley & Morphew, 2008). In addition, our thinking has tended toward structural and functionalist accounts of organizational change, instead of looking more broadly from postmodern and other philosophical perspectives (Kezar, chapter 7; Kezar & Dee, forthcoming).

It also reflects a push toward field-level dynamics in organization theory more broadly, and institutional theory in particular (Bastedo, 2007, 2009a, 2009b; Walsh, Meyer, & Schoonhoven, 2006). As a result, studies of the relationship between public policy and higher education gained even further, and the study of higher education politics has become particularly fruitful in recent years (Bastedo, 2005, 2007; Hearn & McLendon, chap. 3; Lane, chap. 10). The study of college rankings alone has become a minor industry of research (Bastedo & Bowman, 2011; Pusser & Marginson, chap. 4). In turn, topics more internal to higher education, such as organizational culture and loose coupling, have been declining in the literature (Tierney, chap. 6). Decision analysis and psychological models are almost entirely absent.

As Peterson (1985) notes, we have often failed to critique organizational frameworks drawn from management, sociology, and other disciplines for their fit to the higher education context. Instead, an implicit assumption has been that these frameworks apply to higher education without need for substantial revision or elaboration. Often there is good reason to believe this would be true. As I noted earlier in this chapter, the major theoretical frameworks in organizational studies were built upon empirical studies of higher education in diverse forms and contexts, from community colleges to major research universities.

However, there are two major issues to consider. First, the most deeply elaborated versions of these theories were created with many organizational types in mind, across firms, governments, and other nonprofit organizations. So while the empirical base was often higher education, the express purpose was to find the elements of higher education organizations that resonated in a broader range of organizational types. Second, these theories were developed by people outside the field of higher education, with the purpose of creating generalizable theories. Thus these scholars may not share the same depth of interest, concern, or expertise in higher education as scholars within the field or the desire to create theories that are nuanced and adaptive to differences across subunits (e.g., technology transfer, multicultural centers) or across stakeholders (e.g., presidents, staff, faculty, students, alumni).

THE DECLINE OF WORK

We also need to consider how open systems approaches have driven us to understand the influence of environments better than the nature of work itself. Certainly, there is no escaping that all organizations are embedded in field dynamics around resources and norms that influence most of what we do. However, our theorizing seems incapable of escaping environments, to the extent that the nature of the work that we do—the administration, management, teaching, and learning that we do every day—has little influence on our theorizing.

What does it mean to study work? On one level, work is so ambiguous that most sociological studies seem reluctant to define it (Barley & Kunda, 2001). The accepted definitions are thus almost obscenely broad. Thus, "Work tends to be an activity that transforms nature and is usually undertaken in social situations" (Grint, 2009, p. 6). In addition, defining work can be seen as a political act, privileging some forms of "transforming nature" over other forms, particularly along dimensions of class, race, and gender. For our purposes, however, I believe work in higher education is the tasks, problems, and cognitive demands faced by students, faculty, and administrators in the university.

Work itself is an immensely important activity and crucial to a complete understanding of the organizational dimensions of educational practice. Unfortunately, within organization theory, work has become synonymous with administration and connotes an old-fashioned approach to organizations (Barley, 1996; Barley & Kunda, 2001). It connotes dreariness, embedded in notions of bureaucracy, paperwork, and red tape. We have an outmoded impression of work, and this is a serious mistake. The nature of our work—the tasks we face, the problems embedded in those tasks, and their cognitive demands—is often more determinant of organizational outcomes than the demands placed by the environment. The influence of information technology and social networks, changes and developments in the disciplines, emerging understanding of student cognition and learning, the externalization and commodification of low-status work—these are not merely environmental demands. They change the nature of work itself, yet these issues have been deemphasized by organizations scholars in our nearly exclusive focus on externally driven pressures and processes.

How have we moved away from work? The disciplines are studied more for their interlocking networks of journals and professional organizations than for the ways they construct and define knowledge. Academic research is studied more as a form of technology transfer and academic capitalism than as the passionate pursuit of knowledge (Neumann, 2009). Adjunct faculty are studied primarily as unionized negotiators seeking adequate pay and legitimacy. Information technology is treated as a broad spectrum of rapidly evolving environmental demands rather than a cognitive structure that changes the nature of tasks, roles, and rewards.

Our lack of theorizing about work results in a distortion in our understanding of higher education stakeholders. We have a far better understanding of the work of college presidents and trustees than we do of academic deans or vice presidents, much less lower-level administrative and academic managers. We might have almost nothing if it were not for the proliferation of professional communities centered on admissions, technology transfer, registrars, and student affairs administrators, among many others. Even our pedagogical case studies are overwhelmingly focused on presidential leadership, governance, and public policy influences. It is no surprise that students with inherent interests in those stakeholders see organization theory as intellectual leverage for conducting empirical research, and students with interests in other stakeholders—faculty and students in particular—often do not. And the result is that administrators increasingly find the academic study of organizations distant from their problems, concerns, and leadership aspirations.

THE RETREAT FROM PRACTICE

These two interrelated trends—the emergence of open systems models and the decline of the study of work—have resulted in a retreat from educational practice itself. This has had enormous impact on the relevance of our models for the daily work of educators and managers while also impoverishing the quality of our theorizing. As organization theorists in higher education had less and less practical administrative experience, they increasingly sought their idea of disciplinary legitimacy in exciting new areas of theory, and the study of administrative practice became distinctly uncool. Yet to remain useful and relevant, organization theorists in our field must address issues of common concern in education and leverage our deep knowledge of higher education to develop insights that scholars in other disciplines and professions are unlikely to discover (Ball & Forzani, 2007; Heath & Sitkin, 2001).

This is in many ways consistent with the call to develop a distinctive scholarship of higher education organizations (Peterson, 1985) but shifts the focus in a new direction. Few people in higher education are either equipped or inclined to compete with pure theorists who are trained in the disciplines, but the disciplines lack theorists with the nuanced understanding and depth of concern of those who study higher education as the commitment of our professional lives.

Theorists within higher education need to leverage this nuanced understanding by embracing higher education as an applied profession and by deepening our understanding of higher education as an organization that *cannot be duplicated* by scholars from other traditions.

Conceptually, this means a refocusing on educational work and a defocusing or "backgrounding" of environmental dynamics. Practically, this allows for a shift in topical direction toward issues of intense contemporary concern: the inflation of college costs, dilemmas of student access and retention, the need to improve and assess student learning and development, and the need to understand effective processes of knowledge generation and diffusion. All of these have the potential to leverage deep understanding of higher education, develop relevant and useful knowledge for higher education, attract talented people to the field, and develop a vision of higher education with the organizing function at its center.

What Should Be Studied?

Organization theorizing that is relevant to major contemporary concerns in higher education requires reorienting the concerns of organization theorists toward issues of educational work that have effects on these major outcomes in higher education. We can improve the study of educational work by specifying the connection between the micro-level behavior of students, faculty, and administrators within and across institutions with macro-level outcomes in college costs, as well as student learning, access, completion, and diversity. We can be useful to practice by providing sticky ideas (Bastedo, chap. 12; Heath & Heath, 2007) that are memorable and have the potential for lasting impact among practitioners.

STUDENT AND FACULTY LEARNING

The need to understand the depth of learning among college students has been identified as one of the primary challenges of higher education, both within the field and from innumerable outside commissions and commentators. The question is not largely whether we should address the problem but how. We have remarkably little information about what happens inside college classrooms on a broad scale and no consensus on how what is learned (or is not) should be measured.

Similar difficulties plague K–12 education. Yet we have far more organizational knowledge of school learning because scholars have pursued it vigorously. Scholars have wanted to know *how schools can be better designed to promote learning outcomes.* They have studied intensively how principals and school districts can promote instructional leadership; the design of educational interventions that seek to improve student achievement through systemic reform; how teachers respond and resist accountability measures and instructional reform; and the problems of diffusing and "scaling-up" organizational change to other schools (for just a few examples, see Coburn, 2001; Cohen, Raudenbush, & Ball, 2003; Rowan & Miller, 2007).

These are not studies of teaching and learning per se but intensive studies of the context of teachers' work and how these contexts influence student learning. These kinds of studies are exceedingly rare in higher education. Our knowledge of learning generally comes through student psychological development, which has a long and rich history in the field to this day and a great deal to contribute to our understanding of learning (Baxter Magolda & King, 2004). Organizationally, there have been good studies of specific interventions, such as service learning and learning communities (e.g., Tinto, 1997). However, these studies rarely use organization theory or even put organizing at the center of the analysis— although Lounsbury and Pollack (2001) is a notable exception.

Organization theory has a great deal to contribute to our understanding of the nature of professors' work. Sensemaking can contribute to our understanding of how professors interpret demands from students and policies; decision theory can contribute to how professors use (or fail to use) data for instructional improvement; resource allocation and cost-effectiveness studies can help us understand the financial trade-offs of various organizational decisions. But these areas remain largely untouched by organizations scholars because of the nearly exclusive focus on environmental effects and the retreat from the study of educational practice and work. We also have extremely poor quantitative data; there is no source of classroom data across institutions. In addition, as a field we have a weak tradition of studying learning: How often have you seen a higher education researcher studying a college classroom? But the potential is there for rich studies of organizational design, interventions, and technology, as well as for deep studies of faculty scholarly learning, research, cognition, and work (see Neumann, 2009, chap. 11 in this volume) as well as scholarly creativity and innovation (Tierney, chap. 6).

Organization theory also has potential to contribute to the study of student affairs administration, which has been almost entirely divorced from organization theory more broadly. I am happy to say that I am currently working with many students who are addressing this gap in the literature from multiple theoretical perspectives. Their studies include work on the emergency-response routines of residential life administrators (Molina, 2010), the effects of the organized sweatshop social movement on the civic engagement of college students (Barn-

hardt, 2011), and the professional socialization of new student affairs professionals (Perez, forthcoming).

COLLEGE COSTS

Rising college costs are seen by many as the primary threat facing higher education. The financial dynamics are well known: higher education costs are driven
by personnel, costs that almost never decline and generally increase higher than
inflation. There are few economies of scale. States, facing monstrous costs for
Medicaid and prisons, have been reducing support for decades. Students from
upper-income families—the ones who pay the full price of tuition—increasingly
demand the luxury services they enjoyed as children.

Fifteen years ago, Leslie and Rhoades (1995) produced an extensive theory-
driven research agenda for the study of college costs. Very few, if any, of these
studies have been conducted, and there are many cost drivers in higher education
that have the potential for empirical study. For example, there has been a massive
expansion in master's programs throughout American higher education in recent decades, particularly in MBAs and teacher education. The adoption of master's degree programs, however, may be far more related to competitive dynamics
and institutional prestige than workplace demands (Jaquette, 2011). These processes impose huge costs on both individuals and society, and people pursue
master's degrees in fields that are often unnecessary and add little value to individual growth or society in general.

Again, organization theory has enormous potential to contribute to our understanding of college cost drivers. Resource dependence helps us understand how
internal power dynamics among administrative and academic units may lead to
cost escalation. Institutional theory contributes by focusing on the organizational
need for legitimacy that may lead to the adoption of functions without real needs
from students or faculty. Sensemaking and routines allow us to see how administrators or faculty may engage in practices that increase costs unnecessarily. An
analysis of strategy allows us to see how our vision and priorities affect costs and
the degree to which cost reduction is even an institutional goal. On the quantitative side, however, we are often hamstrung by the absence of comprehensive
datasets providing fine-grained financial data about colleges, which would allow
for the nuanced analysis we need to sort out these effects.

STUDENT AND FACULTY DIVERSITY

Although diversity is often examined from an individual perspective, diversity is
by its very nature an organizational concept that requires organizational analysis

and solutions. Daryl Smith (chap. 8) addresses the issue in depth, noting the many accomplishments of researchers to date in studying organizational diversity issues, and laying out an agenda for future research. Undoubtedly, student and faculty diversity is one of the primary challenges facing higher education, and one to which organization theory can contribute.

In addition to the many lines of research noted by Smith (chap. 8), social movement theory has been a recent addition to organization theory, with particular interest in diversity issues (Rojas, chap. 9). In his book, Rojas (2007) analyzes the adoption of black studies programs in the United States as an emerging social movement, examining both the dynamics among black studies faculty and connections to major funders in the environment, particularly the efforts of the Ford Foundation. Slaughter (1997) also has an excellent analysis of the role of social movements in the expansion of higher education curriculum focused on race, class, and gender.

Diversity analysis has been widely studied among business professionals. For example, in the business field there is a rich literature examining the effects of diversity on team dynamics and on the perception of workers and executives. A recent experimental study concluded, for example, that perceptions of the influence of affirmative action cause observers to downgrade the education credentials of black executives (Sauer, Thomas-Hunt, & Morris, 2010). There are many implications for the hiring and retention of minority executives both in business and in higher education; bias against applicants with stereotypically black names has been shown in a famous résumé experiment (Bertrand & Mullainathan, 2004) and against both men and women in executive compensation, even when performance evaluation scores are held constant (Castilla, 2008). There is potential for significant empirical analysis studying administrators in higher education along many dimensions (see Jackson & O'Callaghan, 2009).

STUDENT ACCESS AND COMPLETION

Student access and completion have been the predominant topics of interest in recent years among higher education researchers, students, and external foundations and public policymakers. Yet the focus of our efforts has been almost inclusively at the individual level of the students, rather than the rigorous examination of institutional polices, practices, and attempts at organizational change to improve student access outcomes. In addition, federal and state policy has focused on enrollment as its primary measure of success, rather than student learning, completion, and graduation. As our national agenda has changed toward incentivizing retention and completion, our research agendas as organization theorists should support our understanding of these dynamics as well. We particularly lack knowledge of organizational structures and dynamics at community colleges and nonselective four-year universities, which educate the vast majority of students in U.S. higher education.

While the focus on student learning would examine the context of professors' work and associated learning outcomes, this agenda focuses on the administrative and incentive structures that influence student decisions. Resource dependence theory would focus on the internal power dynamics among units that facilitate or hinder student access and completion. A strategic focus would examine how institutional mission and priorities have adapted, or failed to adapt, to this new national policy need and how institutions balance student success with other stakeholder demands. Sensemaking theory could inform our understanding of how students and administrators interpret the multiple demands placed on them and how they differ in their behavior in the response to obstacles to success, particularly in their use of social networks. Routines could help us understand how students and administrators develop routines both "on the fly" and as standard operating procedures to intervene with at-risk students and how both groups invoke identities that either support or hinder students' educational progress. We particularly need an understanding, whatever theoretical framework is used, of the vast differences between campuses in student completion that are not explained by differences in student background or characteristics.

The potential for organization theory to contribute to our knowledge of higher education is enormous. The study of higher education organizations has been massively generative for organizational theorists, leading to our most exciting and compelling knowledge about how all types of organizations work. Higher education as an organizational form has never been more powerful, and its ideas and values pervade our lives. Yet the problems that higher education faces are unusually challenging, representing deep issues related to how students learn in classrooms and student subcultures, how organizations accommodate a diversity of increasingly autonomous stakeholders, the conditions that enable and constrain creativity and innovation, and how rational action can lead to highly dysfunctional organizational adaptations.

Deep study of the organizational mechanisms underlying these basic organizational issues has immense promise for educational theory and practice. How to develop our understanding of these mechanisms is the subject of the final chapter.

REFERENCES

Abbott, A. (1988). *The system of professions.* Chicago: University of Chicago Press.

Ball, D. L., & Forzani, F. M. (2007). What makes education research "educational"? *Educational Researcher, 36,* 529–540.

Barley, S. R. (1996). Technicians in the workplace: Ethnographic evidence for bringing work into organization studies. *Administrative Science Quarterly, 41,* 404–441.

Barley, S. R., & Kunda, G. (2001). Bringing work back in. *Organization Science, 12,* 76–95.

Barnhardt, C. L. (2011). *Student activism in its contemporary form: Facilitated, fashioned, or reprised?* Unpublished doctoral dissertation, University of Michigan.

Bastedo, M. N. (2005). The making of an activist governing board. *Review of Higher Education 28,* 551–570.

Bastedo, M. N. (2007). Sociological frameworks for higher education policy research. In P. J. Gumport (Ed.), *The sociology of higher education: Contributions and their contexts* (pp. 295–316). Baltimore: Johns Hopkins University Press.

Bastedo, M. N. (2009a). Conflicts, commitments, and cliques in the university: Moral seduction as a threat to trustee independence. *American Educational Research Journal, 46,* 354–386.

Bastedo, M. N. (2009b). Convergent institutional logics in public higher education: State policymaking and governing board activism. *Review of Higher Education, 32,* 209–234.

Bastedo, M. N., & Bowman, N. A. (2011). College rankings as an interorganizational dependency: Establishing the foundation for strategic and institutional accounts. *Research in Higher Education 52*(1).

Baxter Magolda, M. B., & King, P. M. (Eds.). (2004). *Learning partnerships: Theory and models of practice to educate for self-authorship.* Alexandria, VA: Stylus Press.

Bertrand, M., & Mullainathan, S. (2004). Are Emily and Greg more employable than Lakisha and Jamal? A field experiment on labor market discrimination. *American Economic Review, 94,* 991–1013.

Castilla, E. J. (2008). Gender, race, and meritocracy in organizational careers. *American Journal of Sociology, 113*(6), 1479–1526.

Clark, B. R. (1956). *Adult education in transition.* Berkeley: University of California Press.

Clark, B. R. (1960). *The open-door college: A case study.* New York: McGraw-Hill.

Clark, B. R. (1970). *The distinctive college: Antioch, Reed, and Swarthmore.* Chicago: Aldine.

Clark, B. R. (1972). The organizational saga in higher education. *Administrative Science Quarterly, 17,* 178–184.

Clark, B. R. (1983). *The higher education system.* Berkeley: University of California Press.

Clark, B. R. (2008). *On higher education: Selected writings, 1956–2006.* Baltimore: Johns Hopkins University Press.

Coburn, C. E. (2001). Collective sensemaking about reading: How teachers mediate reading policy in their professional communities. *Educational Evaluation and Policy Analysis, 23*(2), 145–170.

Cohen, D. K., Raudenbush, S. W., & Ball, D. L. (2003). Resources, instruction, and research. *Educational Evaluation and Policy Analysis, 25*(2), 1–24.

Cohen, M. D., & March, J. G. (1986). *Leadership and ambiguity: The American college president* (2nd ed.). Boston: Harvard Business School Press.

Ferriss, T. (2009). *The 4–hour work week: Escape 9–5, live anywhere, and join the new rich.* New York: Crown.

Frank, D. J., & Meyer, J. W. (2007). University expansion and the knowledge society. *Theory and Society, 36,* 287–311.

Galinsky, E., Sakai, K., & Wigton, T. (2010). *Workplace flexibility among small employers.* New York: Families and Work Institute.

Goffman, E. (1961). *Asylums.* Chicago: Aldine.

Grint, K. (2009). *The sociology of work* (3rd ed.). Cambridge, UK: Polity Press.

Gumport, P. J. (2000). Academic restructuring: Organizational change and institutional imperatives. *Higher Education, 39,* 67–91.

Hartley, J. M., & Morphew, C. C. (2008). What's being sold and to what end? A content analysis of college viewbooks. *Journal of Higher Education, 79,* 671–691.

Heath, C., & Heath, D. (2007). Made to stick: Why some ideas survive and others die. New York: Random House.

Heath, C., & Sitkin, S. B. (2001). Big-B versus Big-O: What is organizational about organizational behavior? *Journal of Organizational Behavior, 22,* 43–58.

Jackson, J. F. L., & O'Callaghan, E. M. (2009). *Ethnic and racial administrative diversity: Understanding work life realities and experiences in higher education.* San Francisco: Jossey-Bass.

Jaquette, O. (2011). *The effect of financial strain on the adoption and production of graduate degrees.* Unpublished doctoral dissertation, University of Michigan.

Kamens, D. H. (1971). The college "charter" and college size: Effects on occupational choice and college attrition. *Sociology of Education, 44,* 270–296.

Kamens, D. H. (1974). Colleges and elite formation: The case of prestigious American colleges. *Sociology of Education, 47,* 354–378.

Kamens, D. H. (1977). Legitimating myths and educational organization: The relationship between organizational ideology and formal structure. *American Sociological Review, 42,* 208–219.

Kezar, A., & Dee, J. R. (forthcoming). Conducting multi-paradigm inquiry in the study of higher education organization and governance: Transforming research perspectives on colleges and universities. In *Higher education: Handbook of theory and research.*

Leslie, L. L., & Rhoades, G. (1995). Rising administrative costs: Seeking explanations. *Journal of Higher Education, 66,* 187–212.

Lounsbury, M., & Pollack, S. (2001). Institutionalizing civic engagement: Shifting logics and the cultural repackaging of service-learning in U.S. higher education. *Organization, 8,* 319–339.

Meyer, J. W. (1970). The charter: Conditions of diffuse socialization in schools. In W. Richard Scott (Ed.), *Social processes and social structures* (pp. 564–578). New York: Henry Holt.

Meyer, J., & Rowan, B. (1978). The structure of educational organizations. In M. W. Meyer (Ed.), *Environments and organizations* (pp. 78–109). San Francisco: Jossey-Bass.

Meyer, J. W., & Scott, W. R. (1983). *Organizational environments: Ritual and rationality.* Beverly Hills, CA: Sage.

Molina, D. K. (2010). *Sensemaking as a trigger for change in university emergency response routines: Ethnographic and case study analyses of a residential life department.* Unpublished doctoral dissertation, University of Michigan.

Neumann, A. (2009). *Professing to learn: Creating tenured lives and careers in the American research university.* Baltimore: Johns Hopkins University Press.

Perez, R. J. (forthcoming). *Exploring cognitive dimensions of professional preparation and the transition to practice in student affairs.* Unpublished doctoral dissertation, University of Michigan.

Peterson, M. W. (1974). Organization and administration in higher education: Sociological and social-psychological perspectives. *Review of Research in Education, 2,* 296–347.

Peterson, M. W. (1985). Emerging developments in postsecondary organization theory and research: Fragmentation or integration. *Educational Researcher, 14*(3), 5–12.

Peterson, M. W. (1986). Critical choices: From adolescence to maturity in higher education research. *Review of Higher Education, 10*(2), 143–150.

Peterson, M. W. (2007). The study of colleges and universities as organizations. In P. J. Gumport (Ed.), *The sociology of higher education: Contributions and their contexts* (pp. 147–186). Baltimore: Johns Hopkins University Press.

Pfeffer, J. (2005). Developing resource dependence theory: How theory is affected by its environment. In K. G. Smith & M. A. Hitt (Eds.), *Great minds in management: The process of theory development* (2nd ed., pp. 436–459). Oxford: Oxford University Press.

Pfeffer, J., & Salancik, G. R. (1974). Organizational decision making as a political process: The case of a university budget. *Administrative Science Quarterly, 19,* 135–151.

Pfeffer, J., & Salancik, G. R. (1978). *The external control of organizations: A resource dependence perspective.* New York: Harper and Row.

Rojas, F. (2007). *From Black Power to black studies: How a radical social movement became an academic discipline.* Baltimore: Johns Hopkins University Press.

Rowan, B., & Miller, R. J. (2007). Organizational strategies for promoting instructional change: Implementation dynamics in schools working with comprehensive school reform providers. *American Educational Research Journal, 44,* 252–297Salmi, J. (2009). *The challenge of establishing world-class universities.* Washington, DC: World Bank.

Sauer, S. J., Thomas-Hunt, M. C., & Morris, P. A. (2010). Too good to be true? The unintended signaling effects of educational prestige on external expectations of team performance. *Organization Science, 21,* 1108–1120.

Schofer, E., & Meyer, J. W. (2005). The world-wide expansion of higher education in the twentieth century. *American Sociological Review, 70,* 898–920.

Slaughter, S. (1997). Class, race, gender and the construction of post-secondary curricula in the United States: Social movement, professionalization and political economic theories of curricular change. *Journal of Curriculum Studies, 29,* 1–30.

Tinto, V. (1997). Classroomso as communities: Exploring the educational character of student persistence. *Journal of Higher Education, 68,* 599–623.

Walsh, J. P., Meyer, A. D., & Schoonhoven, C. B. (2006). A future for organization theory: Living in and living with changing organizations. *Organization Science, 17*(5), 657–671.

Weick, K. (1976). Educational organizations as loosely coupled systems. *Administrative Science Quarterly, 21,* 1–19.

CHAPTER TWO

Strategic Thinking
in Higher Education Research

PATRICIA J. GUMPORT

Studying colleges and universities as organizations has occupied a central place in the field of higher education over the past four decades. Both in the United States and abroad, as higher education faculty and students have witnessed profound changes in the scale, complexity, and differentiation of higher education, their interest in organizational studies has gained momentum. Moreover, that interest has converged with theoretical and methodological developments within organizational studies to provide leverage for studying these changes. Increased visibility and enthusiasm for organizational research outside our field—across the social sciences and especially in management studies—have lent further momentum and legitimacy to this work, both for organization theory and for particular organizational questions within academic settings.

However, for all its promise, the study of organizations faces the same challenges as our larger field for the precarious position of higher education research and researchers in today's academy. Stated simply and starkly, neither the scholarly nor practical legitimacy of higher education research is assured. Our research is not often cited by scholars in other disciplines, nor is it widely read by university and college leaders (except graduates of our programs). The major consumers are fellow researchers. So, even though our field has grown in established lines of inquiry, academic personnel (i.e., faculty and graduate students), and resources over these several decades, criticism and sometimes outright dismissal persist. The research is not scholarly enough, they say—that is, not sufficiently framed by theory, or in turn not advancing theory. It is not clear enough—that is, not written in an accessible discourse style that identifies the bottom line. Or it falls short of addressing the most pressing issues for practitioners and policymakers in their improvement efforts.[1] These persistent criticisms have high stakes for the study of higher education and so warrant more extensive consideration.

Not surprisingly, organizational studies as a subfield has also been criticized from each end, occupying a visible but uneasy space within the study of higher education. On the bright side, organizational analyses of universities and colleges have focused on significant topics and are evident in peer-reviewed journals, conference presentations, and course requirements of our graduate programs. Most higher education degree programs have faculty with expertise in organizational behavior, management, and/or leadership and administration. But there are also problems. In addition to the fact that research and researchers speak primarily to each other, the external funding base for research is not stable. About a decade ago, several foundations that historically made substantial investments in postsecondary education scaled back or discontinued that part of their grant portfolios. In an interview-based study in 2002, I explored why this was so. Among the reasons, program staff said they were frustrated that their prior funding, whether for research or for programmatic initiatives, did not yield recognizable and sustainable changes in colleges and universities, and they thus concluded their funding was not an effective lever for change.[2] The foundation staff's critique and the limited reach of our field *beyond our own community* remind us that we need to reconsider our intended goals and audiences—not only in writing up our research but also in terms of the questions we consider worthy of study and how we frame them. This chapter addresses some of the pitfalls and promises of these questions in light of the development of organizational studies within higher education into a current legacy: the strategic paradigm.

Before delving into these questions, however, I want to make clear that—these various issues aside—organizational studies have brought enormous value to our field by providing concepts that define the parameters of study and analysis. This observation may seem obvious, but I think it is profound. What we study depends first on what we see. We do not often examine what we take for granted a priori, before embarking on a study.

Consider some examples of how we see everyday life on campus. We may conceive of students as learners to be educated, consumers to be satisfied, young colleagues to be mentored, or community members—like extended family. We may see faculty as primarily instructors or as researchers. We may presume they are motivated by rewards or driven by their professional identities, with internalized norms to maintain quality through self-regulation, or by an abiding passion for ideas or ethos of service. We may see presidents, provosts, and deans as campus officials, administrators, leaders, managers—or as faculty who, like me, take on a broader scope of responsibilities later in their careers.

Finally, and most germane, we may see colleges or universities *as organiza-*

tions. Seeing them as organizations leads us to identify a number of questions as worthy of study. How we frame them depends on where we look. We can look at core processes internal to campus life, such as decision making or leadership. Organizational conflict may be seen as pathological and in need of resolution or as natural and endemic. Or we may move beyond internal organizational dynamics, forgoing the image of a boundary between internal and external, and instead see colleges and universities as situated within wider forces that legitimate academic structures and practices—a foundational conception from institutional theory. A campus is then viewed as a microcosm of societal dynamics, with powerful determinative contexts. In this last framework, how well an organization aligns with widely shared societal expectations determines its legitimacy and therefore its very survival. Much research in this vein examines the homogenizing pressures that produce and maintain structural and normative similarities across colleges and universities, such as long-existing departments that carry on despite low enrollments and few degrees awarded. More recent studies explore different configurations of change and their underlying processes, such as emerging curricula and degree programs (e.g., interdisciplinary) or new kinds of units and personnel. In my own work, I have studied how wider expectations and pressures constitute rationales that are invoked for continuity and change in the organizational structures of colleges and universities. I have examined tensions within organizational change processes as taken-for-granted prescriptions (or logics) become modified, even contested, given divergent understandings of what higher education should be and do as a social institution.

A critique of the institutional framework described above is that it is overly deterministic, presuming the behavior of the organization or individuals to be heavily predetermined by wider expectations, since they need legitimacy to survive. I am drawn to the *neo*-institutional reformulation that sees wider forces as creating a fence, or ground, that delimits organizational and individual behavior and yet leaves room for their agency. But even from this perspective, we need to be explicit about whether we *presuppose* actions to be unconscious, or conscious and possibly even strategic. Research derived from these divergent premises has created an intellectual space with great promise for our field. I mention it here to be explicit about my own conceptual leanings. I will also mention it at the end of this chapter, as a promising future direction.

I also state this up front to drive home my basic point: we must first acknowledge what we presume. What we presume is reflected in how we talk—and how we think—about the phenomena we study. These starting points anchor our conceptual frameworks, frame our analyses, and shape our ending points. They predispose us to generate insights for theory or for practice. They locate us within our field and help us identify potential collaborators. They also generate blind spots—intellectually and professionally. Self-awareness and reflection must be ongoing for each of us and for the field as a whole.

Illustrating the significance of this point, I will elaborate by addressing three questions. First, why have higher education researchers been drawn to organizational studies? Second, how has a strategic paradigm emerged in the study and practice of higher education? And finally, which ideas hold promise for future organizational studies in higher education?

Why Organizational Studies in the Field of Higher Education?

Although the field of organizational studies is now self-identified as such, it is not neatly bounded. It emerged as an interdisciplinary endeavor, primarily from social science disciplines and drawing ideas from scientific management and human relations (Scott, 2004). Early work sought to describe the features of organizations qua organizations, rather than as elements within analyses of broader political or social systems. In subsequent decades, analysts sought to illuminate many "givens" of organizational life, including structural, normative, and cultural dimensions. Research often reflected problems in nonacademic settings, such as business and government (Scott, 2008). According to W. Richard Scott (2007), "Academics look to the world outside for problems meriting study, and practitioners look to scholars of organizations for insights into how to do their work more effectively" (p. 371).

With researchers bringing different interests, backgrounds, and locations to their research, organizational studies have had multiple paradigms. The downside to this is the low consensus within the field, but the upside is the vitality of many lines of inquiry, theories, and methodologies in play.[3] Concepts central to work during these decades have had great staying power to help us consider why organizations look and act the way they do. The classics in the field were intended to have general applicability across all types of organizations.

While organizational studies make up only a small fraction of social science research, they have come to occupy a very visible role in the study of higher education. Researchers have borrowed concepts and models from organizational studies as rationales for their own work. These topics—such as the nature and challenges of leadership, the obstacles to planning and implementation, the persistent need for decision making despite uncertainty, and the processes and consequences of academic restructuring—have moved to the forefront in the field of higher education research and in academic organizations. Several topics are perennial, like leadership and decision making. Others are newer, reflecting changes in higher education, such as initiatives that restructure academic work (by hiring more part-time and off-track faculty and by consolidating academic programs), the pathways to increasing diversity on campuses, new experiments in instructional technology on and off campus, and new organizational forms that reflect interdisciplinary pursuits and novel partnerships between academic organizations and industry. These may be studied in their own right or as windows into more abstract questions about the nature of organizational change and transformation, such as the attendant processes, obstacles, and outcomes—even how new organizational practices have come to be regarded as legitimate. From my perspective, organizational studies have served us well as we have sought to understand emerging challenges from the decades of expansion, differentiation, and specialization to contemporary economic turbulence, public scrutiny, and competitive market forces.

I want to suggest three reasons why the subfield of organizational studies is such a good fit for higher education researchers.

First, we find a deep reservoir of theories, concepts, and methods. We can use them to model—and thus simplify—complex behavior, providing analytical leverage for postulating general theories intended to apply across academic settings. Or we can use findings from organizational studies to describe and diagnose complexities within particular settings, to illuminate them more fully and explain the multiplicity of perspectives and realities on campuses. We can do either or both, as they fit with objectivist or subjectivist epistemologies.

Second, some core assumptions of organizational studies align with properties of U.S. higher education itself. Most characterizations of the U.S. system focus on its magnitude, complexity, and decentralized authority, all of which place the organization at the center of the action. In this the United States differs from countries with a national ministry of higher education and a more centralized authority for policymaking and finance. Formally, the locus of power and decisions in these countries is weighted to the national level, whereas U.S. colleges and universities function with relatively greater independence and more autonomy. Thus different organizational dynamics come to the fore as important and worthy of study.

Third, the decades of growth and increasing momentum for organizational studies correspond directly to the development of higher education as a more scholarly field. By the 1970s, higher education studies clearly extended beyond research at the institutional and state system levels. Research topics expanded and became institutionalized in new journals and professional associations and on campuses as new faculty positions, graduate programs, and research centers. By the 1980s it was apparent that faculty research was also shaped by local cultures and academic reward structures within schools of education. In many places, the expectation was for faculty to contribute insights valuable to practice. In fewer places, like status-seeking education schools, faculty were encouraged to borrow ideas from the disciplines, and even to contribute back to them if they were so inclined.

I was in graduate school at Stanford then, where organizational studies had gained momentum locally through the work of such charismatic figures as James March, John Meyer, and Richard Scott. We were especially drawn to their theoretical ideas and conceptual originality. We also studied the classics of social theory to gain insight into prior thinking on the nature of social change and social institutions: for example, Weber on sources of legitimacy and bureaucratic authority, Durkheim on differentiation and the division of labor in society, and Marx on the nature of conflict in capitalism. We had permission to explore ideas that were illuminating. Instead of having to take problems from practice, we were encouraged to identify problems that were just plain interesting.

As a result, my scholarly sensibility is inspired by these intellectual legacies as well as by my own observations of the daily challenges of academic change on different types of campuses. In my research on academic restructuring, I examined how periods of resource abundance inflated expectations for additive solutions and how conflict was exacerbated when budget cuts dictated priority setting.[4] I became fascinated by tensions over what knowledge matters most, how it should be organized and supported, and who should decide. I drew on organizational studies to anchor and frame empirically grounded studies and historical case studies. Organizational studies also shed light on my concerns about what is at stake—whether for the organization, the fate of academic fields, the trajectory of faculty careers, or higher education's contributions to society. My academic generational peers, and others since, have continued to develop this type of disciplinary-informed research while still focusing on higher education. One result, however, is that this lens has created more ambiguity about the intended audiences for higher education research. Ambiguity is not inherently bad, but it does warrant explicit consideration.

Looking Back: The Emergence of the Strategic Paradigm

For myself as for others, several specific applications from organizational studies have advanced our research, especially those that underscore the capacity of organizations for rationality and purposive action.

CONCEPTS FROM WEBER

Weber's concepts such as bureaucracy, rationality, and legitimacy, as part of his historical argument about the development of rational forms, are at the heart of organizational studies.[5] Weber wrote thoughtfully about big ideas that set parameters for social behavior, including the calculability of rational ends (especially economic prosperity), efficiency as the best means to achieve goals, and authority as embedded in positions and rules that legitimate centralized coordination and control. Just to be clear, Weber did not advocate for the trajectory of rationalization. In fact, he foresaw a rigidifying of rationality's iron cage, and ultimately disenchantment. This is a point that scholars sometimes overlook when they think of Weber's bureaucracy as "an ideal-type," by which term he meant an archetypal form, not a desirable condition.

Since the 1970s and well into the 1980s, scholars studying organizations and higher education have pointed out how the ideal-type bureaucracy does not map well onto academic organizations. This has given rise to alternative conceptions or models. For example, observing the centrality of faculty's professional expertise and ensuing authority to academic life has led many in our field to prefer the model of "professional bureaucracy," where specialists retain considerable control over their work in the organization's operating core (Mintzberg, 1979, 1980). Decision making tends to be highly decentralized, an expectation in academia that is passed along from one generation to the next through professional socialization, especially at research universities. We still hear faculty ask why and how a decision was made, especially when they believe priorities should be elsewhere or their authority should be paramount. The presumptions of an ideal-type Weberian bureaucracy do not hold. Top-down directives fail without faculty buy-in, or at least extensive consultation processes. Academic change is slow, and it is not sustained without faculty ownership.[6]

In other organizational models applied to higher education, faculty authority, power, and interests have each been foregrounded as central. Coupled with a premise of limited rationality, conflicting interests, persistent ambiguity, and struggles for legitimacy, these models include collegial, political, and cultural dynamics. I don't have space here to give these the attention they deserve. But a few strands of organizational studies that focus attention on both rational and nonrational capacities are worth noting as particularly valuable to our field.

THE NONRATIONAL STRAND OF ORGANIZATIONAL STUDIES

In his review of the past fifty years of organizational sociology, our colleague Richard Scott casts the central problem driving organizational studies as this question of rationality (Scott, 2004). While several theories from sociology and economics assumed the rationality of organizations, in the 1950s and 1960s the then nascent field of organizational studies explored the *limits* of rationality. The concepts of unintended consequences of purposive action, bounded rationality, and the importance of myth and ceremony, for example, have each been fundamental to organizational studies in higher education.

Robert Merton and his students identified the "unintended consequences of purposive social action" (Merton, 1936) when they found organizational behavior that could *not* be explained by a rational logic and that instead had resulted accidently from previous actions and decisions. They undertook single-case studies of organizations, utilizing archival, interview, and observational techniques, and they produced holistic accounts of each particular organization under study. Moreover, from then on—in addition to this conceptual legacy—methodologically, the single-case, in-depth treatment of higher education organizations became *the* modal research design in our field.

Bounded rationality, which calls attention to the limitations of individual decision makers, was developed by Herbert Simon initially and expanded upon with James March (March & Simon, 1958) to explore the cognitive and computational limits of rationality. They began with the premise of individuals and organizations as rational but instead found "satisficing" behavior, where people settle for the first solution that is minimally acceptable instead of performing exhaustive searches for optimal solutions.

These ideas were further developed in works such as Michael Cohen and James March's brilliant study of university presidents, *Leadership and Ambiguity* (1974). In this seminal book, Cohen and March applied the "garbage can" model of organizational decision making to universities, where solutions go in search of problems and decision making does not follow an orderly process or rational logic.[7] This picture of universities as "organized anarchies" was a far cry from Weber's bureaucracy.[8]

John Meyer and Brian Rowan (1977) theorized how institutional environments account for structural similarities across organizations and how rational conception itself is a "myth" ceremoniously displayed by organizations to gain legitimacy. Karl Weick (1976) used the concept of "loose coupling" to explain how rational-formal elements of organizations function alongside informal, nonrationalized actions and how more effort is put into the display of competency than into pursuing actual goals. According to Meyer and Rowan (1977), modern societies grant legitimacy to rationalized bureaucracies; therefore organizations must look like rationalized bureaucracies. They point out, however, that looking like a rationalized bureaucracy is not a sufficient condition for behaving and functioning as one. Both "loose coupling" and its close sibling, "decoupling," have run throughout higher education literature and offered persuasive accounts of the origin and reproduction of formal structures. In the same era, Burton Clark's (1972) work on organizational sagas shows how small distinctive colleges may not be rational, but they surely may be quite functional, when they are organized to conform to less visible yet enduring normative legacies and beliefs that constitute the college's character.

RATIONALIST STRANDS

On the other side, several schools of thought with more rationalist premises see organizations as capable of rationality and purposive action. These include resource dependence, contingency theory, and strategic choice approaches. In these "open systems" frameworks, organizations are seen as dependent on their environments for resources, and organizational behavior is shaped by features of the environment.

Some core open systems themes have had a dramatic impact on how we understand the context-dependent "behaviors" of universities. An early example looked at how organizations depend on their environment for crucial resources and how organizations behave in purposive, rational ways to ensure their survival. Two applications of the resource dependence framework are especially noteworthy. One is the idea that organizations cultivate a plurality of resources to reduce their vulnerability to any one of them. The other is that structure follows resources: as new sources of revenue proliferate and grow, organizations create new offices to search for and manage these resources flows. Two examples from the past two decades of the twentieth century are offices of development (also known as "institutional advancement") to coordinate fund-raising activities and offices of technology licensing to oversee technology transfer and help negotiate the complexities of intellectual property.

Contingency theory is another open systems perspective that employs rationalist assumptions. The features of an organization are predicted by the nature of its environment and the technical characteristics of its industry. In contingency theory, effective organizations make rational adjustments to changes in their environments or technologies. In his chapter with David Dill in *Planning and Management for a Changing Environment* (1997), Marvin Peterson portrays numerous institutional challenges as emanating from a turbulent and rapidly changing environment, as well as from changes in the "postsecondary knowledge industry" itself, pushing campuses toward more opportunistic, market-driven choices (see also Peterson, 2000). Yet campuses may respond differently. In a thoughtful piece examining conceptions of strategic responses to external pressures, Oliver (1991) notes that differing views of appropriate responses to the environment reflect divergent assumptions about "the degree of choice, awareness and self-interest that organizations possess for handling external constraints" (p. 148). Thus even in this piece that includes a useful taxonomy of strategic responses, Oliver reminds us of ever present nonrational elements (herein those presumed by institutional theory): "the exercise of strategic choice may be preempted when organizations are unconscious of, blind to, or otherwise take for granted the institutional processes to which they adhere. Moreover, when external norms or practices obtain the status of a social fact, organizations may engage in activities that are not so much calculative and self-interested as obvious or proper" (p. 148).[9]

Although important distinctions can be made between these frameworks, as a whole this body of work brings into sharpest focus the image of an organization as inseparable from its environment and as having the capacity to shape its destiny through strategic decision making. In our field of study and practice, this has been an attractive image. I see this image and its assumptions as having converged with changing realities in higher education to set the stage for and give momentum to what I call "a strategic paradigm."

Several core assumptions from rationalist theory anchor a generic strategic paradigm. Simply stated:

- Colleges and universities *can and should* adapt purposively to a changing environment, on which they depend for many types of resources.
- Rational intentions can be articulated, shared, and carried out.
- Decisions and actions are consequential in that they set processes in motion to bring about desired changes.
- Campus leaders are expected to generate visible, strategic initiatives and will acquire legitimacy for doing so. They are then seen as appropriately forward-looking, even visionary.

These premises echo values and beliefs that have become pervasive in higher education, in both public and private colleges and universities, as in the wider society.

CHANGES IN CONTEXTS

Changes in the *societal, campus,* and *scholarly* contexts for higher education have given the rationalist premises of the strategic paradigm increasing appeal for higher education researchers and practitioners. I see a convergence in the changes across these three contexts, evident in a discourse of change that fuels the legitimacy of a strategic paradigm in higher education. Moreover, this convergence provides a frame for practice that bridges research interests, contributing to its prominence in our field.

At the *societal* level, since the 1980s, researchers have observed and analyzed an increasingly turbulent environment for an increasingly scrutinized higher education enterprise. This includes the now familiar litany of economic, political, demographic, and technological changes. These challenges of "Shock Wave II" include new technology, demographic changes, constraints in public sector resources, the rising popularity of for-profit higher education, and the globalization of the economy (Kerr, 2002). Pervasive accountability pressures have meant that higher education is expected to demonstrate greater transparency and improve institutional performance.

This is evident in the 2006 national report by the Spellings Commission, a blue-ribbon panel convened by the U.S. Department of Education (U.S. Department of Education, 2006). The report critiques higher education's complacency and calls for "urgent reform" (p. ix) and improvement. Comparing higher education to other industries, like railroads and steel manufacturing (p. xii), the panel's message is clear: fail to change at your own peril. Dramatic changes are called for: greater responsiveness to stakeholders, adaptation to changing societal needs, and changes in the organizational character of colleges and universities to become "more nimble, more efficient and more effective" (p. xiii):

> U.S. higher education needs to improve in dramatic ways. . . . American higher education has become what, in the business world, would be called a mature enterprise: increasingly risk averse, at times self-satisfied, and unduly expensive. It is an enterprise that has yet to address the fundamental issues of how academic programs and institutions must be transformed to serve the changing educational needs of a knowledge economy. It has yet to successfully confront the impact of globalization, rapidly evolving technologies, an increasingly diverse and aging population, and an evolving marketplace characterized by new needs and new paradigms. (pp. vi, ix)

Across the United States, similar imperatives have become pervasive, and state leaders direct them specifically to their own public college and university systems.

At the *campus* level, a corresponding discourse of change has been picked up and elaborated by campus leaders—most visibly, senior administrators—during the past two decades. The challenges are depicted as unprecedented and daunting, especially given higher education's *alleged* track record of nonresponsiveness, inertia, and resistance. On different types of campuses, planning reports have identified priorities and formulated initiatives to cut costs, gain efficiency, institute budget discipline, restructure programs, improve flexibility, establish outcomes assessment, and devise performance indicators. Economic rationality has been institutionalized with tools from business, such as strategic planning and budgeting, environmental scanning, enrollment forecasting, and most recently "futuring"—a term borrowed from companies for determining how to cope with uncertainty through scenario building. It is commonly believed that the best way to run colleges and universities is to emulate companies that have gone *from good to great*. After all, our organizations were *built to last*, according to book titles in the contemporary discourse.[10] If ever a time was ripe for higher education leaders to get guidance from organizational analysts with expertise on how to improve the way they do business and manage their organizations in a changing environment, this is it. Even if the writing does not actually tell them what to do, it offers a compelling discourse for cultivating their intentions.

These changes in societal and campus contexts have converged with developments in the *scholarly* context. Academic research grounded in rationality has gained legitimacy within and beyond the academy. In the social sciences, we have seen the rising status of economics above other disciplines and the spread of rational choice theorizing and modeling beyond economics into political science, business, government, and even education (Pfeffer, 1993).

Yet, as I noted earlier, the Janus quality of educational research is sustained by its twin bases for legitimacy, with some of us working on problems with practical relevance and others more on a disciplinary agenda. This leaves open the question of what is best for the research agenda in higher education as a field of study, situated as it is within schools of education. Should it reflect a balance or lean more toward practice, given its location in a professional school? If the recent path of K–12 research is instructive, the stage has already been set for research with rationality assumptions to receive more funding and status in educational policymaking, assessment, and school reform—because, one can surmise, rational choice models from the social sciences are viewed as robust, rigorous, scientific, realistic, and thus more compelling than interpretive, nonrational, and critical approaches.

I see these changes across the above-mentioned three contexts as converging in a discourse of change that directs higher education leaders to face challenges on their campuses by thinking strategically. A strategic paradigm promises to address their urgent needs within a framework of rationality and action, wherein they are presumed to have some agency.

But what about in higher education research? Is the strategic paradigm also pervasive, and if so, what does that mean? This would be worth investigating systematically. An initial informal search we did of primary and secondary literatures led to signs of a strategic paradigm in higher education research.

As expected, the more practice-oriented publications—like the New Directions series and books published by Jossey-Bass—included several pieces aimed at helping campus leaders implement strategic change, planning, decision making, budgeting, leadership, and so on to bring about improvements in performance or quality. Some pieces are grounded in the author's experience at her or his home campus and offered as a local case study.

In the three major U.S. higher education research journals (the *Journal of Higher Education*, the *Review of Higher Education*, and *Research in Higher Education*), we found some articles using a strategic framework for research; some of these were prescriptive as well. To varying degrees they used theoretically framed research and then concluded by promoting strategic approaches.

We also found books by university presses in this category. Arguably the most famous work to date is George Keller's 1983 *Academic Strategy: The Management Revolution in American Higher Education*. While at times cynical in this book, Keller nevertheless urges universities to make better use of concepts from modern management. Why? As he puts it, "To have a strategy is to put your own intelligence, foresight, and will in charge, instead of outside forces and disordered concerns" (p. 75). Moreover, he avows, "Planning makes the implicit, inarticulate, and private explicit, articulate, and public. It brings decision-making out of the closet. It replaces muddling through with purpose" (p. 70). During the same era, strategic choice was proposed as a successful approach to understanding adaptation by higher education organizations, as exemplified by Cameron (1983).

To fast forward two decades, a few titles of recent journal articles further reflect the language and the promise of strategic approaches for rationality and agency (acting), even for best practices:

- "Strategic Planning via Baldridge: Lessons Learned" (Jasinski, 2004).
- "'Incentives for Managed Growth': A Case Study of Incentives-Based Planning and Budgeting in a Large Public Research University" (Hearn, Lewis, Kallsen, Holdsworth, & Jones, 2006).

- "Assessing and Cultivating Support for Strategic Planning: Searching for Best Practices in a Reform Environment" (Welsh, Nunez, & Petrosko, 2006).

Our search also uncovered higher education researchers who, like me, seek to diagnose and critically examine strategic frameworks in use, the organizational discourse, and the rationales offered by campus leaders. The more analytical and critical pieces tend to be from scholars working within social science theoretical frameworks.[11] Beyond the United States, higher education scholars from Europe and Australia analyze the growing prominence of strategic approaches in higher education policy and practice around the world (see, e.g., Allen, 2003; Marginson & Considine, 2000).

Robert Rhoads and Gary Rhoades take the critique of the strategic paradigm a step further by arguing that other perspectives critical of entrepreneurial universities are not being represented in higher education journals, expressing disdain for the journals' role in disseminating prescriptive pieces. They find that "nearly every higher education journal has published articles *promoting* university-corporate partnering" (Rhoads & Rhoades, 2005). If they are pointing fingers, they should point at the peer reviewers—in other words, at some of us.

The range of views on, and different uses of, strategic thinking within higher education practice and research prompt me to consider what it would mean if strategic thinking became *even more* pervasive among members of our research community pursuing organizational studies in higher education. I see some clear merits and potential liabilities of this possible future direction.

Some of the appeal, as stated above, is societal legitimacy. Strategic thinking is taken for granted as not only appropriate but necessary in the current political economic context. Market models and strategic management principles have extremely high societal legitimacy now, compared with models from the public and not-for-profit sectors.

Whether scholarly and practical legitimacy will be forthcoming depends on the intended audiences. If a research question, its conceptual framework, and its methods are theoretical or to some degree adopt "rational choice" assumptions, the question is predisposed to accrue scholarly attention and even credibility. Such a framing could help higher education research reach audiences in the disciplines and other professional schools across university settings. However, if a research question is framed too theoretically, practitioners are not likely to find a scholarly article on the question worth their time. Yet higher education leaders today want their actions to be rational and consequential; they find it necessary to be forward-looking and strategic and to be seen as such. On the other hand, if a problem is taken directly from practice and the research simply feeds it back as such without new insights, the work is not framed for scholarly legitimacy. The merits, then, cannot be presumed across the board in one direction or another.

While a strategic paradigm in higher education organizational studies has support from the contemporary climate, it also has a number of potential liabilities, especially if it becomes dominant or is pursued at the neglect of developing other paradigms. This could be an appropriate caution for any field but is especially apt for ours, given its uncertain status and legitimacy.

In the short run, like Weber's bureaucracy, it would be misleading to promote a strategic paradigm that aspires to have general applicability across colleges and universities. As we know, differences in mission, legacies, and culture matter a great deal in higher education. If the core rationalist assumptions of strategic action are not borne out, this could derail campus leaders by giving them a false and ultimately frustrated vision of rationality, agency, and consequentiality. What about the nonrational features of academic organizations—for example, the bounded rationality, unintended consequences, and myth and ceremony dimensions we looked at earlier? Are these to be cast as simply "constraints" or "obstacles"? It would be a shame to lose the insights from these dynamics, which undeniably function in tandem with rationalist elements and are among the major defining and enduring features of academic organizations. It would also be a liability to miss the opportunity for cultivating practitioners' imaginations to see their problems in new ways.

In the longer term, stated more generally, if our field were to focus too much or too exclusively on working within a strategic paradigm, we would fall short of advancing our understanding of higher education itself. Here I can see three possible field-level consequences.

First, focusing on the organization as actor does not push us to examine the cumulative effect of local incremental decisions, whether for the campus on a longer time horizon, for the higher education system as a whole, or in global terms. This limits the analytical sophistication with which we can speak about the complexity of organizational dynamics—causes, effects, and implications. In essence, it gives us small analytical purchase. To push this point further, we could ask ourselves, why select a campus as the single level of analysis instead of studying colleges and universities as nested within systems or as social institutions in societies around the world? The latter, for example, would be worth exploring the changes in organizational forms that emerged with the transnational mobility of students in the post-Bologna era. Now even prescriptions for case study research guide researchers to design studies that take into account how their cases are embedded in several levels of context.

Second, strategic frameworks in use by scholars and practitioners carry with them broad ideologies, assumptions that those employing them might be unaware of or uncomfortable with. Some of our colleagues are predisposed to applaud work that aims to improve the effectiveness of decision making or overall organizational performance. Others are more inclined to offer an ideological critique of an organizational improvement paradigm that has a corporate and managerial feel to it.

I have written about this in my research on academic restructuring (Gumport, 2000). I found that strategic approaches reflect an "industry logic" that legitimates higher education for its instrumental value to society, especially in economic terms, whether in furthering human capital or economic development. I see this logic as problematic in two ways. First, the premium placed on cost cutting has resulted in cost savings without ensuring that academic quality will be maintained. Second, when priorities are focused on improving a campus's competitive position amid market forces, for gains in efficiency, and in terms of revenue-generating activities, the commercialization and privatization of public higher education are seen as a reasonable—even a natural—next step in the progress of the enterprise. And this leaves in doubt what attention and resources will be devoted to a wide range of democratic and social justice functions of higher education as a social institution (Gumport, forthcoming).

In this sense, our frameworks can inadvertently carry ideological baggage. As I noted at the start of this chapter, how we think about higher education, and the words we use, shape what we study and what insights we draw from our studies, and this matters because both scholars and practitioners socially construct and reinforce the institutional foundations of higher education—not simply the organizational forms that become taken for granted but the character of the organizations: what is valued, how people are treated, what are regarded as acceptable risks, and so on.

Third, the traction in many contexts afforded to—and by—a strategic paradigm suggests its continued prominence. Of course, it may not sustain its legitimacy. But if it does, and if it is promoted as a singularly dominant framework for our field, I am concerned that it could be detrimental to the development of alternative research frameworks.[12] Just as organizational studies has been an interdisciplinary field, the vitality of our ever maturing field of higher education research will be better assured if we continue to nurture its interdisciplinary roots and multiple paradigms for research. This is the case regardless of whether its legitimacy remains contested.

Looking Ahead

To foster the development of many lines of inquiry in higher education's organizational studies, researchers can look to both past and new developments. I will mention five examples to illustrate this potential.

WITHIN A STRATEGIC PARADIGM

Higher education researchers (some of whom also serve as active consultants concurrent with their faculty responsibilities) are already working to refine understandings and applications of strategy, emphasizing the importance of different missions and campus cultures. From my perspective, the role of normative and cultural elements needs to be made more central. Previous work on the limits of rationality could lead to incorporating more interactive dynamics within strategic approaches. Even in business, it is commonly understood that "command and control" assumptions of hierarchical organizations have been displaced by leadership styles that emphasize the necessity of communication and collaboration. A more emergent or ad hoc model of strategic thinking could encourage experimentation and improvisation, wherein plans and directions can be modified as they unfold, yielding the hoped-for benefits of a revitalized sense of purpose. Still the potential for agency and the capacity for control by campus actors must not be overstated.

Following this line of thinking, we could also conceive of strategic deliberations as residing even more *locally,* as decentralized within organizational subunits, each identifying their own intended directions and developing their own plans that reflect their educational values, with the secondary benefit of strengthening collegiality. Of course, the risk of such a self-defined participative approach is that an organization could become more atomized, which may not be viable or prudent in the current climate. Such a perspective also risks missing the cumulative effects of more local decisions—for the organization, the system, and the society.

NEO-INSTITUTIONAL THEORY

Although institutional theory has been developing for forty years in organizational studies, neo-institutional theory is becoming established as a visible line of inquiry in the study of higher education. I see great potential here. Within organizational studies, institutional theorists have focused on the visible regulatory elements that reproduce institutional forms. Yet there is growing recognition that these may be less consequential than normative and cultural-cognitive elements, which are now seen by theorists as "deeper," more resilient, and more ambiguous than the regulatory dimensions that shape organizational behavior (Scott, 2008). Within neo-institutional theory, there is also increased interest in moving from the organization level per se to the field level, and higher education is an ideal arena for doing so (Bastedo, 2009).[13] It would be worth considering whether it is useful to continue to conceptualize higher education as a singular, albeit highly differentiated, field. It would serve us well to ask: What are the consequences of doing so, and what are the other alternatives?

SOCIAL MOVEMENTS

In some exciting work in organizational studies, scholars are examining the role of social movements to explain collective behavior within organizations (Davis, McAdam, Scott, & Zald, 2005). Social movement theories of framing and mobilizing are promising because they explore the nexus between meaning and action. Social movement theories can frame questions on a range of topics in higher education. Several examples are already available, such as curricular change (Slaughter, 1997), affirmative action (Rhoads, Saenz, & Carducci, 2005), and graduate student unionization (Rhoads & Rhoades, 2005). Each of these has explored new terrain in recent years.

POSITIVE ORGANIZATIONAL SCHOLARSHIP

Another promising development in organizational studies could help future higher education scholars probe the nonrational and nonstrategic elements of higher education institutions. Positive organizational scholarship focuses on the affective and social purpose aspects of organizations, offering a strikingly different vision than the strategic paradigm. Kim Cameron, Jane Dutton, and Robert Quinn (2003) argue that the scholarly focus on competition, markets, and instrumental strategies overlooks important arenas for research that could illuminate ways that organizations can contribute to social welfare and bring about the best in human nature.

Positive organizational scholarship in higher education could explore cases in which people in colleges and universities function as integrated communities, working for advances in societal or environmental welfare, such as campuses that effectively use service learning (also known as "community engagement") and foster an ethos of service and collaboration among their students. Or it could be used as a frame to study the resilience of faculty, students, and/or staff working within organizational conditions that would otherwise be trying. Empirical studies within "positive psychology" could fuel this approach, along with the wider cultural interest in the science of happiness.[14]

Finally, and with acknowledged irony in giving a nod to economics as the disciplinary king of rationality, frameworks from economics and economic sociology examine the embeddedness of organizations and their networks to analyze interdependencies between core societal institutions, like the legal system and the market. At the heart of the embeddedness perspective is the claim that the behavior of economic actors is strongly conditioned by the institutional environment instead of purely driven by an instrumental logic. Higher education researchers could make use of tools and findings from this perspective to investigate networks, both human and financial, and relationships between higher education stakeholders and the state. A piece by Brian Pusser, Sheila Slaughter, and Scott Thomas (2006) in the *Journal of Higher Education* employs an embeddedness perspective to investigate the network ties between members of public and private university boards, showing relationships between institution type and board behavior.

In drawing on these approaches in higher education, researchers would expand the analytical focus beyond the organization as level of analysis to more macro investigations of the ties and information flows between higher education institutions and government, industry, and nonprofit sector enterprises. I see this agenda as very timely, in light of global interdependencies, and with growing recognition of the need for comparative and cross-national research.

Conclusion

My broad charge here was to discuss the contributions of organizational studies to higher education research and to reflect upon recent developments and where we may be headed. I have argued that, at this stage in our field's development, our research is still underutilized by practitioners and social scientists alike. The growing legitimacy of a strategic paradigm for higher education has promise for expanding our reach. However, I see serious problems if it becomes our dominant paradigm for research or if it becomes an exclusive frame at a detriment to our developing others. A multiplicity of paradigms has served us well in our field, both in research and in practice. I see this multiplicity as necessary to ensure the continued vitality of our collective research agenda, in addition to providing a variety of generative resources for curricula in graduate programs that educate and socialize the next generation of researchers in our field.

We also must remember that, through our research, we contribute to the social construction of the broader enterprise of higher education—what it is, how it works, and what it can be. Competing logics are at work, signifying divergent views—the ongoing talk of what must change and what must not change, and what is at stake in pursuing alternative directions. I think this is healthy. The diverse views, and the tensions among them, are not a pathology to be eradicated. Rather, they constitute a dynamism essential to the continued vitality of our field and to our understanding of higher education as a changing enterprise.

After all, this is the legacy of academic organizations as sites of contestation and critical thinking, located as we are within, and yet in some ways outside, society. This part of higher education's social charter is not simply an entitlement; it is an obligation. Both in the past and in some newer developments, organizational studies offer a deep reservoir of ideas that help us to understand higher education's complexity as well as to preserve its grand legacies and societal centrality. It would be a disservice to the past—and future—for the field of higher education to narrow itself and let others define the terms of our scholarship, let alone how we go about our daily work within our colleges and universities.

ACKNOWLEDGMENTS

This chapter is adapted from a presentation entitled "Organizational Studies in Higher Education: Insights for a Changing Enterprise" (Dec. 4, 2006) for the University of Michigan's Center for Higher and Postsecondary Education's 50th Anniversary Organizational and Management Lectures. Corrie Potter, PhD candidate at Stanford University, provided valuable research assistance.

NOTES

1. Interestingly, the field of management studies faces some of the same criticisms, but not the same problems of legitimacy within the university. For elaboration on these observations about the study of higher education, see Gumport 2007.

2. The foundation staff also pointed out that their grant funding, even when considered cumulatively, was significantly dwarfed by revenue from large endowments and unrestricted funds, and they believed that campuses could allocate those institutional resources to initiatives for institutional change if it were genuinely a priority (Gumport, 2003).

3. On the lack of consensus in organizational studies, see Pfeffer 1993.

4. See, for example, Gumport 1993a and 1993b for case studies on priority setting in budget cuts, Gumport 2000 on rationales for academic restructuring, Gumport 2002 on

the struggle for legitimacy of academic fields, and Gumport and Snydman 2002 on the significance of academic structure.

5. When the field of organizational studies was gaining momentum, scholars both within and outside sociology noted the important role of Weberian concepts in developing the idea of organizations as objects of study. For example, James March and Herbert Simon (1993) acknowledge the role of Weberian concepts in their classic work *Organizations*, initially published in 1958 by John Wiley. According to March and Simon, "Modern studies of 'bureaucracies' date from Weber (1946, 1947) as to both time and acknowledged intellectual debt" (p. 55).

6. The notion of "ownership" is alternatively referred to as "buy-in," but a continuum of consultation runs from none to extensive. For example, in my research on academic restructuring, I found that faculty express dismay, even disdain, at imperatives to cut costs, establish budget discipline, and cultivate revenue—unless the idea originated with them or they are to some extent involved in the decision-making processes (Gumport, forthcoming).

7. For the original development of the garbage can model and the "organized anarchies" concept, see Cohen, March, & Olsen 1972.

8. The notion of solutions-in-search-of-problems is continued in Robert Birnbaum's (2000) research on higher education management fads, where he observes that a significant time lag occurs between the popularity of a particular solution in the corporate world and its uptake in higher education management.

9. See Gumport and Sporn 1999 for a description of additional frameworks.

10. Two are James Collins's *Good to Great: Why Some Companies Make the Leap . . . and Others Don't* (2001) and Collins and Jerry Porras's *Built to Last: Successful Habits of Visionary Companies* (1997).

11. Indeed, several of us in higher education studies have been looking at how new realities in higher education propel campus leaders to cast their actions as strategic necessity. In this period, they seek to be proactive, to build on their universities' distinctive strengths, and to improve their positions within increasingly competitive markets. For examples of this research, see Clark 1998 and Brint 2005.

12. The rise of a strategic paradigm in higher education research can be seen as part of a larger rationalist/strategic turn in the social sciences. Some scholars claim that these rationalist approaches are particularly imperialist and seek theoretical hegemony over other theoretical approaches. For an example of this argument, see Lichbach 2003.

13. For example, see the discussion of institutional logics by Bastedo (2009) in considering the role of activist governing boards in public higher education.

14. See *Time* magazine's 2005 cover story, "The New Science of Happiness," by Claudia Wallis (Jan. 9, 2005).

REFERENCES

Allen, D. J. (2003). Organizational climate and strategic change in higher education: Organizational insecurity. *Higher Education, 46*(1), 61–92.

Bastedo, M. N. (2009). Convergent institutional logics in public higher education: State policymaking and governing board activism. *Review of Higher Education, 32*(2), 209–234.

Birnbaum, R. (2000). *Management fads in higher education: Where they come from, what they do, why they fail.* San Francisco: Jossey-Bass.

Brint, S. (2005). Creating the future: "New directions" in American research universities. *Minerva, 43*(1), 23–50.

Cameron, K. (1983). Strategic responses to conditions of decline: Higher education and the private sector. *Journal of Higher Education, 54* (July/August), 359–380.

Cameron, K. S., Dutton, J. E., & Quinn, R. E. (2003). *Positive organizational scholarship: Foundations of a new discipline.* San Francisco: Berrett-Koehler.

Clark, B. R. (1972). The organizational saga in higher education. *Administrative Science Quarterly, 17*(2), 178–184.

Clark, B. R. (1998). *Creating entrepreneurial universities: Organizational pathways of transformation.* Surrey: International Association of Universities (IAU) Press/Pergamon.

Cohen, M. D., & March, J. G. (1974). *Leadership and ambiguity: The American college president.* New York: McGraw-Hill.

Cohen, M. D., March, J. G., & Olsen, J. P. (1972). A garbage can model of organizational choice. *Administrative Science Quarterly, 17*(1), 1–25.

Collins, J. C. (2001). *Good to great: Why some companies make the leap . . . and others don't.* New York: HarperCollins.

Collins, J. C., & Porras, J. I. (1997). *Built to last: Successful habits of visionary companies.* New York: Harper Business Essentials.

Davis, G., McAdam, D., Scott, W. R., & Zald, M. N. (2005). *Social movements and organization theory.* Cambridge: Cambridge University Press.

Gumport, P. J. (1993a). The contested terrain of academic program reduction. *Journal of Higher Education, 64*(3): 283–311.

Gumport, P. J. (1993b). Fired faculty: Reflections on marginalization and academic identity. In D. McLaughlin and W. Tierney (Eds.), *Naming silenced lives: Personal narratives and the process of educational change* (pp. 135–154). New York: Routledge.

Gumport, P. J. (2000). Academic restructuring: Organizational change and institutional imperatives. *Higher Education: The International Journal of Higher Education and Educational Planning, 39,* 67–91.

Gumport, P. J. (2002). *Academic pathfinders: Knowledge creation and feminist scholarship.* Westport, CT: Greenwood Press.

Gumport, P. J. (2003). *Higher education research priorities: Perspectives from selected foundations.* A report to Atlantic Philanthropies USA, Inc. Stanford, CA: Stanford Institute for Higher Education Research.

Gumport, P. J. (Ed.). (2007). *Sociology of higher education: Contributions and their contexts.* Baltimore: Johns Hopkins University Press.

Gumport, P. J. (forthcoming). *Academic legitimacy: Institutional tensions in restructuring public higher education.* Baltimore: Johns Hopkins University Press.

Gumport, P. J., & Snydman, S. (2002). The formal organization of knowledge: An analysis of academic structure. *Journal of Higher Education, 73*(3), 375–408.

Gumport, P. J., & Sporn, B. (1999). Institutional adaptation: Demands for management reform and university administration. In J. Smart (Ed.), *Higher education: Handbook of theory and research,* Vol. 14 (pp. 103–145). Bronx, NY: Agathon Press.

Hearn, J. C., Lewis, D. R., Kallsen, L., Holdsworth, J. M., & Jones, L. M. (2006). "Incentives for managed growth": A case study of incentives-based planning and budgeting in a large public research university. *Journal of Higher Education, 77*(2), 286–316.

Jasinski, J. (2004). Strategic planning via Baldrige: Lessons learned. *New directions for institutional research, 123,* 27–31.

Keller, G. (1983). *Academic strategy: The management revolution in American higher education.* Baltimore: Johns Hopkins University Press.

Kerr, C. (2002). Shock wave II: An introduction to the twenty-first century. In S. Brint (Ed.), *The future of the city of intellect: The changing American university.* Stanford, CA: Stanford University Press.

Lichbach, M. I. (2003). *Is rational choice theory all of social science?* Ann Arbor: University of Michigan Press.

March, J. G., & Simon, H. (1958). *Organizations, 1993.* 2nd ed. Oxford: Blackwell.

Marginson, S., & Considine, M. (2000). *The enterprise university: Power, governance and reinvention in Australia.* Cambridge: Cambridge University Press.

Merton, R. K. (1936). The unanticipated consequences of purposive social action. *American Sociological Review, 1*(6), 894–904.

Meyer, J. W., & Rowan, B. (1977). Institutionalized organizations: Formal structure as myth and ceremony. *American Journal of Sociology, 83*(1), 57–77.

Mintzberg, H. (1979). *The structuring of organizations.* Englewood Cliffs, NJ: Prentice Hall.

Mintzberg, H. (1980). Structure in 5's: A synthesis of the research on organization design. *Management Science, 26*(3), 322–341.

Oliver, C. (1991). Strategic responses to institutional processes. *Academy of Management Review, 16*(1), 145–179.

Peterson, M. W. (2000). Emerging developments in postsecondary organization theory and research: Fragmentation or integration. In C. Brown (Ed.), *Organization and governance in higher education* (5th ed., pp. 71–82). (Originally printed in *Educational Researcher 14*(3), 1985).

Peterson, M. W., & Dill, D. D. (1997). Understanding the competitive environment of the postsecondary knowledge industry. In M. W. Peterson, D. D. Dill, & L. A. Metts (Eds.), *Planning and management for a changing environment.* San Francisco: Jossey-Bass.

Pfeffer, J. (1993). Barriers to the advance of organizational science: Paradigm development as a dependent variable. *Academy of Management Review, 18*(4), 599–620.

Pusser, B., Slaughter, S., & Thomas, S. L. (2006). Playing the board game: An empirical analysis of university trustee and corporate board interlocks. *Journal of Higher Education, 77*(5), 747–775.

Rhoads, R. A., & Rhoades, G. (2005). Graduate employee unionization as symbol of and challenge to the corporatization of U.S. research universities. *Journal of Higher Education, 76*(3), 243–275.

Rhoads, R. A., Saenz, V., & Carducci, R. (2005). Higher education reform as a social movement: The case of affirmative action. *Review of Higher Education, 28*(2), 191–220.

Scott, W. R. (2004). Reflections on a half-century of organizational sociology. *Annual Review of Sociology, 30*, 1–21.

Scott, W. R. (2007). Changing contours of organizations and organization theory. In W. R. Scott & G. F. Davis (Eds.), *Organizations and organizing: Rational, natural and open system perspectives.* Upper Saddle River, NJ: Prentice Hall.

Scott, W. R. (2008). Approaching adulthood: The maturing of institutional theory. *Theory and Society, 37*(5), 427–442.

Slaughter, S. (1997). Class, race and gender and the construction of postsecondary curricula in the United States: Social movement, professionalization and political economic theories of curricular change. *Journal of Curriculum Studies, 29*, 1–30.

U.S. Department of Education. (2006). *A test of leadership: Charting the future of U.S. higher education.* Washington: Education Publications Center.

Weick, K. E. (1976). Educational organizations as loosely coupled systems. *Administrative Science Quarterly, 21*(1), 1–19.

Welsh, J. F., Nunez, W. J., & Petrosko, J. (2006). Assessing and cultivating support for strategic planning: Searching for best practices in a reform environment. *Assessment & Evaluation in Higher Education 31*(6), 693.

PART TWO

REINVIGORATING
CORE LITERATURES

CHAPTER THREE

Governance Research

From Adolescence toward Maturity

JAMES C. HEARN AND MICHAEL K. MCLENDON

Governance has long been a topic of intense interest for institutional leaders and faculty. Many of the founders of the colonial colleges, for example, believed that the faculties' control of England's Oxford and Cambridge universities produced excessive sloth and autonomy, so they explicitly chose instead to adopt the Scottish model of placing ultimate institutional authority in the hands of external boards (Thelin, 2004). In the years since, institutional governance styles have evolved further: from de facto board control in the nation's early years, to increasing faculty authority in the late nineteenth through mid-twentieth centuries, to mounting pressures for democratic participation in the 1960s and 1970s, to, finally, the current emphasis on strategic, market-sensitive policymaking in the face of growing resource challenges (see Dill & Helm, 1988; Peterson, 2007; Thelin, 2004). But these generalizations are rough: there is and has always been enormous variation in the ways colleges and universities are governed, and since the earliest years, the relative governing roles and authority of faculty, presidents, boards, and the state have been continually subject to debate and dispute (Carnegie, 1982; Graham, 1989). Whether the issue is the adoption of new degree initiatives, the importance of religious beliefs in a college's faculty hiring, or the appropriate role of intercollegiate athletics, governance has always attracted attention, and many people on and off campus care about it.

That caring, however, has usually taken the form of value assertions regarding what is better or best, rather than empirical, social-scientific investigation of governance structuring and functioning. Systematic research interest in the governance of higher education is a remarkably recent phenomenon. Arguably, effective analytical attention to governance came only in the 1960s, in the wake of not only dramatic growth in attendance, funding, and institutional diversity but also increasing attention to higher education as a distinctive and significant societal institution. As Peterson and Mets (1987) put it, it was in those years that that "the trickle of writing . . . became a deluge" (p. 5).

What, then, have we learned? What fruits has a half century of accelerated analysis of governance borne? What directions seem promising for further work? The questions are far too big for a single book, much less a single chapter. If one wants to examine the college and university governance literature in a new and useful way, and that is the intent of this essay, it seems wiser to selectively craft a reasonably discrete take on a massive topic. Toward that end, we delimit the notion of governance for this essay to focus on the setting of purposes and goals of the organization and the creation of structures, policies, and programs in pursuit of those purposes and goals. Thus, we target the fundamental decision-making processes and arrangements of colleges and institutions. In choosing that approach, we attend little to issues of management (the implementation and execution of governance decisions), and we address leadership (the structures and processes of individual influences on decisions) only to the extent that it intersects with governance.[1]

Also, it would be virtually impossible to cover in a single chapter not only governance research in the United States and Canada but also the burgeoning research literature on governance elsewhere. In the past few decades, perhaps no topic has occupied as much attention among higher education researchers internationally as governance (e.g., see Huisman, 2009; Maassen & Olsen, 2007; Marginson, 2000). The rise of the World Bank in educational analysis and reform, the fall of the Iron Curtain, the rapid expansion of higher education enrollment in East Asia, the emergence of neoliberal governing approaches in Europe, and the signing of numerous international cooperative initiatives (including most notably the Bologna Agreement) have each created remarkable opportunities for rethinking, and researching, governance. Each deserves more intensive treatment than we could offer here.

Finally, we do not address here the legal/judicial bases of governance. The modern university as an organizational form is, at its heart, a legal creation. The medieval origins of the university provided the precursor to the modern legal notion of the corporation (Duryea, 1973), and colleges and universities remain distinctive entities under the law. Institutions operate both under government charter and independently of direct governmental control. This duality benefits institutions but also can create significant governance tensions, as when larger political controversies press on the policies and practices of public universities.

While these issues are significant, covering them would take us well beyond the core organizational concerns of the chapter. Of course, in electing not to address the issues above, we do not presume that we have narrowed the topic to easily manageable dimensions. We are sufficiently daunted to acknowledge that much good work undoubtedly goes unnoted in this essay.

We discuss here the governance literature prior to 1980 and then turn to what has emerged subsequently as numerous scholars turned their attention to the topic. In closing, we consider some potential arenas for the next generation of research on the topic—ideally, such work would contribute substantively to the ongoing research "deluge" first identified by Peterson and Mets.

The Pre-1980 Governance Literature

In a perceptive review of the state of research, Peterson (1985) identified 1963 and 1974 as key turning points in organizational studies in postsecondary education. Peterson characterized 1963 as the beginning of the "infancy" of higher education organizational studies (p. 6). In that same year, McConnell lamented the absence of literature on the organization, administration, and governance of higher education. Over the next decade, the field's first systematic research efforts arose, along with numerous practical and conceptual work. The nascent field began attracting interest from sociologists, social psychologists, political scientists, and management scholars. By 1974, some two hundred research-based publications had been produced (Peterson, 1974). Postsecondary organizational studies, commented Peterson (1985), had reached "pre-adolescence."

Despite these early, noteworthy gains, Peterson (1985) noted four concerns: unsophisticated research designs and methodology, an absence of reliably constructed instruments to support replication, limited theory development, and overreliance on "internal-purposive" theoretical models (viewing colleges and universities as rational and self-directed, the models focused largely on goal attainment and the internal management of organizational activities). These last two held particular relevance for the evolving study of postsecondary governance.

Postsecondary governance came increasingly to be viewed through three lenses in the literature: formal-rational or bureaucratic models, collegial or "professional bureaucratic" models, and political models.[2] With its Weberian underpinnings, the standard model of *machine bureaucracy* conceptualized postsecondary governance essentially as an exercise in rational decision making, in the calculation of the most efficient means by which goals can be achieved, and in the design of systems of managerial control capable of directing the activities of large numbers of personnel within the organization. Accordingly, the model emphasized efficiency, predictability, means-end hierarchies, intentionality, goal attainment, rules and regulations, formal division of labor, patterns of formalization and standardization, top-down information flows, technical competence and performance, managerial control, and clear structural relationships between and among the organization's units. Building on the state of organizational knowledge at the time (e.g., see March, 1965), much of the scholarship on postsecondary governance in the 1960s and 1970s explored the nature and implications of these various elements in the functioning of colleges and universities (e.g., Baldridge, 1971a, 1971b; Blau, 1973; Corson, 1971; Mintzberg, 1979), with analysts often observing how postsecondary organizations tended to defy many of the core assumptions and attributes of the classic machine metaphor.

Conceptions of the college and university as *collegium* arose in the early 1970s, in part as a response to the perceived explanatory failings of the bureaucratic model. Most studies in this tradition sought to examine the nonrational or symbolic side of postsecondary organization. Rooted in cultural analysis and in the empirical case study methods of earlier sociologists, this scholarship conceptualized certain institutions as academic communities defined by broad participation, extensive consultation, collective responsibilities, flattened hierarchies, conformity to norms, adherence to traditions, and egalitarian impulses.

Pioneering contributions to this tradition, notably Clark (1970), focused mainly on certain liberal arts colleges and how the firmly embedded values of those postsecondary institutions shape the organizations' identities, help them form shared accounts and common beliefs, "guide the thoughts and steer the actions" of participants, and, ultimately, condition governance patterns (Clark, 1992, vii). Clark argued that these forces were sufficiently profound to encourage, over time, the development of a distinctive organizational character, which he famously termed an "organizational saga." Clark's was not the first scholarship to focus on institutional culture (e.g., see Pace, 1962), but its theoretical power was seminal (Maassen, 1996), leading to a notable outpouring of research over the next twenty years, including studies of efforts to better define, differentiate, typologize, conceptualize, and assess academic culture (Masland, 1985; Peterson & Spencer, 1993; Tierney, 1988), to manage academic culture (Dill, 1982), and to understand culture's impacts on campus governance (Baird, 1988; Chaffee & Tierney, 1988; Kolman & Hossler, 1987; Tierney, 1989).

Finally, the *political* model arose as a central lens in higher education studies in the 1960s and 1970s. This lens built foundationally on three key concepts deriving from the pluralist school of American politics: dispersion of political power, interest group competition and political bargaining. Political scientists operating in this tradition held to the idea that power to make decisions in American society fundamentally is fragmented. Consequently, public policy is the product of (1) continual struggle between groups that must compete with one another for resources, influence, and power and (2) bargaining or political negotiation between groups and elected officials (e.g., Dahl, 1967). Because no one group can dominate all the others, governance takes the form of compromise among groups. The tendency toward group competition and compromise is the basis for a democratic equilibrium that effectively (if not always efficiently) serves the public weal. As Dahl (1967) once famously observed, "Because constant negotiations among different centers of power are necessary in order to make decisions, citizens and leaders will perfect the precious art of dealing peacefully with their conflicts, and not merely to the benefit of one partisan but to the mutual benefit of all the parties to a conflict" (p. 24).

Borrowing many of these ideas from political science, including the seminal work of Cyert and March (1963), postsecondary researchers conceptualized the college and university as an arena of coalitional activity in which various parties exhibit differing preferences, interests, and goals and in which continual intergroup struggles over resources and power profoundly influence ultimate decisions. In a landmark case study of organizational conflict at New York University, Baldridge (1971b) developed an "interest-articulation" model that emphasized the significance of factions, interests, coalitional activities, and bargaining in shaping institutional governance processes and outcomes. He characterized the political model as providing a more realistic appraisal of university governance processes than either the bureaucratic or collegial models precisely because of the attention it paid to the role of power and group conflict in explaining how decisions are made. Indeed, the differences between the political model and the other two basic governance models of the pre-1974 era are never more evident than on the question of their outlook on conflict. Whereas the bureaucratic and collegial models tend to view dissension as dystopic, the political model regards it as an important factor in promoting needed organizational change. As Thompson (1967) observed, while it might be expected that conflict inescapably would lead to instability, political systems in organizations tend to produce dominant coalitions that can remain stable over time. Disruptive power tends to be minimized because members of the organization belong to more than one group, thus providing a check against instability, a point noted as holding true in universities by both Baldridge (1971b) and Bess and Dee (2008).

The political model holds distinct governance implications. While bureaucratic systems are governed through vertical coordination, and collegial systems through horizontal coordination, political systems are governed through the coordination of conflict (Birnbaum, 1991), hence the many studies of this period that focused on conflict management as key to understanding governance, particularly college and university budgeting and resource allocation (Chaffee, 1983; Pfeffer & Salancik, 1974). Much of this literature also examined the strengths and weaknesses inherent in the political model of governance. As political systems, colleges and universities can function despite goal conflict or ambiguity, and their inefficiency can actually enhance stability as many coalitions and actors effectively counterbalance one another's influence in the larger system. As Baldridge (1971b) wrote, "This may be a better way of grappling with the complexity that surrounds decision processes within a loosely coordinated, fragmented . . . system" (pp. 191–192), such as characterizes many university settings. Yet the political model has its limitations, too. It conceptualizes an organization that often responds ineffectually to problems demanding rational analysis, produces inefficiencies in resource allocation, and fails to account adequately for long-term, routine decision processes because of its episodic focus.

By the mid-1970s, observed Peterson (1985), postsecondary organization theory and research had moved past "early childhood" and entered into an adolescent stage of development, generating a large and growing number of research-oriented studies. Notably, several distinctively new perspectives on governance became increasingly influential, including Cohen, March, and Olsen's (1972) and Cohen and March's (1974) "garbage can" model of organizational choice and Weick's (1976) "loosely coupled systems" model. These publications signaled a shift in the literature toward models grounded in ambiguity, contingent choice processes, and emergent social systems. These approaches often rejected or called deeply into question the assumptions underlying the three principal models of the previous era.

The work of Cohen, March, and Olsen (hereafter, CMO), in particular, left a deep imprint in part because of its groundbreaking conception of the distinctiveness of colleges and universities as organizations. The key distinguishing feature of the CMO model is its conception of the modern university as an organized anarchy. As such, the university organization possesses three distinctive properties. The first is problematic preferences. "The organization," observed the authors, "operates on the basis of a variety of inconsistent and ill-defined preferences" (Cohen et al., 1972, p. 1). Because it is often unclear what preferences decision makers hold, the university resembles more a "loose collection of ideas" than a coherent decision structure. The second organizational property is unclear technology. Although the organization "manages to survive and even produce" (p. 1), members often do not comprehend the organization's decision processes.

Rather, the university tends to operate contingently, haltingly, and often in ways defying straightforward rationalization. The third property is fluid participation. The high degree of autonomy enjoyed by the professionals staffing the university's operating core[3] means participants vary in the amount of time and effort they may choose to dedicate to different activities and roles. Because the involvement of participants varies and the boundaries of the organization are vague and shifting, the decision makers for any particular choice opportunity change irregularly and, often, unpredictably.

Beyond this depiction of the university's underlying organizational properties, Cohen and colleagues (1972) described how the organized anarchy makes choices absent clear, consistent, and shared goals and how its members (and occasional members) direct their attention to certain issues, problems, and solutions. They characterize organizational decision making as a complicated interplay between four "streams" of activity: (1) the development of problems in the organization, (2) the actions and behaviors of participants, (3) the formulation of solutions, and (4) the opportunities for choice (i.e., decision). Problems do not always clearly present themselves. Participants' interest and involvement vary widely from one moment to the next. Solutions do not necessarily flow from the problems to which they eventually become attached; sometimes solutions precede problems. When choice opportunities arise, they may not always correspond with the times when problems need to be solved. Consequently, timing and contingency have notable effects on decision outcomes. They condition the ways in which problems and solutions are introduced into the organization, the manner by which the organization's energy can be deployed, and the impacts of the decision structure itself.

To understand processes within organized anarchies in general, and governance within postsecondary institutions in particular, observed Cohen and colleagues, one can view a choice opportunity as a metaphorical "garbage can" into which "various kinds of problems and solutions are dumped by participants as they are generated" (Cohen et al., 1972, p. 2). Streams of problems, solutions, and participants drift continuously throughout the system but often are independent, very loosely associated, or "partially uncoupled" from one another (p. 16). In such a system, problems linger in search of decision situations in which they can be aired; solutions search for problems to which they may be viewed as the answer; and participants search for status, for issues that will help them build their careers, or for opportunities to shirk or flee. Choice opportunities provoke decisions, but the ambiguity that runs rampant throughout the organized anarchy results in decisions that are highly contingent, unpredictable, and rarely successful in solving problems. In Cohen and March's (1974) memorable phrasing, "The garbage can process is one in which problems, solutions, and participants move from one choice opportunity to another in such a way that the nature of the choice, the time it takes, and the problems it solves all depend on a relatively complicated intermeshing of elements. These include the mix of choices available at any one time, the mix of problems that have access to the organization, the mix of solutions looking for problems, and the outside demands on the decision makers" (p. 16). Consequently, the choice process is nonlinear. As Cohen, March, and Olsen (1972) themselves pointed out, when measured against a conventional model of rational choice, garbage can processes appear "pathological" (p. 16). Yet such standards are inappropriate, maintain the authors: although university garbage can processes do not actually resolve problems very well, they do enable choices to be made under conditions of extreme goal ambiguity and conflict.

Notwithstanding its popularity as an approach to understanding postsecondary organization, the CMO model has attracted sharp criticism. Most pointedly, Bendor, Moe, and Shotts (2001) have argued that despite its great potential and wide-ranging influence, "the theory that has grown up over the years is so complex and confusing, and some of its components are so seriously flawed, that there is little reason for thinking that it can look ahead to a more fertile future. For fundamental reasons, the theory lacks the rigor, discipline, and analytic power needed for genuine progress" (p. 169). To understand the critique, it is important to note, as do Bendor and colleagues, that Cohen, and colleagues provide *both* a verbal description of the features of organized anarchies (most often illustrated with hypothetical and survey- and interview-based examples from university settings) and a computerized simulation of the workings of such settings. Bendor and colleagues suggest that the verbal formulation of the CMO model and the presumably derived computer simulation of the model are at odds with each other in core assumptions, logic, and empirical implications. Indeed, Bendor and colleagues' own explorations of the CMO simulation specifications led to scenarios in which decision makers followed each other in packs, a result essentially opposite the result one would expect under the verbal formulations of the original model. That is, the simulations reveal an organizational world much more orderly than the model's original, colorfully phrased prose presentations would ever suggest. Reviewing their results, Bendor and colleagues conclude: "This is ironic. The informal theory of the garbage can is famous for depicting a world that is much more complex than that described by classical theories of organizational choice. The latter's tidy image of goal specification, alternative generation, evaluation, and choice is replaced by a complex swirl of problems looking for solutions, solutions looking for problems, participants wandering around looking for work, and all three searching for choice opportunities. Yet the simulation depicts almost none of this and in fact creates a world of remarkable order" (p. 182).

Such critiques have not gone unchallenged, however. In a strongly phrased rebuttal, Olsen (2001) countered that Bendor and colleagues had misportrayed both the spirit and the results of Cohen, March, and Olsen's model. Suggesting that proposing "theory" was never their goal, Olsen emphasized instead their more modest, largely heuristic aims. In a related vein, Olsen argued that the simulation results were neither surprising nor defaming for the model because the model never presumed that all decision behavior should be disorderly and atomized. Stressing that repetition and "clumping" were core elements of the model rather than anomalies disconfirming the model's power, Olsen states that what Bendor and colleagues viewed "as a major 'bug' we saw—and still see—as a 'feature.' Namely, the simulation reproduces an experience from our own lives: moving through a series of meetings on nominally disparate topics, reaching few decisions, while talking repeatedly with many of the same people about the same problems" (p. 192). Bendor and colleagues and other critics raise useful points regarding the CMO model, but the undeniably provocative organized anarchy and garbage can ideas have clearly aided understanding of postsecondary organization.

Arising in same period as the CMO model was the complementary concept of loosely coupled systems. Popularized by Weick (1976), the loose-coupling concept built particularly on work by Glassman (1973) and March and Olsen (1975) and on the principles of general systems theory, which was beginning to influence the organizational sciences (Katz & Kahn, 1966). Weick portrayed school and college systems as a counterconventional organizational form characterized by their *lack* of rationality, efficiency, tidiness, and tightly coordinated structures aimed toward goal attainment. Weick drew a vital distinction between loose coupling and a loosely coupled *system*. While the former term may be appropriated to describe the relationship between any two organizational units or entities that are linked to one another weakly or infrequently, a loosely coupled *system*, such as characterizes many schools, colleges, and universities, is one in which minimal interdependence pervades the entire organization over time. Distinctively, loosely coupled systems organizations exhibit an abundance of slack resources, minimal coordination between and among units, high levels of decentralization and delegation, tendencies toward equifinality, and causal independence. Thus, Weick later wrote (1982), loose coupling is evident when elements affect each other "suddenly (rather than continuously), occasionally (rather than constantly), negligibly (rather than significantly), indirectly (rather than directly), and eventually (rather than immediately)" (p. 380).

Viewing educational organizations as loosely coupled systems, noted Weick, is a descriptive and empirical exercise rather than a normative one. Weick (1976) argued that, although traditionalists may regard such systems "as a sin or something to be apologized for" (p. 6), they can provide distinct advantages. Such systems tend to be highly adaptive, mutable, and innovative and can afford the organization a sensitive-sensing mechanism, a capacity for isolating and halting the failures of one part of the system from spreading to other parts, a high degree of self-determination, and lower coordination costs.

The notion of organizations as loosely coupled systems gained widespread popularity throughout the social sciences in the 1970s and the 1980s, although Weick later lamented the concept's drift. Reviewing the literature, Orton and Weick (1990) noted that many later interpretations had lost dialectical quality in the move toward unidimensional understandings. For Orton and Weick, the problem inherent in loose coupling is the demand that it places on analysts to think simultaneously about rationality and indeterminacy, a demand largely unmet in the growing literature on the topic. Regardless, the kind of organization Weick (1976) initially envisioned clearly shared little in common with the bureaucratic and political models of postsecondary governance models so ingrained in the field a decade earlier.

Although certainly less "integrated" than "fragmented" (Peterson, 1985), the postsecondary governance literature of the late 1970s unmistakably had matured in a number of important respects. The range of governance questions, issues, and topics studied had broadened. The conceptualizations had grown in number, richness, and complexity. Because most writings increasingly assumed an open systems, rather than a closed systems, perspective, the literature's principal viewpoint had shifted from purposive, internally oriented models to emergent, adaptive ones. Unpredictability, contingency, and ambiguity had grown more commonplace in the field's thinking on governance, leaving a large imprint on the field's future research and conceptual directions. Methodologically, the field still lacked the development Peterson (1985) had characterized as requisite for full maturation, but scholars had begun to pursue a widening range of techniques beyond the long-dominant case study approach. Indeed, both conceptually and methodologically, the field of the late 1970s had assumed the essential form into which it would grow more completely over the coming decades.

The Emerging Research Literature on Governance

Since the early 1980s, governance research has come to encompass all aspects of U.S. higher education, from institutions' programmatic and departmental levels through to the national level of task forces, associations, commissions, and government agencies. Those levels provide a basis for a review of the profusion of work since that time.

GOVERNANCE AT THE UNIT LEVEL

The most significant governance activity on campuses arguably occurs not at the institutional level but at the level of the academic subunits on campus: programs, departments, and, in large institutions, field-based colleges such as engineering, liberal arts, education, business, and law. Although only a limited number of empirical analyses have tackled governance at this level (Hearn, 2007), theorists have produced ideas well worth researchers' attention.

Clark (1987) stresses that each academic unit is a vehicle through which faculty leverage their professional authority. Professors, he suggests, "use the department as a tool to mediate between the realities of a particular university context and the demands and desires of their own discipline. . . . Forming the base of the structure of faculty power, the department has undergirded the development of a dual authority structure within universities and colleges. . . . The department is the local rock on which the power of voice is based in academia, the organized base for the capacity of academics to exercise influence within the organization to which they belong and to branch out into larger circles" (pp. 64–65).

Massy, Wilger, and Colbeck (1994) follow similar lines of argument, using the term "hollowed collegiality" to capture aspects of the normative climate in departments in which faculty collegially discuss certain issues (especially those relating to facilitating research) while regularly avoiding collegial discussion of such issues as improving teaching and learning. In a similar vein, Massy and Zemsky (1997) argue on the basis of case study evidence that decentralizing governance responsibilities to the departmental level leads to increasing institutional costs, as faculty act to protect their workloads in teaching, preserve resources for research and other prerogatives, and stifle attempts to improve efficiency.[4] This process is the heart of what Massy (1996) terms the "academic ratchet," a problem exacerbated by certain predisposing conditions: "(1) strongly held beliefs about the intrinsic worth of teaching and research programs, (2) a collegial approach to decision making that places consensus at the center and allows little room for alternative points of view, (3) powerful beliefs about academic freedom that are sometimes interpreted as forbidding interference in faculty activities, and (4) the influence of students and alumni who do not want to see the reputation of their program or department negatively impacted" (p. 85). The academic ratchet concept suggests a number of testable propositions, but there appears to have been little empirical follow-up.

The most fundamental decisions in academic units regard who will be allowed to continue as faculty and thus to help shape the unit's future. Hearn and Anderson (2002) found that departments with larger instructional loads and lower levels of internal curricular specialization were more likely to have split votes over promotion and tenure decisions, as were departments from disciplines with a "soft" knowledge base. Thus, consensual unanimity was harder to achieve in units with low levels of disciplinary knowledge development and agreement.

Similarly, Braxton and Hargens (1996) found in a series of studies that departments in high-consensus fields such as physics tend to be more efficient, to be less conflicted, to change and adapt more easily, to exhibit less turnover, to be more collaborative in publications, and to be more effective in achieving certain goals and obtaining financial and human resources, compared with units in low-consensus fields such as sociology. Similarly, Pfeffer (1993), Collins (1994), Smart, Feldman, and Ethington (2000), and others have found evidence that discipline-related factors can influence governance.

Political analysis of unit-level governance is unfortunately rare. Welsh and Slusher (1986) examined the appointment of deans in professional colleges on several university campuses. Their analysis suggested that the level of curricular and research interdependence among faculty in different units mediated the effects of faculty agreement on political activity. When interdependent faculty were in agreement, appointment processes remained relatively unpoliticized, but when non-interdependent faculty were in agreement, political activity blossomed. The authors concluded that political activity serves two purposes: to assist existing coalitions in building advantages, and to facilitate the formation of new coalitions within colleges.

Some analysts (e.g., Kaplan, 2004) have observed that governance arrangements appear to matter little ultimately in departmental and college decisions, but the arena is clearly understudied. If academic units are truly at the heart of

institutional and faculty life, the relative absence of systematic governance research at this level demands redress.

Institutional presidents and provosts must "govern" in addition to managing and
leading. That is, their work involves shaping fundamental directions for the institution. In this, they must act in conjunction with boards above them in the
hierarchy and faculty, staff, and students below them. Leaders' governance concerns appear to be primarily strategic: which curricular areas to emphasize or
deemphasize, which potential revenue-generating markets to embrace or avoid,
which stances to take in response to emerging social, economic, technological,
and political developments, and so forth.

The strategic perspective emerged in the early 1980s in the higher education
literature, and governance was a central concern from the start, addressing the
question of how best to determine institutional directions. The answers varied.
Keller's widely read volume (1983) emphasized the role of leaders, but others
emphasized the role of constituencies, with particular attention to the role of
faculty in the identification of internal programmatic strengths and weaknesses
and external opportunities and threats (e.g., Cope, 1981). After some successes in
other forms of organizations, the strategic movement in higher education has
found widespread acceptance but only debatable success. The relative weakness
of hierarchical and lateral coupling in colleges and universities (e.g., faculty's commitments to shared governance, resistance to central authority, and reluctance to
intercede in the autonomy of faculty in other fields) may hinder effective leader-
driven strategic change (Dill & Helm, 1988; Hearn, 1988; Weick, 1976). Thus,
arguably, strategic change may be most constrained on campuses with the deepest traditions of faculty autonomy.

Also, as Peterson (2007) has noted, the strategic movement ran headlong into
the changing postsecondary knowledge industry of the 1990s and beyond. Earlier challenges had involved such issues as growth, equity, retrenchment, and
quality preservation, but the emerging new era has brought a rapidly changing
marketplace, shifting consumer and stakeholder preferences, and new delivery
models for teaching and research. Peterson argues that, instead of focusing on
responding to environments by identifying key institutional niches, strategic
governance and decision making should now build upon the particulars of a
school's history, internal and external environments, culture, and resources.

Peterson (2007) identifies three elaborations of the strategic framework to fit emerging circumstances: adaptive, contextual, and entrepreneurial models. Sporn and Gumport have taken the adaptive approach, examining how certain institutions have responded effectively to emerging environmental forces by reshaping institutional configurations, processes, and emphases (Gumport & Sporn, 1999; Sporn, 1999). Peterson himself (1997) has pursued the contextual approach, arguing that the emerging context is ill defined, rapidly changing, and unpredictable, with the knowledge industry mediating between larger social forces and specific institutional changes. Finally, Clark (1998) has viewed strategic change through an entrepreneurial lens, with special attention to conditions facing what he terms "the academic heartland" of the core liberal arts and sciences units. In each case, Peterson (2007) suggests, effective institutional leadership and governance are becoming more contingent and more closely tied to particular campus circumstances in time (historical, periodic, and trend contexts) and space (key markets and resources). One might infer that, in such a view, the historical buffering of institutional decision making from external developments and pressures (the "ivory tower" metaphor) loses force by the day.

GOVERNANCE AT THE INSTITUTIONAL LEVEL: SENATES, COMMITTEES, TASK FORCES, AND COMMISSIONS

Faculty from across campuses regularly participate in a variety of governance activities for the institution as a whole, including campus senates, promotion and tenure committees, admissions committees, "blue ribbon" strategic planning task forces, presidential commissions, and the like. Although hortatory essays and books on these activities proliferate, analytical, empirically based literature on the faculty's role in shared institutional governance is scarce (Birnbaum, 1989; Kezar, 2005).

But some high-quality empirical analyses have been produced. Much of that literature focuses on program creation and discontinuation, a topic on the border between faculty and administrative responsibilities (Gumport, 1993). In a series of case studies, Eckel (2000) found that, on campuses facing program closures, faculty participation in shared governance could facilitate difficult choices but that the faculty role was not as initiators of termination processes (largely in the province of administrative leaders) but rather as leaders of choices regarding the fate of particular campus programs, as leaders in opposition to particular termination plans, and, less directly, as effective legitimators of program termination decisions. Similarly, Hardy (1990b) found that shared governance and collegiality can coexist with retrenchment when leaders create structures and processes that ensure communication and consensus and reduce the potentials for political maneuvering.

But politics and power are ever present. Results from a variety of studies (see Hackman, 1985; Pfeffer & Salancik, 1974) suggest that programmatic resource allocations in universities are substantially associated with unit power on campuses. Among the indicators of power such works consider are grants funding and enrollments, the external reputation of academic departments' disciplinary fields, unit representation on key decision bodies, and the campus-level political connections of key unit actors.

In a case study analysis, Gumport (1993) found that "the fate of contending academic fields may have less to do with the ideas themselves (that is, how original, coherent, or brilliant) and more to do with their instrumental value vis-à-vis the broader political economy that tilts toward an explicit service orientation to the state and its ancillary abundant markets (for example, corporations). A significant problem remains in public research institutions: academic ideology promises faculty collegial authority, shared governance, and a meritocracy of rewards, yet economic realities loom large" (p. 305). Reflecting on such results, Gumport and Pusser (1999) suggest that marketplace ideology and the demands of key resource providers can trump internal collegiality and traditional academic values in program-reduction decisions.

Interestingly, faculty participation in campus-level governance may have limited effects. Kaplan's extensive case study work (2004) found that, unsurprisingly, faculty play smaller roles in financial and institutional decisions than in academic decisions on campus. But strikingly, Kaplan also found that levels of faculty participation in campus decisions were unrelated to program closures or ultimate choices in presidential searches. Faculty involvement was nevertheless significantly (albeit slightly) associated with higher salaries, increased chances of adoption of merit-pay policies, and lower teaching loads. Interestingly, Kaplan's work suggested that routinized governance structures and processes have mixed influences: having meetings of the full faculty on a campus was associated with lower rather than higher salary levels, and the existence of academic senates was associated with lower teaching loads but also with lower educational expenditures. Perhaps most striking was Kaplan's finding that in no case was administrative participation in governance associated with outcomes faculty might view less favorably. In sum, Kaplan's work fits with other results suggesting an absence of powerful faculty influences in overall campus governance.

Might faculty governance activities actually work *against* traditional academic values? Talburt's case study analysis (2005) led her to proclaim: "I question claims that faculty inherently serve as a 'check' on the market logic of administrators. . . . [Rapid] changes in ideas about and practices in the university brought on by corporatization create conditions that affect faculty members' understandings of their work and identities—and, thus, their responses to their surroundings in contexts such as governance" (p. 462). Arguing that universities not only serve corporations but emulate them, Talburt suggests that service to corporate interests has reshaped faculty members' perceptions of their governance roles.

Marketized change efforts devaluing established governance approaches may run still larger risks. In an intriguing case study, Kezar (2005) found that radical administration-led reform efforts on a small liberal arts campus threatened symbolic systems and shared understandings while energizing faculty participation in governance. Her case study analysis revealed that even over the longer term, when the hypothesized benefits of radical reorganization on the campus might have been seen as most likely, notable negative consequences persisted. Kezar interprets these findings as supporting earlier work by Birnbaum (1991) and Schuster, Smith, Corak, and Yamada (1994) and directly discrediting calls by Keller (1983), Benjamin and Carroll (1998), and others for movement toward "joint big decision committees" supplanting slower, more established governance structures and processes.

Birnbaum (2004) has observed that most attempts to streamline institutional governance or improve the qualities of decisions have failed because they rely on weak assumptions, for example, that faculty do not care about their institutions, that faculty resist measurement because they fear being discovered, or that faculty deliberation usually means misguided inaction at best or ineffectiveness at worst. Birnbaum proposes that those who see limits to current governance arrangements might more productively focus less on the rationalistic concerns such as structures, rules, and processes and more on the core commitments and values behind governance. Notably, faculty have every right to be concerned over institutions' core academic technologies because that is where their own expertise and interests lie. For Birnbaum, the central concept is thus "soft governance": the notion that all institutional parties respect academic norms and the faculty's historical, culturally rooted role in preserving those norms and will work to preserve those norms in whatever organizational form seems most appropriate to the context. Birnbaum's point echoes that of many others (e.g., Clark, 1983b) in expressing concern that the imposition of rationalistic, managerial ideologies threatens academic institutions' most valuable features: ambiguity of authority, openness to innovation and creativity, and normative commitment to democratic governance.

Clearly, the interplay between rationalistic values, motivations, and interpretations, on the one hand, and symbolic values, motivations, and interpretations on the other profoundly shapes campus governance (Hardy, 1990b), and no single theoretical lens affords definitive insights. Multiple agendas are being pursued, and multiple interpretations are possible. Some (e.g., Lee, 1991) have taken this context as a call for qualitative analysis. As Hardy (1990a) has noted, mere observation is inadequate: "Actions that look rational may be collegial or political, the garbage can may be transformed into a political arena, and so on. This situation is most clear when contrasting collegial and political models. Conflict may occur under a collegial system when different conceptions of the common good exist, which will not necessarily be out of the ordinary in a system of loose coupling and specialization. Conversely, apparent consensus may have been engineered by actors for their own political advantage. The challenge for the researcher is, then, to look beyond the superficial behaviour and understand the motivations and rationales of the various actors" (p. 417).

But work by Pfeffer (1992), Kaplan (2004), and others suggests that at least some aspects of these processes may be amenable to quantitative/positivist analytical tools, and such efforts should not be abandoned. While case studies and similar approaches may better capture understandings and meanings in strategic change, it would be foolhardy to abandon investigations that might shed additional light on the nature and causes of changes in the objective circumstances of various actors in strategic dramas.

INSTITUTIONAL GOVERNING BOARDS

There has been significantly more analysis of institutional governing boards than of senates and other internal governing activities, perhaps because of boards' centrality in choices concerning markets, affordability, accountability, and transparency. Interestingly, though, much of such work has been descriptive or normative, rather than theoretically based and empirically rigorous (Nicholson-Crotty & Meier, 2003).

Still, some intriguing work has emerged. The growing spirit of marketization and entrepreneurialism among boards has attracted increasing research attention. Chait (1995), Lazerson (1997), and Slaughter and Leslie (1997) noted the connections emerging between boards and the new academic capitalism around the same time, and the last stressed a need for theory-driven analysis of the phenomenon. Following that suggestion, Pusser, Slaughter, and Thomas (2006) examined the striking differences in the boards of public and private institutions, finding that private institutions' boards exhibited far more director interlocks with corporations engaged in such emerging arenas as bio-science.

The structuring of university governing boards also has attracted attention. Kaplan (2004) found little consistent relationship between boards' organizational characteristics (size, corporate memberships, meeting frequencies, selection mechanisms, faculty participation) and such outcomes as leadership turnover, program closures, expenditures, and faculty salaries. In related work using principal-agent and public-choice literatures, Toma (1986) investigated why some states choose systemwide board structures while others choose institution-specific boards. Her analyses suggest that larger states were more likely to have consolidated (i.e., across-institution) governing boards, while states with large numbers of private institutions were less likely to have such boards. Thus, she concluded, political costs associated with the interests of educators, taxpayers, and others drive states' governance choices. In later work (1990), Toma found that public institutions with institution-specific boards were more responsive to taxpayer demands than institutions in consolidated governing systems. Notably, institutions governed by their own boards operated more like private institutions in their reliance on tuition, exhibited fewer students per faculty member, and maintained lower proportions of tenured faculty. Toma's cross-sectional methodology precludes causal inferences from her two board-focused studies, but her core questions have been too little considered: What factors drive the ways decision makers structure postsecondary governance arrangements, and what are the implications of those choices?

There has been an increase in attention to the role of boards in dealing with challenges and impending, or at least perceived, crises. Pusser and Ordorika (2001) employ theories of the state, theories of institutions, and theories of power and elite formation to build understanding of these issues. Their work in a Mexican and a U.S. institution suggests that issues of inequality, diversity, elite interests, and ideology play out similarly in board actions in the two settings.

Unfortunately, a number of important board-related topics have attracted little attention. Although aggressive board actions in the avowed pursuit of quality have been frequently lamented and often disparagingly labeled "micromanagement" (Kauffman, 1993), there has been little systematic analysis of that issue. Similarly, while Kerr and Gade (1989) and others have lamented boards' ineffective communication with faculty members and their politicization in public institutions, researchers have not responded with empirical analysis.

STATE-LEVEL GOVERNANCE OF POSTSECONDARY EDUCATION

The literature on postsecondary governance at the state level is large and long standing. That scholarship developed a distinctive identity in the 1950s and 1960s, paralleling the dizzying growth of postsecondary education and the emergence of state postsecondary governance systems in the United States during the postwar era. The arc of the literature proceeds from early descriptive and typological accounts describing the evolution and formalization of state governance systems, through more recent conceptual undertakings aimed at shedding light on governance reform, to the emergence over the past decade of increasingly sophisticated efforts to model governance reform and effects empirically at the state level.

By all accounts, 1959 stands as a watershed year in this literature. That year witnessed publication of two landmark studies—by Moos and Rourke and by Glenny—that powerfully shaped the direction of future study. Against the backdrop of growing concern over the erosion of institutional autonomy at the hands of governmental regulators, Moos and Rourke's *The Campus and the State* (1959) garnered widespread attention for its illumining of the "grave threat" that state centralization posed to "the tradition of the free college or university in America" (p. 3). In it, the authors described the myriad personnel and budgeting controls that were being imposed on higher education by state executive and legislative agencies throughout the nation. Moos and Rourke cautioned against tightly coordinated systems, arguing these forms of control would "leach quality and originality" (p. 226) from public institutions. They concluded that higher education in the United States would thrive only if left to govern itself.

In the same year, Glenny's *Autonomy of Public Colleges* situated itself at the opposite end of debate over autonomy and accountability in U.S. higher education (McLendon, 2003c). In the first comprehensive assessment of state-level higher education planning, coordinating, and governing boards, Glenny studied twelve states that practiced one or another of the three basic forms of statewide organization of higher education: voluntary coordination, statewide coordination, and consolidated governance. Using interviews and case studies, Glenny evaluated board performance in planning, program allocation, and budgeting. In contrast to Moos and Rourke, Glenny (1959) was most critical of the voluntary coordination model, believing it structurally prone toward ineffective coordination and inadequate representation of the public interest. He also expressed significant concern, however, for the increasingly onerous regulatory controls exercised by statewide governing boards, an increasingly adopted governance approach of the era. Glenny implied a preference for coordinating agencies, praising their capability for meeting statewide needs while limiting direct government intrusion. Numerous observers later characterized Glenny's work as landmark, in part because it was the first to assess systematically the strengths and weaknesses of the various modes of statewide organization (Gove & Solomon, 1968; McConnell, 1971).

The following two decades witnessed many other governance assessments. Chambers (1961) extolled the merits of voluntary coordination and railed against what he termed "the blighting effect of [higher education's] immersion in a welter of bureaucratic controls" (p. xi). Glenny himself followed up with numerous works cogently articulating the need for more, and more effectively implemented, statewide coordination (e.g., see Glenny, Berdahl, Palola, & Paltridge, 1971; Glenny & Bowen, 1977). Notably, Glenny and Daglish (1973) contrasted university systems holding constitutional autonomy with statutorily based ones. Their empirical analysis concluded that the procedural autonomy of constitutional universities had eroded but the threat facing statutory universities was far graver: these institutions appeared "destined to become just another agency of state government" (p. 141).

Others contributed importantly to this literature, prominently including Kenneth Mortimer (e.g., see Mortimer, 1971). Berdahl's (1971) examination of institutional coordination in nineteen states was especially influential, providing two key contributions. First, he created what would become the field's standard classification system of governance structures, facilitating analysis of governance trends (McGuinness, 1997) and serving as an analytical resource underpinning future empirical investigations (e.g., Hearn & Griswold, 1994; Lowry, 2001; McLendon, Heller, & Young, 2005). Second, Berdahl drew a useful distinction between "substantive autonomy" (the institution's latitude to decide goals) and "procedural autonomy" (the institution's latitude over how it would accomplish the goals), a distinction taken up in many subsequent studies.

Much of the literature since the 1970s has continued in this vein of describing governance patterns and assessing the merits of various arrangements. The policy context has evolved dramatically, however. In the place of increasing governance centralization and steady state expenditure growth, state governments have begun to face economic transformations (e.g., globalization), mounting budget pressures, and growing calls for more accountability (McLendon, Hearn, & Deaton, 2006). Consequently, many states have restructured governance, often deregulating and decentralizing (McLendon, 2003c). The literature has expanded with studies documenting state governance reform trends (e.g., Hines, 2000; Leslie & Novak, 2003; Marcus, 1997; McLendon, 2003c) and studies examining specific restructuring contexts and reforms (e.g., Berdahl, 1998; Greer, 1998; Hines, 1988; Leslie & Novak, 2003; MacTaggart, 1998; Marcus, Pratt, & Stevens, 1997; McGuinness, 1995; McLendon, 2003b, 2003c; Mingle, 1983; Novak, 1996; Novak & Leslie, 2001). Three prominent reform modalities of this period involved the transfer of decision authority closer to the campus level: (1) the deregulating of state procedural controls, (2) the loosening of state governance and statewide coordination, and (3) the advent of so-called charter, or enterprise, colleges and universities (McLendon & Hearn, 2009).

Paralleling these analyses of policy reform has been the emergence of a conceptually oriented literature on the politics and processes of change (Bastedo, 2005, 2009; Leslie & Berdahl, 2008; McLendon, 2003a, 2003b, 2003c; Mills, 2007; Ness, 2010). These efforts have sought to explain policy change in individual states and, sometimes, across them, applying theoretical frameworks from political science, sociology, and organizational studies and usually employing qualitative research methods. For example, McLendon (2003b) examined the explanatory power of several agenda-setting theories of political science, notably Kingdon's "revised streams" model, in studying the rise of initiatives aimed at decentralizing state governance in the late 1990s in Illinois, Arkansas, and Hawaii. Building on that earlier study, Mills (2007) examined the overhaul of the Florida Board of Regents. Drawing on institutional theory, Bastedo (2009) studied the emergence of activist policymaking by members of the Massachusetts Board of Higher Education.

As the state governance literature has developed, informative case studies have continued to appear (e.g., Richardson, Bracco, Callan, & Finney, 1999), but the emergence of a growing body of *quantitative empirical research* on state governance effects is the most striking recent development. A common element linking these various studies is an effort to model governance impacts across state contexts and, more recently, over time. There are two distinct strands within this vein of scholarship, however, differentiated by whether the phenomenon is studied at the campus or state level.

Volkwein's numerous studies in the 1980s (e.g., see Volkwein 1986, 1987) represent the longest-running program of research on the *campus-level* impacts of state governance. Focusing mainly on public doctoral universities, Volkwein developed an index of state regulatory controls that he deployed in a series of cross-sectional, multivariate analyses of the relationships between state control and the fiscal and academic performance of public universities. His studies generally found the degree of state regulation unrelated to administrative expenditures, salary, or elaborateness; undergraduate quality; faculty reputational quality; faculty productivity; fund-raising success; or the amount universities received in grants and gifts. Using resource dependence theory to explain these findings, Volkwein and Malik (1997) concluded that the "sizes and resource bases" of public universities, rather than their regulatory climates, appear to hold the keys to quality (p. 37).

Lowry (2001) contributed further to the literature on campus-level state governance effects. Drawing on principal-agent theories, Lowry conceptualized state governance structures for higher education as, in effect, systems of political representation because the different institutional arrangements "affect the ability of different actors to influence decisions" (p. 846). Lowry reasoned that regulatory coordinating boards essentially are extensions of governors' capacity to supervise because governors appoint board members. Thus regulatory boards should be found to behave in a manner generally consistent with the preferences of governors (and voters), leading to lower tuition levels. In contrast, governance structures lacking such direct political oversight (e.g., consolidated governing boards) should tend to institutionalize the preferences of faculty and administrators, resulting in higher tuition levels. Using data on 407 public universities for 1995, Lowry found that institutions located in states with regulatory coordinating boards in fact charged significantly lower prices.

Research on *state-level* governance effects, as opposed to campus-level effects, has acquired significant momentum over the past two decades, focusing on the relationship between statewide governance arrangements and various postsecondary policy outcomes (Doyle, 2006; Doyle, McLendon, & Hearn, forthcoming; Hearn & Griswold, 1994; Hearn, Griswold, & Marine, 1996; McLendon, Deaton, & Hearn, 2007; McLendon et al., 2006; McLendon et al., 2005; Mokher & McLendon, 2009; Sabloff, 1997; Zumeta, 1996). This research has examined empirically a wide variety of antecedents of governmental behavior. In general, findings suggest that a constellation of state demographic (e.g., enrollment growth), economic (e.g., changes in tax revenues and employment conditions), political (the ideological proclivities of citizenries and party control of government institutions), and governance conditions drive state policy change and reform in postsecondary education. One surprisingly durable finding across nearly all these studies is the significant effect of governance on state policy behaviors. Although the directions of the effects vary across the different policy domains studied (e.g., finance, accountability, or regulatory policies), there is consistent evidence that governance structure indeed appears to influence the policy decisions a state makes, and in ways that can be empirically assayed.

Our own work, in conjunction with a team of colleagues, appears to be the most prolific program of research in this vein. Drawing on the policy innovation and diffusion literature of political science and using event history analysis,[5] we have examined the factors associated with state adoption of many distinctively new postsecondary policies, including performance-based accountability mandates (i.e., performance funding, budgeting, and reporting policies), state unit-record systems, state eminent-scholars programs, governance reforms, and certain market-oriented college financing schemes (Doyle et al., forthcoming; Hearn, McLendon, & Lacy, 2009; Hearn, McLendon, & Mokher, 2008; McLendon et al., 2007; McLendon et al., 2006; McLendon et al., 2005; Mokher & McLendon, 2009). Notably, this work also includes a longitudinal analysis of influences on states' decisions to change their governance arrangements (McLendon et al., 2007). In this last work, we found that "political instability," in the form of fluctuations in gubernatorial leadership and party control of the legislature, is the key driving force behind the governance shifts observed since the mid-1980s. As earlier noted, these studies overall also point to statewide governance as an important source of influence on the policy decisions of state governments in the postsecondary education arena. For example, we have found that the consolidated governing board arrangement often has a strong, statistically significant effect on governmental adoption of certain new policies, including more rigorous performance-accountability mandates (McLendon et al., 2006). Governance structures, it appears, do seem to matter in shaping public choice for postsecondary education.

Clearly, the state governance literature has evolved notably over the past two decades. Once a body of writings characterized mainly by description and prescription, it has recently acquired increasing scope, depth, and analytical complexity. The range of questions addressed has expanded, conceptual underpinnings have grown more multifaceted and become more deeply anchored in the disciplines, and methodological approaches have been substantially modernized and refined.

GOVERNANCE AT THE REGIONAL, DISCIPLINARY, AND NATIONAL LEVELS

It would seem to be heresy in the U.S. context to suggest that significant governance activity takes place at levels beyond the state. After all, an enduring myth in this country centers on education at all levels being a local responsibility. And the strong resistance to efforts to impose a national quality control regime onto the higher education sector suggests continuing constraints on federal ambitions in the arena (Breneman, 2008). Yet, suprastate governance does exist.

At the regional and national levels, regional accrediting bodies in effect exercise governing control over institutions seeking accreditation within and across academic fields. By imposing standards for undergraduate and graduate education in such matters as faculty-student ratios, library holdings, instructor qualifications, and the like, these bodies exercise some governing control over academic activities in institutions. Participation in accrediting processes is voluntary, but avoiding accrediting associations is a real choice only for institutions with unassailable reputations or highly distinctive strategic niches (Bloland, 2001). Effectively, for the great mass of institutions, the alternatives to accreditation may well be the imposition of some form of governmental quality control or the acceptance of marketplace marginalization.

Although they are neither numerous nor strongly empowered, other formal governing bodies at the national level also exist. For institutions participating in high-level intercollegiate athletics, membership in the National Collegiate Athletic Association is a necessary commitment that clearly shapes institutions' athletic policies, staffing, scholarship practices, and procedures (Thelin, 1996). Similarly, virtually all U.S. institutions participate in the massive federal student-aid programs, and many also receive federal research support, and the respective federal student-aid and research agencies impose regulations and rules that shape institutional structures and actions.[6] Absent such arrangements, it is questionable whether institutions on their own would have established institutional boards to monitor research ethics or imposed strict data transparency and privacy requirements.

But, interestingly, these formal governing mechanisms remain quite weak compared with more *informal* mechanisms. American colleges and universities are indirectly but significantly governed at the national or supranational level. Clark (1983b), Trow (1993), Meyer (Meyer, Ramirez, Frank, & Schofer, 2007), and many others have frequently noted that one can indeed identify a "system" of higher education in the United State. In the main, that system lacks formal reification in rules, regulations, and requirements imposed from the outside, but it can nonetheless be determinative in organizational structures and actions. As Meyer and colleagues (2007) observe, "Organizationally, the existence and legitimation capacity of rulelike external models are crucial to the creation and stabilization of all sorts of everyday structures" (p. 190), including, most prominently, colleges and universities. Forces external to individual institutions profoundly shaped departmental organization, academic cultures, campus missions, levels of professorial autonomy, faculty promotion and tenure standards, the array of disciplines represented on campus, and the curricular requirements for various degrees. Indeed, the word "shaped" may understate the power of these influences. While a potter might shape clay roughly toward an idealized configuration, Meyer's external models stamp molds onto the clay, ensuring minimal variations. In place of guidelines endorsed by fuzzily defined actors from beyond campus walls, Meyer and colleagues envision stern rules imposed by societal actors and fields with little tolerance for dissent.

How do these informal but powerful governing mechanisms impose their rule? Ongoing interactions with people and organizations outside the campus are influential, as are the prior experiences and socialization of faculty hired, promoted, and tenured. Clearly, institutions making decisions that defy the "system's" expectations expose themselves to professional and marketplace sanctions. In this way, nationally or globally institutionalized norms, values, and expectations can literally govern decision making at individual campuses.

There are a number of ways this conception must be elaborated. For one, governing authority can take varied forms, including authority over funding, programs, and approaches to solving problems (Meyer & Scott, 1983). In higher education, the federal government shapes institutional actions through its influences on student-aid and research funding, and the ancillary requirements accompanying those funds, but the government's authority over programming and strategic approaches is much more limited. Also, while institutionalist arguments posit cross-national modeling of organizational forms and processes (Clark, 1983b), one may argue that the national level is most central. Major differences persist between national higher education systems, even across nations with similar socioeconomic characteristics (Ramirez, 2006).

Finally, in addition to governmental and institutionalizing forces, there is a third suprastate force helping direct colleges' and universities' actions. Markets have long been noted as critical agents in coordinating U.S. higher education (Clark, 1983b), but observers (e.g., Kirp, 2003) are now increasingly critiquing their growing importance in campus decision making. This country may be seeing the early scenes of an engrossing three-way drama in which campuses' organizational configurations and processes are shifting toward new forms balancing developments in externally driven market, institutionalizing, and governmental forces (McLendon & Hearn, 2009).

At the same time, as appealing as it is to conceive of organizational action as largely determined externally, it is important to remember that colleges and universities do maintain the capacity to choose. Skillful leaders can effectively employ core values and practices in defense of necessary adaptive change (Bastedo, 2007; Levine, 2000). Market pressures may be ascending, but governance need not be the province of the invisible hand alone.

Governance in a Wider Lens: Some Potential Arenas for Further Research

The preceding review suggests that researchers have made real progress in building understanding of higher education governance. But the progress appears uneven, marked by spirited attention to some topics, limited attention to others, and diversity in methodological rigor and approach. One can also question levels of communication across institutional and disciplinary boundaries on governance research. While the different social science disciplines share interests in such topics as salary determination, resource flows among units, curricular adaptation, program creation and termination, and performance assessment, their respective studies of these topics vary in many respects. Consider, for example, how differently sociologists, psychologists, and economists view questions of faculty salary setting and its implications for institutional effectiveness (see Fox, 1985; McKeachie, 1979; Toutkoushian, 1999). It is also instructive to consider how infrequently citations flow across journals and outlets in different disciplines. It is almost as if separate teams of researchers were bustling around a single, remote native village, observing rituals and traditions, collecting artifacts, and drawing conclusions entirely independently of each other. The results are troubling: duplication of effort, selective inferences, and poor knowledgeability regarding important insights from other fields.

These larger concerns lie well beyond the scope of this chapter (and beyond the capabilities of the present authors), but we can identify a number of arenas that appear understudied and warranting of further attention. The list is far from exhaustive but ideally represents a promising sampler for those hoping to advance this field of study.

A CONTINGENCY APPROACH TO GOVERNANCE STRUCTURES AND PROCESSES

Theoretically informed, empirical analyses of governance remain far too rare.[7] Yet the foundations for such analyses are rich. Bess and Dee (2008), for example, insightfully point to Thompson's (1967) classic conceptualization of organizational action as a potential basis for new work. Thompson suggests that agreement over means and ends (goals) is critical to the nature of decision making. For Thompson, when there is agreement on means and goals, decision making is merely computational: What avenues are most cost-effective given values, probabilities, and the like? When there is agreement on means but not on goals, decision making is a matter of compromise: To what combination of ends may disparate interest groups agree to direct resources, for example? When there is disagreement regarding means but agreement on goals, decision making requires consensus: What approach can like-minded parties agree to pursue? Finally, where there is disagreement on both ends and means, decision making is inspiration driven.

For Thompson, moving individual actors in an anarchical context away from the status quo may require extraordinary creativity, interpersonal skills, and energy.

Adopting Thompson's scheme (also see Thompson & Tuden, 1959), one can infer that classic bureaucratic/rational forms of higher education governance support the computational work necessary when there is agreement over means and ends. Similarly, reliance on the polity fits the political work of compromise when goals are disputed. Finally, collegia appear optimal for consensual decision making when means but not goals are in dispute. Fitting these ideas to research questions regarding effective modes for governance, one can envision intriguing empirical explorations of the match of governance forms and processes to the nature of the issues being confronted. For example, might a threatened institution with unclear and politically disputed paths to restored health be disserved by a hierarchically driven, top-down process of the kind envisioned in some of the field's strategic "bibles"? But is attention to calculations of programmatic cost-effectiveness really maladaptive when extreme challenges loom? The fitting of decision approaches to specific organizational challenges is an ongoing challenge for leaders and has been too little studied. Case studies of "turnaround" efforts, with attention to what seems to have worked best in different circumstances, make good sense.

GOVERNANCE AND INNOVATION

Facing new, market-driven challenges, contemporary higher education needs to adapt creatively in many areas, including its approaches to knowledge transmission, its systems for generating new knowledge, its management practices, and its labor force arrangements. In the spirit of Burton Clark's classic essay (1983a), we may ask, "To what extent are governance systems complicit in the ways institutions and systems innovate in response to emerging, pressing domains? What structures of governance fit best?" There are a variety of approaches to the question.

Long-standing research findings in social and organizational psychology suggest that democratically structured groups can be more effective than hierarchically structured and autocratically led groups for dealing with ill-formed, open-ended problems, while hierarchical structures with clear divisions of labor can be superior for resolving well-defined problems (see the review by Perrow, 1986). It would seem not too great a leap to surmise that current conditions facing postsecondary institutions are ill defined and that shared-governance traditions represent a form of democratic structuring. Thus, if the analogy from small-groups research to university governance holds, we might infer that institutions open to the distinctive problem-solving capabilities of faculty working across units may be especially successful in addressing emerging external challenges and conditions.

Yet that may be too quick and too long a leap. For one, faculty can be largely indifferent to campuswide governance issues, unless there is crisis or threat in the wind (Birnbaum, 2004; Hearn, 1988). At a more fundamental level, many academic constituencies focus on their own subunits' interests and their own professional self-interests rather than those of the larger institution (Kerr, 2001). Thus, to the extent that shared governance contributes to innovation, it may do so more at the level of subunits than at the level of the campus as a whole. As Kerr wryly argues, the only choice that cannot be vetoed at the level of the campus as a whole is to preserve the status quo.

For Collis (2004), the problem centers on a paradox of scope: traditional core units are stable or shrinking, while activities around the periphery are growing (including outsourcing partnerships, vocational courses, sponsored research, licensing and patenting, and affiliated research centers and institutes). To the extent campuswide governance is shaped around the idea that the core represents what is most critical to the institution, governance may falter. Indeed, traditional forms of shared governance that vest authority largely in tenure-line faculty housed in degree-oriented departments may be not only removed from innovative organizational trends on campus but actively resistant to those trends.

Marginson (2000) points to a growing tension between traditional notions of academic governance by a small elite and emerging pressures for adaptation to new organizational values, configurations, and contexts: "Clearly the old idea of collegial governance, whereby academic staff govern the university, administer it and provide some of its auxiliary services, is obsolete" (p. 34). Marginson envisions a new, segmented form of governance and decision making responsive to emerging conditions. His argument is persuasive and merits analytical attention.

However one might view the connections of governance to innovation, it remains a difficult and largely unexplored avenue for empirical work. New research might productively explore the extent to which campuswide governance arrangements may foster or constrain both effective and ineffective innovation.

GOVERNANCE IN EMERGING ORGANIZATIONAL FORMS

In the past few decades, public institutions have increasingly turned to new organizational forms, including university foundations, partnerships with corporations, and new self-governing research centers and labs. Some have argued that research centers and labs are becoming a significant new locus of employment and careers in higher education, to some extent supplanting the academic department (Boardman & Corley, 2008). Without doubt, many new appointments are being made in the centers and labs, and many faculty see those as their true academic home rather than discipline-based departments and programs. Similarly, some analysts see emerging research-oriented units such as university-corporation partnerships and 501c3 organizations as important forms commanding new forms of leadership and governance, as well as empirical attention (Geiger, 1993). Research attention to these developments has been limited.

Perhaps the most notable example of an emerging, underresearched organizational form is the university foundation. The foundation form can help connect more supporters and donors to the institution, provide effective mechanisms for separating gift funds from public funds, provide greater flexibility in the expenditure of funds, and allow publicly chartered institutions to seize opportunities not easily taken under firmer state control (Simic, 1998). Foundations often straddle the line between public and private status and often are focused on such areas as intercollegiate athletics, research activity, and core university academic operations. Establishing legal and functional independence from the institution for which they are organized while appropriately serving its larger purposes represents a major challenge for these entities.

INTERNATIONAL ISSUES IN GOVERNANCE

We had inadequate space to explore international governance issues here, but we can suggest that national distinctiveness in higher education systems is being challenged worldwide by increasing global competitiveness and standardization (Huisman, 2009; Maassen & Olsen, 2007). That these trends are affecting the United States is undeniable. Abundant topics for potential research lie here, including impacts of governance changes on institutional missions, quality, programs, access, and pricing structures; the relationship between changing contexts of governance and academic leadership; and policymaking processes and the role of institutions and governance in shaping public choice for higher education at the subnational, national, and supranational levels. Interestingly, there are numerous U.S. parallels to the simultaneous centralization and decentralization currently taking place in much of Europe.

LOOKING BEYOND GOVERNANCE DECISIONS

Pfeffer (1992) has long argued that organizational research has paid too much attention to decisions themselves and too little attention to the factors preceding and following decisions. The point would certainly seem to apply to higher education governance research. If we focus on evaluating the decisions institutional boards or faculty senates are making, we may exclude a number of intriguing and important issues. Some are arguably foundational to the evaluation of particular decisions. For example, Hammond (2004) has explored the proposition that variations in subunit structures in universities may shape how those units interpret and respond to similar information from central administrators. Structural differences may thus indirectly shape how units communicate with leaders and, in turn, may ultimately contribute to different organizational outcomes. Treating policy decisions as outcomes, rather than as independent variables in evaluative studies, can potentially widen understanding of an arena rather opaque to empirical analysis. And, on the other side of the decision-making timeline, similar policy choices may actually precede quite divergent implementations. In our own work on performance funding (McLendon et al., 2006), for example, we found that characterizing states' policy contexts in dichotomous terms (i.e., a state either has or has not adopted the policy) can mask substantial variations in states' actual funding levels and commitment.

OPENNESS AND TRANSPARENCY

"Sunshine laws" are universal in public higher education and are increasingly influencing private institutions, as well, as governments push for greater transparency in such areas as graduation rate, crime rates, and research funding. College leaders are rarely truly indifferent to the presence of external reporters or to the potential for future public availability of meeting transcripts, but there has been very little attention to openness and transparency as topics for empirical governance research (McLendon & Hearn, 2006a, 2006b). Important questions remain largely unexplored.

Conclusion

In a perceptive essay, Tierney (2004) identified three critical shortcomings in governance scholarship. First, despite some progress since the 1970s, most of it remains nonempirical. As Tierney put it, "what the field needs less of are exhortations and lamentations about the state of governance from either those who want more administrative authority or those who perceive the demise of shared governance" (p. 122). Second, Tierney suggested that far too little research has been conducted on non-four-year institutions and on the governance roles of staff, students, and non-tenure-line faculty. Finally, Tierney lamented inattention by analysts to how well the core purposes of institutional governance are being served.

All three points are well taken, and each poses challenges to the field. Clearly, though, the last question is the hardest. In this essay, we have largely set aside governance's ultimate purposes. Although different parties might agree on a general definition of governance, there is ample room for disagreement on goals. Rosovsky (1990) stresses governance's traditional centrality in shaping teaching and learning on campus, Marginson (2000) focuses on governance's role in helping institutions respond effectively to contemporary conditions, Clark (1983b, 1998) emphasizes governance's role in facilitating institutional innovation, and Trow (1998) highlights governance's role in helping buffer institutions from political interference. The multidimensionality of institutional functioning, and the complexity of the environmental and organizational factors affecting institutional outcomes, confound efforts to discern governance's effects on goal-serving action and health.

Peterson (2007) has observed that "broad environmental forces and conditions shape not just our institutions but also our industry" (p. 180)—that is, the institutionalized forms and processes of higher education itself.[8] In this sense, governance is both shaped itself by external factors and one of a complex array of influences shaping institutional outcomes. In such a contingent context, we are far from isolating its distinctive effects, much less answering questions of effectiveness. But empirical research will bring us far closer to that goal than will a continuing proliferation of data-free opinion. Returning to Peterson's (1985) memorable imagery of a quarter century ago, postsecondary governance studies clearly have evolved beyond the stage of "advanced adolescence—maturing rapidly, capable of extremes of sophistication and foolishness, and alternately confident and uncertain" (p. 6). Whether the field continues its march toward adulthood will depend largely on its growing more confident in its own identity and commitment to substantive, conceptual, and methodological multidimensionality.

NOTES

1. Distinctions between governance, management, and leadership have been emphasized by Marvin Peterson (e.g., see Peterson & Mets, 1987) and many others and are quite helpful in understanding postsecondary organization and parsing research on these issues. College and university management and leadership are covered in depth elsewhere in this volume and in the broader literature.

2. Baldridge (1971a, 1971b) may have been the first to identify and label these three strands in the literature. Hardy (1990a) and Birnbaum (1991) have noted that it increasingly became paradigmatic in the field to characterize governance theories and models through such lenses.

3. A few years later, Mintzberg (1979) developed these ideas further in his description of the modern research university as a professional bureaucracy.

4. In an early, comprehensive essay on decentralization, Peterson (1971) examined the nature, causes, and implications of this core concern in governance.

5. Event history analysis is a regression-like, longitudinal technique that originated in biostatistics but has since been widely adopted by political scientists. See McLendon & Hearn 2007 and Hearn, McLendon, & Mokher 2008 for discussions of the methodology and its distinctive advantages and limitations in studying state governance and policy behavior.

6. For more on these issues, see Gumport 1991 regarding research policies and practices and Hearn 1993 regarding student financial aid.

7. The point has been made by Tierney (2004) and many others.

8. The point addresses the "capital I" sense of institutions in higher education: the contours of the enterprise as a *societal* institution spanning the thousands of specific colleges and universities engaged in it.

REFERENCES

Baird, L. L. (1988). The college environment revisited: A review of research and theory. In J. C. Smart (Ed.), *Higher education: Handbook of theory and research,* Vol. 4 (pp. 1–52). New York: Agathon Press.

Baldridge, J. V. (1971a). Introduction: Models of university governance—bureaucratic, collegial, and political. In J. V. Baldridge (Ed.), *Academic governance: Research on institutional politics and decision making.* Berkeley, CA: McCutchan Publishing.

Baldridge, J. V. (1971b). *Power and conflict in the university.* New York: Wiley.

Bastedo, M. N. (2005). The making of an activist governing board. *Review of Higher Education, 28*(4), 551–570.

Bastedo, M. N. (2007). Sociological frameworks for higher education policy research. In P. Gumport (Ed.), *Sociology of higher education: Contributions and their contexts* (pp. 295–316). Baltimore: Johns Hopkins University Press.

Bastedo, M. N. (2009). Convergent institutional logics in public higher education. *Review of Higher Education, 32*(2), 209–234.

Bendor, J., Moe, T. M., & Shotts, K. W. (2001). Recycling the garbage can: An assessment of the research program. *American Political Science Review, 95*(1), 169–190.

Benjamin, R., & Carroll, S. (1998). The implications of the changing environment for higher education governance. In W. Tierney (Ed.), *The responsive university* (pp. 92–119). Baltimore: Johns Hopkins University Press.

Berdahl, R. O. (1971). *Statewide coordination of higher education.* Washington, DC: ACE.

Berdahl, R. O. (1998). Balancing self interest and accountability: St. Mary's College of Maryland. In T. J. MacTaggart (Ed.), *Seeking excellence through independence: Liberating colleges and universities from excessive regulation* (pp. 59–83). San Francisco: Jossey-Bass.

Bess, J. L., & Dee, J. R. (2008). *Understanding college and university organization: Theories for effective policy and practice* (Vols. 1 and 2). Sterling, VA: Stylus.

Birnbaum, R. (1989). The latent functions of the academic senate: Why senates do not work but will not go away. *Journal of Higher Education, 60*(4), 423–443.

Birnbaum, R. (1991). *How colleges work.* San Francisco: Jossey-Bass.

Birnbaum, R. (2004). The end of shared governance: Looking ahead or looking back. In W. G. Tierney & V. M. Lechuga (Eds.), *Restructuring shared governance in higher education.* New Directions for Higher Education, No. 127 (pp. 5–22). San Francisco: Jossey-Bass.

Blau, P. (1973). *The organization of academic work.* New York: Wiley.

Bloland, H. G. (2001). *Creating the Council for Higher Education Accreditation (CHEA).* Westport, CT: Greenwood Publishing and the American Council on Education.

Boardman, P. C., & Corley, E. (2008). University research centers and the composition of research collaborations. *Research Policy, 37*(5), 900–913.

Braxton, J. M., & Hargens, L. L. (1996). Variations among academic disciplines: Analytical framework and research. In J. C. Smart (Ed.), *Higher education: Handbook of theory and research,* Vol. 11 (pp. 1–45). New York: Agathon Press.

Breneman, D. (2008, February 15). Elite colleges must stop spurning critiques of higher education. *Chronicle of Higher Education, 54,* 23.

Carnegie Foundation for the Advancement of Teaching. (1982). *The control of the campus: A report on the governance of higher education.* Washington, DC: Author.

Chaffee, E. E. (1983). The role of rationality in university budgeting. *Research in Higher Education, 19*(4), 387–406.

Chaffee, E. E., and Tierney, W. G. (1988). *Collegiate culture and leadership strategies.* New York: American Council on Education and Macmillan.

Chait, R. P. (1995). *The new activism of corporate boards and the implications for campus governance.* Occasional Paper #26. Washington, DC: Association of Governing Boards of Universities and Colleges.

Chambers, M. M. (1961). *Voluntary statewide coordination.* Ann Arbor: University of Michigan.

Clark, B. R. (1970). *The distinctive college: Antioch, Reed and Swarthmore.* Chicago: Aldine.

Clark, B. R. (1983a). Governing the higher education system. In M. Shattock (Ed.), *The structure and governance of higher education* (pp. 19–43). Guildford, UK: Society for Research into Higher Education.

Clark, B. R. (1983b). *The higher education system.* Berkeley: University of California Press.

Clark, B. R. (1987). *The academic life: Small worlds, different worlds.* Princeton, NJ: Carnegie Foundation for the Advancement of Teaching.

Clark, B. R. (1992). *The distinctive college.* Edison, NJ: Transaction Publishers.

Clark, B. R. (1998). *Creating entrepreneurial universities: Organizational pathways of transformation.* New York: Pergamon.

Cohen, M. D., & March, J. G. (1974). *Leadership and ambiguity: The American college president.* New York: McGraw-Hill.

Cohen, M., March, J., & Olsen, J. (1972). A garbage can model of organizational choice. *Administrative Science Quarterly, 17*, 1–25.

Collins, R. (1994). Why the social sciences won't become high-consensus, rapid-discovery science. *Sociological Forum, 9*(2), 155–177.

Collis, D. J. (2004). The paradox of scope: A challenge to the governance of higher education. In W. G. Tierney (Ed.), *Competing conceptions of academic governance: Negotiating the perfect storm* (pp. 33–76). Baltimore: Johns Hopkins University Press.

Cope, R. G. (1981). *Strategic planning, management, and decision-making.* AAHE-ERIC Higher Education Research Report, No. 9. Washington, DC: AAHE.

Corson, J. (1971). The modernization of the university: The impact of the function of governance. *Journal of Higher Education, 42*(6), 430–441.

Cyert, R. M., & March, J. G. (1963). *A behavioral theory of the firm.* Englewood Cliffs, NJ: Prentice-Hall.

Dahl, R. (1967). *Who governs? Democracy and power in an American city.* New Haven, CT: Yale University Press.

Dill, D. D. (1982). The management of academic culture, notes on the management of meaning and social integration. *Higher Education 11,* 303–320.

Dill, D. D., & Helm, K. P. (1988). Faculty participation in strategic policy making. In J. C. Smart (Ed.), *Higher education: Handbook of theory and research,* Vol. 4 (pp. 319–355). New York: Agathon Press.

Doyle, W. R. (2006). Adoption of merit-based student grant programs: An event history analysis. *Educational Evaluation and Policy Analysis, 28*(3), 259–285.

Doyle, W., McLendon, M. K., & Hearn, J. C. (forthcoming). The adoption of prepaid tuition and savings plans in the American states. *Research in Higher Education.*

Duryea, E. D. (1973). Evolution of university organization. In J. A. Perkins (Ed.), *The university as an organization* (pp. 15–37). New York: McGraw-Hill.

Eckel, P. D. (2000). The role of shared governance in institutional hard decisions: Enabler or antagonist? *Review of Higher Education, 24*(1), 15–39.

Fox, M. F. (1985). Publication, performance, and reward in science and scholarship. In J. C. Smart (Ed.), *Higher education: Handbook of theory and research,* Vol. 1 (pp. 255–282). New York: Agathon Press.

Geiger, R. L. (1993). *Research and relevant knowledge: American research universities since World War II.* Oxford: Oxford University Press.

Glassman, R. B. (1973). Persistence and loose coupling in living systems. *Behavioral Science, 18,* 83–98.

Glenny, L. A. (1959). *Autonomy of public colleges: The challenge of coordination.* New York: McGraw-Hill.

Glenny, L. A., Berdahl, R. O., Palola, E. G., & Paltridge, J. G. (1971). *Coordinating higher education for the 70's.* Berkeley: Center for Research and Development in Higher Education, University of California.

Glenny, L. A., & Bowen, F. M. (1977). *State intervention in higher education.* Cambridge, MA: Sloan Commission on Government and Higher Education.

Glenny, L. A., & Dalglish, T. K. (1973). *Public universities, state agencies, and the law.* Berkeley: Center for Research and Development in Higher Education, University of California.

Gove, S. K., & Solomon, B. W. (1968). The politics of higher education: A bibliographic essay. *Journal of Higher Education 39*(4), 181–195.

Graham, H. D. (1989). Structure and governance in American higher education: Historical and comparative analysis in state policy. *Journal of Policy History 1*(1), 80–107.

Greer, D. (1998). Defining the scope and limits of autonomy: New Jersey. In T. J. MacTaggart (Ed.), *Seeking excellence through independence: Liberating colleges and universities from excessive regulation* (pp. 84–108). San Francisco: Jossey-Bass.

Gumport, P. J. (1991). The federal role in American graduate education. In J. C. Smart (Ed.), *Higher education: Handbook of theory and research*, Vol. 7 (pp. 102–134). New York: Agathon Press.

Gumport, P. J. (1993). The contested terrain of academic program reduction. *Journal of Higher Education, 64*(3), 283–311.

Gumport, P. J., & Pusser, B. (1999). University reconstructing: The role of economic and political contexts. In J. C. Smart (Ed.), *Higher education: Handbook of theory and research*, Vol. 14 (pp. 146–200). New York: Agathon Press.

Gumport, P. J., & Sporn, B. (1999). Institutional adaptation: Demands for management reform and university administration. In J. C. Smart (Ed.) *Higher education: Handbook of theory and research*, Vol. 14 (pp. 103–145). New York: Agathon Press.

Hackman, J. D. (1985). Power and centrality in the allocation of resources in colleges and universities. *Administrative Science Quarterly, 30,* 61–77.

Hammond, T. H. (2004). Herding cats in university hierarchies: Formal structure and policy choice in American research universities. In R. G. Ehrenberg (Ed.), *Governing academia* (pp. 91–138). Ithaca, NY: Cornell University Press.

Hardy, C. (1990a). Putting power into university governance. In J. C. Smart (Ed.), *Higher education: Handbook of theory and research*, Vol. 6 (pp. 393–426). New York: Agathon Press.

Hardy, C. (1990b). Strategy and context: Retrenchment in Canadian universities. *Organization Studies, 11*(2), 207–237.

Hearn, J. C. (1988). Strategy and resources: Economic issues in strategic planning and management in higher education. In J. C. Smart (Ed.), *Higher education: Handbook of theory and research*, Vol. 4 (pp. 212–281). New York: Agathon Press.

Hearn, J. C. (2007). Sociological studies of academic departments. In P. Gumport (Ed.), *Sociology of higher education: Contributions and their contexts* (pp. 222–265). Baltimore: Johns Hopkins Press.

Hearn, J. C., & Anderson, M. S. (2002). Conflict in academic departments: An analysis of disputes over faculty promotion and tenure. *Research in Higher Education, 43*(5), 503–529.

Hearn, J. C., & Griswold, C. P. (1994). State-level centralization and policy innovation in U.S. postsecondary education. *Educational Evaluation and Policy Analysis, 16*(2), 161–190.

Hearn, J. C., Griswold, C. P., & Marine, G. M. (1996). Region, resources, and reason: A contextual analysis of state tuition and student-aid policies. *Research in Higher Education, 37*(3), 241–278.

Hearn, J. C., McLendon, M. K., & Lacy, T. A. (2009, April). *Analyzing the origins of state "Eminent Scholar" programs: An event-history analysis.* Paper presented at the annual meeting of the Midwest Political Science Association, Chicago.

Hearn, J. C., McLendon, M. K., & Mokher, C. (2008). Accounting for student success: An empirical analysis of the origins and spread of state student unit-record systems. *Research in Higher Education, 50*(1), 665–683.

Hines, E. R. (1988). *Higher education and state governments: Renewed partnership, cooperation, or competition?* ASHE-ERIC Higher Education Report, No. 5. Washington, DC: George Washington University.

Hines, E. R. (2000). The governance of higher education. In J. C. Smart (Ed.), *Higher education: Handbook of theory and research,* Vol. 15 (pp. 105–155). New York: Agathon Press.

Huisman, J. (Ed.). (2009). *International perspectives on the governance of higher education: Alternative frameworks for coordination.* New York: Routledge.

Kaplan, G. E. (2004). Do governance structures matter? In W. G. Tierney & V. M. Lechuga (Eds.), *Restructuring shared governance in higher education.* New Directions for Higher Education, No. 127 (pp. 23–34). San Francisco: Jossey-Bass.

Katz, D., & Kahn, R. L. (1966). *The social psychology of organizations.* New York: Wiley.

Kauffman, J. F. (1993). Governing boards. In A. Levine (Ed.), *The higher learning in America: 1980–2000* (pp. 222–239). Baltimore: Johns Hopkins University Press.

Keller, G. (1983). *Academic strategy: The management revolution in American higher education.* Baltimore: Johns Hopkins University Press.

Kerr, C. (2001). *The uses of the university* (5th ed.). Cambridge, MA: Harvard University Press.

Kerr, C., & Gade, M. L. (1989). *The guardians: Boards of trustees of American colleges and universities.* Washington, DC: Association of Governing Boards of Universities and Colleges.

Kezar, A. (2005). Consequences of radical change in governance: A grounded theory approach. *Journal of Higher Education, 76*(6), 634–668.

Kirp, D. L. (2003). *Shakespeare, Einstein, and the bottom line: The marketing of higher education.* Cambridge, MA: Harvard University Press.

Kolman, E. M., & Hossler, D. (1987). The influence of institutional culture on presidential selection. *Review of Higher Education, 10*(4), 319–333.

Lazerson, M. (1997, March/April). Who owns higher education? The changing face of governance. *Change,* 10–15.

Lee, B. A. (1991). *Campus leaders and campus senates.* New Directions for Higher Education, No. 75 (pp. 41–61). San Francisco: Jossey-Bass.

Leslie, D. W., & Berdahl, R. O. (2008). The politics of restructuring in Virginia: A case study. *Review of Higher Education 31*(3), 309–328.

Leslie, D. W., & Novak, R. J. (2003). Substance vs. politics: Through the dark mirror of governance reform. *Educational Policy, 17*(1), 98–120.

Levine, A. (2000, March 13). The soul of a new university. *New York Times.*

Lowry, R. C. (2001). Governmental structure, trustee selection, and public university prices and spending: Multiple means to similar ends. *American Journal of Political Science 45,* 845–861.

Maassen, P. (1996). The concept of culture and higher education. *Higher Education, 1*(2): 153–159.

Maassen, P., & Olsen, J. P. (Eds.). (2007). *University dynamics and European integration.* Dordrecht, Netherlands: Springer.

MacTaggart, T. J. (Ed.). (1998). *Seeking excellence through independence: Liberating colleges and universities from excessive regulation.* San Francisco: Jossey-Bass.

March, J. G. (1965). *Handbook of organizations.* Chicago: Rand McNally.

March, J. G., & Olsen, J. P. (1975). *Choice situations in loosely coupled worlds.* Unpublished manuscript, Stanford University.

Marcus, L. R. (1997). Restructuring state higher education governance patterns. *Review of Higher Education, 20*(4), 399–418.

Marcus, L. R., Pratt, B., & Stevens, J. L. (1997). Deregulating colleges: The autonomy experiment. *Educational Policy, 11*(1), 92–110.

Marginson, S. (2000). Rethinking academic work in the global era. *Higher Education Policy and Management, 22*(1), 23–35.

Masland, A. T. (1985). Organizational culture in the study of higher education. *Review of Higher Education 8*(2), 157–168.

Massy, W. F. (1996). Productivity issues in higher education. In W. F. Massy (Ed.), *Resource allocation in higher education* (pp. 49–86). Ann Arbor: University of Michigan Press.

Massy, W. F., Wilger, A. K., & Colbeck, C. (1994, July/August). Overcoming "hollowed" collegiality. *Change, 26*(4), 10–20.

Massy, W. F., & Zemsky, R. (1997). A utility model for teaching load decisions in academic departments. *Economics of Education Review, 16*(4), 349–365.

McConnell, T. R. (1963). Needed: Research in college and university organization and administration. In T. Lunsford (Ed.), *Study of academic organizations.* Boulder, CO: Western Institute Commission on Higher Education.

McConnell, T. R. (1971). *The redistribution of power in higher education: Changing patterns of internal governance.* Berkeley: Center for Research and Development in Higher Education, University of California.

McGuinness, A. C. (1995). *Restructuring state roles in higher education: A case study of the 1994 New Jersey Higher Education Restructuring Act.* Denver, CO: Education Commission of the States.

McGuinness, A. C. (1997). *State postsecondary education structures handbook.* Denver, CO: Education Commission of the States.

McKeachie, W. J. (1979). Perspectives from psychology: Financial incentives are ineffective for faculty. In D. R. Lewis & W. E. Becker, *Academic rewards in higher education* (pp. 3–20). Cambridge, MA: Ballinger.

McLendon, M. K. (2003a). The politics of higher education: Toward an expanded research agenda. *Educational Policy, 17*(1), 165–191.

McLendon, M. K. (2003b). Setting the governmental agenda for state decentralization of higher education. *Journal of Higher Education, 74*(5), 1–37.

McLendon, M. K. (2003c). State governance reform of higher education: Patterns, trends, and theories of the public policy process. In J. C. Smart (Ed.). *Higher education: Handbook of theory and research,* Vol. 18 (pp. 57–143). London: Kluwer.

McLendon, M. K., Deaton, R., & Hearn, J. C. (2007). The enactment of reforms in state governance of higher education: Testing the political-instability hypothesis. *Journal of Higher Education, 78*(6), 645–675.

McLendon, M. K., & Hearn, J. C. (2006a). Mandated openness and higher education governance: Policy, theoretical, and analytic perspectives. In J. C. Smart (Ed.), *Higher education: Handbook of theory and research*, Vol. 21 (pp. 39–97). Norwell, MA: Kluwer.

McLendon, M. K., & Hearn, J. C. (2006b). Mandated openness in public higher education: A field study of state sunshine laws and institutional governance. *Journal of Higher Education, 77*(4), 645–683.

McLendon, M. K., & Hearn, J. C. (2009). Viewing recent US governance reform whole: "Decentralization" in a distinctive context. In J. Huisman (Ed.), *International perspectives on the governance of higher education: Alternative frameworks for coordination* (pp. 161–181). New York: Routledge.

McLendon, M. K., Hearn, J. C., & Deaton, R. (2006). Called to account: Analyzing the origins and spread of state performance-accountability policies for higher education. *Educational Evaluation and Policy Analysis, 28*(1), 1–24.

McLendon, M. K., Heller, D. E., & Young, S. (2005). State postsecondary education policy innovation: Politics, competition, and the interstate migration of policy ideas. *Journal of Higher Education, 76*(4), 363–400.

Meyer, J. W., Ramirez, F. O., Frank, D. J., & Schofer, E. (2007). Higher education as an institution. In P. Gumport (Ed.), *Sociology of higher education: Contributions and their contexts* (pp. 187–221). Baltimore: Johns Hopkins University Press.

Meyer, J. W., & Scott, W. R. (1983). *Organizational environments: Ritual and rationality.* Beverly Hills, CA: Sage.

Mills, M. (2007). Stories of politics and policy: Florida's higher education governance reorganization. *Journal of Higher Education 78*(2), 162–187.

Mingle, J. R. (Ed.). (1983). *Management flexibility and state regulation in higher education.* Atlanta: Southern Regional Education Board.

Mintzberg, H. (1979). *The structuring of organizations.* Englewood Cliffs, NJ: Prentice-Hall.

Mokher, C., & McLendon, M. K. (2009). Uniting secondary and postsecondary education: An event history analysis of state adoption of dual enrollment policies. *American Journal of Education, 115*(2), 249–277.

Moos, M. C., and Rourke, F. E. (1959). *The campus and the state.* Baltimore: Johns Hopkins Press.

Mortimer, K. (1971). The dilemmas in new campus governance structures. *Journal of Higher Education, 42*(6), 467–482.

Ness, E. C. (2010). The politics of determining merit aid eligibility criteria: An analysis of the policy process. *Journal of Higher Education 81*(1), 33–60.

Nicholson-Crotty, J., & Meier, K. J. (2003). Politics, structure and public policy: The case of higher education. *Educational Policy, 17*(1), 80–98.

Novak, R. J. (1996). Methods, objectives, and consequences of restructuring. In T. MacTaggart (Ed.), *Restructuring higher education* (pp. 16–49). San Francisco: Jossey-Bass.

Novak, R. J., & Leslie, D. W. (2001). A not so distant mirror: Great Depression writings on governance and finance of public higher education. *History of Higher Education Annual, 20*, 59–78.

Olsen, J. P. (2001). Garbage cans, the new institutionalism, and the study of politics. *American Political Science Review, 95*(1), 191–198.

Orton, J. D., & Weick, K. E. (1990). Loosely coupled systems: A reconceptualization. *Academy of Management Review, 15*(2), 203–223.

Pace, C. R. (1962). Methods of describing college culture. *Teachers College Record, 63,* 267–277.

Perrow, C. (1986). *Complex organizations: A critical essay.* New York: Random House.

Peterson, M. W. (1971). Decentralization: A strategic approach. *Journal of Higher Education, 42*(6), 521–539.

Peterson, M. W. (1974). Organization and administration in higher education: Sociological and social-psychological perspectives. In F. Kerlinger (Ed.), *Review of research in education,* Vol. 2 (pp. 296–347). Itasca, IL: Peacock.

Peterson, M. W. (1985). Emerging developments in postsecondary organization theory and research: Fragmentation or integration? *Educational Researcher, 14*(3), 5–12.

Peterson, M. W. (1997). Using contextual planning to transform universities. In M. W. Peterson, D. D. Dill, L. A. Mets, & Associates (Eds.), *Planning and managing for a changing environment* (pp. 127–157). San Francisco: Jossey-Bass.

Peterson, M. W. (2007). The study of colleges and universities as organizations. In P. Gumport (Ed.), *Sociology of higher education* (pp. 147–184). Baltimore: Johns Hopkins University Press.

Peterson, M. W., & Mets, L. W. (1987). An evolutionary perspective on academic governance, management, and literature. In M. W. Peterson & L. A. Mets (Eds.), *Key resources on higher education governance, management, and leadership* (pp. 1–20). San Francisco: Jossey-Bass.

Peterson, M. W., & Spencer, M. G. (1993). Qualitative and quantitative approaches to academic culture: Do they tell us the same thing? In J. C. Smart (Ed.). *Higher education: Handbook of theory and research,* Vol. 9 (pp. 344–388). New York: Agathon Press.

Pfeffer, J. (1992). *Managing with power: Politics and influence in organizations.* Cambridge: Harvard Business School Press.

Pfeffer, J. (1993). Barriers to the advance of organizational science: Paradigm development as a dependent variable. *Academy of Management Review, 18,* 437–455.

Pfeffer, J., & Salancik, G. (1974). Organizational decision making as a political process: The case of the university budget. *Administrative Science Quarterly, 19*(2), 135–151.

Pusser, B., & Ordorika, I. (2001). Bringing political theory to university governance: A comparative analysis of governing boards and the Universidad Nacional Autónoma de México and the University of California. In J. C. Smart (Ed.), *Higher education: Handbook of theory and research,* Vol. 16 (pp. 147–194). New York: Agathon Press.

Pusser, B., Slaughter, S., & Thomas, S. L. (2006). Playing the board game: An empirical analysis of university trustee and corporate board interlocks. *Journal of Higher Education, 77*(5), 747–775.

Ramirez, F. O. (2006). Growing commonalities and persistent differences in higher education: universities between globalization and national tradition. In In J. W. Meyer & B. Rowan (Eds.), *The New Institutionalism in education: Advancing research and policy* (pp. 123–142). Albany, NY: SUNY Press.

Richardson, R. C., Bracco, K. R., Callan, P. M., & Finney, J. E. (1999). *Designing state higher education systems for a new century.* Phoenix, AZ: Oryx Press.

Rosovsky, H. (1990). *The university: An owner's manual.* New York: Oryx Press.

Sabloff, P. L. (1997). Another reason why state legislatures will continue to restrict public university autonomy. *Review of Higher Education, 20*(2), 141–162.

Schuster, J., Smith, D., Corak, K., & Yamada, M. (1994). *Strategic academic governance: How to make big decisions better.* Phoenix, AZ: Oryx Press.

Simic, C. R. (1998). *The role of the foundation board.* A report in the Board Basics series. Association of Governing Boards of Universities and Colleges [AGB]. Washington, DC: AGB.

Slaughter, S., & Leslie, L. (1997). *Academic capitalism: Politics, policies and the entrepreneurial university.* Baltimore: Johns Hopkins University Press.

Smart, J. C., Feldman, K. A., & Ethington, C. A. (2000). *Academic disciplines: Holland's theory and the study of college students and faculty.* Vanderbilt Issues in Higher Education. Nashville: Vanderbilt University Press.

Sporn, B. (1999). *Adaptive university structures: An analysis of adaptation of socioeconomic environments of US and European universities.* London: Jessica Kingsley.

Talburt, S. (2005). Ideas of a university, faculty governance, and governmentality. In J. C. Smart (Ed.), *Higher Education: Handbook of Theory and Research,* Vol. 20 (pp. 459–505). New York: Agathon Press.

Thelin, J. R. (1996). *Games colleges play: Scandal and reform in intercollegiate athletics.* Baltimore: Johns Hopkins University Press.

Thelin, J. R. (2004). *A history of American higher education.* Baltimore: Johns Hopkins University Press.

Thompson, J. D. (1967). *Organizations in action.* New York: McGraw-Hill.

Thompson, J. D., & Tuden, A. (1959). *Comparative studies in administration.* Pittsburgh, PA: University of Pittsburgh Press.

Tierney, W. G. (1988). Organizational culture in higher education: Defining the essentials. *Journal of Higher Education, 59,* 2–21.

Tierney, W. G. (1989). Symbolism and presidential perceptions of leadership. *Review of Higher Education, 12*(2), 153–166.

Tierney, W. G. (2004). A cultural analysis of shared governance: The challenges ahead. In J. C. Smart (Ed.), *Higher education: Handbook of theory and research,* Vol. 19 (pp. 85–131). New York: Agathon Press.

Toma, E. F. (1986). State university boards of trustees: A principal-agent perspective. *Public Choice, 49,* 155–163.

Toma, E. F. (1990). Boards of trustees, agency problems, and university output. *Public Choice, 67,* 1–9.

Toutkoushian, R. K. (1999). The status of academic women in the 1990s: No longer outsiders, but not yet equals. *Quarterly Review of Economics and Finance, 39,* 679–698.

Trow, M. (1993). Federalism in American higher education. In A. Levine (Ed.), *Higher learning in America: 1980–2000* (pp. 39–67). Baltimore: Johns Hopkins University Press.

Trow, M. (1998). Governance in the University of California: The transformation of politics into administration. *Higher Education Policy, 11,* 201–215.

Volkwein, J. F. (1986). State financial control of public universities and its relationship to campus administrative elaborateness and cost. *Review of Higher Education, 9*(3): 267–286.

Volkwein, J. F. (1987). State regulation and campus autonomy. In J. C. Smart (Ed.), *Higher education: Handbook of theory and research*, Vol. 3 (pp. 120–154). New York: Agathon Press.

Volkwein, J. F., & Malik, S. M. (1997). State regulation and administrative flexibility at public universities. *Research in Higher Education, 38*(1), 17–42.

Weick, K. E. (1976). Educational organizations as loosely coupled systems. *Administrative Science Quarterly, 21*(1), 1–19.

Weick, K. (1982). Management of organizational change among loosely coupled elements. In P. S. Goodman and Associates (Eds.), *Change in organizations* (pp. 375–408). San Francisco: Jossey-Bass.

Welsh, M. A., & Slusher, E. A. (1986). Organizational design as a context for political activity. *Administrative Science Quarterly, 31*(3), 389–402.

Zumeta, W. (1996). Meeting the demand for higher education without breaking the bank: A framework for the design of state higher education policies for an era of increasing demand. *Journal of Higher Education, 67*(4), 367–425.

CHAPTER FOUR

The Elephant in the Room

Power, Politics, and Global Rankings in Higher Education

BRIAN PUSSER AND SIMON MARGINSON

An interesting puzzle at the heart of the study of higher education institutions is the apparent inability of postsecondary organizations to meet goals that have been central to their missions for several decades (Birnbaum, 2000; Marginson & Considine, 2000; Readings, 1996).

For example, what accounts for the increasing stratification of students by family income in selective colleges and universities that seek a more egalitarian student array (Astin & Oseguera, 2004)? How does one explain the continued lack of success in attempting to significantly increase the number of traditionally underrepresented students at selective institutions (Bowen, Kurzweil, Tobin, & Pichler, 2005)? Perhaps related to that question, why have postsecondary organizations been unable to preserve affordability and control the cost of college, or at the very least present a compelling rationale in the broader political economy for the proposition that rising costs are appropriate (Ehrenberg, 2000)? Why can we not account for the persistently low rates of baccalaureate completion by students who begin in community colleges, an issue that Burton Clark brought to prominence nearly forty years ago (Levin, 2007)?

As demands grow for universities to train a more specialized and professionalized labor force for the twenty-first century, what explains the continuing erosion of professional status among faculty (Rhoades, 1998)? Why, when administrations and academic leaders have long proclaimed the importance of the role of universities in relation to new knowledge (Kerr, 2001) and research and scholarship are seen as central to faculty life in the age of the "knowledge economy," is funded research activity an oligopoly of a small minority of faculty?

At the same time, there are a number of areas of higher education in which postsecondary organizations can point to significant success. The proportion of women graduates has greatly increased over the past four decades, not just in the United States but in nearly all developed higher education systems around the world (Organisation for Economic Co-operation and Development, 2008). The total amount of funded research has greatly increased and with it higher education's contribution to scientific advancement in a variety of fields (Geiger, 2004). Technology is now employed on college and university campuses in ways that encourage new forms of knowledge production and link scholars across the world (Altbach, 2007).

Higher education is a mix of policy successes and policy failures. Given higher education's legitimacy in many sectors of the global political economy, how is it that such prominent organizations have had such a checkered record of organizational performance for so long? And how is it that scholars cannot better account for that performance?

We argue that scholars who specialize in the study of postsecondary organizations, particularly in the United States, have generally been unable to account for this poor fit between intention and effect because they have failed to take into account the explicit and implicit forces at work. In particular they have pursued an approach to understanding postsecondary organizations that is lacking in attention to theories that address the nature and sources of power. This is not the case for social theorists writ large. Significant attention has been turned to power in organizations by the work of Weber (1947), Blau (1955, 1970), C. Wright Mills (1956), Zald (1970), Bourdieu and Passeron (1977), Foucault (1977, 1980), Mintzberg (1983), Lukes (1986, 2005), and Clegg (1989). There is also a significant body of scholarship on organizations other than postsecondary institutions that has utilized critical theory (Burrell & Morgan, 1979; Clegg & Dunkerley, 1980), state theoretical models (Campbell & Pedersen, 2001; Harvey, 2005; Rhoads & Torres, 2006; Skocpol, 2003), critical historical approaches (Perrow, 1986), and postmodern perspectives (Casey, 2002, among others), all of which have been centrally interested in problems of power.

This chapter presents a case for employing the analysis of power in the study of postsecondary organizations and illustrates that argument by applying the approach to a topic of growing importance worldwide: the role and character of global rankings in higher education. Rankings allocate rewards, stratify institutions, establish hierarchies between nations, and impose agendas, norms, and values on all who come within their purview. Yet few of the millions of words written about rankings each year treat questions of power as explanatory. We find that global higher education rankings have much to say about the dynamic relations of power between postsecondary organizations, states, market actors, and social interests, particularly when those ranking systems are interrogated using the methods of critical research.

Power and Disciplinary Approaches to Higher Education Organizations

In contrast to the diverse set of critical perspectives applied to the study of institutions writ large, research on postsecondary organizations has relied on a smaller set of conceptual frameworks that includes positivist and rational choice models (Baldridge, 1971; Hammond, 2004; Volkwein, 1989), functionalist approaches (Balderston, 1974; Dill & Sporn, 1995; Hines, 2000), institutionalist approaches (Clark, 1993; DiMaggio & Powell, 1983; Pfeffer & Salancik, 1978), and, more recently, entrepreneurial and new managerialist models of postsecondary organization (Kezar & Lester, 2009; Maassen, 2003; Reed, 2002). The construction of normative conceptions of the purposes of higher education organizations and their relationship to the wider political economy is underdeveloped. Power is either not addressed in any significant way or presented as a factor in what are consistently constructed as internal political challenges to organization and governance.

The dearth of attention to power in studies of postsecondary organization can be attributed in no small measure to the evolution of organizational studies in higher education out of the sociology of organizations. While the pioneering work on organizations by Weber, Blau, Lipsett, Perrow, and others constituted a distinctive political sociology, relatively little of that work's attention to power is manifest in subsequent research in higher education. Research drawing upon the sociology of higher education organizations has addressed such key topics in the field as differentiation and stratification (Clark, 1983, 1993; Gumport & Sporn, 1999; Hearn, 1991; McDonough, 1997), professional expertise and legitimacy (Rhoades, 1998), organizational culture and leadership (Chaffee & Jacobson, 1997; Cooper & Kempner, 1993; Horvat, 2000; Neumann & Larson, 1997), multidimensional models of governance (Berger & Milem, 2000; Birnbaum, 1988), resource dependence frameworks (Pfeffer & Salancik, 1978; Slaughter & Leslie, 1997), and new institutionalist approaches to organizational structure (Bastedo, 2007; Brint & Karabel, 1989; Morphew, 2002). The work of Pierre Bourdieu (1984, 1996) is central to a great deal of contemporary research in the sociology of higher education, but his treatment of power is rarely invoked in detail. A related arena of socio-anthropological work has also contributed significantly to understanding culture and leadership in higher education (Margolis, 2001; Tierney, 1988, 1991, 2006; Villalpando & Solarzano,

2005). While the sociology of organizations, and the institutionalist approach in particular, have provided substantial insight into higher education organizations, and to a lesser degree into power in organizations, they have rarely adopted the inherently political approaches that address questions of power directly (Ordorika, 2003; Pusser, 2004).

Terry Moe (1996) has argued that the lack of political models in the study of public institutions is due to a traditional divide in the field of political science between the study of political institutions and the study of public administration. Educational institutions, to the extent that they were addressed at all from a political standpoint, were studied early on as part of the field of public administration. In the latter part of the twentieth century, political scientists and economists using positive theories of institutions and modeling the new economics of organizations (Weingast & Marshall, 1988) became increasingly influential in the study of public institutions, including schools (Chubb & Moe, 1990; Masten, 1995). While these developments brought political scientists more centrally into the study of educational organizations, they predominantly applied pluralist frameworks and rarely addressed the state, ideology, or relations of power (Pusser, 2008).

One of the earliest works of significant influence on the study of power in postsecondary organizations was J. Victor Baldridge's *Power and Conflict in the University* (1971). Baldridge's model of the "political university" (p. 16) relied on conflict theory drawn from Dahrendorf (1959) and Gamson (1968), research on community power (Dahl, 1961; Polsby, 1963), and interest-articulation analyses of postsecondary organizational conflict (Blau & Scott, 1962; Selznick, 1949). Baldridge's work, which has been instrumental in the development of the political frame in multidimensional models of organizational behavior (Bolman & Deal, 2008), offers a rational, pluralist, and positivist approach to contest. While Clark (1983) and Kogan (1984) added the role of the university as an institution of the state as an essential element for understanding postsecondary organizational authority relations, their approach to contest is similar to that of Baldridge.

POWER AND CRITICAL RESEARCH

Over the past twenty years a new school of critical postsecondary research has emerged, one that—as it moves away from functionalist and rational choice models— has opened new perspectives on race, gender, social class, discourse, and standpoint in higher education (Iverson, 2007; McDonough, 1997; Morrow, 2006; Solarzano, 1998; Tierney, 1991). The critical approach has, for the most part, not been applied to issues of power and organizational behavior in higher education, and, as we have argued elsewhere (Marginson, 1997; Pusser, 2008), the study of organization and governance in higher education has been limited by a lack of critical political theory. The term "critical political theory" is used here to distinguish postsecondary work that encompasses contest, ideology, social movements, the mobilization of bias, and structural inequalities from the pluralist, rational choice, interest-driven approaches that dominate much of contemporary work on postsecondary organizations in various contexts. Criticality is invoked in the spirit of Paolo Freire (1985), who noted, "[W]e must adopt a critical view, that of the person who questions, who doubts, who investigates, and who wants to illuminate the very life we live" (p. 190). We do not argue that only critical scholars who are skeptical about the claims of existing elites can study power in higher education. However, in general, an explicit focus on power is both a central feature of the critical political approach and one that is utilized comparatively rarely in the study of postsecondary education. Interestingly, there are few equivalents in studies of higher education to the neorealist and conservative traditions in research on foreign policy and international relations, which do focus explicitly on power.

In using a more direct approach to the analysis of power in higher education organizations and in their relationships with the larger society and political economy, the critical school has been able to develop a more theoretically grounded and nuanced understanding of postsecondary organizations. Critical scholars have used a combination of social theory and empirically grounded studies to address issues central to postsecondary organization, such as the commodification of knowledge production and market/corporate forms of organization (de Sousa Santos, 2006; Marginson, 1997), "academic capitalist" approaches to postsecondary revenue generation and allocation (Slaughter & Leslie, 1997; Slaughter & Rhoades, 2004), the role of the state in shaping postsecondary organization and governance (Ordorika, 2003; Ordorika & Pusser, 2007; Pusser, 2008), critical perspectives on globalization and higher education (Kempner & Jurema, 2006; Levin, 2001; Torres & Rhoads, 2006), and the rise of neoliberal state practices in higher education (Levin, 2007; Marginson, 1997).

Arguably, the breakthrough text was Sheila Slaughter's *The Higher Learning and High Technology* (1990). In her critique of pluralist approaches to postsecondary behavior, Slaughter noted the importance of social context, class structures, and the role of the state in shaping the relations of power in higher education. Slaughter's model focused on ideology and the ways in which powerful actors in the policy process shape information, discourse, and beliefs about social class and power relations in postsecondary organizations. Michael Parsons (1997) usefully articulated a broad view of power in *Power and Politics: Federal Higher Education Policymaking in the 1990s,* albeit a view not explicitly situated as "critical." Simon Marginson (1997) applied Foucault's (1980) concept of "relations of power"—whereby individual conduct and the relations between individual and state are shaped by ideology, economic relations, and knowledge production—to the "power-knowledge" strategies of the state in the government-driven reorganization of postsecondary institutions as business organizations operating in quasi markets. Ordorika (2003) and Pusser (2004) brought together the study of conflict, interest group competition, ideology, and class relations in case studies of political contests in higher education that pointed to the need to incorporate more inherently political models into the study of postsecondary organizations.

Critical scholarship on higher education organizations, and the particular insights and concepts it has generated, have had an undeniable influence on the larger field during this relatively short period. Some of the work is among the most highly cited in the field, being extensively used by scholars from outside the critical school itself—for example, the two books by Slaughter and collaborators on academic capitalism (2086 Google Scholar citations as of this writing) and Marginson and Considine's *The Enterprise University* (653 Google Scholar citations). We suspect that the critical work on power has gained widespread traction even among those who would not self-identify as "critical" precisely because power matters. Yet working directly with notions of power remains problematic for many scholars, requiring conceptual models and theoretical frameworks that can be difficult to reconcile with the normative claims of the institutional administrations and state agencies that continue to exercise substantial influence in the field. In other words, power is the elephant in the room. It would seem to be too consequential to miss, but many do. Scholarship in higher education has been slow to embrace the concept openly. Perhaps this is partly because of the dominance of neoliberal market models in global policymaking since the mid- to late 1980s, which evade the question of power by presenting postsecondary education institutions as largely shaped by markets. The recent collapse of global financial markets and the consequent revelation of inherent contradictions in the neoliberal market models that have dominated global postsecondary policymaking over the past quarter century should give us pause and serve as a reminder that the time is right to more deeply consider the nature and sources of power in higher education organizations.

Universities as Political Institutions of the State

We begin by proposing that postsecondary organizations in the United States (and elsewhere) are usefully conceptualized as political institutions of the state, where the state is understood as encompassing political institutions, laws, rules and regulations, judicial systems, and formal systems of power including law enforcement and military organizations, as well as a variety of other formal organizations that serve to shape collective activity and protect individual rights (Carnoy, 1984; Skocpol, 1992). Colleges and universities—both public and private—are chartered by state action as sites for the production of key public and private benefits, outcomes central to broader state goals (Kaul, 2008; Pusser, 2008). The form of those benefits and the allocation of the costs that attend them are determined by political and social contest. At the same time, states are also actors in political struggles, with interests of their own (Schumpeter, 1942/1976). Public and private institutions are therefore both sites of contest over key state functions and instruments in broader contests over the nature of the state (Gramsci, 1971). For all these reasons the nature of postsecondary organizations and the ways in which power is exercised in those institutions cannot be decoupled from an understanding of the role of postsecondary institutions in a given state context.

POSTSECONDARY ORGANIZATIONS AND THE STATE

How, then, do we understand the role of contemporary postsecondary organizations within a given state? Few questions in our field are more complex. State projects must be viewed through a variety of lenses: social, economic, cultural, historical, and political modes of interpretation. Given that, one discovers an array of findings on central questions within the field. David Labaree (1997) has pointed to three essential goals that drive the American educational system: democratic equality, social efficiency, and social mobility. This suggests that the state, through its demands for particular outcomes, and contest over state purposes more generally shape educational institutions. At the same time, Ordorika and Pusser (2007) have argued that in many instances and across national contexts universities have conditioned and nurtured the development of the state through the production of knowledge, through training of professionals, and as a site of individual transformation. Carnoy and Levin (1985) have noted that education is a key site for the redress of inequality generated by state efforts in support of capital accumulation. Persell and Cookson (1990) point to the role of college access in social reproduction and the formation of elites, while Slaughter and Rhoades (2004) have argued that colleges and universities serve a key role in state efforts to privilege economic development.

What these multiple and conflicting perspectives point to is the centrality of contest in understanding the relationship of the state and higher education organizations. Understanding how those contests are shaped, and competing demands adjudicated, requires that we equip ourselves with a theory of power and higher education.

Power in Social Thought

The nature of power has been one of the most contested topics in social theory.[1] A variety of authors have noted that while there is general agreement on some aspects of power, it is exceedingly difficult to precisely define the concept (Dahl, 1961; Lukes, 2005; Marginson & Considine, 2000; Morgan, 1997). Lukes (2005) credits Bertrand Russell (1938) with defining power as the ability to produce intended effects. Russell's invocation of intentionality, consistent with historical understandings, requires scholars of higher education to offer a more nuanced version of administrative agency than has been heretofore offered. Following Russell, powerful actors produce intended outcomes, ergo, power cannot be gauged without first understanding intention. Much of the prior research on higher education organizations has been vaguely normative, relying on mission as polestar, and concepts such as adaptation to external demands or ensuring student success are treated as proxies for organizational intention.

Central to the Weberian notion of power is the powerful actor's ability to impose his will in spite of resistance. C. Wright Mills (1956) and Talcott Parsons (1967) turned Weber's (1947) model to the study of community power and leadership. They argued that power ultimately is embedded in elite and coercive structures, the institutionalization of authority and leadership. The structural model of authority is essential to thinking about power in higher education because it turns attention to the distinction between normative understandings of authority relations, such as shared governance, and the formally codified exercise of authority by rules, legal authority, and legislative action.

Michel Foucault emphasized relations of power rather than concentrations of power. His work turned attention to "disciplinary" forms of power (Foucault, 1977)—the governance of human behaviors in school systems, state institutions, and work organization, in which conventions, words, practices, and knowledge are more important than legal decrees—in contrast to the conventional focus on power as sovereign force (Foucault, 1980). Foucault focuses on the manner in which people are subjugated not by robbing them of agency power but by forming them as self-actualizing agents who carry out orthodox agendas on a voluntary basis. Pierre Bourdieu (1984, 1996) drew out the manner in which the capacity to define legitimacy and shape agendas is a matter of continuous unequal contestation between different social groups, who possess unequal amounts of economic, political, social, and cultural capital. In Bourdieu's universe power relations are zero-sum and the subject of a continuous contest for position in which individuals from the different social groups use a variety of positional strategies. The content of these strategies reflects their inherited positions in the social hierarchy and the interior cultural lessons or "habitus" installed by generations of social practice. While resistance is possible, there is a limited scope to break with the reproduction of the status quo.

The question of how, or whether, to separate structure from agency in power relations has also long been debated in social theory. Hannah Arendt (1958) conceptualized a more pervasive view of power in which embedded structures shape power, agency, and action, as she argued that political institutions stand as formations born of the exercise of authority, which in turn shape the outcomes of contest and resistance. Work on education and class formation has long addressed the role of educational institutions as sites for the reproduction of powerful elites (Bowles, 1971; Domhoff, 1978), and occasionally this model has been applied to higher education as well (Aronowitz, 2000; Kingston & Lewis, 1990; Sacks, 2007; Slaughter, 1990). Bourdieu and Passeron (1977) argued that educational institutions contribute to social reproduction through maintaining, recycling, and successively institutionalizing status quo power relations in society. They suggest that this activity, which is deeply reflective of the structures of social class, has become so embedded in cultural consciousness that it has become an internalized norm—a concept that is consistent with Bourdieu's notion of "habitus." "The concept of 'misrecognition' captures the idea that while the pedagogic actions of an educational institution serve existing power relations and class interests, this interest remains invisible and therefore seemingly neutral" (Bourdieu and Passeron, as cited in Mann, 2008, p. 77). However, there is disagreement over the degree to which this reproductive effect of educational institutions is inevitable. Antonio Gramsci (1971) and critical theorists of education following his lead, Carnoy and Levin (1985) and Ordorika (2003), argue that, instead of serving inexorably as sites of the reproduction of class inequalities, political institutions, such as postsecondary organizations, also serve as sites of contest and change. Higher education has ambiguous potentials. Not only does it reproduce existing relations of power, but under some circumstances it can contribute to the loosening and transformation of power. Its potentials might be more open with respect to global power than within single nations (Marginson, 2008b). For example, there is considerable policy space for particular nations to shift the balance of power between the world's research universities. China, Germany and France are all currently engaged in major research and development investment programs that will lift their research university sectors in the next generation. On the other hand, there is less policy space within particular nations to dramatically advance the relative power of research universities in one corner of the country at the expense of others. This is because of the disciplinary effects of intranational competition and distributional politics at the national level. There is no global state—and there are no constraining distributional politics—at the world level. Individual nations and institutions have more scope for taking initiatives and breaking old policy paradigms in their global dealings with each other than they do in dealing with other institutions at home.

LUKES'S THREE-DIMENSIONAL MODEL OF POWER

The conceptual frame provided by Steven Lukes for a critical consideration of power is very usefully applied to understanding contest in postsecondary organizations (Lukes, 1986, 2005). He begins with the premise that "to have power is to be able to make a difference to the world" (1986, p. 5). That standpoint leads to a three-dimensional view of power that enables two lines of inquiry, one addressing the characteristics of the difference that is made by power, the other addressing the locus of power.

Lukes traces the one-dimensional view of power to the work of Weber (1947), Dahl (1961), and Polsby (1963), as it encompasses the rational behavior of actors in decision making and pluralist views of authority and power. According to Sadan (1977), the rational, pluralist view, in which power is exercised in a process through which interests are revealed by political participation in interest group contests, remains the most prevalent in organizational literature. While noting the limitations of the one-dimensional view, Lukes suggests that it does turn attention to authority relations and the nature of contested decision processes and political participation.

Lukes's second dimension of power relies upon Bachrach and Baratz (1970), who argued for an approach to power that moved beyond pluralism to incorporate forms of power that shape context, control agendas, direct issue attention, and define the nature of contest. Where a one-dimensional analysis focuses on decision making, the second dimension interrogates the nature of decision making and also the exercise of power to prevent contest and the need for a decision. From that standpoint, power is exercised through both decision making and "non-decision making," in each case serving as a constraint on others' ability to participate meaningfully in the decision-making process (Lukes, 2005). Central to a two-dimensional view of power is Bachrach and Baratz's concept of the "mobilization of bias," a process they defined this way: "Political systems and sub-

systems develop a 'moblization of bias,' a set of predominant values, beliefs, rituals and institutional procedures ('rules of the game') that operate systematically
and consistently to the benefit of certain persons and groups at the expense of
others" (1970, p. 43). While one-dimensional views of power do turn attention to
an array of activities designed to shape pluralist competition, Lukes suggests that
the two-dimensional view goes well beyond the classic pluralist formulation of
"agenda control" in an effort to understand "the power to decide what is decided"
(2005, p. 11). A two-dimensional analysis of power also offers a limited critique
of rational models of political behavior and opens space for both covert conflict
and interests unrevealed by pluralist processes.

Lukes's three-dimensional view of power incorporates and moves beyond the
first two dimensions as it suggests that there is unrecognized conflict between
those in power and the larger interests of civil society. To uncover this latent conflict scholars are called upon to go beyond traditional norms of intentionality in
rational and pluralist models of power and influence and to consider issues that
are not currently contested. Lukes (2005) notes, "[T]he bias of the system can be
mobilized, recreated and reinforced in ways that are neither consciously chosen
nor the intended result of particular individuals" (p. 25).

Lukes's three-dimensional model of power entails a direct challenge to behav-
ioralist views of power, including rational choice theory and the notions of homo
economicus that have influenced education policymaking in the neoliberal era,
as it opens the possibility that power may, under certain conditions, transcend
decision-making processes. It also moves beyond interest group theories and
principal-agent models by turning attention to the importance of forces that are
not formally codified within the political system, the constraints on conflict, and
issues that do not appear on decision-making agendas. A three-dimensional approach to power enables the contemplation of both "subjective and real interests"
(Lukes, 2005, p. 29), as it opens space for consideration of the role of ideology in
shaping power and authority relations, with or without contextual conflict.
Lukes's model also allows us to consider the role of archetypal values and myths
that determine what is persuasive in the exercise of power, assumptions about
the equity of competition and its Darwinian benefits, and primal beliefs in the
superiority of a way of life or of particular forms of organizational behavior.

The State, Higher Education Rankings, and Power

We now turn to an application of the three-dimensional model of power to a key
arena shaping postsecondary organizations: the relationship of states and sys-

tems of postsecondary institutional rankings (Marginson, 2007a, 2009). We will focus not only on *U.S. News and World Report* (*USNWR*) but also on the range of global rankings as a whole, which allows us to identify more general implications for the framing of the roles of the state and power dynamics in higher education. Rankings offer a useful lens for the study of power in higher education because they incorporate all three of Lukes's dimensions. They enable us to talk about contest, the role of the state and external actors, ideology, and relations of power.

In relation to global rankings and state purposes, a three-dimensional approach to power requires analysis of three key concepts:

1. Intentionality: A one-dimensional view of power predicts that the mission and purposes of higher education organizations in a particular state context drive the outcomes generated by those institutions. While much can be learned about normative state intentions for higher education from the elements of the national and global rankings recognized by that state and its institutions, a broader view of power may offer considerably more explanatory effect.

2. Legitimacy: From a one-dimensional view, state power privileges those functions of higher education that are consistent with broader national purposes, and those purposes are revealed in the choices of resource allocation, legitimation, and policies made by a particular state. This suggests, on the one hand, that global rankings contribute to the state's shaping of the legitimate purposes of higher education organizations and, on the other hand, that rankings legitimate the purposes, choices, and outcomes generated by postsecondary organizations in the most powerful states. It further suggests that the hierarchy of institutions valorized by a particular ranking system is both a source of legitimation for the outcomes of the stratification effects of state policies and consistent with the policy objectives of states. A multidimensional view of legitimacy may problematize the construction of rankings and the legitimacy of existing hierarchies of postsecondary organizations.

3. Ideology and myth: From a one-dimensional perspective on state power, it follows that, given the different forms and purposes of state relations to higher education, there should be some significant variation in the elements of ranking/accountability systems and the attention paid to such assessments within different states. That is, state approaches to global rankings, and the ways in which state power is arrayed in support of higher education, should be consistent with fundamental state ideology and with

core myths of the national culture that states foster and tap into as means of motivating action and securing consent. A three-dimensional view of power offers space for a critique of predominant ideological norms and embedded sagas framing state purposes for higher education by conceptualizing them as instruments in a broader process of the mobilization of bias and by giving voice to those constituents of postsecondary education long marginalized in state and institutional decision-making processes.

Our contention is that rankings serve as a key source of power and legitimacy in broader state contests. The diversity of rankings reflects the different purposes and agendas that are advanced by ranking processes. This encompasses not only the different groups that seek to benefit directly from them (elite universities, research communities, scientific disciplines, international educators) or utilize rankings to secure particular outcomes, or have a hand in their operation, but also the roles that are played by rankings in relations of power in national and global higher education. What is ranked and what is not ranked provide a window into contemporary power in higher education. What rankings measure offers insight into the hegemony of particular values and practices in contemporary universities and into the role of state policies and practices in shaping discourse, resource allocation, and power relations in contemporary postsecondary organizations.

We first examine what rankings measure and how rankings are constructed, which necessitates brief details on the main ranking system. Then we consider where the ranking systems connect to the agendas of states and powerful institutions, before situating the rankings-power nexus within Lukes's three dimensions of power.

RANKINGS: HISTORICAL AND CONTEMPORARY ROLES

Rankings are not a new phenomenon in higher education. Comparative data on European universities have been published for more than 150 years. Formal rankings, based on such metrics as faculty's earned degrees and institutional reputation, were first published in the United States a century ago (Stuart, 1995). A recurring element is the use of reputational surveys to establish a single hierarchy or "league table," with such tables presented without reference to contextual elements; that is, each organization is presented as if it were competing for a position in the "table" with all other organizations on the basis of equivalence. In the United States the most prominent ranking is the *U.S. News and World Report*'s annual compendium, America's Best Colleges. The *USNWR* rankings have transcended the assessment arena and achieved the status of a cultural phenomenon reported by nearly every major media outlet in the country (Ehrenberg, 2003). The *U.S. News* rankings have become such a central part of the political economy of U.S. colleges and universities that not only do they measure institutional behaviors, but they also shape them (Ehrenberg, 2000; Kirp, 2003). Rankings are both a reflection of the relative power and influence of postsecondary organizations and a source of that power and influence. Over time ranking systems have demonstrated an impressive (though not always welcome) potential to redefine and reify the core purposes of organizations. Kirp (2003) provides examples that illustrate what every university president knows: that *USNWR* encourages universities to enhance the role of merit aid at the expense of needs-based aid because the more academically selective the university, the higher its *USNWR* ranking position.

Not just national but global comparisons of higher education have become increasingly important in the goals and policies of states (Marginson, 2007b). This has created a many-layered culture of comparison. Thus in the United States, those rankings conducted by the national academies—for example, the National Research Council's Assessment of Research-Doctorate Programs—have significant legitimacy within disciplines and research universities. The commercial rankings done by *Barron's, Princeton Review,* or *U.S. News* are required reading for university administrative leaders and are widely read and employed by students and parents (McDonough, Antonio, Walpole, & Perez, 1998). At the same time, international comparisons of national postsecondary performance are used by political leaders to promote agendas, and these comparisons also highlight the contribution of each institution to the ranking position of the nation (Adelman, 2009). In a 2009 address to a joint session of Congress, President Barack Obama used America's global ranking for degree attainment as part of a rallying call for higher postsecondary achievement. "That is why we will provide the support necessary for you to complete college and meet a new goal: by 2020, America will once again have the highest proportion of college graduates in the world," (The White House, 2009). In France, Germany, China, and elsewhere the performance of the nation's universities in the annual Shanghai Jiao Tong comparison of research performance is a primary driver of accelerated investment in research (Salmi, 2009).

RANKINGS AND POSTSECONDARY ORGANIZATIONS

Hazelkorn (2008), in a study for the Paris-based Organization for Economic Cooperation and Development (OECD), demonstrates that the new body of comparative information, especially institutional rankings and research output metrics, has rapidly become installed in the thought processes, performance systems, and funding decisions of national governments, higher education organizations, corporations, philanthropists, and donors. Hazelkorn gathered data from institutional leaders in forty-one countries. Almost universally, respondents testified that "rankings are a critical factor underpinning and informing institutional reputation," affecting applications, especially from international students; university partnerships; government support; and employer valuation of graduates (Hazelkorn, 2008, p. 196). Most university leaders had set in place strategies to lift rankings, especially the organization's position in the Shanghai Jiao Tong University comparison. Only 8% of respondents had taken no action in response to rankings. Many institutions had stepped up data collection on research in both their own and peer institutions. Some universities had "taken a more aggressive approach, using rankings as a tool to influence not just organizational change but institutional priorities" (pp. 199–201). In many universities around the world strategic activity is focused on the constituent elements that constitute the Jiao Tong ranking—for example, by recruiting Nobel Prize winners and high-citation researchers ("HiCi" in the Shanghai Jiao Tong nomenclature) and providing incentive funding for faculty who publish in prestigious journals. A May 2009 study of institutions in Australia, Canada, Germany, and Japan by the Institute for Higher Education Policy confirms the centrality of rankings in strategy and planning and their significance in attracting international students (Institute for Higher Education Policy, 2009, p. 28).

WHO DOES THE RANKING?

Most countries with a large higher education component now have their own national ranking (Salmi & Saroyan, 2007). The rankings are conducted in varied ways by a variety of entities, including national ministries, accreditation agencies, universities, associations of higher education organizations, and commercial publications. Whereas national ministries often manage national rankings, there is no global state (though the OECD conducts worldwide comparisons of school student performance and is testing possible comparisons in higher education). The relationship between global rankings and state projects is played out not in instrumental fashion but in the way states use these rankings to advance control agendas, performance regimes, ideologies, and legitimation functions.

One influential global ranking system, based in the United Kingdom, resembles the *USNWR* exercise in being conducted by a commercial media player: the *Times Higher Education* (2008). In comparisons of research performance, the most prominent rankings are managed by autonomous academic units: China's Shanghai Jiao Tong University Institute of Higher Education (2009), and the Leiden University's Centre for Science and Technology Studies (2011) in the Netherlands, which specializes in metrics of science publication and citation. The Higher Education Evaluation and Accreditation Council of Taiwan (2008), a state instrumentality, also ranks institutional research performance. The Shanghai ranking has achieved greater credibility than the Taiwan ranking, though there is no great difference between them in data validity. The Jiao Tong is an independent project, which confers a more powerful legitimation function. The shaping role of states is more directly obvious in the 2009 decision of the European Union nations to create a Europe-wide classification system and "multi-purpose ranking" that will include teaching and student satisfaction as well as research performance (Kehm, Huisman, & Stensaker, 2009; van Vught, 2009).

WHAT'S BEING RANKED?

There is some variation in what rankings assess (Salmi & Soroyan, 2007; Usher & Savino, 2006). The two commercial media rankings claim to be holistic evaluations of what higher education organizations do, while in practice they focus on factors that, as the rankers see it, are signs of competitive position. In *U.S. News* academic reputation, student selectivity and faculty resources (based on such factors as compensation, prestige of terminal degree, student-faculty ratio) together constitute 60% of the ranking. This makes *USNWR* the most "student focused" of the major rankings and explains why it is mistakenly portrayed as the most "market driven." The *Times Higher Education* bases 50% on reputational surveys among faculty and graduate employers. It also covers student-faculty ratios, research citations per faculty, and the internationalization of the faculty and student body. In Germany, the Centre for Higher Education Development (CHE) rankings, conducted in collaboration with the media organization Die Zeit, rely on surveys of students and faculty on the academic program and on student services. Each data component is to be separately evaluated at discipline level for the purposes of comparison. CHE does not provide a single league table hierarchy of institutions but lists them in three broad bands of achievement (CHE, 2006).

The Shanghai Jiao Tong ranking emphasizes faculty publication, especially in science and nature, and privileges institutions that either trained or employ winners of the Nobel Prize in the sciences and economics and those that employ the top 250–300 high-citation researchers in each field. While the Jiao Tong rankings are an improvement on reputational assessments in that they are grounded in actual performance, they are limited to research productivity. This is different from measuring a "top university" in the broader sense defined by, say, the *Times Higher Education* (Marginson, 2007a).

Taken together, the commercial media rankings and the league tables of research outputs and productivity embody most of the elements found in other national and international rankings (Ehrenberg, 2000). One additional player is Webometrics, which ranks the global communications power of universities, recording the number of Web pages; external hits; "rich pages," such as pdfs and Word documents attached to Web sites; and publication and citation counts in Google Scholar. The last constitutes 50% of the index (Webometrics, 2009). Like the Shanghai Jiao Tong and *Times Higher Education* rankings, Webometrics is increasingly cited by policymakers (Marginson, 2009).

Scholars at the Universidad Nacional Autónoma de México (UNAM, the national university of Mexico) have developed a nonhierarchical presentation of data from Mexican universities to compare institutional performance in domains significant to universities and the Mexican state. UNAM includes a wide range of metrics designed to address public and private purposes in Mexican higher education (Ordorika, Rodriguez Gómez, Lozano Espinosa, & Márquez Jiménez 2009).

IMPLICATIONS OF RANKINGS FOR POWER IN
POSTSECONDARY ORGANIZATIONS

It is significant that far more is written about institutional efforts to adapt to ranking system criteria (Ehrenberg, 2000; Marginson, 2007a) than about institutional efforts to change ranking systems (Hoover, 2007). The volume of literature in both areas is greatly overshadowed by work, some in scholarly journals, that addresses the overriding issue of how to lift ranking performance.

Rankings identify and codify winners and losers. They are a key factor in building prestige and legitimacy. The rankings of flagship public and private research institutions bestow legitimacy on, and provide resources for, their research activities and their elite roles in undergraduate education. Prestigious schools possess the attributes of "high-ranking" institutions everywhere, including institutional wealth, faculty with high reputations and above average salaries, and, most important of all in the United States, students with advanced preparation, as measured by SAT scores and class rank. It is not surprising that wealth and prestige, and the students who seek both, are increasingly concentrated in fewer, more powerful postsecondary organizations. States are complicit in prestige competition, implicitly or explicitly, and are ready and willing to use the legitimizing device of rankings to bolster system stratification and elite formation.

Two examples illustrate this point. Our first is the tie-in between rankings and the outcomes of the government-driven British Research Assessment Exercise (RAE). The RAE (which was abolished in 2009) compared the measured research performance of UK institutions and allocated research-designated funding to institutions and disciplines on the basis of the comparison. A large proportion of total UK funds for higher education were distributed this way; for example, US$8.6 billion in 2001 (Salmi, 2009, p. 89). The RAE further concentrated resources on a group of universities with a broad range of high-caliber research activities. At the other end of the system were institutions with little research presence. The RAE also created a faculty transfer market. Institutions enhance their RAE rating by attracting mobile researchers with strong records, further augmenting institutional concentration. Concurrently with the RAE, news outlets such as the *Times* and the *Guardian* developed unofficial, widely utilized institutional rankings. These rankings embodied a variety of criteria, not just research performance, but it was noticeable that Cambridge, Oxford, and the other universities doing well in the RAE also led the newspaper rankings. Whether conceived for the purpose or not, the rankings functioned as a brilliant vehicle for publicly legitimizing what might otherwise be seen as a highly inequitable distribution of public research funds. The rankings recycle research power as prestige power and widen the gap between the haves and the have-nots in a process that becomes self-fulfilling. Under this regime the top group of UK universities sustained a strong research performance—the United Kingdom is second in research output after the United States, while spending only one-seventeenth of what the United States spends on higher education (Marginson, 2008b).

A second example is the effect of *U.S. News* on patterns of institutional selectivity. Between 1986 and 2003, while *U.S. News* rankings gained increasing salience in the postsecondary political economy, the number of schools *U.S. News* rated as "highly selective" increased by 21%, the number of "selective" institutions increased by 30%, and the number of schools with "open admissions" policies declined by 33% (Sacks, 2007, pp. 151–152). It could be argued that demographic shifts during the period also augmented selectivity, but in a rankings environment institutions have no incentive to compensate for those demographic effects by moving to sustain access. Rather, they have strong motivations to enhance selectivity. Rankings and selectivity are inextricably linked. Selectivity and prestige are similarly linked, as are prestige and power. As Pfeffer (1992) concluded, "Strategic behavior consciously intended to demonstrate performance and build reputation is helpful in the effort to develop sources of power" (p. 145). The prestige of the leading institutions at home and abroad underpins not just American pride but American state-building projects. Consider the contribution of the training of foreign elites in U.S. universities to U.S. foreign policy. Prestige rankings draw foreign students into the leading U.S. universities and deepen the impact of the American values that are inculcated there.

Another powerful effect of rankings is to embed in postsecondary organizations the core neoliberal state-driven messages: that higher education is a competitive market in the economic sense, that it primarily generates private benefits rather than common benefits, and that higher education organizations, which must resource themselves, are primarily focused on their own interests. Rankings are the most compelling instrument yet devised for imposing both the ideology and the practices of the competitive model. Rankings do so more effectively because in most cases they are seen to come from outside government itself.

At the same time, as we have seen, rankings do not cover all the goals of higher education. A key problem of ranking systems is that they primarily address goals and practices related to prestige competition and to competitive advantage within and between states but are indifferent to public state (and civil society) goals. Rankings cause both government and institutions to shift from public to private outcomes (whether of institutions or graduates) and from those private benefits without implications for the competitive position of institutions, such as the real quality of teaching, to reputational effects or proxy measures of quality. In the *USNWR* 2009 National Universities table, no public university was ranked in the top twenty.

RANKINGS AND POLICY FAILURES

Rankings draw and channel power not only from ideologies they install but also from pre-given myths they reflect. Rankings lock into potent notions at the historical roots of cultures as they reinstall a familiar, inherited institutional hierarchy. They standardize status competition and build upon existing sagas of entrenched excellence. That universities entrusted with the lion's share of moneys for science are worthy of such largesse becomes a self-replicating norm. In a similar fashion, admissions policies feeding elite preparation reinforce the notion that privileged students merit further benefits through higher education. This reification of institutional prestige and selectivity is supported by another neoliberal tenet wherein success is attributed to the state and its institutions but failure is the fault of individuals. Harvey (2005) notes that individual accountability is an essential component of neoliberalism: "Individual success or failure are interpreted in terms of entrepreneurial virtues or personal failings (such as not investing significantly enough in one's own human capital through education) rather than being attributed to any systemic property (such as the class exclusions usually attributed to capitalism)" (pp. 65–66).

The lack of linkages between rankings and such potentially transformative state projects as the redress of inequality or the preservation of a public sphere through higher education (Pusser, 2006) helps to explain the intractable challenges presented at the outset of this chapter. Few of those persistent challenges enter rankings criteria. Increasing diversity, ensuring affordability, or promoting leadership development do not rate. It is unsurprising that many higher education organizations prefer to pursue policy goals, such as increasing research funding, that can move them up the rankings. Always, whatever generates higher rankings is privileged (Hazelkorn, 2008; Marginson, 2007a, 2007b). The organizational behaviors that improve rankings position include what Slaughter and Rhoades (2004) have described as "a combination of market and prestige orientations" (p. 280). In this case the market is for highly prepared students, faculty with high potential for generating research funding, licensing opportunities, and scientific publications and activities that increase institutional wealth, including building endowments with alumni support. Many of these activities generate primarily private goods, or perhaps a mix of private and public goods. However, the range of postsecondary outcomes defined as contributing to private and/or public goods could be considerably expanded, as could the metrics for ranking those contributions. Imagine a postsecondary arena in which the fundamental criterion for rankings was an institution's contribution to social justice. What does it say about the nature of power in higher education that such a concept, even for the U.S. postsecondary system, with 70% of all students enrolled in public institutions, appears beyond utopian? In answer we return to our three key propositions.

INTENTIONALITY

We have suggested that a state theoretical approach is essential for understanding power in relation to rankings and the persistent inability of postsecondary organizations to meet essential public goals outside the rankings process (Marginson, 2007a). We contend that (1) states shape institutional actions and institutions shape state actions; and (2) contemporary postsecondary organizations in the United States are shaped by the neoliberal state and contest over neoliberal policies. In general, rankings of postsecondary organizations in a given state reflect fundamental purposes of higher education in that state project. This happens in at least two ways.

The first is system organization. Rankings, together with a classification system, serve as a device for establishing boundaries, defining a hierarchy based on mission, resources, and prestige, while locking institutions into common state-vectored purposes. *U.S. News* and the Carnegie classification together give form to the U.S. "market" of institutions (not least by defining postsecondary education as a competition based on a hierarchy of institutions and a hierarchy of benefits) and thereby perform an indispensable service to governments, spared the task of making politically controversial decisions on rankings and classifications. The example has not gone unnoticed. China has introduced national classifications and national rankings. The European Union is creating both a continent-wide classification of institutions and a multipurpose ranking covering all of teaching, research, and service that promises to be a more sophisticated policy tool than *U.S. News* (van Vught, 2009). Thus China and the EU both hope to compete more effectively with the American knowledge economy while opening up postsecondary education to industry investment.

Second, there is a "rankings effect": rankings drive an increasing focus by both institutions and the state on goals pertinent to prestige building through competitive rankings. In nations other than the United States, global rankings play a "disciplinary" role (Foucault, 1977; Sauder & Espeland, 2009), encouraging institutions in those nations—despite differences in resources, stage of development, national histories, traditions, languages, and cultures—to adopt the template of the globally dominant universities that lead rankings: comprehensive research-intensive institutions with selective admissions, emphasizing science and technology and elite professional schools. Thus despite the multiple and at times conflicting state goals embedded in institutional missions around the world, there is a global trend to postsecondary strategic convergence (Marginson, 2007a, 2007b). In the United States, the same process of convergence is occurring around the activities measured by *U.S. News*, such as the drive to attract highly rated students.

Yet because states and their institutions are sites of contest, rankings—powerful as they are—do not settle the matter of intentions for all time. Other missions and goals are part of the state postsecondary project, and these continue to be rallying points inside states, within postsecondary organizations and in the public sphere.

LEGITIMACY

The disproportionate allocation of state resources to those institutions most successfully conducting research for economic development, and the privileging of knowledge production linked to capital markets, have been widely discussed in research (Bok, 2003; Geiger, 2004; Marginson, 1997; Slaughter & Rhoades, 2004). To the extent that the most prominent sector of higher education can be understood as a competitive, prestige "market," global rankings define relative organizational success and secure its legitimacy. Rankings are exceptionally effective in legitimating prestige-seeking behaviors while excluding other goals. Without the legitimizing effect of ranking systems, states would have to make overtly political and thus contestable arguments for merit and selectivity, elite training, and "close to the market" research. Rankings serve as a useful buffer for states.

At the same time, global rankings legitimize state policies that enhance global competitiveness, further privileging strong institutions. Simultaneously national rankings are mobilized by states to support research concentration and stratification programs such as 985 in China, the Excellence Initiative in Germany, the French mergers, and the UK RAE (Salmi, 2009). Rankings foster a policy environment that facilitates state-managed quasi markets and new public management reforms designed to secure state influence and augment performance using accountability, audit, and quality assurance techniques (Marginson, 2008a). This litany of forces begs the question: What is the source of power/prestige/legitimacy for postsecondary education in those states that have state goals for higher education that fall beyond the boundaries of formal rankings?

IDEOLOGY AND MYTH

Our third proposition begins with the assertion that state theory predicts variation in state goals and purposes for higher education due to the evolution of ideological approaches in different state contexts. States and postsecondary systems exhibit varying stages of development, historical legacies, and cultural variations (Altbach, 2007). Similarly, the metrics of national rankings should also vary in accordance with the distinctive missions and goals of institutions in different state contexts. Surprisingly, institutional reactions to global rankings suggest that rankings are not as state-specific as would be expected (Hazelkorn, 2008; Marginson, 2007a, 2009). Rankings appear to install common expectations and assessments generally associated with a neoliberal state approach to postsecondary organization (Bensimon & Ordorika, 2006; Canaan, 2008; Torres & Rhoads, 2006). In other words, the legitimation functions, which are homogenizing in form, are also homogenizing in contents. Building a state project entails new myths and sagas (Meyer & Rowan, 1977) that shape understandings of legitimate institutional forms, behaviors, and aspirations (Harvey, 2005; Ordorika & Pusser, 2007). But here a common global reification is at work, grounded in a narrow set of legitimate metrics.

How, then, does a state that values equity, diversity, and a range of public goods, with a history of contestation over these values in higher education, reconcile them with the market competition, individualism, and deregulation associated with the neoliberal project (Harvey, 2005)? It is not enough to continually offer the promise of incremental improvement or future success or to suggest that slow progress toward equity and universal access is ameliorated by vast gains in research productivity or economic development. Where dominant ideologies and sagas that define the most legitimate postsecondary forms and behaviors diverge significantly from the lived experiences of individuals, contest and challenges to the state and its institutions will persist.

Conclusion

We conclude with remarks on the benefits of theorizing rankings and power and the utility of critical and multidimensional approaches to power and postsecondary organizations.

Lukes's typology of power can help scholars to understand the relationship between state goals and postsecondary organization. For example, a one-dimensional view of power relations might suggest that the balance between need-based financial aid and merit-based aid in the United States is the result of rational choices made on the basis of professional expertise and pluralist competition. A two-dimensional view would go further, adding that as the postsecondary project in the United States has moved from the more egalitarian New Deal and Great Society commitments to the meritocratic and competitive constructions of the neoliberal state, bias has been shifted from collective values to individual performance with individual merit measured in tests. A three-dimensional view might question the construction of merit, the attributes of prestige, the nature of public and private goods produced by state institutions, and the challenge of reconciling "elite" and "public."

Applying critical models of power to global postsecondary rankings helps us to locate higher education organizations in broader state relations of authority. Ranking is primarily an extrastate project that works in tandem with contemporary state policies. The potency of rankings is much enhanced by their origins and operations outside government offices. Rankings are an agenda-setting device par excellence, a powerful legitimator of executive action, and it is very difficult for higher education organizations to stand outside them. For the most part research universities have more autonomy than other types of higher education institutions, but less autonomy in relation to rankings. Only a move to substantial plurality in the ranking instruments is likely to reduce the normalizing power of rankings and their increasingly effective lock on state regulation.

However, the extrastate character of the most influential ranking systems, coupled with the global character of rankings, also suggests limits to state power in and through higher education. "Market"-oriented rankings such as *US News* and the *Times Higher Education* promote the autonomous authority of universities positioned at the top. Whereas at a national level these must contend with states that are in many respects supreme, there is no global state, and the power of leading universities builds in the vacuum (lesser institutions are less fortunate, more likely to be disempowered than empowered by globalization). Universities are partly "disembedded" from states in research production and dissemination and internationally generated income, increasingly important in many countries (Marginson, 2007b). This gives the most prominent institutions more room to negotiate with their national states, not least because those states need stronger research universities to advance the states' own global position.

It could be that in the longer run, at the global level, the relationship between higher education rankings and state power and state building will be reversed. Rather than fastening onto existing relations of power as at the national level, global rankings may help to foster multilateral regulation of higher education through the dovetailing of national accreditation and quality assurance systems, and possibly even global state building further down the track. These tendencies are apparent within the multilateral European zone, with the Bologna synchronization of programs and diplomas, and the emerging European ranking and classification system. Significantly, emerging systems of institutional rankings in Europe combine a more comprehensive set of public and private objectives in higher education than does *US News*, with less dependence on multiple indicators and purpose-built comparisons.

The analysis of power serves as an essential lens for illuminating the relationship between rankings and postsecondary organizations in various state contexts. Future research on other central challenges facing higher education will benefit from turning attention to contest, the role of the state, and the multiple dimensions of power. Given their potential for increasing our understanding of postsecondary organizations and their importance in other domains of social science, we believe it is time to bring analyses of power into closer relation with other research programs in higher education. While it may take some time to fully comprehend the implications, we are confident that once attention is turned to power, our scholarship and our institutions will be better for it.

NOTE

1. For a definitive treatment of power in social theory, see Lukes 2005.

REFERENCES

Adelman, C. (2009). International comparisons: What your fourth-grade math can reveal. *International Higher Education, 55,* 21–23.

Altbach, P. G. (2007). Empires of knowledge and development. In P. G. Altbach & J. Balan (Eds.), *World class worldwide: Transforming research universities in Asia and Latin America* (pp. 1–30). Baltimore: Johns Hopkins University Press.

Arendt, H. (1958). *The human condition.* Chicago: University of Chicago Press.

Aronowitz, S. (2000). *The knowledge factory: Dismantling the corporate university and creating true higher learning.* Boston: Beacon Press.

Astin, A. W., & Oseguera, L. (2004). The declining "equity" of American higher education. *Review of Higher Education, 27,* 321–341.

Bachrach, P., & Baratz, M. S. (1970). *Power and poverty: Theory and practice.* London: Oxford University Press.

Balderston, F. E. (1974). *Managing today's university: Strategies for viability, change and excellence.* San Francisco: Jossey-Bass.

Baldridge, J. V. (1971). *Power and conflict in the university: Research in the sociology of complex organizations.* New York: Wiley.

Bastedo, M. N. (2007). Bringing the state back in: Promoting and sustaining innovation in public higher education. *Higher Education Quarterly, 61,* 155–170.

Bensimon, E., & Ordorika, I. (2006). Mexico's estímulos: Faculty compensation based on piecework. In R. A. Rhoads & C. A. Torres (Eds.), *The political economy of globalization: The university, state and market in the Americas* (pp. 250–274). Palo Alto, CA: Stanford University Press.

Berger, J. B., & Milem, J. (2000). Organizational behavior in higher education and student outcomes. In J. C. Smart (Ed.), *Higher education: Handbook of theory and research,* Vol. 15 (pp. 268–338). New York: Agathon Press.

Birnbaum, R. (1988). *How colleges work: The cybernetics of academic organization and leadership.* San Francisco: Jossey-Bass.

Birnbaum, R. (2000). *Management fads in higher education: Where they come from, what they do, why they fail.* San Francisco: Jossey-Bass.

Blau, P. M. (1955). *The dynamics of bureaucracy.* Chicago: University of Chicago Press.

Blau, P. M. (1970). A formal theory of differentiation in organizations. *American Sociological Review, 35,* 201–218.

Blau, P. M., & Scott, W. R. (1962). *Formal organizations.* San Francisco: Chandler.

Bok, D. (2003). *Universities in the marketplace.* Princeton, NJ: Princeton University Press.

Bolman, L. G., & Deal, T. E. (2008). *Reframing organizations: Artistry, choice and leadership* (4th ed.). San Francisco: Jossey Bass.

Bourdieu, P. (1984). *Distinction: A social critique of the judgment of taste.* London: Routledge and Kegan Paul.

Bourdieu, P. (1996). *The state nobility: Elite schools in the field of power* (L. C. Clough, Trans.). Palo Alto, CA: Stanford University Press.

Bourdieu, P., & Passeron, J. (1977). *Reproduction in education, society and culture.* Beverly Hills, CA: Sage.

Bowen, W. G., Kurzweil, M. A., Tobin, E. M., & Pichler, S. C. (2005). *Equity and excellence in American higher education* (Thomas Jefferson Foundation Distinguished Lecture Series). Charlottesville: University of Virginia Press.

Bowles, S. (1977). Unequal education and the reproduction of the social division of labor. In J. Karabel & A. H. Halsey (Eds.), *Power and ideology in education* (pp. 137–153). New York: Oxford University Press.

Brint, S., & Karabel, J. (1989). *The diverted dream: Community colleges and the promise of educational opportunity in America, 1900–1985.* New York: Oxford University Press.

Burrell, G., & Morgan, G. (1979). *Sociological paradigms and organizational analysis: Elements of the sociology of corporate life.* London: Heinemann Educational Books.

Campbell, J. L., & Pedersen, O. K. (2001). The rise of neoliberalism and institutional analysis. In J. L. Campbell & O. K. Pedersen (Eds.), *The rise of neoliberalism and institutional analysis* (pp. 1–23). Princeton, NJ: Princeton University Press.

Canaan, J. E. (2008). A funny thing happened on the way to the (European social) forum: Or how new forms of accountability are transforming academics' identities and possible responses. In J. E. Canaan & W. Shumar (Eds.), *Structure and agency in the neoliberal university* (pp. 256–278). New York: Routledge.

Carnoy, M. (1984). *The state and political theory.* Princeton, NJ: Princeton University Press.

Carnoy, M., & Levin, H. M. (1985). *Schooling and work in the democratic state.* Stanford, CA: Stanford University Press.

Casey, C. (2002). *Critical analysis of organizations: Theory, practice, revitalization.* London: Sage.

Centre for Higher Education Development [CHE]. (2006). University rankings, published in association with Die Zeit. Retrieved December 16, 2006, from www.daad.de/deutsch land/studium/hochschulranking/04708.en.html

Chaffee, E. E., & Jacobson, S. W. (1997). Creating and changing institutional cultures. In M. W. Peterson, D. D. Dill, L. A. Mets, & Associates (Eds.), *Planning and management for a changing environment* (pp. 230–245). San Francisco: Jossey-Bass.

Chubb, J. E., & Moe, T. (1990). *Politics, markets and America's schools.* Washington, DC: Brookings Institution.

Clark, B. R. (1983). *The higher education system: Academic organization in cross-national perspective.* Berkeley: University of California Press.

Clark, B. R. (1993). The problem of complexity in modern higher education. In S. Rothblatt & B. Wittrock (Eds.), *The European and American university since 1800* (pp. 263–279). Cambridge: Cambridge University Press.

Clegg, S. R. (1989). *Frameworks of power*. London: Sage.

Clegg, S., & Dunkerley, D. (1980). *Organization, class and control*. London: Routledge and Keegan Paul.

Cooper, J., & Kempner, K. (1993). The lord of the flies community college. *Review of Higher Education, 16*, 419–437.

Dahl, R. A. (1961). *Who governs? Democracy and power in an American city*. New Haven, CT: Yale University Press.

Dahrendorf, R. (1959). *Class and class conflict in industrial society*. London: Routledge and Keegan Paul.

de Sousa Santos, B. (2006). The university in the 21st century: Toward a democratic and emancipator university reform. In R. A. Rhoads & C. A. Torres (Eds.), *The university, state, and market: The political economy of globalization in the Americas* (pp. 60–100). Stanford, CA: Stanford University Press.

Dill, D., & Sporn, B. (1995). The implications of a postindustrial environment. In D. Dill & B. Sporn (Eds.), *Emerging patterns of social demand and university reform: Through a glass darkly* (pp. 1–19). Oxford: Pergamon Press.

DiMaggio, P. J., & Powell, W. W. (1983). The "iron cage" revisited: Isomorphism and collective rationality in organization fields. *American Sociological Review, 48*, 147–160.

Domhoff, G. W. (1978). *Who really rules? New Haven and community power reexamined*. New Brunswick, NJ: Transaction Books.

Ehrenberg, R. G. (2000). *Tuition rising: Why college costs so much*. Cambridge, MA: Harvard University Press.

Ehrenberg, R. G. (2003). *Method or madness? Inside the USNWR college rankings*. Cornell Higher Education Research Institute Working Paper #39. Retrieved July 27, 2009, from digitalcommons.ilr.cornell.edu/workingpapers/42

Foucault, M. (1977). *Discipline and punish: The birth of the prison*. New York: Pantheon.

Foucault, M. (1980). *Power/knowledge: Selected interviews and other writings, 1972–1977* (C. Gordon, Ed.). New York: Pantheon.

Freire, P. (1985). *The politics of education*. South Hadley, MA: Bergin and Garvey.

Gamson, W. A. (1968). *Power and discontent*. Homewood, IL: Dorsey Press.

Geiger, R. L. (2004). *Knowledge and money: Research universities and the paradox of the marketplace*. Palo Alto, CA: Stanford University Press.

Gramsci, A. (1971). *Selections from prison notebooks*. New York: International Publishers.

Gumport, P. J., & Sporn, B. (1999). Institutional adaptation: Demands for management reform and university administration. In J. C. Smart (Ed.), *Higher education: Handbook of theory and research*, Vol. 14 (pp. 103–145). New York: Agathon Press.

Hammond, T. H. (2004). Herding cats in the university hierarchies: Formal structure and policy choice in American research universities. In R. G. Ehrenberg (Ed.), *Governing academia* (pp. 91–138). Ithaca, NY: Cornell University Press.

Harvey, D. (2005). *A brief history of neoliberalism*. London: Oxford Press.

Hazelkorn, E. (2008). Learning to live with league tables and ranking: The experience of institutional leaders. *Higher Education Policy, 21,* 193–215.

Hearn, J. C. (1991). Academic and nonacademic influences on the college destinations of 1980 high school graduates. *Sociology of Education, 64,* 158–171.

Higher Education Evaluation and Accreditation Council of Taiwan. (2008). 2007 performance ranking of scientific papers for world universities. Retrieved September 1, 2008, from www.heeact.edu.tw/ranking/index.htm

Hines, E. (2000). The governance of higher education. In J. C. Smart (Ed.), *Higher education: Handbook of theory and research,* Vol. 15 (pp. 105–155). New York: Agathon Press.

Hoover, E. (2007, April 20). Anti-rankings campaign stirs new criticisms of U.S. News guides. *Chronicle of Higher Education, 53,* A41.

Horvat, E. (2000). Understanding equity and access in higher education: The potential contribution of Pierre Bourdieu. In J. C. Smart & W. Tierney (Eds.), *Higher education: Handbook of theory and research,* Vol. 16 (pp. 195–238). New York: Agathon Press.

Institute for Higher Education Policy. (2009, May). *Impact of college rankings on institutional decision making: Four country case studies.* Retrieved July 27, 2009, from www.ihep.org/assets/files/publications/g-l/ImpactofCollegeRankings.pdf

Iverson, S. V. (2007). Camouflaging power and privilege: A critical race analysis of university diversity policies. *Educational Administration Quarterly, 43,5* 586–611.

Kaul, I. (2008). Providing (contested) global public goods. In V. Rittberger & M. Nettesheim (Eds.), *Authority in the global political economy* (pp 89–115). New York: Palgrave Macmillan.

Kehm, B., Huisman, J., & Stensaker, B. (Eds.) (2009). *The European higher education area: Perspective on a moving target.* Rotterdam: Sense Publishers.

Kempner, K., & Jurema, A. L. (2006). Brazil's local solutions to global problems. In R. A. Rhoads & C. A. Torres (Eds.), *The university, state and market: The political economy of globalization in the Americas* (pp. 221–249). Stanford, CA: Stanford University Press.

Kerr, C. (2001). The uses of the university (5th ed.). Cambridge, MA: Harvard University Press.

Kezar, A. J., & Lester, J. (2009). *Organizing higher education for collaboration: A guide for campus leaders.* San Francisco: Jossey-Bass.

Kingston, P. W., & Lewis, L. S. (1990). Undergraduates at elite institutions: The best, the brightest, and the richest. In *The high-status track: Studies of elite schools and stratification* (pp. 105–120). Albany: State University of New York Press.

Kirp, D. L. (2003). *Shakespeare, Einstein and the bottom line.* Cambridge, MA: Harvard University Press.

Kogan, M. (1984). The political view. In B. R. Clark (Ed.), *Perspectives on higher education* (pp. 56–78). Berkeley: University of California Press.

Labaree, D. F. (1997). Public goods, private goods: The American struggle over educational goals. *American Educational Research Journal, 34,* 39–81.

Leiden University Centre for Science and Technology Studies. (2011). The Leiden Ranking. Retrieved June 16, 2011, from www.socialsciences.leiden.edu/cwts/products-services/leiden-ranking-2010–cwts.html#world

Levin, J. S. (2001). *Globalizing the community college*. New York: Palgrave.

Levin, J. S. (2007). *Nontraditional students and community colleges: The conflict of justice and neoliberalism*. New York: Palgrave Macmillan.

Lukes, S. (1986). Introduction. In S. Lukes (Ed.), *Power* (pp. 1–18). Washington Square: New York University Press.

Lukes, S. (2005). *Power: A radical view* (2nd ed.). London: Macmillan.

Maassen, P. (2003). Shifts in governance arrangements: An interpretation of the introduction of new management structures in higher education. In A. Amaral, V. L. Meek, & I. M. Larsen (Eds.), *The higher education managerial revolution?* (pp. 31–53). Dordrecht, Netherlands: Kluwer.

Mann, S. J. (2008). *Study, power and the university*. New York: Open University Press.

Marginson, S. (1997). *Markets in education*. Melbourne: Allen and Unwin.

Marginson, S. (2007a). Global university rankings. In S. Marginson (Ed.), *Prospects of higher education: Globalization, market competition, public goods and the future of the university* (pp. 79–100). Rotterdam: Sense Publishers.

Marginson, S. (2007b). The new higher education landscape: Public and private goods, in global/national/local settings. In S. Marginson (Ed.), *Prospects of higher education: Globalization, market competition, public goods and the future of the university* (pp. 29–77). Rotterdam: Sense Publishers.

Marginson, S. (2008a). Academic creativity under new public management: Foundations for an investigation. *Educational Theory, 58*, 269–287.

Marginson, S. (2008b). Global field and global imagining: Bourdieu and relations of power in worldwide higher education. *British Journal of Sociology of Education, 29*, 303–316.

Marginson, S. (2009). Open source knowledge and university rankings. *Thesis Eleven, 96*, 9–39.

Marginson, S., & Considine, M. (2000). *The enterprise university: Power, governance, and reinvention in Australia*. Cambridge: Cambridge University Press.

Margolis, E. (2001). *The hidden curriculum in higher education*. New York: Routledge.

Masten, S. E. (1995). Old school ties: Financial aid coordination and governance of higher education. *Journal of Economic Behavior and Organizations 28*, 23–47.

McDonough, P. M. (1997). *Choosing colleges: How social class and schools structure opportunity*. Albany: State University of New York Press.

McDonough, P. M., Antonio, A. L., Walpole, M., & Perez, L. X. (1998). College rankings: Democratized college knowledge for whom? *Research in Higher Education, 39*(5), 513–537.

Meyer, J. W., & Rowan, B. (1977). Institutionalized organizations: Formal structure as myth and ceremony. *American Journal of Sociology, 83*, 340–363.

Mills, C. W. (1956). *The power elite*. New York: Oxford University Press.

Mintzberg, H. (1983). *Power in and around organizations*. Upper Saddle River, NJ: Prentice Hall.

Moe, T. (1996). *The positive theory of public bureaucracy*. New York: Cambridge University Press.

Morgan, G. (1997). *Images of organization*. Thousand Oaks, CA: Sage.

Morphew, C. C. (2002). A rose by any other name: Which colleges became universities. *Review of Higher Education, 25*, 207–224.

Morrow, R. (2006). Critical theory, globalization, and higher education: Political economy and the cul-de-sac of the postmodernist cultural turn. In R. A. Rhoads & C. A. Torres (Eds.), *The university, state and market: The political economy of globalization in the Americas*, pp. xvii–xxxiii. Stanford, CA: Stanford University Press.

Neumann, A., & Larson, R. S. (1997). Enhancing the leadership factor in planning. In M. W. Peterson, D. D. Dill, L. A. Mets, & Associates (Eds.), *Planning and management for a changing environment* (pp. 191–203). San Francisco: Jossey-Bass.

Ordorika, I. (2003). *Power and politics in university governance: Organization and change at the Universidad Nacional Autónoma de México*. New York: RoutledgeFalmer.

Ordorika, I., & Pusser, B. (2007). La máxima casa de estudios: The Universidad Nacional Autónoma de México as a state-building university. In P. G. Altbach & J. Balan (Eds.), *World class worldwide: Transforming research universities in Asia and Latin America* (pp. 189–215). Baltimore: Johns Hopkins University Press.

Ordorika, I., Rodriguez Gómez, R., Lozano Espinosa, F. J., & Márquez Jiménez, A. (2009). Desempeño de universidades mexicanas en la función de investigación: Estudio comparativo. Cuadernos de Trabajo de la *Dirección General de Evaluación Institucional*, año 1, no. 2. *Dirección General de Evaluación Institucional*, Universidad Nacional Autónoma de México. Mexico, DF.

Organisation for Economic Cooperation and Development. (2008). *Education at a glance 2008: OECD indicators*. Paris: OECD Directorate for Education.

Parsons, M. D. (1997). *Power and politics: Federal higher education policymaking in the 1990s*. Albany: State University of New York Press.

Parsons, T. (1967). *Sociological theory and modern society*. New York: Free Press.

Perrow, C. (1986). *Complex organizations: A critical essay* (3rd ed.). New York: McGraw-Hill.

Persell, C. H., & Cookson, P. W., Jr. (1990). Chartering and bartering: Elite education and social reproduction. In P. W. Kingston & L. S. Lewis (Eds.), *The high-status track: Studies of elite schools and stratification* (pp. 25–50). Albany: State University of New York Press.

Pfeffer, J. (1992). *Managing with power: Politics and influence in organizations*. Boston: Harvard Business School Press.

Pfeffer, J., & Salancik, G. R. (1978). *The external control of organizations: A resource dependence perspective*. New York: Harper and Row.

Polsby, N. W. (1963). *Community power and political theory*. New Haven, CT: Yale University Press.

Pusser, B. (2004). *Burning down the house: Politics, governance and affirmative action at the University of California*. Albany: State University of New York Press.

Pusser, B. (2006). Reconsidering higher education and the public good: The role of public spheres. In W. Tierney (Ed.), *Governance and the public good* (pp. 11–28). Albany: State University of New York Press.

Pusser, B. (2008). The state, the market and the institutional estate: Revisiting contemporary authority relations in higher education. In J. C. Smart (Ed.), *Higher education: Handbook of theory and research*, Vol. 23 (pp. 105–139). New York: Agathon Press.

Readings, B. (1996). *The university in ruins*. Cambridge, MA: Harvard University Press.

Reed, M. (2002). New managerialism, professional power and organisational governance in UK universities: A review and assessment. In A. Amaral, G. A. Jones, & B. Kersath

(Eds.), *Governing higher education: National perspectives on institutional governance* (pp. 163–186). Dordrecht, Netherlands: Kluwer.

Rhoades, G. (1998). *Managed professionals: Unionized faculty and restructuring academic labor.* Albany: State University of New York Press.

Rhoads, R. A., & Torres, C. A. (2006). *The university, state, and market: The political economy of globalization in the Americas.* Palo Alto, CA: Stanford University Press.

Russell, B. (1938). *Power: A new social analysis.* London: Allen and Unwin.

Sacks, P. (2007). *Tearing down the gates: Confronting the class divide in American education.* Berkeley: University of California Press.

Sadan, E. (1997). *Empowerment and community planning: Theory and practice of people-focused social solutions.* Tel Aviv: Hakibbutz Hameuchad Publishers.

Salmi, J. (2009). *The challenge of establishing world class universities.* Washington, DC: World Bank.

Salmi, J., & Saroyan, A. (2007). League tables as policy instruments: Uses and misuses. *Higher Education Management and Policy, 19,* 31–68.

Sauder, M., & Espeland, W. (2009). The discipline of rankings: Tight coupling and organizational change. *American Sociological Review, 74,* 63–82.

Schumpeter, J. A. (1942/1976). *Capitalism, socialism and democracy.* London: Taylor and Francis Books.

Selznick, P. (1949). *TVA and the grass roots.* Berkeley: University of California Press.

Shanghai Jiao Tong University Institute of Higher Education. (2009). Academic Ranking of World Universities. Retrieved May 12, 2009, from www.arwu.org/

Skocpol, T. (1992). *Protecting soldiers and mothers: The political origins of social policy in the United States.* Cambridge, MA: Harvard University Press.

Skocpol, T. (2003). *Diminished democracy: From membership to management in American civic life.* Norman: University of Oklahoma Press.

Slaughter, S. (1990). *The higher learning and high technology: Dynamics of higher education policy formation.* Albany: State University of New York Press.

Slaughter, S., & Leslie, L. L. (1997) *Academic capitalism.* Baltimore: Johns Hopkins University Press.

Slaughter, S., & Rhoades, G. (2004). *Academic capitalism and the new economy.* Baltimore: Johns Hopkins University Press.

Solorzano, D. (1998). Critical race theory, racial and gender microaggressions and the experiences of Chicana and Chicano scholars. *International Journal of Qualitative Studies in Education, 11,* 121–136.

Stuart, D. L. (1995). Reputational rankings: Background and development. *New Directions for Institutional Research, 88,* 13–20.

The White House. (2009, February 24). Remarks of President Barack Obama—Address to Joint Session of Congress. Retrieved February 24, 2009, from www.whitehouse.gov/the_press_office/remarks-of-president-barack-obama-address-to-joint-session-of-congress/

Tierney, W. G. (1988). Organizational culture in higher education: Defining the essentials. *Journal of Higher Education, 59,* 2–21.

Tierney, W. G. (1991). Ideology and identity in postsecondary institutions. In W. G. Tierney (Ed.), *Culture and ideology in higher education* (pp. 35–58). New York: Praeger.

Tierney, W. G. (2006). *Trust and the public good: Examining the cultural conditions of academic work*. New York: Peter Lang Publishing.

Times Higher Education. (2008). World university rankings 2008. Retrieved March 30, 2008, from www.timeshighereducation.co.uk/hybrid.asp?typeCode=243&pubCode=1&navcode= 137

Torres, C. A., & Rhoads, R. A. (2006). Introduction: Globalization and higher education in the Americas. In R. A. Rhoads & C. A. Torres (Eds.), *The university, state, and market: The political economy of globalization in the Americas* (pp. 3–38). Stanford, CA: Stanford University Press.

Usher, A., & Savino, M. (2006, January). A world of difference: A global survey of university league tables. Retrieved July 27, 2009, from www.educationalpolicy.org/pdf/World-of-Difference-200602162.pdf

van Vught, F. (Ed.) (2009). *Mapping the higher education landscape: Towards a European classification of higher education*. Heidelberg: Springer.

Villalpando, O., & Solorzano, D. (2005). The role of culture in college preparation programs: A review of the research literature. In W. Tierney, Z. Corwin, & J. Colyar (Eds.), *Preparing for college: Nine elements of effective outreach* (pp. 13–28). Albany: SUNY Press.

Volkwein, J. F. (1989). Changes in quality among public universities. *Journal of Higher Education, 60*, 136–151.

Weber, M. (1947). *The theory of social and economic organization*. Glencoe, IL: Free Press.

Webometrics. (2009). Ranking web of world universities. Retrieved May 1, 2009, from www.webometrics.info/index.html

Weingast, B. R., & Marshall, W. J. (1988). The industrial organization of Congress; or, why legislatures, like firms, are not organized as markets. *Journal of Political Economy, 96*, 132–163.

Zald, M. N. (1970). Political economy: A framework for comparative analysis. In M. N. Zald (Ed.), *Power in organizations*, pp. 221–261. Nashville, TN: Vanderbilt University Press.

CHAPTER FIVE

Institutional Strategy

Positioning for Prestige

J. DOUGLAS TOMA

Despite the impressive diversity of institution types, the relative autonomy of individual universities and colleges, and the vast differences in respective resources available to them, higher education institutions in the United States tend to arrive at a common aspiration. They are eerily similar in vision, in fact, seemingly obsessed with "moving to the next level." Their common goal is legitimacy through enhanced prestige—and with it access to greater resources, recognizing that the most prestigious institutions also tend to be the wealthiest. They not only portray their ambitions using similar rhetoric but also operationalize them through a rather generic set of approaches. Even significant differences in prestige or resources among institutions do not seem to matter, as they seemingly all endeavor so purposefully to become more like those directly above them on the prestige hierarchy (Toma, 2008). There is an increasingly similar ubiquity worldwide in institutions and systems fixating on rankings, with even some similarity in tactics, such as entering the competition for researchers perceived to be able to attract meaningful resources. Institutional theory anticipates universities and colleges across types adopting just such a similar strategic approach. But writing on corporate strategy emphasizes differentiation in developing aspirations and approaches, as opposed to such isomorphism. In higher education there is some differentiation, but it is more at the surface or margins, with few institutions stepping away from the herd in meaningful ways, the pull of legitimacy being so powerful.

I begin my exploration of strategy at universities and colleges by considering what constitutes strategy, recognizing the relative dearth of work directly within higher education. Employing the Atlanta market, I illustrate aspirations of and approaches by institutions across types—what universities and colleges are actually doing. In doing so, I draw on data from my own research involving thirty-eight institutions representative of types across American higher education (Toma, 2008, 2010a). I then consider theory on competitive strategy, which emphasizes differentiation more than isomorphism, even if sometimes merely at a surface level. I continue by exploring why these institutions arrive at the same basic vision and pursue it utilizing such similar tactics, employing institutional theory to suggest legitimacy and autonomy as motivating forces. I conclude by commenting on the applicability of theory drawn from corporations to higher education and suggest that universities and colleges may underemphasize differentiation in their endeavors to move to the "next level."

I explore these ideas within the context of writing about the entrepreneurial university. As Americans have embraced neoliberal notions, understanding higher education in terms of gains for individuals and contributions to local economic development—as opposed to solely the advancement and dissemination of knowledge for the overall good of society—universities and colleges are increasingly seeking resources in new markets and viewing knowledge as a commodity. In doing so, they are deemphasizing their traditional academic core in favor of seeing revenues at their more agile peripheries; expanding management capacity and the influence of managers; restructuring the composition of the faculty to lower instructional costs; subsidizing researchers (who themselves are increasingly focused on individual gain); aggressively recruiting accomplished students; and obsessing over meaningless measures, such as those associated with rankings (Bok, 2002; Slaughter & Rhoades, 2004). As a result, institutions are less able to control spending and have become more expensive (Ehrenberg, 2002; Geiger, 2004; Zemsky, Wegner, & Massy, 2005). Such trends in strategy are increasingly familiar worldwide.

These maneuvers are occurring in the context of institutions fixated on their upward mobility—and are likely accelerated by it. Positioning for prestige is the standard strategic direction chosen across higher education, at least at institutions that are selective or have such ambitions. It is logical for institutions to concentrate their strategic efforts on achieving the enhanced legitimacy and likely greater autonomy likely available at the "next level." Universities and colleges with the highest status are usually the wealthiest, and perceptions of being associated with a leading institution making it easier to accomplish more are likely correct. Prestige is to higher education as profit is to corporations. In addition to concrete benefits like reducing resource dependency and other kinds of exposure, there are more psychological ones, as with individuals connecting their own identity with the organizations with which they affiliate (organizational identification) and firms gaining the tangible benefits that accompany a strong brand (brand equity) (Aaker, 1991; Dutton, Dukerich, & Harquail, 1994; Toma, Dubrow, & Hartley, 2005). In addition, positioning strategies may be so prominent because there is not a set status hierarchy in higher education, and few structural barriers, if any. There is thus always the hope of moving up—winning the lottery, in effect—and just enough examples of institutions across types doing just that.

But universities and colleges cannot simply wish themselves to become more legitimate, with the autonomy that tends to accompany prestige and resources. Writing on competitive strategy in the corporate sector contends that firms are most successful when they differentiate themselves in the interest of capturing a greater or more attractive portion of a given market segment—or, as in higher education, even move into a more promising segment. But institutions tend to concentrate only on the latter in developing strategy, through common aspirations and generic approaches toward enhancing prestige, suggesting that isomorphism is the preferred route to increased legitimacy and autonomy—and the greater resources perceived to accompany these. The mere appearance of differentiation is sufficient, with the distinctiveness that institutions claim being more superficial than actual. Regardless of marketing claims by institutions, academic programs among them are rarely different in meaningful ways, and the student experience away from the classroom at residential institutions is relatively standard. For instance, seemingly every selective university or college has established an honors program and learning communities, is enhancing study abroad opportunities and offering freshmen seminars, and is constructing a building for teaching science and has invested in a fitness center and student residences. From one selective institution to the next, are courses arrayed and delivered in ways that are really different? Is the student affairs (or external affairs) infrastructure any different, or are there the same units doing roughly the same work? While universities and colleges represent themselves as distinctive, differences are modest—matters more related to look and feel. They prefer the security that comes with following standard approaches, pursuing similar goals in roughly the same manner.

Greater attention to real differentiation—strategy as opposed to legitimacy—would ultimately be a better result, as opposed to the academic drift and mission inflation that drive positioning for prestige. Morphew (2009) and Birnbaum (1983) argue that the diversity of institution types in U.S. higher education is declining, as are the advantages that accompany it, as institutions leave one sector to enter a more crowded one in the search for prestige and resources (Riesman, 1956). But there is no opting out of the reputation race, it seems. Among institutions that even make a pretense to being selective, it is difficult to identify an institution that has done so. Could a president realistically offer the status quo relative to institutional reputation as his or her vision, even accompanied by real progress in other areas? It is a given, including increasingly worldwide, that institutions will pursue common aspirations of legitimacy and autonomy through a remarkably standard set of approaches. I thus do not ask whether such strategies and tactics are flawed but instead explore strategy as a concept, in operation, and as influenced by the security of isomorphism and the potential competitive advantages of differentiation.

What Is Strategy?

Strategy is not only a plan toward attaining missions and achieving aspirations but is also a pattern and thus consistent over time; a position, locating particular products in particular markets; a perspective, or the fundamental ways an organization does things; and a ploy, a specific maneuver intended to outwit an opponent or competitor (Mintzberg, 1987a). Mintzberg (1987b) notes that organizations need strategy to (1) set a direction for themselves and outsmart competitors (or at least enable themselves to maneuver through threatening environments); (2) focus effort and promote coordination of their activities; (3) define the organization; and (4) reduce uncertainty and provide consistency (however arbitrary these may be) in order to aid cognition, satisfy intrinsic needs for order, and promote efficiency under conditions of stability (by concentrating resources and exploiting past learning).

Chafee (1985), in considering universities and colleges, similarly contends that strategy includes both the organization and its environment, is complex in substance, affects the overall welfare of the organization, involves both content and process, is not purely deliberate, exists on different levels, and involves both conceptual and analytical thought processes. Keller (1983) argues that strategy is grounded in an institution shaping its own destiny, focused on keeping pace with the current environment, influenced by markets and competition, oriented toward action, both rational and tolerant of ambiguity, and obsessed with the fate of the institution. It considers the traditions and values of an institution, as well as its aspirations and priorities, while taking into account strengths and weaknesses, both academic and financial, and the external environment. I thus frame strategy as aspirations, such as heightening legitimacy and enhancing autonomy

through moving to the "next level," as well as the actual approaches toward positioning for greater prestige, such as the activities that institutions are undertaking to attract more-accomplished students.

Camillus (2008) frames strategy as a means to tame, but not necessarily solve,
"wicked" problems. These are challenges, often unprecedented, where there are
not only multiple stakeholders with different values and priorities but also complex and varied bases such that they are difficult even to formulate. Such "wicked"
problems are complicated, do not suggest a right answer, and tend to change with
attempts to solve them. Camillus suggests involving stakeholders, defining identity, focusing on action, and assuming problems in advance as approaches. Jacobides's (2010) response to turbulent environments is to frame strategy not as a
formal plan but instead as a "playscript" with plots, subplots, and narratives. Collis and Rukstad (2008) also offer counsel on developing strategy, encouraging
finding a strategic "sweet spot" through considering questions of objective,
scope, and advantage—the ends the strategy is designed to achieve, the part of
the landscape in which the organization will operate, and what it will do better or
differently than others.

Writing on strategic management considers not only developing strategy but
also implementing it. Mintzberg, Ahlstrand, and Lampel (2005) categorize the
multiple conceptual and intellectual traditions in strategic management into
three "prescriptive" schools, concerned with what strategy should be, and seven
"descriptive" ones. (The discussion here is not grounded in a single one of these
traditions, nor does it dismiss any of them.) Prescriptive approaches feature design, such as SWOT analysis (strengths, weaknesses, opportunities, and threats)
(Andrews, 1987; Selznik, 1957); planning, as with operational plans developed
from objectives, budgets, and programs (Ansoff, 1965); and positioning, selecting one of a few generic strategies upon analyzing an industry. For instance,
Porter (1979) focuses on how competition influences strategy, arguing that a firm
gains advantage through positioning. Positioning involves differentiating from
rivals and having interlocked activities, even those diverse in nature, which are
difficult for competitors to match (Porter, 1996, 1987, 2008b). When applied in
higher education, each of these so-called prescriptive approaches has been criticized as a poor fit with the diffuse nature of universities and colleges and the
complex environment within which they function, with earlier design and planning approaches considered overly rigid and linear.

Among the descriptive schools, the cognitive school stresses subjectivity and
creativity in formulating strategy over mapping reality in some more or less objective manner—there is no perfect outcome and no ideal approach (March &

Simon, 1958; Mintzberg et al., 2005; Simon, 1997). Given the complexity of organizations, the learning school contends that strategy is a process that is incremental, emergent, and learned in character, as opposed to comprehensive visions
and exact plans, so formulating and implementing strategy intertwine (Prahalad
& Hamel, 1990; Quinn, 1980). The power school considers strategy as the product of bargaining, persuasion, and confrontation, within organizations as well as
between and among them (Allison, 1971; Astley, 1984; Pfeffer & Salancik, 1978).
Strategy is an emergent social process based on common interests and integration, according to the culture school, and thus rooted in the culture of an organization (Normann, 1977; Rhenman, 1973). The environmental school approaches
strategy as being reactive to the external context of the organization, rather than
initiated from within the organization (Hannen & Freeman, 1977). The entrepreneurial school is focused more on the charisma and intuition of the chief executive officer (Cole, 1959; Schumpeter, 1950). Finally, what Mintzberg and colleagues (2005) term the configuration school combines the others to some
extent, arguing that organizations exist in "states of being," with strategy as the
process of transformation from one state to another.[1]

Institutional Aspirations and Approaches toward Realizing Them

Those writing about U.S. higher education have long recognized what O'Meara
(2007) terms "striving" institutions, those attempting through a variety of approaches
to reposition themselves toward greater prestige—and, they assume, increased resources (Berdahl, 1985; Brewer, Gates, & Goldman, 2002; Clotfelter, 1996; Ehrenberg, 2003; Massy & Zemsky, 1994; Riesman, 1956; Winston, 2000). Common
strategic approaches include enrolling more-accomplished students, increasing
emphasis on research, adding graduate programs, enhancing spending on administrative support and infrastructure, and articulating messages about the institution being "on the move" (O'Meara, 2007). Before delving into competitive
strategy and institutional theory to consider what may be driving such positioning for prestige, I begin with a brief review of how moving to the "next level" as
a standard aspiration across universities and colleges within the Atlanta market
differs across institution types. I then consider the approaches institutions are
employing toward realizing their ambitions, which are also common across institution types, perhaps indicating there are only so many realistic ways to reposition an American institution.[2]

The Atlanta study involved interviewing presidents, gathering documentary data, and observing campus life during early 2008 at thirty-eight institutions connected with the Atlanta market. Atlanta is an ideal laboratory, with essentially all major institution types in American higher education represented—public and private, research and teaching, larger and smaller, urban and rural, general and special focus, and so on. As part of my case study methods course in May 2008, I directed a group of doctoral students who conducted interviews with several senior administrators and faculty at four public institutions within the set of thirty-eight, including a research university, large comprehensive institution, a liberal arts college, and a community college. Examining a market representing the continuum of institutions in U.S. higher education extends discussions about prestige beyond the elite universities and colleges on which they typically focus. It also introduces the idea that, in strategy, institutions with few claims to prestige and little to differentiate themselves still must make a plausible set of assertions as they position within a market segment.

ASPIRATIONS

The status hierarchy in American higher education is reasonably clear, as captured each year in *U.S. News and World Report* rankings. Institutions know there is a "next level" and understand fairly well the steps required to reach it. They are also not bashful about announcing their intentions, even if only marginally plausible, as simply doing so tends to place an institution among others, thus adding legitimacy. Georgia State University, for instance, aspires to progress (as it sees it) from a "commuter" institution established to serve Atlanta students to a destination for the most accomplished students seeking a residential collegiate experience in an urban setting. Georgia State is also interested in continuing to advance as a research university, becoming recognized as similar to the more developed Georgia Institute of Technology and University of Georgia (UGA). It thus employs various approaches toward attempting to realize these aspirations, investing in infrastructure in areas such as housing and developing its research capacity, both in staffing and facilities.

Comprehensive institutions are also interested in the "next level." They also understand that attracting more-accomplished students is reflected in the reputational rankings. For instance, UGA has leveraged the increasing standardized test scores of its entering undergraduates to move into the leading twenty public universities in the annual *U.S. News and World Report* survey. Comprehensives are also adding, as permitted by the state system, the graduate programs and research activity also associated with more prestigious flagship institutions. There is a robust competition, for example, between Kennesaw State University and Georgia Southern University, two larger comprehensives, for both suburban Atlanta students and permission from the university system to add master's and doctoral degree programs, particularly in professional fields like education. Pursuing both approaches moves them closer to their aspiration of assuming the characteristics of a state flagship. These institutions continue to serve their local market, as with Kennesaw drawing from the suburbs north of Atlanta, but they are also interested in extending their reach to be more like Tech or UGA, beginning to offer the trappings, such as campus residences, needed to do so.[3]

Some smaller private institutions within the Atlanta market are also extending their academic programs as they attempt to realize their institutional ambitions. Mercer University, Piedmont College, and Brenau University have expanded over several years beyond their traditional liberal arts core to include graduate professional programs and develop satellite campuses. As they attract nontraditional students into academic programs on the institutional periphery, these institutions employ some of the resources they generate there to invest in the collegiate experience expected by traditional students on the home campus. These institutions are competing in two markets simultaneously, one for traditional students who appreciate the appeal of liberal arts colleges and one involving professional programs and based on student convenience. Additionally, although financial stability, always a concern at less selective smaller private colleges, is the purpose of these professional programs, some prestige attaches to them when in fields such as business. In addition to advancing in the small college hierarchy, being more comprehensive is thus part of the "next level" for these hybrid institutions.

Even aspirations at community colleges, while expressed in terms of access, are akin to those at other kinds of institutions. Several Georgia community colleges, such as Dalton State College, are adding four-year degree programs—the "next level" for them—successfully contending that there is a need, as with responding to mission drift by other institutions. Young Harris College, a rare private two-year institution, is becoming a four-year college. At nonselective institutions like community colleges, there is also a prestige advantage in increasing in size. In representing itself, Georgia Perimeter College, a large community college in suburban Atlanta, certainly cites enrollment growth as fulfilling its purposes. But it also emphasizes possibilities for transfer to prestigious institutions, having formalized relationships with several institutions, including leading public and private ones locally and nationally.

At the other end of the spectrum, the prestige ladder in the United States is most associated with traditional liberal arts colleges (along with research universities). These institutions are interested in improving in ranking, but their overarching strategies tend to concentrate as much on maintaining position, recognizing the difficulty associated with advancing in the rankings. Davidson College is acutely aware of the investments needed to maintain its top ten national ranking, just as Emory University simply cannot tolerate falling from the top fifteen among private (and thus all) research universities. Similarly, the University of the South (Sewanee) must maintain its top forty ranking; Agnes Scott College and Spelman College have to remain in the top seventy-five; and Berry College needs to continue in tier one in the *U.S. News* rankings. Imagine the distraction for a president if an elite institution slips in the rankings, not to mention the added burden on the admissions staff.

The investments in collegiate infrastructure and the like thus necessitated by their aspirations represent institutions both playing offense and minimizing risk by also playing defense. The emphasis on constructing facilities is a classic arms race, with moves by one competitor matched or exceeded by others, prompting an even greater commitment by the first competitor. Given the premium price they charge, liberal arts colleges should offer students substantive advantages. But the quality of the faculty or curriculum is a "black box," difficult for prospective students and other outsiders to ascertain. The look and feel of an institution is more apparent—and liberal arts colleges are making significant strategic investments in this respect, needing to keep pace in looking the part.

Other smaller private institutions also focus on their collegiate character in attracting residential students, needing also to underscore their distinctiveness more than institutions atop the rankings. Oglethorpe University, for instance, is attempting to leverage greater prestige—and, once again, the resources so commonly thought to follow—through its developing identity as a liberal arts college in a dynamic urban setting. The Savannah College of Art and Design (SCAD), a relatively new private institution, has prospered while aggressively developing new undergraduate programs and transforming downtown Savannah into an appealing college town. Similarly, Southern Polytechnic State University, a public institution, is also interested in increasing in stature, as well as size, offering distinctive academic programs. Finally, colleges with a pronounced religious orientation, such as Covenant College and Toccoa Falls College, focus on their cultural distinctiveness but still must pay attention to developing the appealing academic programs and attractive campus facilities considered to draw even devout students.

APPROACHES

The approaches that institutions have available to actually position for greater prestige are relatively limited, with institutions within and across types tending to develop similar approaches. These approaches are both academic and collegiate in nature and emphasize recruiting the kinds (or numbers) of students that advance institutional aspirations. Universities and colleges have thus professionalized and expanded student recruiting as an initial matter.[4] They are also concentrating more on marketing. Georgia Southern, for instance, is advertising aggressively in suburban Atlanta, including larger banners at upscale shopping malls.

In order to appeal to the accomplished prospective students they hope to attract, universities and colleges have also launched or enhanced innovative or unusual academic programs, study abroad opportunities, service learning efforts, honors options, and undergraduate research initiatives. Such efforts can enliven curricula, even if driven more by strategic interests than purely academic values. For instance, a group of faculty interested in establishing any such effort will appeal for resources on grounds that the initiative advances both academic and strategic ends.

Institutions are also seeking advantage in attracting the students (and even faculty and administrators) they desire by updating the infrastructure devoted to collegiate life. Necessities such as dormitories, dining halls, and gymnasiums have become amenities—luxury apartments, upscale food courts, and deluxe fitness centers (Toma, 2008; Winston, 2000). Universities and colleges across types are in a construction arms race, competing with one another. Georgia Tech, for instance, has recently completed a spectacular fitness center on the site of the former Olympic swimming pool. It addressed the dearth of a shopping district adjacent to campus earlier in the decade by constructing storefronts below its new business school and conference center and hotel facility across I-75 from the main campus. Georgia State has constructed loft-style apartments; suburban Kennesaw State and Armstrong Atlanta State University in Savannah also transformed their "commuter" campuses into residential ones; and UGA has added an atrium to its student center.

In addition, institutions are constructing academic buildings, especially science buildings, in another arms race. There is also some attention to "amenities" for the broader community, such as the new art museum facility at Auburn University. Universities and colleges are engaged in similar efforts in intercollegiate athletics, improving facilities, "upgrading" to Division I, and seeking entry into better conferences as they position themselves for greater prestige (Toma, 2003, 2008, 2010b). Georgia State, responding to student demand for a critical marker of a "real" American university, voted to tax students $85 per semester to launch a football team to compete at the Division I-AA level (now called the Football

Championship Subdivision). (The university also voted for a fee increase to fund a library renovation.) Troy University in Alabama, which is heavily involved in distance education, has built a Division I-A (Football Bowl Subdivision) football program of some note to provide its students around the world with a collegiate touchstone. LaGrange College, which is also enhancing its library, added Division III football recently, intending to enhance both student recruitment and alumni and community relations. Savannah State and Kennesaw State have also moved to compete in Division I.

Research universities continue to hire noteworthy faculty and invest in needed infrastructure to building their research programs, including buildings and personnel (Clotfelter, 1996; Ehrenberg, 2003). Georgia Tech, UGA, Georgia State, and the Medical College of Georgia (MCG) are participating in the robust national market for faculty thought to be able to attract resources through grants and contracts. UGA is adding a medical school, partnering with MCG, and enhancing its engineering programs, knowing both fields are significant drivers of research funding.

These approaches across institution types, and the aspirations that drive them, are thus essentially generic, fixed to whatever a university or college decides is the "next level." Whether these aspirations need to be realistic, or assertions about prestige and distinctiveness need to be accurate, especially when received by less sophisticated audiences, is an open question. In sales, accuracy is sometimes a secondary concern. There are also important concerns about access for less affluent and other underrepresented students being deemphasized as institutions seek the more-accomplished students, who are also likely to be more affluent (O'Meara, 2007).

Universities and colleges continue to express such values, especially in efforts to enhance diversity. But even these have a strategic component, as diversity is another arms race, with institutions aggressively competing for a relatively small number of accomplished minority faculty and students. The neoliberal thought now so established in American society and its higher education privileges such strategies more than these values. Ideas such as return on investment and gains for individuals increasingly eclipse traditional purposes grounded in serving the broader societal good. Higher education has become more of a commodity, with competition intense and consumerism rampant (Bok, 2002; Marginson, 2006; Slaughter & Rhoades, 2004). For reasons anticipated by both institutional theory and competitive strategy, given the choice between access and prestige, institutions would likely find the latter to be more desirable.

But aspirations can also be productive. They can energize a campus, making it more dynamic. Everyone on campus can appreciate the enhanced facilities, and often faculty find working with more-accomplished students to be appealing (O'Meara, 2007). But moving toward the "next level" works best when it causes institutions to differentiate themselves. For instance, Columbus State University has developed its fine arts program into a regional leader; Georgia College and State University has adopted the public liberal arts college mission; Morehouse College is especially mindful of its identity as a selective, all-male, historically black college when setting aspirations and crafting approaches; and Fort Valley State University and Savannah State University, both historically black universities, have continued to emphasize their historical mission while also enhancing their academic profiles. Nevertheless, few institutions—not even these, really— truly separate themselves from the pack, as isomorphism is a particularly strong pull in higher education.

Competitive Strategy as an Influence on Strategy

The foundation of competitive strategy is differentiation. But universities and colleges, like those in the Atlanta market, tend to differentiate only to the extent that they must, with the comfort that comes with conformity and thus legitimacy proving compelling. The logic of competitive strategy is nevertheless accepted within higher education, with institutions underscoring in their marketing what makes them attractive relative to competitors. Writing on competitive strategy considers matters such as (1) positioning, whether through pursuing different activities or similar activities in different ways—and avoiding straddling multiple positions; (2) deciding whether to diversify or expand based on the fit among various activities; (3) considering how favorable the structure of a given industry is before entering; (4) increasing competitive advantage through increasing the willingness of consumers to pay or lowering the costs of production; (5) developing a brand and realizing the equity that comes with a strong one. These can conflict with notions such as network influences, legitimacy and efficiency, isomorphism, and rational myths and satisficing. But even with these forces, universities and colleges must compete in relevant markets. Doing so pushes them toward differentiation—or, at least, its appearance.

POSITIONING

In asking "what is strategy?" Porter (1996) explains that it is not mere operational effectiveness—performing similar activities better than rivals. Rather, strategy requires positioning: a firm outperforming rivals by establishing a difference that it can preserve, either pursuing different activities or similar activities in different ways. Different approaches to positioning include serving only (a) an aspect of an industry (such as oil changes within the automotive repair industry); (b) a particular customer type (such as the home furnishing needs for younger, urban customers); or (c) a given area (such as a chain of theaters concentrated in small towns) (Porter, 1996). Porter (1985) also developed the idea of generic strategies, suggesting that firms attempt to position for advantage over competitors in one of three ways: offering a standard product at a lower cost; marketing differentiated products that can attract a higher price (often luxury brands); or focusing on a targeted (or niche) market (Porter, 2008b). Treacy and Wiersema (1993) term these value disciplines, framing them as operational excellence (as a means to lower costs), product leadership (through cutting edge products), and customer intimacy (to meet their specific wants and needs).[5]

Different higher education institutions tend to position along these lines, concentrating on a given segment of the overall market. Community colleges and nonselective four-year institutions offer standard products at low prices, the first position type. These universities and colleges tend to serve a local market, appealing to students motivated by location and cost. These institutions still must compete in that local market, so they attempt to underscore their attractiveness. Only instead of garnering prestige through admissions, endowment, or research, nonselective institutions feature enrollment growth, relevant programs, and personal accomplishments. Distinctiveness thus matters less than convenience and accessibility, as with institutions marketing through success stories. These universities and colleges may have aspirations to reach the "next level," but they understand that their relevance to an immediate audience requires attention.

Institutions that are even somewhat selective must sell more than just affordable cost. In the Atlanta market, most competition occurs among institutions having established a niche, the second type of position. This might be a particular customer type or aspect of the overall industry. These universities and colleges offer a set of attributes that are appealing to a certain type of prospective student, attempting to enhance these to improve their position among competitors. The public institutions among these are similar in price and reputation, as well as academic program. But their respective approaches to collegiate life, and thus institutional culture, can be distinctive. And that is the difference they feature: whether the urban experience at Georgia State, the small-town residential one at Georgia Southern, the suburban character of Kennesaw, or the liberal arts college feel of North Georgia. (At institutions with some commuting students, such as Georgia State and Kennesaw, location remains the primary motivator for students in choosing to attend.) The strategies that they employ accentuate these characteristics, such as building loft-style dorms at Georgia State or renovating the historic core campus at Georgia College.

But the extent to which these institutions are engaged in different activities or conducting the same activities in different ways is primarily limited to these surface factors, as well as the occasional unusual program, such as military training at North Georgia. There are some niche institutions, primarily privates, offering a product differentiated on substance, such as specialized programs at SCAD or Southern Poly. In the same manner, programs at Covenant or Toccoa Falls appeal to evangelicals, as does the culture of the institutions. There are also universities and colleges that serve a particular type of "consumer," as with Piedmont College targeting students unlikely to gain admission to UGA but still desiring a collegiate experience in Athens, or satellite programs serving adult students at a variety of Atlanta institutions.

Within the third position type, product leadership, liberal arts colleges and private research universities can attract a higher price because they provide something akin to a luxury product, offering a premium experience to which prestige attaches. With any luxury product, there is the belief that with price comes additional quality. Both a BMW and a Kia will get the driver to his or her destination, but the ride is likely smoother and certainly more stylish in the former. What matters is whether such advantages are worth the additional cost of acquiring a BMW. Similarly, is a Gucci bag that is ten times more expensive than an undifferentiated one really ten times better? Much of what the consumer purchases is intangible, connected with notions such as status. Nevertheless, institutions such as Davidson and Emory offer advantages, such as generous staffing in student affairs, attention from accomplished faculty, or access to networks of influential alumni. They can differentiate along such lines—as well as based on the prestige attached to them, which can also be tangible—enabling them to charge the premium price afforded luxury goods. Examples of such tangible prestige are access to leading graduate programs and desirable employment through alumni networks.

State flagships have sufficient prestige that they tend have some elements of a luxury experience but at a regular price. (They thus have a significant advantage in the market over other publics and all but the leading privates.) Because enrolling—and, to some extent, retaining—accomplished students is primary in determining prestige at selective universities and colleges, institutions focus on what they perceive is most appealing to these students, enhancing their collegiate character and developing attractive academic programs.[6] But strategies at these institutions tend to emphasize not only campus look and feel. They also emphasize the advantages associated with a leading institution. The latter can be as simple, especially in the Atlanta market, as access to Southeastern Conference football at Auburn and the University of Georgia. These institutions also offer more diverse academic programs, with degrees in areas like engineering, and their research programs add prestige.[7]

Porter (1996) notes that reaching a sustainable strategic position requires trade-offs—organizations cannot straddle types of positions, as they must keep a consistent image or reputation, configure their products in a logical manner, and have limits in their internal coordination and control. When a selective research university or small private residential college offers professional courses to returning students at a satellite campus, it may so straddle positions. These institutions are not only selling convenience at their periphery but also extending the particular brand they have developed over time, risking inconsistency. Can Mercer really be a luxury good for traditional students in Macon while also having graduate professional programs in law and medicine, as well as convenience programs for adults in suburban Atlanta?

Coherence and coordination also present challenges with programs at the periphery, as marketability can be more important than neatly fitting into the entire curriculum, and managers tend to control these programs, as opposed to regular faculty back on the home campus. Collis (2004) cautions against mission creep, whereby "each succeeding tier of the periphery pursues new directions of its own accord" (p. 63), thus risking expanding everywhere into the periphery and failing to commit a sufficient amount of scarce resources to any one venture—the inability to prioritize, in other words.[8]

DIVERSIFICATION AND EXPANSION

The idea of fit is instructive in answering the Mercer question. Fit is important in strategic success, whether defined as having consistency between and among activities within a firm; activities that reinforce one another; or optimizing effort, as through coordination and communication. Positioning is thus not just excellence in individual activities according to Porter but also about alignment: combining activities into an entire system—one that is hard for a rival to match. Collis and Montgomery (1997) ask whether a firm is more than the sum of its parts, concluding that corporate advantage results from creating value through developing an integrated whole—configuring and coordinating the activities of various units.

Fit can diminish with growth in an organization, especially as it emphasizes programs at its periphery. But it can also be enhanced. For instance, the convenience programs in Atlanta can align somewhat with the liberal arts core in Macon, as is the case when it is possible to have regular faculty drive in to teach. Also, the peripheral programs can generate revenue to support the institutional core. Piedmont College can support its core campus in Demorest with revenues from its Athens branch. Nevertheless, peripheral programs may not optimize effort, as they make the institution more complex and diffuse.

In the corporate setting, such questions of diversification and expansion are central in competitive strategy. The classic approach within firms to integration is developing multiple units competing in different markets, creating value through configuration and coordinating across these activities (Piskorski, 2005). Using core faculty at satellite campuses is an illustration. Another is the University of Georgia partnering with the Medical College of Georgia to add a medical branch in Athens. In developing the new unit, UGA enters the market for medical education, joining other flagship universities nationally. It also can draw on faculty from the arts and sciences college in teaching, as well as enhancing its research in the biological sciences, in which collaboration with medical faculty can prove useful. Even though different academic units operating within a research university may compete with one another for resources, they also tend to complement one another. Among other examples in the Atlanta market, the University of West Georgia emphasizes joint enrollment and early admission programs for accomplished high school students, some of whom may complete degrees there; Columbus State has built a performing arts infrastructure including performance space, academic programs, and student residences in downtown Columbus; and Mercer diversified its revenues and extended its brand over the past two decades by adding graduate professional programs in medicine, nursing, business, education, theology, and music, already having law and pharmacy schools.

The decision to expand, according to Piskorski (2005), is first whether entering a new market improves the competitive advantage of other business units. An institution with fragile finances thus may view satellite programs as necessary to generate revenue needed to support the home campus. Or a comprehensive institution may add graduate programs to enhance its prestige, thus improving its possibilities in recruiting more-accomplished undergraduate students. The second test is if ownership of a given unit is more advantageous than making another arrangements, such as outsourcing or partnering. Institutions across types have determined that functions such as dining and bookstores can be outsourced. At public institutions, the decision may be complicated by state-level coordination, with partnerships resulting from political necessity. The MCG-UGA medical partnership is the product of interests in Augusta resisting UGA establishing a medical school that might compete with the established MCG program. A similar situation would be a state, having allocated graduate education to its flagship, allowing a comprehensive to enter the area only in partnership with that flagship. The public-private partnership between Emory and Georgia Tech in bioengineering takes advantage of respective strengths at the institutions, as Tech does not have medicine and Emory does not have engineering.

Corporations also consider advantages of horizontal diversification—simultaneous ownership of multiple units that utilize a similar set of tangible or intangible resources—and vertical integration, in which the outputs of some units (upstream) are inputs for other units (downstream). For instance, Coca-Cola diversifies horizontally when it adds water to its soft drink lines, employing the same production facilities and distribution networks. A paper company that owns its own forests is seeking advantage in vertical integration. In higher education, state systems represent horizontal strategies, with institutions established to serve various localities and other interests, with coordination among them to avoid needless repetition of programs. With transfer and articulation agreements within systems, as within the University System of Georgia (USG), there is also vertical integration within the system.

Day (2007) frames the question of whether to enter a market in three parts: Is it real (both the product and market)? Can we win (both the product and company being competitive)? And is it worth doing (the product is profitable at acceptable risk and makes strategic sense)? Also relevant are whether diversification will break up assets that need to be kept together, and what the firm can learn by diversifying and whether it is sufficiently organized to do so. Ritson (2009) examines the hazards of launching a product to compete with an established brand in a stable and profitable market, such as cannibalizing existing successful brands and concentrating more on what the competitor is doing than on developing the new product. Kim and Mauborgne (2005) encourage moving into uncontested spaces in the market, which they call the "blue ocean," as opposed to those heavily occupied by others within the industry ("red ocean").

These questions underscore the difficulty associated with entering a new market, particularly in a competitive industry such as higher education where attractive markets are likely saturated. For instance, there are numerous executive MBA programs in Atlanta at various price points—at Emory, Georgia Tech, the University of Georgia, Georgia State, Kennesaw State, and Mercer (as well as various for-profit institutions). Were another institution to enter the seemingly "red ocean" Atlanta space, before it could even address whether it could "win" in the market, it would need to ask questions about simple viability. Perhaps the most important question is whether, given the competitive environment, it could fund the project without impoverishing the rest of the university or college.

INDUSTRY STRUCTURE

Porter (1987) argues that diversification works only when the industries that a firm enters are attractive or can be made so, the cost of entry does not capitalize all future profits, and the new unit gains advantage from its link with the firm as a whole.[9] The structure of an industry tends to shape competitive strategy, with organizations establishing a position that will enable them to defend against various threats or influence them favorably. Porter (1979, 2008a) identifies four types of threats of entry within industries: barriers to entry, powerful suppliers, powerful buyers, the threat of substitute products, and rivalries between existing competitors. Accordingly, some industries have intense competition and low returns, while others have mild competition and high returns as the norm (Porter, 1979). In higher education, there are aspects of each threat, but these tend to be less acute at institutions with greater prestige, with the convenience sector most turbulent, tending to justify "next level" strategies.

Private institutions have few formal barriers to entry, while public universities and colleges must convince coordinating boards to enable the establishment of academic programs to enter new markets. As a practical matter, there are significant barriers to entry in higher education, as well as some advantages. For instance, pursuing the strategy of moving into the market for more-accomplished, residential students at Kennesaw State has required overcoming several disadvantages, such as needing to make large-scale investments in areas like student residences and building brand identification. Kennesaw State also needed to overcome resistance from the USG to its expanding into certain areas. Competitors such as Georgia Tech and the University of Georgia also enjoy incumbency advantages, as with having established brands and preferred access to the best students. There are network effects offering established institutions similar competitive advantage—buyers become more interested in a product when they know others are interested. In addition, simply being more comprehensive enables Georgia Tech and UGA to spread costs over more units and take advantage of other economies of scale. If the overall market for accomplished students is expanding and there are not other new competitors (such as Georgia State and Georgia Southern), these disadvantages are less daunting. But if not, Kennesaw must displace its more established competitors and battle other new entrants, like a new product securing finite shelf space at a supermarket through lowering prices or promotional activities. Finally, there may also be retaliation by those already in the desired space, perhaps through infrastructure investments or additional tuition discounting.

Kennesaw, like other universities and colleges, may be better positioned against the threats of powerful suppliers and powerful buyers. Faculty members, as a rule, have limited leverage, especially with the shift toward temporary appointments and employment markets being saturated. In addition, faculty members are essentially undifferentiated across much of higher education, with only a relative few attracting a premium and most compensated modestly. As buyers, students have several options among institutions, as academic programs are relatively standard across universities and colleges, particularly those within a given market segment. Those students most in demand can play one institution against others toward lowering their price. Among most students, there is a significant degree of price sensitivity. Switching costs are modest once a student is enrolled, as transfer is common. But there are some advantages. Students, apart from a sophisticated group targeting elite institutions, are commonly poorly informed about matters such as the quality of academic programs, with institutions able to shape perceptions through marketing and "curb appeal." Furthermore, no one student has the power of a large volume purchaser in another industry, and there is no risk of buyers integrating backward to produce the product themselves, as in many industries.

There is some risk of substitute products, such as distance education, among those students primarily seeking convenience, but no ready alternative option for those interested in a residential experience. In other industries, the presence of substitute products, such as Skype for long-distance service, causes profitability to suffer, especially when switching costs are low. Residential higher education is relatively immune from substitutes. But the final determinant of industry structure, rivalries between existing competitors, is acute in higher education, with numerous competitors constantly jockeying for position. Products such as courses are perishable and lack differentiation; fixed costs and exit barriers are high; and rivals have "aspirations for leadership . . . [with] goals that go beyond economic performance [such as] prestige" (Porter, 2008a, p. 85). Furthermore, rivals tend to compete on the same dimensions, which can cause them to spend aggressively and lower prices. However, institutions are able to predict the strategies and read the signals of competitors, and there is modest growth in the industry. Another advantage is that there is some segmentation, with different institutions serving different niches—and thus protecting their market share.

Not only the structure of an industry matters, but also the status. McGahan (2004) identifies four trajectories along which industries evolve, based on both their core activities and core assets (such as resources, knowledge, and brand): (1) radical (both core activities and core assets are threatened, as with travel agencies); (2) intermediating (activities are threatened, but assets are safe, as with auto dealerships); (3) creative (activities are safe, but assets are threatened, as with motion pictures); and (4) progressive (neither are threatened, as with commercial airlines). Residential higher education tends to be progressive, neither its core activities nor its core assets threatened—again, a pull toward positioning for greater prestige. However, core activities in the convenience sector are challenged, as different means of delivery are increasingly available. Additionally, Porter and Rivkin (2000) suggest that industries transform when there are changes in technology, customers needs or wants, or regulation. These triggers are followed by experimentation within an industry and eventually convergence as most experiments fail and dominant designs emerge. Once again, residential higher education is relatively immune to such changes, with even increased regulation within state systems a relatively mild threat. But there is more turbulence in the convenience sector, especially with the advances in distance teaching.

Finally, Kim and Mauborgne (2005) argue that industry structure is not a given—strategy can define an environment, as opposed to being defined by it. Even in a competitive industry, doing so requires a departure from the standard approach of an organization choosing either differentiation or low price—and, instead, accomplishing both through innovation, as with Apple iTunes.

COMPETITIVE ADVANTAGE

Regardless of industry structure, competitive advantage occurs one of two ways (Ghemawat & Rivkin, 2006). The first is increasing the difference between what people will pay for a service or product and what it costs a firm to produce it. Firms can either increase willingness to pay without significantly increasing costs (differentiation strategies), lower their price and reduce their costs (low cost strategies), or produce superior products at lower cost (dual advantage). Most universities and colleges prefer differentiation strategies, although community colleges such as Georgia Perimeter adopt low-cost strategies. Positioning for prestige involves some investments in areas such as physical infrastructure in order to attract more-accomplished students and thus increasing willingness to pay (or the tuition discount required)—for instance, when Clemson raised its price as it increased markedly in ranking. Morehouse and Spelman offer another example of differentiation strategies, as they compete directly with institutions that offer a more attractive price—and even greater prestige—but afford students an experience unavailable elsewhere. They are thus able to beat the Ivy League in attracting certain students, having increased their willingness to pay.

The second approach is aligning the various functions of an organization to do something unique and valuable. For instance, SCAD has kept its costs low and its price high while providing an unusual and attractive set of programs in an appealing environment. But few institutions are so distinctive. The discipline required to configure in such a way is also challenging at loosely coupled organizations such as universities and colleges, especially given the pull of isomorphism. Collins (2001) offers another conceptualization, encouraging firms to become hedgehogs (and not foxes, engaged in several areas), focusing on understanding, and not just envisioning, what they can be the best at, what drives their economic engine, and what they are passionate about. His approach can certainly apply to universities and colleges. An example is Sewanee, which concentrates on being a liberal arts college with particular characteristics and appealing to a certain kind of student (and faculty member).

Collis and Montgomery (1997, 2008) offer a resource-based approach to competitive advantage. They argue that strategically valuable resources—what enables a corporation to perform activities better or more cheaply than rivals—provide competitive advantage. These might be physical assets (such as location), intangible assets (such as a strong brand or employee loyalty), or capabilities (such as an exemplary manufacturing process or leadership). Such resources are difficult to copy; depreciate slowly; are controlled by the firm, and not customers, suppliers, and employees; cannot be easily substituted; and are superior to parallel resources at competitors. Elite higher education institutions tend to have such resource advantages, along with financial assets such as endowments. Replicating the infrastructure, brand, and talent present at Emory or Davidson is not impossible but would require substantial investment—and a fair amount of good fortune. The competitive advantage in resources that these institutions enjoy tends to be stable, especially as they tend to continue to upgrade their assets and capacities.

But Gourville (2003) offers the reminder that strategy is not simply structural but also psychological. For instance, consumers irrationally overvalue existing products, even more than ones that offer substantial improvements, given high psychological switching costs (people overweigh or overvalue things they already have). In other words, prospect theory suggests that psychological reactions to gains and losses drive behavior far more than objective gains and losses themselves, as people are more averse to losses. D'Aveni (2007) notes that customers tend to value intangible benefits in a product, apart from its performance, such as the aura of a certain brand of motorcycle, with firms pricing accordingly. Even if an institution can match the resource advantages of a competitor at the "next level," it may take even more than that to actually move there.

BRAND EQUITY

Concepts such as branding are important in gaining competitive advantage. Brands develop as rather durable cultures, acquiring meaning and connotations that circulate in society, eventually becoming conventional and accepted as truths— and even icons. They thus shape how customers experience a product in a sensory manner (Holt, 2003). They are also slow to become established. Brand equity—a brand's tangible value to a firm—includes several advantages. Leading universities and colleges, having developed the strongest brands, realize benefits such as brand loyalty (which creates awareness and reassurance in customers), brand awareness (familiarity providing an anchor to which to attach other associations), perceived quality (new products being easier to sell when attached to an established brand), and brand associations (that allow for differentiation with other brands) (Aaker, 1991; Toma et al., 2005). The strongest brands reduce risk and simplify choices for consumers, can be trusted by them in the future, and offer symbolic values through expressing values and identities (Holt, 2003). These benefits make it difficult for even the most adept competitors to catch up. Keller (2000) focuses on measuring such advantages, asking questions about whether a brand delivers benefits customers desire, stays relevant, is priced based on consumers' perceptions of value, and so on. These advantages are considerable, and "next level" strategies by universities and colleges are sensible in trying to realize them, as institutions with more prestige tend to have stronger brands.

Finally, positioning for prestige is not only associated with resources. There are intangible advantages associated with prestige within organizations. Because people come to understand themselves in reference to the organizations with which they associate, they are more likely to celebrate their connections with prestigious institutions, making just about everything on campus easier to achieve (Dutton et al., 1994; Toma et al., 2005). When the advantages of enhanced identification combine with the promise of greater resources and the security of increased legitimacy, an institution aspiring to enhance prestige is seemingly obligatory, no matter the institution type.

Legitimacy as an Influence on Strategy

Strategic approaches, and the aspirations that drive them, are so standard for reasons suggested by institutional theory. In their quest for the perceived greater resources that accompany increased legitimacy and autonomy, universities and colleges tend to pursue common strategies because they (1) are subject to influences within various networks; (2) are less interested in seeking efficiency than in legitimizing themselves through reference to other organizations; (3) become more homogeneous over time, believing that doing so will enhance the resources that lead to greater autonomy and stability; (4) can develop narratives to support strategies that sometimes have little connection with reality—rationalized myths—but reassure themselves and others; and (5) "satisfice," limiting the solutions they view as legitimate to a few possible paths, with isomorphism prominent among these strategies. I simplified these theories somewhat for the purpose of exploring them below, again through the experience of the institutions across the Atlanta market.

NETWORK INFLUENCES

Organizations, and thus the strategy they develop, are subject to influences within a network, especially when, like universities and colleges, outputs such as administrative efficiency and student success are difficult to evaluate (Meyer & Rowan, 1977). There is a well-established overall higher education network in the United States. The same is increasingly the situation worldwide, driven somewhat by the emergence of global rankings. Institutions are aware of trends and issues across higher education, through professional associations and meetings and trade publications such as the *Chronicle of Higher Education* and *Inside Higher Ed*—and even the education section of the *New York Times* in the United States. Universities and colleges have a particularly clear sense of what is going on strategically at the leading institutions, on which most attention focuses. For instance, a curricular reform at Harvard, administrative restructuring at Stanford, or financial retrenchment at Berkeley is soon familiar to those across U.S. higher education. If replicating market leaders lends legitimacy to institutions, as institutional theory contends, then U.S. universities and colleges tend to have the information they require in doing so.

There are also clear subnetworks within U.S. higher education that also influence strategy. Institutions group themselves into consortia, such as the Association of American Universities (the leading research universities nationally, including Emory), Atlantic Coast Conference (state flagships and other major athletic powers, such as Georgia Tech and Clemson), the Associated Colleges of the South (selective liberal arts colleges such as Sewanee and Davidson), or the Council of Public Liberal Arts Colleges (including Georgia College). Entrance into the AAU, ACC, ACS, and COPLAC has associational benefits, thrusting a university or college into a prestigious group. There is nothing the University of Georgia desires more than AAU membership; LaGrange College understands the benefits that would come with being in the ACS; and COPLAC membership immediately delivered a significant degree of legitimacy to Georgia College, given its new mission. Similarly, when Virginia Tech, Boston College, and the University of Miami recently joined the ACC, they instantly became a peer with several of the leading research universities and athletic programs in the region, such as Duke, the University of North Carolina, and the University of Virginia.[10]

Universities and colleges are also grouped, as by the University System of Georgia, which divides its thirty-five institutions into research universities, regional universities, state universities, state colleges, and two-year colleges. Because resource implications and perceived prestige are associated with these categories, they practically invite institutions to seek to move to the "next level." Systems, such as the USG, thus carefully monitor institutions attempting to extend academic programs toward positioning for greater prestige. U.S. higher education is notable for its segmentation—the impressive institutional diversity that offers most prospective students several options. But segmentation invites mission creep, as institutions seek the advantages that they perceive are at the "next level." A purpose of state-level coordination is to combat impulses by individual institutions that diminish diversity across a system, leaving gaps within it, particularly in the areas of the market with which the least prestige attaches (Collis, 2004; Morphew, 2009).[11]

Institutions are also active in benchmarking. In formulating strategy, they are typically able to readily identify their peer institutions, as well as the "aspirational" ones they seek to emulate. For instance, Auburn and Clemson can reference state flagships nationally with similar student compositions, research profiles, and endowment holdings, just as LaGrange College and Oglethorpe University can look to other moderately selective liberal arts colleges in the Southeast, and Dalton State can pattern itself after the state colleges in Georgia. Data are reasonably good and easily available to make such comparisons. These enable institutions to chart progress relative to those similarly situated—as well as direct competitors. For example, through the standardized testing services, institutions know their admissions overlap group—where students who applied to them also applied and ultimately attended. They also know more qualitatively the institutions with which they are competing through their direct interaction with prospective students. There are also the annual *U.S. News* rankings that factor in how presidents (or those completing their survey) at other institutions consider an institution.

Each also has a carefully defined set of "aspirational" institutions. Auburn can look to the next tier of land grant institutions, such as Iowa State and Virginia Tech, and Clemson has universities like Georgia Tech and Illinois at the "next level"; LaGrange and Oglethorpe consider ACS colleges, with their greater selectivity, as "aspirational" institutions; and Dalton State strives to be more like the state universities in Georgia, such as West Georgia. Not only does all of higher education thus constitute a network, but institutions can also locate with relative ease and certainty their relative position within it with some precision. Unlike cross-national comparisons, as in Europe, which are challenging given differences across systems, institutions in one state can readily compare themselves with institutions in other states, and even private and public institutions are comparable.

The challenge here is that because outputs are so difficult to measure in higher education, benchmarking is incomplete, typically relying on measures associated more with prestige than actual results. Benchmarking does not sufficiently approach questions such as whether an institution is producing outputs of high quality, matters such as whether its academic programs are having a satisfactory impact or its administration is efficient and effective. In fact, even the definition of the term "quality" is often nebulous, especially when applied to cross-institution comparisons. These tend to focus on measures that are more superficial, like average standardized test scores for students. There are also measures like retention rates, which are a decent surrogate for prestige (Zemsky, Shaman, & Iannozzi, 1997), and student satisfaction, as through the National Survey of Student Engagement. But even these are not particularly satisfying. Is retention really a surrogate for effectiveness, or do inputs—more-accomplished students enrolling—tend to be stronger influences? Are the opinions of students really that telling when measuring academic quality?

What matters here is not necessarily that the measures are inconclusive but instead that benchmarking leads institutions to stress measures associated with prestige. Institutions are subject to the influences of the networks they are within—and that they aspire to be in. They know just what is required to move to the network at the "next level" of prestige—and, if nothing else, what they must do to maintain their current position. Through such mobility or maintenance, institutions perceive that their access to resources is less likely to be disrupted, reducing turbulence and maintaining stability (Meyer & Rowan, 1977). The path to increased prestige is not through quality, which is typically a black box. Rather, it is through enrolling more-accomplished students, building endowments, and (where applicable) developing research.

LEGITIMACY AND EFFICIENCY

Institutional theory contends that organizations are less interested in seeking efficiency than in legitimizing themselves through reference to other organizations (DiMaggio & Powell, 1983). Organizations perceive that legitimacy, as opposed to efficiency, is the catalyst that ensures resources and enhances stability. Accordingly, they thus act to "increase their legitimacy and their survival prospects, independent of the immediate efficacy of the acquired practices and procedures" (Meyer & Rowan, 1977, p. 340).

Efficiency is rarely, if ever, articulated as an aspiration and thus does not reach the level of strategy. There are ever more institutional effectiveness efforts across institutions, as in the Atlanta market, but these tend to be responses to external accountability mandates, as from states or accrediting agencies. Universities and colleges comply with reporting requirements and schedule regular program reviews, but it is debatable whether these are mostly just paperwork exercises. It is difficult to imagine the president of a selective university or college defining efficiency as the cornerstone of his or her ambitions for the institution—and certainly not unaccompanied by the standard "next level" rhetoric. Claiming efficiency as the strategic emphasis for an institution, even if particularly needed, would likely be seen as the president having no vision at all.

Especially as American higher education is so dependent on private giving—and increasingly so—institutions must be perceived to be moving forward. Donors are unlikely to contribute to "keeping the lights on," instead preferring to attach their support to projects such as facilities, professorships, or scholarships—those intended to enhance prestige. Community colleges, which are much less reliant on private giving, do tend to focus more on effectiveness, especially if it enables them to keep their costs lower and prices affordable. But even there, faculty and senior administrators also tend to view more progress-focused aspirations as appealing. Private institutions, with boards predominantly composed of business leaders, also devote much less attention to operations than positioning. Even though efficiency is a comfortable concept for those in business, as it increasingly is for those in government, they are hardly influencing institutions to focus on that concept, finding the promise of the "next level" to be more alluring.

Even if not articulated at the level of institutional ambitions, efficiency has tactical importance across institution types. The neoliberal ethos that has come to characterize higher education in the United States substitutes the logic of external markets and potential for internal efficiency for traditional support from the state. Institutions across types, including those in the Atlanta market, are aggressively reducing instructional costs, expanding management capacity, and seeking revenue at their peripheries. But they are doing so to enable robust spending on enhancing prestige, motivated by the pursuit of legitimacy and autonomy. Positioning for greater prestige is expensive—and institutions have had to find resources somewhere.

In Atlanta, as elsewhere, significantly increasing tuition price is not an option (Zumeta, 2001), except perhaps in response to the most extreme budget crisis. For instance, as the state higher education system sets tuition price in Georgia— and the legislature directly funds that tuition for many students through the HOPE scholarship—meaningful increases are unrealistic. In addition, state appropriations, in real terms, have declined nationally (Geiger, 2004; McGuinness, 2005), and nondiscretionary costs, as for health benefits and energy consumption, have increased for institutions, sometimes markedly (Ehrenberg, 2002; Lee & Clery, 2004; Society for College and University Planning, 2005). Nevertheless, states expect public institutions to balance, and increasingly to demonstrate, access, affordability, and quality (Newman, Couturier, & Scurry, 2004). Meanwhile, expectations related to furthering local, state, and national economic development have never been greater (Geiger, 2004; McGuinness, 2005). At private institutions, there is the question of what the market will tolerate and limits to how much they can discount tuition, as well as the same nondiscretionary cost pressures.

Discretionary spending is also increasing as institutions develop strategies to position for greater prestige (Bok, 2002; Clotfelter, 1996; Geiger, 2004; Kirp, 2003; Slaughter & Rhoades, 2004; Zemsky et al., 2005). These strategies are not focused on efficiency but instead intended to enhance legitimacy and, it follows, autonomy. Research universities (and those aspiring to that status) are recruiting and subsidizing researchers thought to be able to attract resources through grants and contracts (Slaughter & Leslie, 1997; Slaughter & Rhoades, 2004). Even modestly selective universities and colleges are employing pricing strategy—tuition discounting—to the extent they can afford toward attracting more-accomplished students (Ehrenberg, 2002; Geiger, 2004; McPherson & Schapiro, 1998). But success in the ever more intense competition for the most accomplished students requires institutions to lower their price, thus reducing the institutional bottom line (Ehrenberg, 2002; Geiger, 2004; McPherson & Schapiro, 1998). Doing so has also shifted emphasis from need-based toward "merit" student aid.

Other strategies aimed at attracting more accomplished students are also costly: building admissions offices, launching popular undergraduate majors, adding or augmenting graduate programs, encouraging faculty research, emphasizing honors programs, and enhancing study abroad opportunities (Geiger, 2004; Kirp, 2003). (Investments enhancing campus infrastructure, such as student residences, dining commons, fitness centers, and even shopping districts, are also expensive but tend to have a revenue stream attached.) Universities and colleges across types are also increasing their commitment to athletics, with most directly subsidizing the activity (Toma 2009). Obsessively pursuing prestige provides a useful surrogate for increasing shareholder value or bottom line profits as an outcome consistent with a neoliberal frame. It has also caused the price of higher education to increase, as raising funds and recruiting students is expensive. But students have been willing to pay for perceived benefits, at least at more selective institutions (Ehrenberg, 2002).

Once again, institutions have attempted to increase efficiency elsewhere to fund these efforts toward increasing legitimacy and autonomy. In essence, they have deemphasized their traditional core in favor of seeing revenues at their more agile peripheries. One approach has been to seek efficiencies in areas such as campus services, drawing on private sector management ideas, such as outsourcing, that have permeated the public sector (Kirp, 2003; Zemsky et al., 2005). Institutions have also sought to generate resources through corporate partnerships involving research, instruction, and training. In focusing on finances, undergraduates, research, and industry ties at research universities, Geiger (2004) argues that as government support declines, they are less able to control their own activities and engage less in public service. He contends that with the ascent of the market in higher education there is a marked and increasing inequality among institutions, with public universities disadvantaged, given limits on what price they can charge.

Another strategy has been for universities and colleges to expand, sometimes significantly, activities at their seemingly more efficient—and profitable—peripheries. Institutions across types are establishing satellite campuses to serve part-time students studying in professional fields (Bok, 2002; Newman et al., 2004; Slaughter & Rhoades, 2004; Zemsky et al., 2005). The Atlanta market offers several illustrations:

- The University of Georgia is emphasizing master's degrees in fields such as education in the northern Atlanta suburbs.
- Mercer University preserves its selective liberal arts core in Macon, in part,

though part-time professional programs in Atlanta (and through developing full-time graduate professional programs in Macon).

- Kennesaw State and Georgia State aggressively market their part-time
  MBA degrees to professionals in Atlanta and its suburbs.
- Less selective Piedmont College has developed a campus in Athens (as has
  Gainesville State, to some extent) to serve students interested in the univer-
  sity town experience that UGA is not serving.
- Brenau University has considerable activity on its periphery, with profes-
  sional programs at several sites, with protecting a small traditional core
  women's college as one purpose.
- Troy University has invested heavily in establishing programs around the
  world, including traditional instruction and e-learning.

These universities and colleges, as is the case nationally, are responding to perceived markets, launching programs based on student convenience with entrepreneurial ends, as opposed to democratizing ones (Bok, 2002). There is demand for such programs, especially as individuals and employers recognize the
greater need for training and credentialing in a knowledge economy (Collis,
2004; Newman et al., 2004; Zemsky et al., 2005). But the impetus for these efforts is the additional revenue that can support and advance the legitimacy of the
core campus (or, in the worst case scenario, to keep the core campus afloat).

There has also been an overarching strategy of cutting expenses and seeking
greater organizational dexterity through shifting faculty staffing away from tenure-
significant positions toward temporary, part-time, and adjunct ones (Bousquet,
2008; Collis, 2004; Lee & Clery, 2004). Not only do contingent faculty members
teach peripheral academic programs, but they also provide an increasing proportion of instruction within the traditional institutional core, with research universities making more extensive use of graduate students. Non-tenure-track faculty
members now constitute nearly one-half of all faculty members nationally, compared with 22% in 1970 (Collis, 2004). According to Rhoades (2005), academic
capitalism "depends on a mode of production that fosters the growth of contingent faculty and non-faculty professionals relative to full-time, tenure-track professors. It also gives rise to a mode of management that strengthens the governance role of central academic managers relative to that of faculty" (p. 38; see also
Slaughter & Rhoades, 2004).

As institutions have added managers, there are now as many administrators
across higher education as regular faculty—a change from there being twice as
many faculty members as administrators in 1976 (Collis, 2004; Zemsky et al.,

2005). While administrative and professional staff increased by 15% between 1993 and 2001, full-time faculty expanded by only 3.4% (Lee & Clery, 2004). Whether adding administrators and reducing regular faculty have made universities and colleges more efficient is an open question. Traditional values, which have hardly been abandoned, are challenged within the neoliberal university. Institutions have not dismantled traditional structures of faculty governance but have increasingly supplanted them with new arrangements. For instance, managers have greater discretion related to academic programs at the institutional periphery taught by temporary faculty or core faculty on overload. Strategic planning and administrative flexibility are increasingly esteemed, with the clear possibility for market criteria and revenue generation to trump educational standards (Bok, 2002; Keller, 1983; Rhoades, 2005). Academic programs that are inclined to view students as clients and that can be readily closed if viewed as losing money mark a meaningful cultural shift away from traditional faculty influence (Bousquet, 2008; Rhoades, 2005; Slaughter & Rhoades, 2004; Zemsky et al., 2005).

The fundamental idea in strategy at the entrepreneurial university is that the periphery, through generating resources, can protect the less agile core of the institution. Despite the promise of new revenues at their periphery and efficiencies within their cores, resources generally remain strained across institutions, often significantly so, especially during downturns in the national or local economy. The legitimacy and autonomy that institutions aspire to generate through various strategic approaches are expensive. They are also, ultimately, inefficient.

ISOMORPHISM

As they seek legitimacy and autonomy through reference to others, organizations across types become more homogeneous over time, eventually adopting the innovations of leading organizations as these become the prevailing wisdom (DiMaggio & Powell, 1983). Such isomorphism is driven by both responding to markets (competitive isomorphism) and competition for legitimacy, both political and organizational (institutional isomorphism). Institutions, as across the Atlanta market, tend not only to develop parallel aspirations but also to pursue them in through similar strategies. There are some differences based on institution type, of course. For instance, at Agnes Scott College, the "star faculty" system at research universities would not likely work in the more collegial setting of an elite liberal arts college. But the parallels between institutions connected with Atlanta are considerably more striking than the differences.

Institutional isomorphism, according to DiMaggio and Powell (1983, 1991), is coercive, mimetic, or normative. Coercive pressures can come from those on whom institutions depend for resources or through formal regulation. Gornitzka (1999) explains how government policies and programs influence organizational change in higher education. Slaughter and Leslie (1997) apply resource dependency theory to higher education, arguing that institutions and individuals within them seek prestige and resources, the two being linked, toward increasing their autonomy (Pfeffer & Salancik, 1978; Slaughter & Rhoades, 2004). Mimetic isomorphism is grounded in reducing uncertainty by imitating market leaders, as there is less risk when universities do not step out from the herd. Normative forces come from those within an organization having been, and continuing to be, acculturated as professionals as graduate students or within practitioner networks, thus acquiring a sense of what structures and processes are legitimate. Here, there is a particular pull toward research (Blackburn & Lawrence, 1995; Tierney & Bensimon, 1996).[12]

There are coercive, mimetic, or normative bases for the common aspirations and generic approaches across the Atlanta market. Beginning with coercive pressures, the donors who have become more important across higher education, especially at more selective institutions, are much more interested in projects that advance the reputation of the institutions they choose to support. The primary strategies for positioning for prestige tend to be those that attract private support, including merit scholarships, endowed professorships, innovative programs, signature facilities, and spectator sports. Universities and colleges expressly reference "aspirational" institutions in fund-raising for these, encouraging donors to adopt—and compel—a "next level" strategic mentality.

The University of Georgia connects such fund-raising with stability. The institution has reached the level of its aspirants, such as Berkeley and Wisconsin, on several measures connected with legitimacy, such as undergraduate selectivity. But the relatively low endowment at UGA is well below competitor institutions, and the percentage of the budget from the state is around one-third, which is high for a public research university. Unusually for a state flagship, the university does not have a medical or engineering school, thus hindering its research funding. UGA is consequently more vulnerable—less stable—because it lacks these two drivers of prestige, knowing also that the Georgia general assembly can reduce its annual state appropriation. Its strategy is to become more like other state flagships that have already positioned themselves more solidly through using research and endowment to diversify and augment their resources.

The need to secure annual state appropriations also has a coercive effect on the strategic actions of universities and colleges. Within the University System of

Georgia (as at Auburn in Alabama), there is a benefit in the funding formula for having more graduate education, thus contributing to the desire to inflate missions. The state system does present a drag on such activity through its program approval process. A similar coercive effect is the potential for blowback from traditional constituents associated with mission inflation. For instance, when Dalton State adds four-year programs or Georgia Southern increases its admission selectivity, concerns are raised among some longtime supporters. But institutions tend to be able to manage such challenges—they are not too great a drag on their aspirations. A challenge particular to special-focus USG institutions such as Georgia College, which has a liberal arts mission recognized by the state, and Southern Poly, which focuses on applied technology, is the opposite of coercive pressure. Both are funded by the USG as smaller comprehensive institutions when what the state charges them to do is more expensive.

There are also mimetic pressures that lead institutions to become more isomorphic over time, as reflected in strategy. Imitating market leaders enables colleges and universities to reduce uncertainty and reassure themselves. The latter may be as simple as Armstrong Atlantic, having decided on a strategy of building student residences, now being able to count itself among residential universities, which are more prestigious than commuter campuses. Doing so is comforting, as leading institutions tend to experience less turbulence than do less affluent ones. The more interesting question is whether the risk in having aspirations or approaches that are decidedly different is such that institutions simply cannot envision moving in that direction. States and donors tend to be conservative— and likely more comfortable with traditional programs.

In addition, there is the possibility of losing the validation that comes with the rankings, which reward conformity. Rankings such as *U.S. News* are also divided into so many subgroups that most institutions can claim some distinction—an attractive outcome for them. For instance, being ranked among the top sixty master's universities in the Southeast is of strategic importance for North Georgia College and State University. At Emory, its ranking is so important in attracting students and faculty, as well as resources, that it simply cannot allow itself to slip. The university has the challenge of developing its own identity, emphasizing programs in which it excels, such as public health, while needing to compete in all areas with the wealthiest universities nationally.

Spelman and Morehouse, the leading institutions nationally devoted to serving African American women and men, respectively, similarly have to compete for students who could attend, often at a more discounted price, any number of leading universities or colleges. They must balance their distinctiveness with offering, at least to some degree, what is available at research universities in the Ivy League or elite liberal arts colleges such as Swarthmore, Williams, and Amherst. For overtly Christian colleges, such as Covenant and Toccoa Falls, the challenge is more straightforward. Students and parents looking specifically for a Christian environment may be forgiving if such an institution lacks certain programs or amenities. Nevertheless, there is competition within that sector—and between it and secular institutions—that moves Christian institutions to also position for prestige in order to reduce uncertainty and provide reassurance.

There are also normative pressures toward the isomorphism. Few faculty members tend to object to aspirations and strategies connected with increasing prestige. Most became acculturated—coming to understand what makes a university legitimate—within a graduate program that is both more prestigious than where they are now employed and devoted to research. Presidents thus not only have a willing audience among faculty but also may risk criticism from them if they do not express increased prestige as an institutional ambition. The psychological need to be a "real" university is strong. Troy University, which expanded significantly through distance education, began to emphasize its football team, which served as a marker of a traditional university. Georgia State, a campus spread across downtown Atlanta, more on the European model, also recently added a football program for similar reasons.

The information about other institutions, especially those with greater prestige, that results from benchmarking and rankings also presents normative pressures. For instance, Clemson knows precisely not only where it ranks but also how far it has moved up in a given amount of time. The tendency to identify "aspirational" institutions is a particular normative force. For example, Young Harris College has identified Elon University in North Carolina as a model in its move to become a four-year institution. Elon has attracted attention for transforming itself into a selective liberal arts college, concentrating particularly on matters such as campus beautification and enhancing athletics (Keller, 2004). Young Harris accordingly has a clear target.

RATIONALIZED MYTHS AND SATISFICING

Institutions do not always behave in ways they purport to or perhaps even want to, developing "rationalized myths." These are narratives that sometimes have little connection with reality, often decoupled from the technical core of the organization (Zucker, 1987). But they are reassuring to those inside and outside the organization, while also connecting with stated institutional purposes (Meyer & Rowan, 1977). Institutions similarly rely on ceremony to signal legitimacy, again to both themselves and others (Jepperson, 1991). It is not necessary for the notions that these ceremonies represent to be proven effective, but simply believed in (March & Olsen, 1989). Such practices tend to be deeply internalized within organizations and thus highly resistant to change.

For instance, a small college may frame itself as a traditional liberal arts college both internally and externally when the bulk of its activities consist of teaching professional degree courses to part-time, adult students on a satellite campus (Kraatz & Zajac, 1996). There is nothing to prevent an institution from claiming the liberal arts title, provided it can make a plausible case. Doing so is relatively simple, as most prospective students and their parents operate with limited information about institutions and insight into higher education. It may be enough for a college to simply look the part of a liberal arts college, sending the appropriate signals through its physical campus (and even its price), reinforced by messages through text and images on Web sites and in print materials. In other words, an undifferentiated small college can be made to look and sound like Williams or Amherst, with only savvy consumers discerning the disconnects. Those within universities or colleges tend not to be troubled about perceiving and announcing their institution as more significant than it necessarily or completely is. For instance, faculty members, often having acculturated at more prominent institutions, can find such embellishment to be heartening.

Such rationalizations influence the establishment of impressive ambitions and later pronouncements about having realized them. There is no penalty for aspiring to reach the "next level" or stretching from reality in determining and demonstrating how close the institution is to getting there. In fact, doing so is reassuring to those connected with an institution. Additionally, as creative as institutions are in developing rationalized myths (a concept from sociology), they commonly represent the opposite in limiting themselves to a few familiar strategic paths viewed as legitimate, thus "satisficing" (an idea from social psychology) (Simon, 1997). Defaulting to a "next level" set of aspirations is a familiar and comfortable direction. Satisficing is most pronounced in stable organizations, such as universities and colleges. It may also be exacerbated in a competitive environment in which the margin for error is increasingly slim. Just as there is safety in the herd, there is also comfort in the familiar.

It is important to remember that organizations, especially those as complex as universities and colleges, are hardly singular in their responses. Institutions are loosely coupled, with different parts often operating within different contexts, sometimes significantly so, resulting in limited consistency and coordination between and among them (Meyer & Rowan, 1977; Scott, 2003). Loosely coupled organizations can thus claim prominence in particular areas. For instance, a department at a research university, such as fisheries at Auburn, can reach national or international standing apart from the stature of the broader institution. Meanwhile, academic units, like the institutions that house them, tend to compete for prestige, as it provides them with leverage in seeking resources internally (Ehrenberg, 2002; Slaughter & Silva, 1985). There is thus a "next level" game within the broader game.

There is also the risk that even the richest visions and sharpest strategies may be implemented differently—or not at all—within various parts of the loosely coupled organization, and outcomes may differ across areas. In addition, behavior is situational within organizations, occurring as much within informal structures and processes as formal ones (Scott, 2001). Presidents, as a result, may have less control over strategy and tactics than it might seem.

Conclusion

Applying corporate models to higher education requires one to ask whether they are relevant, given the clear differences between the two areas. Ideas in institutional theory clearly have explanatory power in understanding organizational issues, including strategy at universities and colleges as elsewhere. In both corporate and higher education settings, organizations are subject to influences within various networks, are less interested in seeking efficiency than in legitimizing themselves through reference to other organizations, and become more homogeneous over time in the belief that doing so will enhance the resources that lead to greater autonomy and stability. The same is true of concepts such as rationalized myths and satisficing. Accordingly, those exploring organizational issues in higher education have employed institutional theory since its emergence.

Fewer have considered higher education in terms of competitive strategy. But these concepts also can frame an analysis of the aspirations and approaches of various university and colleges. While strategy in higher education fits neatly into notions in institutional theory, universities and colleges are more comfortable with legitimacy and isomorphism than they are with differentiation and synergies. Higher education institutions are interested in positioning to realize greater prestige—status serving as a proxy for profit—but they are not as inclined to actually pursue different activities or similar activities in different ways. Their preference is to differentiate only on the surface. Institutions also risk straddling positions as they move activities, especially academic programs, to the periphery. A particularly interesting question is whether a university or college that would actually differentiate would be in a better competitive position. Would it thus earn the legitimacy and stability that drive isomorphic behaviors through real differentiation?

Other issues in competitive strategy may also be instructive in considering strategy at universities and colleges, as with deciding whether to diversify or expand based on how well the new activity fits among various existing ones. The loosely coupled nature of institutions may complicate such approaches but hardly renders them inapplicable. For instance, expanding into medical education is a logical strategy at the University of Georgia given its connection with strategically critical existing research activities in the biological sciences. The same is true in calculating competitive advantage in determining aspirations and approaches, considering how to increasing the willingness of consumers to pay, or lowering the costs of production, as with developing a brand and realizing the equity that comes with a strong one.

Marginson (2006) argues that social competition for status by individuals and institutions alike within a competitive economic market, exacerbated by the neoliberal ideology, is more pervasive in higher education than traditional market competition. The pursuit of status (and human capital) overrides other concerns for students, such as avoiding lackluster teaching and paying a high price. Institutions spend accordingly on efforts thought to enhance reputation and prestige. There is a purely commercial sector in higher education, according to Marginson, but it is rather small—essentially foreign students at English-speaking universities and for-profits like the University of Phoenix.

But writing specific to corporations, as in the competitive strategy literature, may still be applicable. In adapting his corporate model to the social sector, Collins (2001) perhaps offers an answer, contending that great, as opposed to simply good, social organizations, such as universities and colleges, have four features. They have results in relationship to their mission (research, for example, at a research university); impact, which Collins defines in terms of distinctiveness (would there be a hole that would be difficult to fill if the institution closed down tomorrow); esteem, both from those within the organization (like students) and from experts in the field; and endurance—they last over time. Even the most entrepreneurial university or college remains influenced by its traditional values. Considering competitive strategy, as well as other ideas borrowed from business, in the context of these values may prove useful to those interested in why institutions generate generic aspirations and standard approaches toward realizing them. It may also be instructive to institutions themselves in pushing them to be more creative in doing so.

NOTES

1. Across these traditions, there are various strategic management frameworks. Toma (2010a) proposes one specific to higher education that outlines the elements required to build the administrative foundation needed to establish and sustain various initiatives associated with realizing the vision of an institution. Like all strategic management approaches, it provides leaders and senior managers with a means to organize planning and implementation—a checklist, of sorts (Collis & Montgomery, 1997; Connolly & Lucas, 2002; Kaplan & Norton, 1996, 2004; McKinsey & Company, 2001).

2. I included an earlier version of this discussion in an article in the Fall 2009 annual report of the Institute of Higher Education.

3. Accompanying such an approach is typically a change in requirements for promotion and tenure toward stressing research. Synthesizing the literature in the area, O'Meara (2007) suggests that comprehensives such as these, as well as less selective liberal arts colleges and research universities just outside the top tier, are most likely to focus on striving for greater prestige.

4. Among elite institutions, early admissions programs are a strategy to attract accomplished, affluent students who may require less of a discount, if any, to attract them (Ehrenberg, 2003). These institutions have also extended their recruiting nationally.

5. In exploring the structure of the higher education industry, Zemsky, Shaman, and Ianozzi (1997) argue that the market is a continuum between traditional-aged students on largely residential campuses and user-friendly institutions that stress convenience and value for those across ages who mix work and study. At one end of the continuum is name-brand, private institutions that provide a medallion for those who graduate and thus can charge a premium and be quite selective. Other institutions target less selective students and can be more competitive on cost or more focused on student needs. Most universities and colleges are somewhere in the middle.

6. Research universities and liberal arts colleges also concentrate on building endowment and developing research, as not just admissions and retention numbers influence national reputation.

7. Nevertheless, in positioning for greater prestige, advancement in student numbers is more readily achievable than progress in research or endowment. Georgia State, Georgia Southern, and Georgia College, for instance, each increased their average SAT to around 1,100, enough to put them near the top of institutions of their type.

8. In summarizing the criticisms of Porter's positioning approach, Mintzberg, Ahlstrand, and Lampel (2005) suggest it can be overly deliberate, narrow, and formulaic, as well as too divorced from organizational learning—it is too much about staying home and calculating and not enough about getting out there and learning, as the authors put it.

9. He recommends integrating either good but undervalued or struggling but fixable companies, or finding synergies through similarities or efficiencies through sharing between and among units.

10. The same would be true if the Russell Group in the United Kingdom announced it was taking new members or if people began to consider as Sandstone Universities in Australia institutions other than the current eight.

11. Birnbaum (1983) suggests that population ecology explains why institutions decrease in diversity over time, becoming more homogeneous when responding to the same stimuli over time. Morphew (2009) also argues that diversity has declined, although he is more persuaded by institutional theory as an explanation.

12. Organizational institutionalism is the dominant theory in organizations and management, with citations to Meyer and Rowan (1977), DiMaggio and Powell (1983), and Pfeffer and Salancik (1978) related to institutional theory and resource dependency only increasing over the past decade (Greenwood, Oliver, Sahlin, & Suddaby, 2008). Subsequent research has only made institutionalism more complex and applicable as a theory, as with expanding consideration of questions of isomorphism and legitimacy into areas such as institutional entrepreneurship (active change within organizations) and institutional logics (influence of broader belief systems, such as capitalism) (Friedland & Alford, 1991).

REFERENCES

Aaker, D. A. (1991). *Managing brand equity: Capitalizing on the value of a brand name.* New York: Free Press.

Allison, G. T. (1971). *Essence of decision: Explaining the Cuban missile crisis.* Boston: Little, Brown.

Andrews, K. R. (1987). *The concept of corporate strategy.* Homewood, IL: Irwin.

Ansoff, H. I. (1965). *Corporate strategy.* New York: McGraw-Hill.

Astley, W. G. (1984). Toward an appreciation of collective strategy. *Academy of Management Review, 9*(3), 526–533.

Berdahl, R. O. (1985). Strategy and government: U.S. state systems and institutional role and mission. *International Journal of Institutional Management in Higher Education, 9*(3), 301–307.

Birnbaum, R. (1983). *Maintaining institutional diversity in higher education.* San Francisco: Jossey-Bass.

Blackburn, R. T., & Lawrence, J. H. (1995). *Faculty at work: Motivation, expectation, satisfaction.* Baltimore: Johns Hopkins University Press.

Bok, D. C. (2002). *Universities in the marketplace: The commercialization of higher education.* Princeton, NJ: Princeton University Press.

Bousquet, M. (2008). *How the university works: Higher education and the low-wage nation.* New York: New York University Press.

Brewer, D., Gates, S. M., & Goldman, C. A. (2002). *In pursuit of prestige: Strategy and competition in U.S. higher education.* New Brunswick, NJ: Transaction Press.

Camillus, J. C. (2008). Strategy as a wicked problem. *Harvard Business Review, 86*(5), 99–106.

Chafee, E. E. (1985). From concept of strategy: From business to higher education. *Higher education: Handbook of theory and research,* Vol. 1 (pp. 133–171). New York: Agathon Press.

Clotfelter, C. T. (1996). *Buying the best: Cost escalation in elite higher education.* Princeton, NJ: Princeton University Press.

Cole, A. H. (1959). *Business enterprise in its social setting.* Cambridge, MA: Harvard University Press.

Collins, J. (2001). *Good to great: Why some companies make the leap—and others don't.* New York: Harper Business.

Collis, D. J. (2004). The paradox of scope: A challenge to the governance of higher education. In W. G. Tierney (Ed.), *Competing conceptions of academic governance: Navigating the perfect storm* (pp. 33–76). Baltimore: Johns Hopkins University Press.

Collis, D. J., & Montgomery, C. A. (1997). *Corporate strategy: A resource-based approach.* New York: McGraw-Hill.

Collis, D. J., & Montgomery, C. A. (2008). Competing on resources. *Harvard Business Review, 84*(7), 143–150.

Collis, D. J., & Rukstad, M. G. (2008). Can you say what your strategy is? *Harvard Business Review, 86*(4), 82–90.

Connolly, P., & Lukas, C. (2002). *Strengthening nonprofit performance: A funder's guide to capacity building.* St. Paul, MN: Amherst H. Wilder Foundation.

D'Aveni, R. A. (2007). Mapping your competitive position. *Harvard Business Review, 85*(11), 110–120.

Day, G. S. (2007). Is it real? Can we win? Is it worth doing? Managing risk and reward in an innovation portfolio. *Harvard Business Review, 85*(12), 110–120.

DiMaggio, P. J., & Powell, W. W. (1983). The iron cage revisited: Institutional isomorphism and collective rationality in organizational fields. *American Sociological Review, 48,* 147–160.

DiMaggio, P. J., & Powell, W. W. (1991). Introduction. In W. W. Powell & P. J. DiMaggio (Eds.), *The new institutionalism in organizational analysis* (pp. 1–38). Chicago: University of Chicago Press.

Dutton, J. E., Dukerich, J. M., & Harquail, C. V. (1994). Organizational images and member identification. *Administrative Science Quarterly, 39,* 239–263.

Ehrenberg, R. (2002). *Tuition rising: Why college costs so much.* Cambridge, MA: Harvard University Press.

Ehrenberg, R. G. (2003). Reaching for the brass ring: The U.S. News and World Report rankings and competition. *Review of Higher Education, 26*(2), 145–162.

Friedland, R., & Alford, R. R. (1991). Bringing society back in: Symbols, practices, and institutional contradictions. In W. W. Powell & P. J. DiMaggio(Eds.), *The new institutionalism in organizational analysis* (pp. 232–266). Chicago: University of Chicago Press.

Geiger, R. (2004). *Knowledge and money: Research universities and the paradox of the marketplace.* Stanford, CA: Stanford University Press.

Ghemawat, P., & Rivkin, J. W. (2006). Creating competitive advantage. Harvard Business School Note 798–062.

Gornitzka, Å. (1999). Governmental policies and organisational change in higher education. *Higher Education, 38*(1), 5–31.

Gourville, J. T. (2003). Why consumers don't buy. Harvard Business School Note 504–056.

Greenwood, R., Oliver, C., Sahlin, K., & Suddaby, R. (2008). Introduction. In R. Greenwood, C. Oliver, K. Sahlin, & R. Suddaby (Eds.), *The SAGE handbook of organizational institutionalism* (pp. 1–46). Thousand Oaks, CA: Sage.

Hannan, M. T., & Freeman, J. (1977, April). Structural inertia and organizational change. *American Sociological Review, 49*, 149–164.

Holt, D. B. (2003). Brands and branding. Harvard Business School Note 503–045.

Jacobides, M. G. (2010). Strategy tools for a shifting landscape. *Harvard Business Review, 88*(1), 77–84.

Jepperson, R. L. (1991). Institutions, institutional effects, and institutionalism. In P. J. DiMaggio & W. W. Powell (Eds.), *The new institutionalism in organizational analysis* (pp. 143–163). Chicago: University of Chicago Press.

Kaplan, R. S., & Norton, D. P. (1996). *The balanced scorecard: Translating strategy into action.* Boston: Harvard Business School Press.

Kaplan, R. S., & Norton, D. P. (2004). *Strategy maps: Converting intangible assets into tangible outcomes.* Boston: Harvard Business School Press.

Keller, G. (1983). *Academic strategy: The management revolution in American higher education.* Baltimore: Johns Hopkins University Press.

Keller, G. (2004). *Transforming a college: The story of a little-known college's strategic climb to national distinction.* Baltimore: Johns Hopkins University Press.

Keller, K. L. (2000). The brand report card. *Harvard Business Review, 78*(1), 147–157.

Kim, W. C., & Mauborgne, R. (2005). *Blue ocean strategy: How to create uncontested market space and make the competition irrelevant.* Boston: Harvard Business School Press.

Kirp, D. (2003). *Shakespeare, Einstein, and the bottom line: The marketing of higher education.* Cambridge, MA: Harvard University Press.

Kraatz, M.S., & Zajac, E. J. (1996). Exploring the limits of the new institutionalism: The causes and consequences of illegitimate organizational change. *American Sociological Review 61*(5), 812–836.

Lee, J., & Clery, S. (2004). Key trends in higher education. *American Academic, 1*(1), 21–36.

March, J. G., & Olsen, J. P. (1989). *Rediscovering institutions: The organizational basis of politics.* New York: Free Press.

March, J. G., & Simon, H. A. (1958). *Organizations.* New York: Wiley.

Marginson, S. (2006). Enabling democratic education in the neoliberal age. *Educational Theory, 56*(2), 205–219.

Massy, W. F., & Zemsky, R. (1994). Faculty discretionary time: Departments and the "academic ratchet." *Journal of Higher Education, 65*(1), 1–22.

McGahan, A. M. (2004). How industries change. *Harvard Business Review, 82*(10), 86–94.

McGuinness, A. C. (2005). The states and higher education. In P. G. Altbach, R. O. Berdahl, & P. J. Gumport (Eds.), *American higher education in the twenty-first century: Social, political, and economic challenges* (pp. 198–225). Baltimore: Johns Hopkins University Press.

McKinsey & Company. (2001). *McKinsey capacity assessment grid.* vppartners.org/learning/reports/capacity/assessment.pdf

McPherson, M. S., & Schapiro, M. O. (1998). *The student aid game: Meeting need and rewarding talent* Princeton, NJ: Princeton University Press.

Meyer, J. W., & Rowan, B. (1977). Institutionalized organizations: Formal structure as myth and ceremony. *American Journal of Sociology, 83*(2), 340–363.

Mintzberg, H. (1987a). The strategy concept I: Five Ps for strategy. *California Management Review* 30(1), 11–24.

Mintzberg, H. (1987b). The strategy concept II: Another look at why organizations need strategies. *California Management Review* 30(1), 25–32.

Mintzberg, H., Ahlstrand, B., & Lampel, J. (2005). *Strategy safari: A guided tour through the wilds of strategic management.* New York: Free Press.

Morphew, C. C. (2002). A rose by any other name: Which colleges became universities. *Review of Higher Education, 25*(2), 207–224.

Morphew, C. C. (2009). Conceptualizing change in the institutional diversity of U.S. colleges and universities. *Journal of Higher Education, 80*(3), 243–269.

Newman, F., Couturier, L., & Scurry, J. (2004). *The future of higher education: Rhetoric, reality, and the risks of the marketplace.* San Francisco: Jossey-Bass.

Normann, R. (1977). *Management for growth.* New York: Wiley.

O'Meara, K. (2007). Striving for what? Exploring the pursuit of prestige. In J. C. Smart (Ed.), *Higher education: Handbook of theory and research,* Vol. 22 (pp. 121–179). New York: Agathon Press.

Pfeffer, J., & Salancik, G. R. (1978). *The external control of organizations: A resource dependence perspective.* New York: Harper and Row.

Piskorski, M. J. (2005). Note on corporate strategy. Harvard Business School Note 7-5-449.

Porter, M. E. (1979). How competitive forces shape strategy. *Harvard Business Review, 57*(2), 137–145.

Porter, M. E. (1985). *Competitive strategy: Techniques for analyzing industries and companies.* New York: Free Press.

Porter, M. E. (1987). From competitive advantage to corporate strategy. *Harvard Business Review, 65*(3), 43–59.

Porter, M. E. (1996). What is strategy? *Harvard Business Review, 74*(6), 61–78.

Porter, M. E. (2008a). The five competitive forces that shape strategy. *Harvard Business Review, 86*(1), 78–93.

Porter, M. E. (2008b). *On competition.* Boston: Harvard Business School Press.

Porter, M. E., & Rivkin, J. W. (2000). Industry transformation. Harvard Business School Note 701-008.

Prahalad, C. K., & Hamel, G. (1990). The core competencies of the corporation. *Harvard Business Review, 68*(3), 79–91.

Quinn, J. D. (1980). *Strategies for change: Logical incrementalism.* Homewood, IL: Irwin.

Rhenman, R. (1973). *Organizational theory for long range planning.* London: Wiley.

Rhoades, G. (2005). Capitalism, academic style, and shared governance. *Academe, 91*(3), 38–42.

Riesman, D. (1956). *Constraint and variety in American education.* Lincoln: University of Nebraska Press.

Ritson, M. (2009). Should you launch a fighter brand? *Harvard Business Review, 87*(10), 87–94.

Schumpeter, J. A. (1950). *Capitalism, socialism, and democracy* (3rd ed.). New York: Harper and Row.

Scott, W. R. (2001). *Institutions and organizations* (2nd ed.). Thousand Oaks, CA: Sage.

Scott, W. R. (2003). *Organizations: Rational, natural and open systems* (5th ed.). New York: Prentice Hall.

Selznick, P. (1957). *Leadership in administration: A sociological interpretation*. Evanston, IL: Row, Peterson.

Simon, H. (1997). *Administrative behavior: A study of decision-making processes in administrative organizations* (4th ed.). New York: Free Press.

Slaughter, S., & Leslie, L. L. (1997). *Academic capitalism: Power, politics and the entrepreneurial university*. Baltimore: Johns Hopkins University Press.

Slaughter, S., & Rhoades, G. (2004). *Academic capitalism and the new economy*. Baltimore: Johns Hopkins University Press.

Slaughter, S., & Silva, E. (1985). Towards a political economy of retrenchment: The American public research universities. *Review of Higher Education, 8*(4), 295–318.

Society for College and University Planning. (2005). *Trends in higher education*. Ann Arbor, MI: SCUP.

Tierney, W. G., & Bensimon, E. M. (1996). *Promotion and tenure: Community and socialization in academe*. Albany: State University of New York Press.

Toma, J. D. (2003). *Football U.: Spectator sports in the life of the American university*. Ann Arbor: University of Michigan Press.

Toma, J. D. (2008). *Positioning for prestige in American higher education: Case studies of strategies at four public institutions toward "getting to the next level."* Paper presented at the Association for Research on Higher Education (ASHE) Annual Meeting, Jacksonville, Florida.

Toma, J. D. (2009). The business of intercollegiate athletics. In D. Siegel & J. Knapp (Eds.), *The business of higher education, Vol. 3 (pp. 179–216)*. Santa Barbara, CA: Praeger.

Toma, J. D. (2010a). *Building organizational capacity: Strategic management in higher education*. Baltimore: Johns Hopkins University Press.

Toma, J. D. (2010b). Intercollegiate athletics, institutional aspirations, and why legitimacy is more compelling than sustainability. *Journal of Intercollegiate Athletics, 3*(1), 51–68.

Toma, J. D., Dubrow, G., & Hartley, J. M. (2005). *The uses of institutional culture: Strengthening identification and building brand equity in higher education*. ASHE Higher Education Reports, 31(3). San Francisco: Jossey-Bass.

Treacy, M., & Wiersema, F. (1993, January/February). Customer intimacy and other value disciplines. *Harvard Business Review*, 84–93

Winston, G. (2000). *The positional arms race in higher education*. Williams Project on the Economy of Higher Education, Discussion Paper 54. Williamstown, MA: Williams College.

Zemsky, R., Shaman, S., & Iannozzi, M. (1997, November/December). In search of strategic perspective: A tool for mapping the market in higher education. *Change*, 23–38.

Zemsky, R., Wegner, G. R., & Massy, W. F. (2005). *Remaking the American university: Market-smart and mission-centered*. New Brunswick, NJ: Rutgers University Press.

Zucker, L. G. (1987). Institutional theories of organizations. *Annual Review of Sociology, 13*, 443–464.

Zumeta, W. (2001). Public policy and accountability in higher education: Lessons from the past for the new millennium. In D. E. Heller (Ed.), *The states and public higher education policy: Affordability, access, and accountability* (pp. 155–197). Baltimore: Johns Hopkins University Press.

CHAPTER SIX

Creativity
and Organizational Culture

WILLIAM G. TIERNEY

What role does organizational culture play in developing and sustaining creativity and innovation? We know that some organizations thrive on stability and a commitment to the status quo (Tierney, 1999, 2006). A significant amount of evidence exists that colleges and universities now face a great many changes, not the least of which are transformations brought about by technology and the changing nature of the workforce (Duderstadt & Womack, 2003). A commitment to the status quo without a sense of how to meet the changing needs of the twenty-first-century economy strikes many as a recipe for disaster. The point is not simply to discard traditions and rush into the future. To continue in a pattern that has been developed over decades simply because such activities are part of a tradition is evidence of a dying enterprise. Any organization needs to adapt; the question is whether such adaptations are minuscule or significant, and for the purposes of this chapter, what role organizational culture might have in advancing creativity and innovation.

Some have argued that a question pertaining to management is off-target insofar as a discussion of culture is essentially a theoretical undertaking. Culture is seen as an ideological notion, so why assume that an understanding of culture will have any impact on performance? Research on organizational culture came onto the stage a generation ago, and although there has never been conceptual agreement about the meaning of culture, in an initial burst of enthusiasm many authors suggested that culture had a role in increasing the effectiveness and efficiency of an organization (Peters & Waterman, 1982). The argument went along the following lines: strong cultures have a greater likelihood of success than weak cultures; if leaders manipulate a cultural variable, they might succeed where others fail. The problem is that there has been very little evidence to support such claims, and there has been equally little agreement with regard to the meaning and parameters of culture. The result has been that the literature on organizational culture in general has receded. Those interested in theory have moved on, and those concerned about organizational performance have eschewed culture in favor of more scientific notions.

I have three goals for this chapter. I first elaborate on how we might think about organizational creativity and discuss why the idea is important, suggesting that creativity will be a defining concept for educational organizations in the twenty-first century. I then review the arguments pertaining to organizational culture. Although I acknowledge the lack of agreement about what we mean by organizational culture, I disagree with the idea that some sort of grand agreement needs to come about with a term that has motivated anthropological and sociological thought since the inception of those disciplines. I then relate the ideas of creativity and culture not as yet another management fad but as a way to think about organizational life. I suggest that even though individuals frequently have different conceptions of organizational life, the possibility exists for developing a common conception of an organization's culture and, through this, building the conditions for creativity.

Creativity and Innovation

How societies change, how cultures change, and how organizations change have accounted for numerous scholarly treatises that range from suggestions that change can be managed and purposeful (Peters & Waterman, 1982) to those that it is anarchical and whimsical (March, 1984; Weick, 1982). Leaders may be able to bring about change, or they may be irrelevant (March & Cohen, 1974; Sample, 2002). Change is likely due to environmental conditions (Levinthal, 1991), or it derives from strategic decision making. Change may be destructive and bring about decline (Haveman, 1992), or it may unleash renewal.

Given the wide swings in the literature about how to think about change, one wonders what might be said with any sense of certainty other than that there is a great deal of uncertainty about how change occurs. We know that organizations have different needs because of their foci and their life span. Some organizations thrive on stability, and others have a greater need to change. Karl Weick's research on loose coupling plays into the idea of stability and change (Weick, 1976). Tightly coupled organizations are more top-down and directive; loosely coupled organizations are more decentralized. Managers of McDonald's restaurant franchises, for example, are more likely to know what their workers are doing and what the output for the day, month, and year will be; the president of a university may not know what or how a particular instructor is teaching in a class or what the "output" will be. A university produces graduates, and to a certain extent, the institution may be direct with regard to estimating how many students are likely to be retained and eventually graduate, but the precision will be less than that of an organization in which stability is a necessary ingredient for success. The research activity of the faculty and the hiring of new appointments are also more likely to impact the organization than when a fast-food chain hires a new worker to replace someone else.

We also know that organizations have different needs based on their time frame. Start-up companies operate in a different manner than do long-standing institutions. The transition of a longtime leader is likely to be different from the situation in an organization that experiences change at the top every few years. A company that merges has different challenges than one that files for bankruptcy.

Those who work in universities acknowledge the importance of changing various aspects of academic work even though colleges and universities have existed for centuries (Chaffee, 1988). Even though individuals like to criticize postsecondary institutions as reluctant to change, over the past generation a great deal of reform has occurred. The manner in which we conduct research has been reconfigured. How we interact with one another has moved in a manner entirely unexpected only a decade ago. What one means by the "library" and how we undertake scholarship has experienced a sea change; technology makes a trip to the library today as a rare occurrence rather than routine. Who populates higher education also continues to change with regard to race and gender. More contingent faculty are now hired than tenure-track staff. How academe funds itself, the relationship between the state and public institutions, and the rise of for-profit institutions all signal an environment rife with change.

One way to understand the environment is through mechanisms such as environmental scanning. Although not always accurate, a concern for organizational externalities or a consideration about future trends frequently is useful. An additional way to think about change is by way of the internal structure of the organization and an assessment of how well it is configured to deal with change. From this perspective we are not merely concerned with understanding change but instead trying to put forward ideas toward positive and planned change. We do not seek an explanatory model of why change brought about failure but instead consider how change might be able to engender successful outcomes.

Hence, I am interested in the idea of creativity. Creativity is a bit like other elusive terms such as leadership—its meaning is unclear and its variables uncertain. Just as some scholars old and new suggest that the traits of a leader are something with which an individual is born, creativity is frequently thought of as a unique characteristic of someone (Carlyle, 1897). Creativity is seen as a positive asset: "She's very creative" has as positive a ring, as does "He's a great leader." Such perspectives paint a picture of an individual. The organization is irrelevant. As Williams and Yang (1999) note, "The major focus in creativity research has been on the individual creator and his or her personality, traits, abilities, experiences, and thought processes" (p. 378). When we consider organizations, a discussion of creativity most often is painted in negative terms: the organization stifles creativity. The assumption is that a creative individual enters the organization, but through bureaucratic procedures the individual is made to conform. Creativity dies (Whyte, 1956).

What if creativity is not a unique trait of an individual? What if an organization is able to foster creativity in all workers? Such questions turn the lone wolf portrait of creativity on its head. From this perspective creativity can be enhanced in many individuals by means of the social environment (Amabile, Conti, Coon, Lazenby, & Herron, 1996, p. 1155). What would it mean if we referred not only to creative individuals but also to creative organizations? Woodman, Sawyer, and Griffin (1993) have defined organizational creativity as "the creation of a valuable, useful new product, service, idea, procedure or process by individuals working together in a complex social system" (p. 293). The definition is useful for it thinks of creativity as the development of something new by a group. Sternberg and Lubart (1999) offer a slightly different interpretation by defining creativity as "the ability to produce work that is both novel (i.e., original, unexpected) and appropriate (i.e., useful, adaptive concerning task constraints)" (p. 3).

The import remains on a new creation, but the expectation is not that it must come only from a group; organizations can foster creativity in individuals. Such a distinction is useful for loosely coupled systems, such as a college, in which a professor may be working in isolation from colleagues. If we are to think of creativity in universities, we will look for organizations in which individuals or groups are able to develop a new product, idea, or process. One key aspect of the organization, then, becomes the development of talent. Such an observation suggests that, from a cultural perspective, socialization is important.

Laird McLean (2005) makes the useful point that a creative organization needs to be an innovative one. Creativity and innovation are related, but distinct, terms. Creativity refers to inventions and breakthroughs. Innovation pertains to the implementation of the idea. McLean goes on to state: "The focus here, particularly . . . is on taking a creative idea and bringing it to fruition. . . . [In] the life of an organization, many brilliant ideas never see the light of day. To bring an idea from concept to market, it must be recognized for its potential" (p. 227). Amabile and colleagues (1996) follow this line of thinking by stating, "[W]e define creativity as the production of novel and useful ideas in any domain. We define innovation as the successful implementation of creative ideas within an organization" (p. 1155). Such a point is important because it highlights some of the more critical issues facing postsecondary institutions. A generation ago the linkage of creativity and innovation would have been relatively unimportant. In the twenty-first century, however, issues such as technology transfer, intellectual property, and the relationship between postsecondary organizations and businesses have taken on increased importance. Whereas a university once may have been thought of as a repository and conveyor of knowledge, the new stance suggests that the institution needs to be more engaged with the external environment such that it not only creates new products but also helps bring them to market.

The interrelationship between creativity and innovation is different for a postsecondary organization. When a college fosters an environment for experimentation in the classroom, or a philosopher works on a topic in solitude, creativity is focused on an act (writing a poem) or an event (teaching a class). Those who work at the cutting edge of biotechnology or neuroscience are likely to find avenues not simply for the creation of a novel idea but also for its implementation. Those who write a series of poems may publish a book, just as those who teach an innovative class may take the curriculum design public. Individuals also may be creative in their research or pedagogy, but the creativity does not go beyond the boundary of the campus or the printed page.

Richard Florida details the import of creativity for the country to maintain its economic and social well-being (Florida, 2002, 2004). He maintains that the university plays a critical role not merely in being creative itself but in fostering creativity in the larger environment. While Florida, Gates, Knudsen, & Stolarick (2006) acknowledge that a university should have a creative role to play in economic development, they argue that the creation of talent and the fostering of new ideas and diversity are also central activities for a university. "Our findings suggest," they conclude, "that the role of the university goes far beyond the 'engine of innovation' perspective. Universities contribute much more than simply pumping out commercial technology or generating startup companies. . . . In short, the university comprises a potential—and in some places, actual—creative hub that sits at the center of regional development" (p. 38). The import of the university to be creative is not merely so that as an organization it can remain relevant; the well-being of the country is in part dependent upon the ability of a postsecondary institution to be creative. Creative universities, then, are places (a) where an individual is creative, (b) where a creative act or invention may be implemented, and (c) where ideas and people help generate creativity in the larger environment. Such an observation moves us far afield from a portrait of a cloistered community that passes truths down from one generation to the next.

Most scholars of innovation will point out that more often than not creativity is stifled rather than supported (Amabile, 1998). The argument is that organizations function because of coordination, productivity, and control—and those very measures frequently destroy creativity. How, then, do we create an organizational culture of creativity? Is such a question even appropriate, or as foolhardy as previous cultural questions linked to organizational performance? To answer these questions I turn to an overview of how we have thought about culture, and then I consider how creativity and culture interact.

Perspectives on Culture

Most students of organizational culture will acknowledge that formal and informal structures and interactions help define organizational culture (Tierney, 1988b). However, to go much further and provide a concrete definition of organizational culture has proven elusive. My purpose here is not to offer a history of organizational culture, but it is useful to acknowledge that at least since the early 1980s a great many theorists have been arguing about the meaning of culture in formal organizations (Hallett, 2003). Jelinek, Smircich, and Hirsch (1983) stated that the quarrels and differences over the meaning of organizational culture in part reflected the tensions in fields such as anthropology, where structural, functional, and interpretive definitions of culture had vied for prominence since World War II (Jelinek et al., 1983). Franz Boas, the preeminent anthropologist of the early twentieth century, proposed the idea of cultural relativism that held sway for some time; cultural relativism, however, had been eschewed by the 1940s, and no other singular definition of culture had come to take its place.

Conceptual confusion also pertained to what one studied in an organization. Most individuals acknowledged that symbolic forms, such as nomenclature, fell into the cultural column. Symbolic artifacts such as rituals could be investigated from a cultural framework (Tierney, 1989). The result was that researchers collected data about whether leaders used first or last names when they spoke with individuals. But was an organization's budgeting process also part of an organization's culture? When the board developed a strategic plan, was that a cultural act? And if budgeting and strategic planning were part of an organization's culture, then what was not? Or were organizational culture and the organization synonymous?

Two additional topics arose that further confused the issue about how to define culture. As I noted above, some authors made claims about the utility of culture in increasing organizational performance. Among the best-selling business books of the 1980s, for example, were Peters and Waterman's *In Search of Excellence* (1982) and Deal and Kennedy's *Corporate Cultures* (1982). Because the idea of culture appears deceptively simple, the books appeared as a primer for "good" cultural behavior and "bad" cultural behavior. "Management by walking around" came into fashion as an example of "good" cultural actions. Effective managers were ones who had an open door policy and interacted informally with their staffs, and ineffective managers had a top-down, linear management and decision-making style (Mitroff & Kilmann, 1975; Smircich & Morgan, 1982). Unfortunately, many such claims lacked empirical evidence. Nevertheless, the assumption existed that the main reason to study culture was to unearth lessons to improve organizational performance.

How one studied culture also placed the topic within the methodological debates of the time (Morgan & Smircich, 1980). The study of culture was at first claimed by qualitative methodologists, but organizational studies had become increasingly quantitative. Not only was the argument concerned with how one defines culture, or whether culture could be used to increase organizational effectiveness, but it also centered on the ability of qualitative researchers to reinsert themselves in the field's mainstream. How one studied a topic became almost as important as the topic that was studied.

To further confuse the matter, neither topic was static. Qualitative methodologists, for example, started to become concerned with the idea of reflexivity—to what extent the researcher's values, opinions, and standpoints should be considered in the development of a text (Clifford & Marcus, 1986). Textual experimentation became the vogue in anthropology; more discrete methods such as life history rose in import (Behar, 1993; Frank, 2000). Each methodological experiment fed back on how one might study culture in an organization.

Similarly, in the 1980s the Japanese economy was strong and the Americans suffered through a recession. Individuals looked to the culture of Japanese organizations for clues about how to turn around the American economy. Theories of leadership focused on interpretive aspects of "good" leaders and posited that the ability to interpret the organization's culture was paramount. And yet when the Japanese economy sank and the American economy started to improve, organizational culture did not seem to have the explanatory power once hoped for by its proponents.

The result was that by the early twenty-first century there was a decided decrease in the use of culture as an analytical tool employed to understand organizational life either on a theoretical or a practical level. Harold Silver (2008), opting for one interpretation of culture, went so far as to say, "In terms of definitions derived in recent decades from theoretical assumptions about shared norms, values and assumptions, as well as symbols, myths or rituals, universities do not have a culture. Individual perceptions of the university are ones of chaos or anarchy or a system of subcultures in perpetual, erratic and damaging tensions" (p. 167). Although I am hard pressed to think of anyone who thinks of culture as "shared norms" to the point that everyone interprets and acts in a similar fashion in an organization, such a critique opts for the closing down of analyses that utilize what Silver thinks of as a cultural framework.

At the same time, in part because of judgments similar to Silver's, fewer analyses focused on organizational culture in the first decade of the twenty-first century than in the 1980s. Was the study of culture in organizations at an end or merely experiencing a timeout? In a recent book by Joanne Martin (2002), after acknowledging that much of the organizational culture literature has offered a confusing morass of conflicting findings, she states, "The purpose of a social science theory is not to comfort managers with promises of relatively easy solutions but to capture and perhaps even construct organizational experiences, in all their discomforting complexity, conflict, ambiguity and flux. . . . Cultural theory and research have more to offer than easy promises of culture as a key to profitability" (p. 9). Martin returns organizational culture, then, to an intellectual domain rather than one focused on practice. What needs to be answered, of course, is if Martin is correct that cultural research in organizations is of any worth.

Before suggesting what cultural research has to offer, it is useful to delineate how the study of culture has been defined. One utility of a slowing down in a particular area of inquiry is the ability to take a collective breath and to create a conceptual map of the field. Frequently, during a time of intellectual ferment it is difficult to take stock of the field. An intellectual pause enables scholars to analyze various propositions, to offer a review of the literature, and to see where different authors and frameworks overlap or contradict with one another. Joanne Martin has done the most thoughtful review. She creates ideal types and divides them into three conceptual views of organizational culture: integration, differentiation, and fragmentation.

AN INTEGRATION FRAMEWORK

Integration tries to understand the underlying elements of an organization that binds participants together. Beliefs and values are a significant focus of such studies, and the manner in which one looks for these concepts is by way of organizational artifacts such as rituals and stories. Critical stages in an organization's or individual's life—such as the creation of the organization, a merger, or the retirement of another—are clues to understanding the ethos of the place. How people communicate is also important. Researchers look at written and verbal forms as well as formal and informal communicative frameworks. One generic view of an integrationist perspective might be derived from the question "What's this place like?" Presumably, a researcher will ask such a question of multiple employees. Based on the redundancy of responses the author might conclude that seniority is valued more than participation by everyone, or that the leader tends to function by means of more formalized mechanisms such as mandatory monthly meetings than informal means such as discussions around the proverbial water cooler.

Insofar as the driving question of integrationists is frequently "What holds this place together?" researchers often face a methodological conundrum (Chaffee & Tierney, 1988). Qualitative studies are never generalizable; those who employed qualitative methods in their work were not after a unifying metaphor for a culture. Some studies may merely have attempted to describe what a particular culture was like. The description itself was sufficient. Other studies may have tried to understand if there were underlying constants or deep structures, but the way these forms got enacted varied from culture to culture. Thus, a great deal of studies tried to come to grips with deep forms and types of a ritual, for example. Over time we have come to understand that initiation rituals differ from other forms of rituals, and how one defines an initiate matters. But no attempt has been made over the past half century to go the next step and say that traditional cultures interpret and enact initiation rituals in a similar manner, or that one type of ritual is more effective than another.

Any individual who has done more than three interviews on the same topic knows that individuals never mirror exactly what someone else says. The idea of trust, for example, may be a concept that permeates an organization for an integrationist. However, would anyone actually assert that every individual in any organization trusts a leader in precisely the same manner? We know that individual behaviors help shape one's attitude toward different phenomena, so it would be remarkable if all employees trusted one another in exactly the same way. More important, the meaning of an abstruse construct such as trust also defies precision. A statement such as "I trust the president " might mean that an individual believes what the president says, and to another person it might mean the president has agreed with the respondent on a variety of issues, and hence the person trusts the leader.

Some methodologists might say that such problems are simply bad method. Geertz's well-worn phrase of "thick description" highlights the importance of understanding the meanings of respondents (Geertz, 1973). Others will suggest that the drive to find common interpretations encourages a researcher to discard inconvenient responses. Thus, if someone interviews sixty individuals in an organization and fifty respondents say some version of "I trust the president," the reality is that ten people did not give a statement expressing trust. Oftentimes, however, the import of explicating statements is to find an overriding ethos. When combined, frankly, with page restrictions in journals, diverse ideas get collapsed into an overriding theme.

At the same time, we also know that different themes, concepts, and ideas do pervade organizations just as they do traditional cultures. Americans are different from the French; Tocqueville made this observation well over a century ago, and any American or French person would agree. The Navajo are different from Anglos. The Navajos' conception of nature, life, and death differs from that of European Americans, and we can see these differences in the manifestations of the different cultures. Similarly, the University of Southern California, where I currently work, has a different culture than Pennsylvania State University, where I once worked.

What, then, are we to make of the integrationist perspective? Perhaps the major problem with such a framework is the underlying push to offer simple generalizations that might be employed in other organizations. Again, a challenge for many authors who work in professional disciplines such as business or education is that in part they want their work to be useful. Scholars want business organizations to improve; they want schools and universities to better serve various communities. But anyone who has studied organizational life will know that simple generalizations do not exist. Although it might be seductive to encourage leaders to act in a particular manner, to suggest that all leaders act in a similar way is foolhardy. At the same time, I have often found that individuals have little understanding of the cultures in which they exist. Is it not possible to suggest that an understanding of culture is useful? If the answer is that an understanding of culture is useful, then we return to perhaps, not what to understand or how to act, but how to understand.

However, critics have charged that integrationists' overriding concern is to downplay organizational ambiguity and to present organizational consensus. When consensus does not exist, or when ambiguity pervades the organization, the conclusion is that the culture is weak, not strong, and clarity needs to be implemented. As Martin (2002) has summarized: "What makes a study congruent with the integration perspective is a prevalence of descriptive material consistent with the integration view (consistency, organization-wide consensus, and clarity), plus a normative position: Deviations from integration are portrayed as regrettable shortfalls" (p. 99). While I agree with Martin's point, I offer the caution that an opposite perspective is equally implausible. Surely some individuals agree on some tasks or outcomes. If no one agrees on any process or goal, is it also not possible to conclude that the organization is likely to be troubled? My simple point here is that if the ideal type painted of integrationists is one mistaken vision of organizational life, then surely the other end of a continuity-discontinuity continuum is equally mistaken.

A DIFFERENTIATION FRAMEWORK

If clarity is the norm to be developed by integrationists, the opposite comes to the fore in differentiation studies. Subcultures have different interpretations of the organizational world based on their perspectives. The assumption that a leader can take any particular action that will provide cohesion is foolhardy. As opposed to prescriptive recommendations for organizational reform, the focus is on getting to implicit and frequently unstated meanings. Not surprisingly, interest group power and politics are the main themes.

Differentiation is useful in pointing out how different groups coalesce either because of some sort of membership external to the organization or because of their positions within the organization. Christian members might form a Bible study group prior to work, and they may have one interpretation if the division vice president brings his same-sex partner to the Christmas party, whereas gay members might have another interpretation and feel more comfortable lobbying that vice president for a nondiscrimination policy. Membership in either group might defy one's standing in the organization such that a Christian janitor might form a common bond with an upper-level manager, just as a lesbian secretary might befriend a gay staff worker.

Similarly, we know that faculty frequently have a different interpretation than staff about a host of issues. Science faculty see the world differently than those in the humanities. My point here is not that even all members of subcultural groups see the world similarly because differences always exist—working-class Christians may have different issues than wealthy Christians, for example. Differentiationists have brought to life the competing conceptions of organizational reality (Clark, 1998). As Martin, Frost, and O'Neil (2004) note, "differentiation studies define culture in terms of inconsistency, consensus and clarity—only within subcultural boundaries" (p. 15).

If one steps back from the researcher's struggle to understand the organization, one can easily see how such a perspective functions. Different people have different perspectives based on different standpoints. Some people see issues similarly because they have a shared background. By no means do those who subscribe to this framework believe that all subgroups act alike. Women may share some commonalities, for example, but simply being a woman or a man, gay or straight, and the like does not ensure that all individuals within a particular subgroup will behave in the same way. Indeed, what motivates those who work from this perspective is inconsistency. Rather than cohesion and clarity, they seek to understand, perhaps even applaud, differences and dissent.

Whereas integrationists tend to downplay interest group politics and the portrait may be negative when groups disagree, differentiation supporters are more likely to try to understand differing perspectives and acknowledge that rather than the amelioration of differences there will be dissensus. Integrationists see difference as a weakness; differentiationists see difference as the way the world works. Unions might be thought of as obstructionists from an integration perspective, whereas an opposing interpretation would be that those in a union have a fundamentally different perspective of the organizational world. Rather than a negative portrait, the challenge is to offer understanding to the various competing conceptions of organizational reality. If integrationists had an overriding concern to offer recommendations for organizational improvement, perhaps the most that can be said of fragmentationists is that they at least want individuals to have an understanding of the different positions within an organization. How the organization moves forward based on these different positions is usually not discussed.

A FRAGMENTATION FRAMEWORK

Fragmentation focuses on ambiguity. The assumption that anyone knows what he or she is doing in the organization is a mirage, and researchers who search for unitary understandings or cohesion on any level are on a fool's errand. Organizational ambiguity is more than assuming that a particular act or event is unclear to a few individuals because if something is unclear, the possibility exists that the confusion can be clarified. Consensus is elusive and fleeting; some individuals cohere on one issue at one point in time and disagree on the next issue or the same issue at a later date. If integration's goal is to create unities, and differentiation's goal is to understand the differences, then fragmentation's goal is simply to exist in a chaotic environment. To make sense of that environment is impossible.

Of the three frameworks, fragmentation might be thought of as the most playful. Irony, paradox, and contradiction are highlighted, and that confusion exists is not seen as something to be fixed or necessarily understood (Cohen & March, 1974). Paradox and organizational chaos are normal. Instead of trying to fix a problem, individual actors "muddle through." Individuals act out scripts in a play that may have no meaning. Because the individual has a role—such as president or vice president—he or she plays that role. The assumption that someone can make a difference is seen as absurd.

Given the underlying assumptions of this framework, it is not surprising that some of the primary areas of investigation are topics such as humor and irony. If we cannot make sense of the organizational environment as researchers because there is no sense to be made of it, then why not study the playfulness of language codes and interactions? Culture is a puzzle that has no solution. Individuals inhabit multiple identities, and how one responds to environmental stimuli depends upon context, temporality, and location. Fragmentation at all levels—the organization, the unit, and the individual—defines culture.

HIGHER EDUCATION AND THE FRAMEWORKS

Cultural analyses of academe parallel research in the organizational arena with two significant differences. Most of the research has called upon the integration framework. Burton R. Clark's work is the forerunner of much of this research even though he was speaking of a subset of American colleges—those that he labeled "distinctive" (Clark, 1970, 1971, 1980). His theme of an institution that had an overarching saga is a perfect fit for the assumption that organizations have an overriding ideology that gives meaning to the participants. Clark's work, however, was not intended as an indicator for effectiveness. Those institutions he studied as distinctive—Reed, Swarthmore, and Antioch—were most certainly not exemplars of effective or efficient decision making. What he posited was that they were examples of distinctive institutions in ways that a large state university was not.

Some of my earlier work also followed in the vein of Clark's (Chaffee & Tierney, 1988; Tierney, 1988a). We made the claim that culture might be seen as organizational glue, and to the extent that people need to hang together, the greater synthesis that existed, the more effective the institution would be. David Dill (1982), Andrew Masland (1985), and George Kuh and Elizabeth Whitt (1988) also fall into the integrationist higher education camp.

Although Clark's work falls squarely within a cultural tradition, albeit from a sociological perspective, those authors who might subscribe to a differentiation or fragmentation perspective actually predate cultural analyses in organization theory. Scholars such as Bolman and Deal (2008) and Pfeffer and Salancik (1978) worked from the perspective of power and politics. They did not claim that their work was cultural and made little, if any, effort to critique cultural frameworks. Nevertheless, the ideas that frame their research fall into the domain that I have defined as a differentiation perspective, and those who have utilized this for their own cultural analyses of higher education frequently cite them.

Similarly, perhaps the most influential work that falls into the fragmentation framework is by James March (1981). March's (1980) concept of a university as an "organized anarchy" is precisely what fragmentationists state is a culture. March and Cohen's (1974) discussion of presidential leadership in a university also parallels what those who subscribe to this framework think of with regard to administration. The concept of the leader as a great man or woman is absurd and the assumption that the leader is able to orchestrate organizational action a fallacy. Thus, one significant departure in cultural work in higher education is that two of the three frameworks utilize work as foundational that is not explicitly cultural.

The second significant departure is that cultural studies of academe often have highlighted faculty culture, rather than that of the organization (Becher, 1981). If one looks at traditional investigations of a "culture," the unit of analysis might be a tribe or group. And certainly in traditional or organizational studies of culture issues such as socialization or gender might be investigated. However, rarely is one group in an organization accorded as much analysis as the faculty have been given in cultural studies of higher education. A similar literature, for example, does not exist in studies of organizational culture or traditional cultures. Although subcultures are always ripe for investigation—especially from the differentiation perspective—the work on faculty culture frequently does not think of it as a *sub*culture but rather a culture unto itself. In part, the subculture is also a discipline and a profession. Clark wrote of the four cultures of the faculty—organization, discipline, profession, and nation—and the irony was always that where individuals played out these various identities was on a campus. Again, differentiationists might argue that these various cultural identities prove their point: within an organization any one individual carries within him- or herself various identities, and how he or she reacts to a particular topic depends upon one's subject location.

Cultural Interpretation and a Unified Model

What often is overlooked when analysts discuss the ideal types of the frameworks that I have outlined is not the differences between the frameworks but their similarities. The most important similarity is the underlying epistemological stance of those who consider the culture of an organization. Culture is interpretive. Indeed, the culture of an organization is interpreted by three different constituencies—those within the organization, the researchers who study the organization, and those who read the research that derives from the studies.

Consider this example: A university president walks into a meeting of faculty and shakes the hands of the men and not the women. The researcher notes the act and writes that if the president wants to be more inclusive he should shake the hands of everyone. A male reader agrees with the interpretation and concludes that if he ever were to become president he would be sure to shake the hand of all male and female faculty. Would a researcher provide a different interpretation and a reader reach a different conclusion if the university was in the United States or Afghanistan? The culture of Afghanistan and other conservative Islamic countries assumes that men should not shake the hand of a woman unless the woman proffers it. Thus, one might conclude that the university president was being culturally sophisticated and to proffer one's hand would be a cultural gaffe. Or perhaps the American president in Afghanistan was deliberately breaking a cultural rule to signal not simply a greeting but that the university needed to change the gender relations that ruled the institution and country.

An integrationist might assume that individuals interpret such acts in a similar way and whether the president shakes hands or does not shake hands depends upon the president's intent. Those who work from the differentiation perspective will point out that men and women are likely to interpret the handshake similarly, and to state that the president should or should not shake the hand will most likely not be an effective act. Someone who utilizes the fragmentation framework will go further. Some men may have been educated in the United States and appreciate if the president is trying to equalize gender relations; other men may find such an action deeply offensive. Some of the men who have been educated in the United States may understand what the president is trying to do, but they still interpret it as an act of American imperialism and resent it. Still others may not care one way or the other but oppose the president on some other measure and decide to support or oppose the handshake in order to ally with a particular group. The result is that to assume that the handshake can be interpreted in a singular manner or according to interest group politics will be seen as absurd.

One integrationist observation might be that I have purposefully chosen a symbolic act that is clearly controversial. The differences between a university in the United States and one in Afghanistan are significant, and if I had chosen most institutions in the United States, the act would indeed be interpreted in a similar manner—and the president should shake everyone's hands. A methodological differentiationist would claim that any unitary perspective is simply bad method—that the situation has been misinterpreted regardless if the setting is the United States or Afghanistan. The reasons for agreement or disagreement will vary based on different situations in the countries, but there will still be no consensus. Those who subscribe to a fragmentation framework will go even further: there is no way that the researcher will be able to assume that he or she interprets situations in a manner that the various individuals do, and further, readers will have multiple interpretations as well. A text really can be little more than a private diary that at best reveals the complexity of organizational life.

I need to offer two critical points. First, my example highlights the agreement that proponents of each framework share. Unlike empiricists who assume that organizational phenomena can be agreed upon, a cultural epistemology does work from the perspective that the organization is interpretive. The ability of someone to interpret a situation varies, of course, but it is no small matter that a cultural framework begins with the assumption that whatever is to be analyzed will be interpretive. If we know that interpretation is the raison d'être of the undertaking, then the import of methodology arises. Yes, a radical stance will be that no understanding can occur because of individual differences, but even to ensure that no understanding is possible demands that the researcher be able to hear differences across individuals and groups. The critique of integrationists is that they fail to interpret situations correctly, and the integrationists' basic goal is to find symbolic patterns in an environment by way of interpretive interviews and observations.

The second point pertains to the handshake. That president is still going to walk into that meeting at the Afghanistan (or U.S.) university. He is either going to shake hands or not. Assume that in the anteroom to the meeting place sit three people. The president asks, "What should I do?" Presumably the integrationist will offer an answer. The differentiation supporter may hesitate and caution about the multitude of challenges the handshake will engender, but the president is likely to decide based on the information either to shake or not shake hands with the women faculty. The scholar who sees the world as fragmented, however, is likely to shrug his or her shoulders and say that any act will do insofar as the result will be impossible to predict. Regardless of the interpretation that the president accepts, he is still going to have to make a decision—to shake or not to shake hands.

Insofar as culture is an interpretive act, it is inherently a subjective undertaking of ideational and material concerns. If we step back from the idealist versions of the frameworks, one can find much to agree with in each version of culture. In an organization some, perhaps many, individuals share commonalities at particular points in time. Who has not worked in a college or university and found broad agreement on some topics? Similarly, who does not acknowledge that subcultures exist, just as differentiation proponents point out? That subcultures exist seems to be almost self-evident; what one needs to discover is the degree to which they are in harmony with, in conflict with, or independent of one another. The fragmentation perspective's focus on ambiguity also seems apparent to anyone who has worked in academe over time. Perhaps ambiguity is not a constant, but surely there are moments in an organization when lack of clarity is apparent and the point is less to try to clarify the situation than simply exist with it. The point, then, is less to wage conceptual war on a particular framework and more to see how these competing frameworks might provide a fuller description of organizational life than simply one perspective. What might this more complete description look like? To answer the question I return to a discussion of creativity and think about what that means from a cultural perspective.

Creativity and Culture

If we believe that colleges and universities need to move toward creativity and innovation, what sorts of actions might be proposed? Such a question hinges on how the respondent defines "we." Integrationists from an earlier era might jump in with a variety of cookbook-style recipes that any manager who is geared toward creativity could employ. Someone wedded to the differentiation perspective will caution that no unified response is possible. A college president will view creativity from his or her perspective that dramatic change needs to occur in the organization; a by-product will be that the president will garner attention and get a better job at a more prestigious institution. A fragmentation proponent will flatly reject that "we" exists in an organization and instead may analyze communicative actions. Those who do not work from a cultural perspective will suggest a series of instrumental actions. From this viewpoint culture is irrelevant, and instead a series of empirically based actions might be employed that will enhance organizational creativity.

The strength of using a cultural perspective, however, is to think about creativity neither as a set of instrumental activities that need to be developed nor as a fool's errand because it is impossible to orchestrate. An integrated approach suggests that change agents need to hold multiple points of view. Tim Hallett (2003) defines "organizational culture as a negotiated order that emerges through interactions between participants, a negotiated order influenced by people with symbolic power—the power to define a situation" (p. 135). Hallett suggests that symbolic power is the ability to define the situation as it is contextualized and negotiated. Contextualization refers to the larger enacted environments in which the organization resides, and negotiation is an ongoing interaction that is often invisible and unclear. Such a point of view, although clearly nonlinear and nonfunctional, captures a more protean view of culture. "We" exists in an organization, although how "we" gets defined is in constant rearrangement and rearticulation. Beliefs are not necessarily shared as if everyone interprets an act or communicative message in the same manner; rather, different perspectives are viewed such that integration and conflict are in coexistence with each other. Because the researcher acknowledges that symbols and interpretation are key to organizational life, an understanding of instrumental activities is viewed as more than simply bureaucratic actions or segmented decisions.

The result is that I return to what I stated at the outset: colleges and universities are not static entities; they are in constant redefinition. The presumption that everyone will agree or care about a particular definition is as presumptuous as to conclude that differences are so significant that no one will understand or agree with one another. Bertalanffy (1968), the founder of general systems theory, posited that an end (rather than a goal) may be reached by various routes. To be sure, causality exists in certain scientific, or empirical, situations. If I turn the light switch on, light appears. If it does not, something is wrong. In culture, however, systems operate quite differently. Different early experiences in an organization may have similar outcomes; similar experiences and interpretations by individuals may have different outcomes. Organizational predictability becomes difficult, if not impossible.

However, the ability to take into account the constructed environments in which a postsecondary institution exists also suggests clues for organizational transformation. In organizations in which respondents have a significant degree of latitude, what Weick (1976) called loosely coupled, the point differs from organizations in which a strict chain of command exists, what Goffman (1961) labeled a total institution. A university is loosely coupled; a mental institution or prison is tightly coupled. Thus, I have argued here for a more complicated view of the organization, one that acknowledges constant reinterpretation but also suggests that concerted action is possible.

REFERENCES

Amabile, T. M. (1998). How to kill creativity. *Harvard Business Review*, 76(5), 77–89.
Amabile, T. M., Conti, R., Coon, H., Lazenby, J., & Herron, M. (1996). Assessing the work environment for creativity. *Academy of Management Journal*, 39(5), pp. 1154–1184.
Becher, T. (1981). Toward a definition of disciplinary cultures. *Studies in Higher Education*, 6, 109–122.
Behar, R. (1993). *Translated woman: Crossing the border with Esperanza's story*. Boston: Beacon Press.
Bertalanffy, L. V. (1968). *Organismic psychology and systems theory*. Worcester, MA: Clark University Press.
Bolman, L., & Deal, T. (2008). *Reframing organizations: Artistry, choice and leadership*. San Francisco: Jossey-Bass.
Carlyle, T. (1897). *Heroes and hero-worship*. London: Chapman and Hall.
Chaffee, E. E. (1988). Listening to the people we serve. In W. G. Tierney (Ed), *The responsive university*. Baltimore: Johns Hopkins University Press.
Chaffee, E. E., & Tierney, W. G. (1988). *Collegiate culture and leadership strategies*. New York: Macmillan.
Clark, B. (1970). *The distinctive college*. Chicago: Aldine.
Clark, B. (1971). Belief and loyalty in college organization. *Journal of Higher Education*, 42(6), 499–520.
Clark, B. (1980). The organizational saga in higher education. In H. Leavitt, L. Pondy, & D. Boje (Eds.), *Readings in managerial psychology*. Chicago: University of Chicago Press.
Clark, B. R. (1998). *Creating entrepreneurial universities: Organizational pathways of transformation*. Kidlington, Oxford: Elsevier Science.
Clifford, J., & Marcus, G. (Eds.) (1986). *Writing culture: The poetics and politics of ethnography*. Berkeley: University of California Press.
Cohen, M. D., & March, J. G. (1974). *Leadership and ambiguity: The American college president*. New York: McGraw-Hill.
Deal, T., & Kennedy, A. (1982). *Corporate cultures: The rites and rituals of corporate life*. Reading, MA: Addison-Wesley.
Dill, D. (1982). The management of academic culture: Notes on the management of meaning and social integration. *Journal of Management*, 2, 83–98.
Duderstadt, J. J., & Womack, F. W. (2003). *The future of the public university in America: Beyond the crossroads*. Baltimore: Johns Hopkins University Press.
Florida, R. (2002). *The rise of the creative class*. New York: Basic Books.

Florida, R. (2004). *Cities and the creative class*. New York: Routledge.

Florida, R., Gates, G., Knudsen, B., & Stolarick, K. (2006). *The university and the creative economy*. Retrieved February 2009 from Creative Class Group, Web site: creativeclass .com/rfcgdb/articles/University_andthe_Creative_Economy.pdf

Frank, G. (2000). *Venus on wheels: Two decades of dialogue on disability, biography, and being female in America*. Berkeley: University of California Press.

Geertz, C. (1973). *The interpretation of cultures*. New York: Basic Books.

Goffman, E. (1961). *Asylums: Essays on the social situation of mental patients and other inmates*. Garden City, NY: Random House.

Hallett, T. (2003). Symbolic power and organizational culture. *Sociological Theory, 21*(2), 128–149.

Haveman, H. (1992). Between a rock and a hard place: Organizational change and performance under conditions of fundamental environmental transformation. *Administrative Science Quarterly, 37*, 48–75.

Jelinek, M., Smircich, L., & Hirsch, P. (Eds.). (1983). Organizational culture. *Administrative Science Quarterly, 28*(3), 331–495.

Kuh, G. D., & Whitt, E. J. (1988). *The invisible tapestry: Culture in American colleges and universities*. ASHE-ERIC Higher Education Report No. 1. Washington, DC: Association for the Study of Higher Education.

Levinthal, D. (1991). Organizational adaptation and selection—interrelated processes. *Organizational Science, 2*(1), 140–145.

March, J. G. (1981). Footnotes to organizational change. *Administrative Science Quarterly, 26*(4), 563–577.

March, J. (1984). How we talk and how we act: Administrative theory and administrative life. In T. J. Sergiovanni & J. E. Corbally (Eds.), *Leadership and organizational culture* (pp. 18–35). Urbana: University of Illinois Press.

March, J., & Cohen, M. (1974). *Leadership and ambiguity*. New York: McGraw-Hill.

Martin, J. (2002). *Organizational culture: Mapping the terrain*. Thousand Oaks, CA: Sage.

Martin, J., Frost, P. J., & O'Neill, O. A. (2004). *Organizational culture: Beyond struggles for intellectual dominance* (Research Paper No. 1864). Palo Alto, CA: Stanford University Graduate School of Business.

Masland, A. (1985). Organizational culture in the study of higher education. *Review of Higher Education, 8*(2), 157–168.

McLean, L. D. (2005). Organizational culture's influence on creativity and innovation: A review of the literature and implications for human resource development. *Advances in Developing Human Resources, 7*, 226–246.

Mitroff, I. I., & Kilmann, R. H. (1975). Stories managers tell: A new tool for organizational problem solving. *Management Review, 64*, 18–28.

Morgan, G., & Smircich, L. (1980). The case for qualitative research. *Administrative Science Quarterly, 25*, 605–622.

Peters, T., & Waterman, R. (1982). *In search of excellence: Lessons from America's best-run companies*. New York: Harper and Row.

Pfeffer, J., & Salancik, G. R. (1978). *The external control of organizations: A resource dependence perspective*. New York: Harper and Row.

Sample, S. B. (2002). The contrarian's guide to leadership. San Francisco: Jossey-Bass.

Silver, H. (2008). Does a university have a culture? *Studies in Higher Education, 28*(2), 157–169.

Smircich, L., & Morgan, G. (1982). Leadership: The management of meaning. *Journal of Applied Behavioral Science, 18*, 257–273.

Sternberg, R. J., & Lubart, T. I. (1999). The concept of creativity: Prospects and paradigms. In R. J. Sternberg (Ed.), *Handbook of creativity* (pp. 3–15). Cambridge: Cambridge University Press.

Tierney, W. G. (1988a). Organizational culture in higher education: Defining the essentials. *Journal of Higher Education, 59*(1), 2–21.

Tierney, W. G. (1988b). *The web of leadership*. Greenwich, CT: JAI Press.

Tierney, W. G. (1989). Symbolism and presidential perceptions of leadership. *Review of Higher Education, 12*(2), 153–166.

Tierney, W. G. (1999). *Building the responsive campus: Creating high performance colleges and universities*. Thousand Oaks, CA: Sage.

Tierney, W. G. (2006). *Trust and the public good: Examining the cultural conditions*. New York: Peter Lang.

Weick, K. E. (1976). Educational organizations as loosely coupled systems. *Administrative Science Quarterly, 21*(1), 1–19.

Weick, K. E. (1982). Management of organizational change among loosely coupled elements. In Paul Goodman & Associates (Eds.), *Change in organizations* (pp. 375–408). San Francisco: Jossey-Bass.

Whyte, W. H. (1956). *The organization man*. New York: Simon and Schuster.

Williams, W. M., & Yang, L. T. (1999). Organizational creativity. In R. J. Sternberg (Ed.), *Handbook of creativity* (pp. 373–391). Cambridge: Cambridge University Press.

Woodman, R. W., Sawyer, J. E., & Griffin, R. W. (1993). Toward a theory of organizational creativity. *Academy of Management Review, 18*(2), 293–321.

CHAPTER SEVEN

Organizational Change in a Global, Postmodern World

ADRIANNA KEZAR

It is commonly assumed that change in higher education is infrequent, slow, and labor-intensive. Change related to faculty is often described as "herding cats." Foundations bemoan the slow pace of change, and critics often assail higher education for being unresponsive (Tierney, 1999). This common image does reflect the institutional status of colleges and universities that are meant to be organizations that maintain long-standing and deeply held values and that will be maintained even though environmental conditions fluctuate (Kezar, 2001). One of the defining features of institutions is that they stay true to their mission and carry out an important societal purpose. Yet the common stereotypes about the inability of postsecondary institutions to change also hide important (and potentially destructive) and ongoing changes that are constantly occurring within the higher education sector.

One only needs to look at the history of higher education, worldwide or in the United States, to see the vast array of changes: the institutional types that have emerged, the shift in curriculum, the different types of students, and the new missions that have developed over time. Colleges and universities are anything but static institutions (Clark, 1998). The popular image of higher education as a removed "ivory tower" is not consistent with the historical record and does not help us to explore and understand change. But to suggest that some changes are institutionalized within higher education more easily than others would certainly be accurate.

However, this issue of what type of changes are integrated into institutions and which ones become stifled or rejected has not been addressed until more recently through political and cultural theories of change and critical and interpretive approaches to the study of change. If scholars of postmodernism and globalization are correct, organizational change is likely to be more common as technology and cultural exchange allow for greater sharing of ideas that may lead to innovation—or so the claim goes (Berquist, 2007; Carnoy & Rhoten, 2002; Clark, 1998). Change, I argue, is an unavoidable part of organizational life, and the more we understand it, the better we can negotiate, resist, and facilitate it. I also suggest that change itself is neither good nor bad (but some ideas for change are better and some worse, depending on who you are) (Macdonald, 1997). The consequences of various changes need to be evaluated quite carefully, and more recent paradigms and theories of change help to better analyze and critique change proposals and will be the focus of the discussion.

In this chapter, first I introduce readers to four different paradigms that have emerged for understanding change and describe how they fundamentally differ in terms of their assumptions. I highlight paradigms as they have been largely unexamined, particularly in higher education research. Furthermore, I argue that unexamined assumptions about change have lead to narrowly focused studies that hide the complexity and underlying interests in change. Second, I review five schools of thought (encompassing similar theories of change) related to change that emerged within these different paradigms. Over time, the field of organization theory has developed new insights into how to understand the concept of change. I demonstrate how a multifaceted and complex approach to change will better serve to explain and facilitate change.

Research Paradigms: Fundamentally Different Beliefs about Change

Paradigms are the underlying assumptions that drive all the decisions about studying and theorizing organizational change and affect the questions asked, methodology and study design, focus of research, basic assumptions, definitions of change, and outcomes (Collins, 1998). Many researchers have noted that assumptions are often absent or not transparent in studies of change. For example, Quattrone and Hopper (2001) note that, "despite widespread research on why and how organizations change, what constitutes change is often taken for granted. Its definition is avoided" (p. 403). Collins (1998) notes that one of the key problems in the study of change is that authors do not explicitly discuss their theoretical assumptions; uncritical perspectives on change have continued to guide our thinking and analysis.

While authors argue that certain paradigms are better for understanding organizational change (see Collins, 1998), I think that all paradigms add insight and can be used to better understand this complex process. Others have also taken this perspective. For example, Joanne Martin (1992) examines organizational culture using three different paradigms. Four main paradigms have been used to understand change: (1) the positivist or functionalist paradigm; (2) the interpretive paradigm; (3) the critical paradigm; and (4) the postmodern paradigm. While it is difficult to fit all theories within these four paradigms because some theories include assumptions from more than one paradigm, these broad distinctions help to identify some underlying differences in assumptions. Table 7.1 summarizes some of the main differences between different paradigms for understanding organizational change and should be referred to throughout this section.[1] What becomes clear in reviewing paradigms is that researchers are fundamentally looking at organizational change in different ways. If you believe that change typically represents the imposition of elite's interests, you will frame a change scenario in quite different ways than if you believe that change occurs to increase the effectiveness of an organization.

FUNCTIONALIST PARADIGM

Of the four paradigms, the functionalist paradigm is more commonly used by researchers and practitioners than the other paradigms. The functionalist paradigm is guided by some of the following assumptions: change can be explored through causal relationships between phenomena; empirical evidence is favored over conceptual arguments; change is a discoverable, observable, and measurable phenomenon; and change can be predicted and is episodic. Readers are likely familiar with concepts such as total quality management, business process reengineering, and strategic planning—all part of the popular business literature.[2] The representation of change within the functionalist paradigm is found in the charismatic leader—typically a person in power; change occurs because of strategic planning, management techniques, and careful implementation of a rational and linear process.[3] I will provide more examples of the functionalist paradigm in the section "Schools of Thought Related to Change."

Because functionalist images of change tend to be familiar to readers, I provide an overview of some less common paradigms and describe some studies that help to articulate and make concrete the interpretive, critical, and postmodern paradigms as they are more likely to be unfamiliar to readers.

INTERPRETIVE PARADIGM

Interpretive studies foreground language, discourse, and communication patterns: the interpersonal meaning of change, the symbolic significance; the implications of change for affected cultures and individuals, social background of ac-

TABLE 7.1.

Comparison of underlying assumptions about change across different paradigms

Paradigms	Functionalist	Interpretive	Critical	Postmodern
Beliefs about change—epistemological and ontological	Change is a finite phenomenon that can be readily documented, measured, and observed; change is controllable and can be predicted; change is episodic.	Change can be perceived only by varying actors who may perceive it differently (reality and socially constructed); change is elusive and hard to pin down; change is more continuous.	Change represents the imposition of elites' interests or contestation and negotiation of different interests between groups; while it may sometimes be observable, because political interests are often implicit, it is often difficult to document; change is episodic.	Questions whether change is truly a phenomenon and holds that the world is constantly in flux and that to identify, isolate, and document a particular change is difficult. Tends to see the world as continuously in flux—adrift. Closest analogy is improvisation. Change is very difficult to control, or identifying whose interests are served is challenging.
Theories of change	Evolutionary, teleological, or scientific management, life cycle	Social cognition, sensemaking; cultural; institutional theory	Political; social movement; dialectical; critical race theory; feminism	No real theories have emerged because this paradigm for postmodernism suggests some sense of prediction and control postmodernists do not believe in.
Beneficiaries of and focus of change	Typically comes from the perspective of those in management and authority; fixity is the norm as elites' interests tend to be served by existing structures.	Investigates multiple perspectives and interests; changes are natural and ongoing.	Those in power control change; change is often a co-optation of power for any advances made by nonelites; focus on those without power and authority and how change affects them or changes that will benefit those without power.	Often sees that changes benefit those in positions of authority and questions this privileging; however, constant shifting of power makes it difficult to understand who is in power and whose interests are served by change.

Why change occurs	In order to maximize effectiveness and efficiency	Cognitive dissonance. People are inclined to make meaning of their worlds, and if they see that conditions exist that do not make sense, they attempt to change or manage the conditions.	Due to the elites or bottom-up interests. As a particular interest emerges, a change may occur; because any change is likely to serve only one group, conflict is inherent.	Often because of the interests of those in power. However, changes occur randomly and are often not tied to any particular reason. Collision of forces.
How change occurs	Through planning, through external pressures; rational and linear; purposeful	By changing mental frameworks; through learning; by appealing to people's values; inquiry and dialogue; action learning	Through negotiation, agenda setting, coalitions and contestations of power; tends to be collective in social movements	As a result of random interactions of people, through networks, or by people who can exert their will
Outcome of change	New structures, processes, and organizing principles	New organizational identity, frame of mind, or culture	New organizational ideology	Never fully instantiated—ongoing alterations in structure, culture, and ideology; does not conceive of institutionalization; often difficult to predict outcome given the randomness of how change occurs.
Agency	Some theories suggest a great deal of agency for leaders; others suggest a strong role of outside forces and more limited agency.	Agency differs for varying groups.	Agency more limited for bottom-up leaders; in some theories there is a strong structuralism that impedes agency for those not in authority.	Limited agency, constrained yet free

(continued)

TABLE 7.1. *continued*

Paradigms	Functionalist	Interpretive	Critical	Postmodern
Role of context and history	Not conceptualized as impacting change strongly.	Context and history strongly affect the way change processes unfold.	Context and history can affect the way change processes unfold.	Context and history can affect the way change processes unfold; hard to see at that time period.
Boundedness of change	In many theories bounded by the organization.	Tends to be bounded within the organization.	Examines larger power structures that go beyond organization that shape change.	Examines larger power structures and trends that go beyond organization that shape change but sees great interactivity.
Role of power	Does not conceptualize power.	Power can affect the change process depending on how people interpret their context and agency.	Power plays a major role in how and why change occurs; structure of power—tenure, maintaining employment, etc., often make people not become involved in bottom-up change: institutions serve elites' purposes.	Power plays a role in how and why change occurs, but other random occurrences also affect process.
Purpose of research	To identify ways to predict and control change; provide tools for top-down leaders.	To identify the ways that people react to and are affected by change; to understand how people make meaning of change; action research—to work with actors throughout organization to create change.	To understand whose interests are served by changes and to critically examine those interests; to document change approaches by nonelites; participatory action research—create collective change.	To demonstrate the complexity of change and resist certainty; importance of multiple voices for change; question assumptions of change; break down hierarchies; develop critique toward social reconstruction—even social justice can go wayward.

Role of values	Value-free stance, but neutral stance hides support of elites in change processes.	Change tends to be conceptualized as neutral, but different views within the organization are examined in order to understand ethical considerations.	Because change is typically about serving different interests, it has an inherent value component.	Because change sometimes serves different interests, it has an inherent value component, but the randomness and flow of events make values judgments difficult.
Major insights	Helps to develop advice about processes and systems for creating change.	Adds insight into the characteristics of individuals and the human aspects of change; helps understand implementation problems and resistance; through the importance of language and discourse suggests new possibilities for social order.	Helps to illuminate sexism, racism, classism, and other issues often in the change proposals; helps understand power dimension and interests involved in change.	Ambiguity; importance of deconstruction to see change anew; complexity of perspective
Limitations	Does not critically examine change initiatives and the interests they serve. Does not examine conflict and resistance as they relate to change. Does not conceptualize the role of context. Problems are of implementation – not ideas, some often not overcome.	Individual stories and context may not translate into other situations; may not identify other larger structures and power conditions that are operating and shaping change.	Any gains are typically reversed by those in power by another change that disempowers this group. Role of agency often minimized.	May reemphasize the status quo by deemphasizing agency; complexity can be overwhelming to understand, and often there are few practical implications.

tors and the role of history and culture; and performance of organizational actors (Antonacopoulo & Gabriel, 2001; Boyce, 1996, 2003; Brown, 2006; Burke, 1995; Ferlie, 1997; Gioia, Schultz, & Corley, 2000; Heracleous, 2002; McWilliam & Ward-Griffin, 2006; Rhodes, 1996, 1997; Weick & Quinn, 1999). Through phenomenological[4] approaches to change, interpretivists have been able probe more deeply into the human psyche to understand resistance, coping strategies, cognitive dissonance, mental maps and frameworks, differing beliefs and ideologies, and ways agents interpret and make sense of change (Andrews, Cameron, & Harris, 2008; Baldridge & Deal, 1983; Berman, Ford-Gilboe, & Campell, 1998). Through ethnographic accounts, they have also been able to examine the role of culture, history, ideology, and language and more shared structures in which people make sense and are shaped by change.

The interpretive tradition places great emphasis on discourse and language (Finstad, 1998; Kelly, 1998). Language is seen as a way to shape social conditions and is also an expression of different interpersonal meanings of change (Dill, 1982). A variety of studies have looked at metaphors and storytelling as a way to facilitate organizational change (Heracleous & Barrett, 2001; Palmer & Dunford, 1996). For example, changes that are outside people's experience might be better understood if leaders use well-known metaphors or stories that capture experiences that are familiar to people. Interpretive studies also examine the difference between managers and staff as they describe a change process and the sense of agency that top-down leaders have and the lack of empowerment that the language of staff reflects (Rhodes, 1996, 1997). Also, studies have documented how staff and managers see the alteration in underlying ideology for the change quite differently: the staff seeing it as a way to save money and the managers noting that it improves quality (Palmer & Dunford, 1996). Therefore, key concepts such as the interpersonal meaning or symbolic significance of change are grasped through the focus on language and discourse—a central principle for reconceptualizing change (Chaffee, 1983).

Prior studies of change are often centered on leaders or those in authority who are considered agents of change. As noted above, interpretive studies focus on those experiencing the change, trying to understand their perspective and how they make meaning of a change process (Luscher, Lewis, & Ingram, 2006). These studies help illuminate the role of resistance or barriers to change because changes are not well understood or are considered poor by others in the organization (Rhodes, 1996, 1997). Through these investigations of other actors, interpretive studies also identify new agents of change—without positions of authority—and demonstrate how they are part of a shared or distributed change process. (Kezar,

Carducci, & McGavin, 2006; Pearce & Conger, 2003). Studies have also shown how these newly identified agents initiate change processes that have not been identified in prior studies.

Interpretive studies also give prominence to the social background of people within the organization and help identify the ways social class, ethnicity, or gender affect the way people make meaning of a particular type of change. Mandatory sexual harassment training will be seen by some women as creating a more positive climate, whereas some men may find it develops a surveillance culture (Antonacopoulou & Gabriel, 2001). In addition to social background, the theory emphasizes the culture and history of people related to change (Dawson, 1994; Pettigrew, 1987). The struggle for human rights (a changed focused on by many interpretive scholars) is an ongoing struggle but is seen as shaped by different historical factors and cultural conditions. Interpretive researchers draw on the lessons and experience of the humanities, such as history and cultural studies, to put change processes in context and understand how the focus, aim, strategies, and outcomes may differ by these contextual conditions (Gergen & Thatchenkcry, 2004). For example, reactions to sexual harassment training have changed over the past thirty years as norms about what is appropriate have changed. As new generations of people come into the workplace and have experienced less overt discrimination, they may be less open to training, seeing it as unnecessary, but with a greater appreciation of a diverse workforce that makes them more open to seeing the value of training.

Interpretive researchers also believe it is important to ascertain more about the inner life of actors who respond to change and as well as the way they perform as a result of these internal meaning-making struggles (Aune, 1995). For example, a staff member might present a particular perspective in meetings with those in power (front stage), but with other colleagues he or she might describe resistance to the change (backstage), and then when individually thinking about the change, he or she might have some beliefs that are shared with those in power but also other views that resist the change (under the stage).

A helpful study for understanding the interpretive paradigm of change in higher education is a study by Trowler—*Academics Responding to Change: New Higher Education Frameworks and Academic Cultures* (1998). The author examines how academic staff in a British university responded to a rapid change process that included the expansion in the number of students and the creation of a new curriculum and credit framework structure. Coming from an interpretive tradition, he shifts the focus from those in positions of authority creating change to the way individuals perceive and make meaning of changes that occur to them.

Previous studies from a more functionalist perspective have been unable to understand resistance to change and the way that actors throughout the organization shape and alter a change initiative coming from the top down. As Trowler notes, "the manager's job becomes much harder and the process of change much more uneven as change is interpreted in and reacted to in different ways within the organization" (p. 29). The author identifies several different perspectives about the ways academics responded to this top-down change, including swimming, coping strategies, policy reconstruction, and sinking.

Through the interpretive paradigm, Trowler (1998) examines differences in responses related to various social identities and based on culture and history. Those who held a perspective that the change allowed them to swim (often women who had not been allowed to play a leadership role in the previous policy environment) believed that they were able to thrive in the new environment, and some of these individuals were able to gain leadership positions as a result of the new credit framework. Those who reported coping strategies tried to deal with the increasing number of students and declining resources by retreating from innovation and work in some areas. Those who held a policy reconstruction perspective rebelled against the new credit framework and created their own innovations to deal with the new environment. They created their own reinterpretations of policies and took the change in different directions than intended. This course of action allowed the staff to look as if they may have been responding to the change, but instead they were creating other changes that resisted and flew in the face of the change but were not readily identifiable. Both of these perspectives demonstrate the agency that is often present but typically not made visible through functionalist studies. Sinking suggests that some people were mutely accepting the change even though they thought it was personally damaging and they suffered many negative consequences such as stress and illness. The author also identifies different factors that appear to be affecting whether people adopted these perspectives from disciplinary background, personal background, race and gender, potential for profitability within the academic area, and external entities that impacted educational perspectives.

This study highlights some of the underlying assumptions listed in Table 7.1—the study provides information about resistance, agency among faculty, implementation problems, personal attributes that impact change, importance of interpretation of individual actors, and the varying ways people within organizations make meaning. Other examples of change research within an interpretive paradigm in higher education include Neumann's (1995) work on the way people socially construct changes that are presented to them, Levin's (1998) work on how culture and context shape and frame change, and Lueddeke's (1999) constructivist framework for guiding change.

Overall, the interpretive paradigm helps add more information about the human dimensions of change—individuals' thinking, feeling, beliefs, and perspective. This paradigm highlights the role of the broader human context—embedded in history and culture. Also, interpretive scholars focus on ways to capture the insights about culture, perspective, values, and discourse through language and gathering multiple perspectives.

CRITICAL PARADIGM

Researchers who adopt a critical perspective for examining change question the instrumental reason within functionalist theories (Dehler, Welsh, & Lewis, 2001; DePaula, 2004; Grubbs, 2000; Linstead, Brewis, & Linstead, 2005; Magala, 2000; Morley, 1997). Change from the top is seen as a type of imperialism, cultural domination, or imposition (Grubbs, 2000). Collins (1998), and others have critiqued traditional theories of change for their value-free orientation in which researchers approach change as if it did not represent any particular interest. Researchers that claim to be value-free do not examine how change tends to come from the top down or can be understood only from the top down, reinforcing that power lies with elites (Smircich & Calás, 1982). Also, the consequences of change are never examined for those who have to implement or live with the change process. For example, restructuring and reengineering typically resulted in many employees losing their positions or being put into positions that they neither were interested in nor had skills in (Caroli & Van Reenen, 2001). The consequences for participants within the organization were largely ignored or considered unimportant (Morgan, 1997). Critical theorists also question the techniques, such as surveillance and accountability mechanisms, used by managers in order to maintain control as the change is implemented.

Critical studies tend to highlight the desired changes by groups that have been historically oppressed in society (Astin & Leland, 1991; Benjamin, 1996; Meyerson, 2003). For example, studies have examined historically underrepresented groups within organizations and their desire to create policies such as cultural sensitivity training to develop inclusive environments because of discrimination they have experienced in the workplace (Linstead et al., 2005). One of the most common frameworks for understanding the desired change from historically underrepresented groups is participatory action research in which the community defines the type of change, not a group of elites (DePaula, 2004). While change processes have been dominated by elites and those in positions of authority, critical theorists suggest and document that others have agency to create change.

Meyerson's (2003) "tempered radicals framework" is an example of a theory of change that has been developed within the critical paradigm. Meyerson argues that many undocumented types of changes occur from the bottom up but are not observable because of the current way that we conceptualize and think about change. She chooses to study individuals who have an interest in creating change but are not in positions of authority, and she examines the way that they create change (through resistance, educating others, networks), negotiate power structures, and maintain resiliency within change processes that often take much longer than change initiatives by those in positions of authority who can mandate change. Building on Meyerson's work, Kezar and Lester's (2009, 2011) research on grassroots leaders in higher education demonstrates a critical perspective on change. Their study challenges the predominant focus on presidents, provosts, and other positional leaders in studies of change in higher education. Instead, her research examines faculty and staff grassroots leaders who pursued a variety of changes that are largely undocumented and not well understood, such as creating an environmental studies program, starting a child-care center, improving the environment for underrepresented students, and addressing staff equity. Their research identifies a collective change process that occurs through very different strategies such as partnering with student activists, integrating activities into campus curriculum, and hiring like-minded activists. These strategies differ from top-down leaders who can use rewards, strategic planning, evaluation and accountability.

The study also demonstrates the way bottom-up leaders, particularly custodial and secretarial staff, navigate intense power conditions that they face (Kezar & Lester, 2009). Bottom-up leaders are labeled troublemakers and often fired, their job threatened, or they are demoted. In order to create change, they developed ways to fly under the radar and create effective coalitions to protect themselves. This type of change and leadership has been mostly invisible on campus, since making it visible would invoke the imperialistic tendencies of those in power. Not only is this change invisible, but it is less common because the structure and norms of colleges work to dissuade people from being involved in collective action that would forward their interests. Faculty worried about being involved in grassroots efforts because it might impede their chances for tenure and promotion. Non-tenure-track faculty worried about obtaining a contract year to year. Staff were controlled by managers who did not allow them the time off to meet with others and to participate in staff development and threatened to lower evaluation and raises. The study uncovers ways faculty and staff support each other in their collective change efforts through networks and off-campus activities. A few other scholars have also enriched our understanding about change from a critical perspective, including Rhoades's (1998) work on students activists and Rhoades's (1996) work on faculty activism and unionization.

The main contribution of the critical paradigm is to fundamentally alter *who* and *what* are studied as part of the change process—looking at bottom leaders and change processes that have been invisible for decades. Furthermore, this paradigm illuminates power, interests that are in play, and reasons why certain groups might support or be against a change process. Researchers using a critical paradigm reconceptualize resistance to change as agency by those poorly served by the change. Previous studies from an elite, more managerial perspective described these actions as more irrational fears to change.

POSTMODERN PARADIGM

There are two different bodies of literature on change that describe themselves as postmodern, but only one reflects a postmodern paradigm and will be the focus of this section (often termed epistemological postmodernism).[5] At the most basic level, postmodernists question the notion of organizations or institutions themselves and whether concepts such as organizational change can really exist, seeing organizations as modernist constructions (Hassard & Parker, 1993). If such organizations do exist, they are more fluid, heterogeneous, and less predictable than represented in earlier modernist studies. The static description of organization serves to reinforce elites' interests and should be challenged. Postmodernism suggests that this emphasis on the fixed and orderly character of organizations helps to support the elites and managerial interests (Beeson & Davis, 2000). Postmodern critics believe that earlier models that emphasize the central role of management worked to make people believe that these actors also had this type of control. For example, postmodernists reject systems theory for reinforcing the status quo through principles such as equilibrium and homeostasis that reinforce traditional power relationships and homogeneity (Clegg, 1989).

Change is seen as natural and ongoing; control and authority are seen as unnatural structures that limit the agency and creativity of individuals within organizations (Berquist, 1993, 1998). Postmodern scholars reject any generalized factors or conditions that lead to change and focus on the self-organizing and organic qualities of organizations that are constantly in flux (Kondakci, 1998). Weick's (1989) notion of improvisation is a good analogy for thinking about change within environments that are unknowable, unpredictable, fast moving, and messy (Crossan, Lane, White, & Klus, 1996; Hassard & Parker, 1993). Change is likened to an improvisational theater where there are no scripts, the cast is interchangeable, and there are no sets or minimal props and costumes (Crossan et al., 1996). Postmodernists employ several analytical techniques including Foucauldian analysis, Derridean deconstruction, and Lyotard language games (Hassard & Parker, 1993). Foucault's (1975) analysis of change identifies endless series of power games (control technologies, surveillance practices) without any enduring institutional rationale to maintain the existing order. Change generally occurs to reinforce existing norms. However, because Foucault sees power relationships as in flux, the existing organization is not a static entity, and occasionally those who traditionally have less power can gain advantage. One of the main tools of postmodernism is deconstructionism. Researchers using deconstructionism identify ways managers colonize employees' subjectivity as part of change process by including employees in decision making and attempting to empower the worker and to dismantle the hierarchy (Boje, Gephart, & Thatchenkery, 1996; Hancock & Tylor, 2001). Therefore, even organizational changes that appear positive for those in nonmanagerial roles typically still serve elites' interests. Derridean analysis (1976) would question the term "change" and its opposite, "stagnation," suggesting that it hides existing power relationships. Instead, postmodern scholars offer different terms for change, such as enactment, drift, and flow, that suggest constant opportunity for shifting the organizational direction. Lyotard illustrates that overarching stories of progress and eventual emancipation often underlie studies of change, making managers look heroic and creating an idealism around current perspectives on organizational change (Hassard & Parker, 1993). In order to better understand change, researchers using a postmodern approach interview people throughout an organization to understand the varying and contested ways that they express and understand the change. Postmodernists see the value in talking with and understanding the perspectives of as many people as possible within an organization, similar to interpretive and critical paradigms (Atkinson, 2002).

Postmodernism scholars see the value in situating knowledge locally; change processes are best understood among the people who "create" and experience the change (Boje & Dennehym, 1993; Boje et al., 1996). Postmodern scholars do not see the value in creating generalized patterns for understanding why change occurs, how change occurs, or the consequences of change. All these concepts are deeply embedded within the specific organizational contexts. For example, a learning community curriculum might be a gimmick on one campus and at another campus could be a profound change in the nature of learning, depending on how the change process unfolds and the beliefs of people on campus.

Postmodernism overlaps with the critical and interpretive paradigms and in many ways combines these assumptions. Similar to critical theory, postmodernism sees organizations as political entities in which conflict and power are constantly occurring. Postmodernists also believe that changes generally work to reproduce existing power and authority relationships. Similar to the interpretive scholars, postmodern scholars see language and discourse as important for understanding basic assumptions about change processes and underlying ideologies that need to be deconstructed and examined (Hassard & Parker, 1993; Boje et al., 1996). Like interpretive approaches, postmodernism emphasizes the multiplicity of organizational actors/viewpoints that are both creative and contentious within change processes (White & Jacques, 1995). Different interpretations represent varying interests that need examination and critique.

A study that examines organizational change from a postmodern perspective is William Tierney's *Building Communities of Difference* (1993).[6] The book examines the culture of different postsecondary institutions reflecting different potential and limitations for creating more inclusive environments for historically underrepresented groups. The book foregrounds the language, history, and local conditions that shape these unique institutions. In order to examine the potential for creating more inclusive campuses where students from all demographic background can be successful, Tierney explores new campuses such as California State San Marcos that are not deeply embedded in traditional structures to see how higher education might look and change in the future. He interviewed people throughout the campuses and system, speaking to those often left out of studies such as students and bottom-up leaders. These new and innovative campuses have more interaction among faculty and staff, lack hierarchy, and have fewer siloed structures and more interdisciplinary environments. Campus leaders attempt to leave roles open and flexible and lines of communication between faculty and administration open.

Tierney (1993) demonstrates how forces both from within and outside campus eventually created a more centralized structure, roles became less flexible because the campuses are part of the state system, and the structure imposed by the state began to overwhelm the agency of the new campuses. As the state experienced financial crisis and began to invoke more controls, the campuses had to adapt and change to become more like other campuses in the system. Over time the campus changed, and "it created an organizational straitjacket and made everyone there conform to the parameters of the state" (p. 123). Tierney's postmodern analysis demonstrates how change happens more ambiguously—not because the state is consciously trying to break down the flexible structures that support innovation that helps create a more inclusive environment, but through a series of random events. He deconstructs how elites' interests are served by the turn of events that make campuses less responsive to students and that include faculty and staff less in decision making. He carefully analyzes people's stories and languages about change to demonstrate the chaotic and often random forces and impulses. He also highlights contextual and historical features in play that lead to the change process. The study also demonstrates how, given agency and freedom, people in organizations innovate, improvise, and work together collectively to serve broader interests. The limited and precarious agency of people within broader state and organizational systems demonstrates how important changes are eclipsed as normative forces and institutionalized patterns that are mostly unnoticed shatter potential for innovation and change. The study also shows how change is constant; people in organizations strive for changes in the system, and the system pushes for other counteractive changes that reinforce conformity.

One of the major contributions of postmodern thought to change is to help emphasize complexity, ambiguity, continuous change, disorder, and nonlinear processes (Atkinson, 2002). Previous functionalist theories emphasize the maintenance of order and the linearity of change processes, which have become the norm when thinking about organizational processes (Boje & Dennehym, 1993).

While I have presented these paradigms as separate, some researchers are combining insights from the paradigms to enrich our understanding. Interaction between paradigms helps to create new insights into understanding change. In recent years, many scholars have suggested that organizational learning has grown into dominance as a way to explain and promote organizational change. Magala (2000) suggests that organizational learning's growth is a result of this theory being able to integrate aspects of a functionalist paradigm (ways to enable change or the creation of structures to promote planned change) and combine them with insights from interpretive paradigm (importance of individual meaning making, bottom-up nature of change, and agency of individuals). In the future, I believe that the ability to deepen our understanding of change will come from working across and integrating insights from paradigms.[7] At the end of the chapter, I present institutional theory as an example of the potential of multiparadigm analysis.

DIVERSITY AND TECHNOLOGY

Two contrasting examples of changes (diversity and technology) in higher education will help to demonstrate the importance of these paradigms for understanding and explaining change processes. Diversity and technology have advanced at
different paces and been met with different amounts of resistance; research paradigms offer some insight into why. Let me say more. Many institutions across
the country are trying to create an environment in which all students feel welcome and included, which is often termed a "diversity initiative." While hundreds of campuses are trying to create more inclusive campuses, change has
been slow and uneven. Many campus leaders have created strategic plans, altered
campus priorities, and developed structures and processes in order to institutionalize this important change. Although leaders have followed many of the principles outlined in the functionalist paradigm, they have had limited success (Kezar,
Eckel, Contreras-McGavin, & Quaye, 2008). In addition, campuses have faced
pressures to change campus operations and teach in new ways through the integration of technology. While there has certainly been some resistance to technology, there has been greater integration and penetration of technology within
colleges and university. Examining these two changes from the interpretive, critical, and postmodern paradigms can help us to better understand why the functionalist paradigm has been unable to explain the different success of these two
change initiatives.

From an interpretive perspective, we might find that diversity initiatives are
much more complex to comprehend than technology. Diversity can have many
different definitions; people have varying experience and background with diverse populations. Technology is open to less interpretation about its nature.
People's experience with technology can vary, but likely in more predictable ways
(it worked or did not work). There are also generally fewer values and less emotion associated with technology.[8] Diversity may be perceived symbolically as a
much more fundamental change to a campus than technology, which is an extension of an existing infrastructure. By talking to people and gaining these insights,
the difference in the nature of the change initiative becomes more apparent. In
addition, while many people do not understand technology, most understand the
need to integrate technology. As a result, the logic for diversity-oriented changes
likely needs more careful consideration and thought. Many individuals need to
undergo a learning process to fully appreciate diversity. Interpretive researchers
help describe the mental maps of people in relationship to diversity and technology so that the fears, concerns, and values related to these issues can be made

visible and potentially be overcome. The backgrounds of people on campus and local culture significantly shape the way people respond to these changes. Interpretive scholars show how campuses that lack a technology history or infrastructure and yet are more diverse may in fact struggle more with integrating technology than diversity.

From a critical perspective, diversity does not necessarily serve elites' interests; meanwhile, technology may serve elites' interest by speeding up work and increasing productivity. Technology initiatives tend to be led by campus leaders, while diversity initiatives are often first embraced by bottom-up leaders such as a student affairs staff member or student. Diversity initiatives might bring up an assortment of political interests that need to be negotiated in the change process. For instance, white alumni may not support diverse groups (Kezar, 2007). Because of various interests represented and competing agendas, traditional functionalist prediction and control often do not work well in understanding the change. Also, a critical analysis would illuminate the institutional racism that makes diversity initiatives face greater barriers than other change initiatives. Structures that support and privilege whites would be examined and brought to light. In addition to institutional racism, this lens would help to identify power structures within the system that support and/or resist technology and diversity and ideology they use to support their views. For example, the board of trustees, president, and key faculty and administrators may support technology but resist diversity because they believe it will take faculty and staff away from important priorities and will reduce quality on campus.

The postmodern paradigm can help us to see the diversity initiative as part of an ongoing struggle—not a separate change process. Inclusion and technology are long-term historical trends that, when placed in historical context, are easier to understand. Technology has typically been embraced by elites, and systems that support its integration are prevalent, whereas groups that differ from the majority have long struggled for representation, rights, and power. The deconstructivist techniques would make apparent the infrastructure in support of technology (such as the values pertaining to efficiency and quantification) and the absence of support and even barriers to diversity. One barrier to diversity that is embedded in academy is the notion of a singular knowledge/truth or belief in foundationalism rather than embracing multiple epistemologies or knowledge systems. The deconstructivist analysis would show how deeply embedded many of these assumptions are and how most campus organizational participants are unaware of any bias in their beliefs. This unawareness makes the inclusion process invisible to most and hard to investigate. Like interpretive scholars, postmodern researchers would also highlight how each campus has differential openness to diversity and technology, the differential based on local histories and conditions.

This contrast between diversity and technology helps to demonstrate what each paradigm has to offer in terms of better understanding change as a phenomenon. Functionalism has provided linear change roadmaps that do not capture the complex and subtle aspects of change. Furthermore, functionalism reinforces maintaining order and elites' interests by not questioning or deeply examining politics and power. Interpretivism, critical theory, and postmodernism scholars interrogate hidden and subtle process and explain the differential success of various change initiatives.

Schools of Thought Related to Change

Five schools of thought are often represented in the literature in higher education (and across various disciplines): evolutionary, teleological, social cognition, cultural, and political.[9] These various schools of thought (constellation of related theories) have guided the study of change to date. The evolutionary and teleological schools of thought have been used most often to study change and are part of the functionalist paradigm.[10] However, studies in higher education demonstrate that political, social cognition, and cultural schools of thought are helpful for understanding the change process in higher education and that they are underutilized. These three schools of thought represent the interpretive (social cognition and cultural), critical (political), and postmodern (some social cognition, political and cultural) paradigms. In this section, I review the main assumptions of these five schools of thought and provide an example of one or two theories to make the assumptions more concrete (see Kezar, 2001, for a fuller description of these schools).[11] A summary is provided in Table 7.2.

FUNCTIONALIST PARADIGM: EVOLUTIONARY THEORY

There are many evolutionary models and theories ranging from adaptation, resource dependence, self-organizing, contingency and systems theory, strategic choice, punctuated equilibrium, and population ecology. The main assumption underlying all these theories is that change is dependent on circumstances, situational variables, and the environment faced by each organization (Morgan, 1986). Social systems as diversified, interdependent, complex systems evolve over time naturally (Morgan, 1986). But evolution is basically deterministic; people have only a minor impact on the nature and direction of the change process (Hrebiniak & Joyce, 1985). These models focus on the inability of organizations

TABLE 7.2.
Five schools of thought related to change

	Evolutionary: functionalism	Teleological: functionalism	Political: critical and postmodern	Social cognition: interpretive and postmodern	Cultural: interpretive and postmodern
Why change occurs	External environment	Leaders; internal environment	Dialectical tension of values, norms, or patterns	Cognitive dissonance; appropriateness	Response to alterations in the human environment
Process of change	Adaptation; slow; gradual; nonintentional	Rational; linear; purposeful	First order followed by occasional second order; negotiation and power	Learning; altering paradigms or lens; interconnected and complex	Long term; slow; symbolic process; nonlinear; unpredictable
Outcomes of change	New structures and processes first order	New structures and organizing principles	New organizational ideology	New frame of mind	New culture
Key metaphor	Self-producing organism	Change master	Social movement	Brain	Social movement
Examples	Resource dependency; strategic choice; population ecology	Organizational development, strategic planning; reengineering; TQM	Empowerment; bargaining; political change; Marxist theory	Single and double loop learning; paradigm shifting; sensemaking	Interpretive strategy; paradigm shifting; processual change
Criticisms	Lack of human emphasis; deterministic quality	Overly rational and linear; inability to explain second-order change; plasticity of people	Deterministic; lack of environmental concerns; little guidance for leaders	Deemphasizes environment; overemphasizes ease of change; ignores values and emotions	Impractical to guide leaders; focus on universalistic culture; mostly untested
Benefits	Environmental emphasis; systems approach	Importance of change agents; management techniques and strategies	Change not always progressive; irrationality; role of power	Emphasizes socially constructed nature; emphasis on individuals; habits and attitudes as barriers	Context; irrationality; values and beliefs; complexity; multiple levels of change

to plan for and respond to change and on managing change as it occurs. Change happens because the environment demands that systems change in order to survive; however, some later models suggest adaptation can be proactive and anticipatory (Cameron, 1991).

The key concepts of evolutionary theory reflect biological systems such as systems, interactivity between the organization and environment, openness, homeostasis, and evolution (Birnbaum, 1991; Morgan, 1986). The concept of systems reflects how organizations are perceived as having interdependent and interrelated structures. Impacting one part of the structure has implications for other parts. Openness refers to the relationship between the environment and internal transformation and tends to characterize change as highly dependent on the external environment. Open systems exhibit interdependence between internal and external environments (Berdahl, 1991). The concept of homeostasis refers to self-regulation and ability to maintain a steady state by constantly seeking equilibrium between the system and environment (Sporn, 1999). Processes are inherently less important within the evolutionary models, and change is mostly unplanned; rather, change is an adaptive process (or based on selection). Over time, it has become commonplace to assume the environment affects the structure and culture of an organization, but this was a contested issues up until twenty years ago, as these models developed.

Resource dependence theory is a common evolutionary approach to understand change. Leaders make choices to adapt to their environment; the organization and environment have an interdependent relationship, and the focus is on transactions that occur as part of this relationship (Gumport & Pusser, 1999). This model differs from natural selection in its focus on leaders as active agents able to respond to and change the environment (Goodman, 1982). Resource dependence theory presupposes that organizations are not self-sustaining and need to rely on external resources; organizations are dependent on other organizations, leading to an interorganizational and political view (Gumport & Sporn, 1999; Sporn, 1999). Mergers are an example of organizational response to outside forces. This approach generated great interest, since it stresses a more interactive evolutionary approach whereby human agency can impact the change process.

A recent revival of evolutionary models of change is chaos theory applied to change, popularized by Margaret Wheatley in her book *Leadership and the New Science: Discovering Order in a Chaotic World* (1999). Change here is seen as inherent to biological systems; all organizations are constantly changing. The emphasis, as in earlier open systems models, is on being aware of solutions inherent in the system: feedback loops, resiliency, and self-organizing, allowing structures to emerge within the system. Chaos models suggest that planned changed is mostly irrelevant and unhelpful. Instead, organizations should organically respond. In other words, solutions emerge in real time as the problem unfolds with an understanding of existing resources and conditions. Planning ahead when conditions of the future are unknown is seen as unhelpful.

The contribution of this school of thought is illustrating the impact of the context and environment on change, since formerly organizations were conceptualized as self-contained entities (El-Khawas, 2000; Levy & Merry, 1986; Morgan, 1986). Assuming that organizations are systems advances thinking about change, identifying new reasons for and approaches to change. There are many empirical studies that illustrate the strength of evolutionary models with certain type of changes (Burnes, 1996; March, 1994; Phillips & Duran, 1992; Sporn, 1999). Also, examining how change is often unplanned and emerges from outside organizations was a novel insight.

FUNCTIONALIST: TELEOLOGICAL SCHOOL OF THOUGHT

The teleological school of thought focus on several related models and theories of change including planned change, scientific management, and rational approaches. Strategic planning, organizational development, and adaptive learning approaches are contained within the teleological umbrella (Van de Ven & Poole, 1995). Researchers within this school of thought assume that organizations are purposeful and adaptive (Cameron & Smart, 1998; Carnall, 1995; Peterson, 1995; Van de Ven & Poole, 1995). Change occurs because leaders, change agents, and others see the necessity of change (Eckel, Hill, Green, & Mallon, 1999; Peterson, 1995). According to teleological theories, the change process is rational and linear, as in evolutionary models, but individual managers are much more instrumental to the process (Carnall, 1995; Carr, Hard, & Trahant, 1996; Curry, 1992; Nevis, Lancourt, & Vassallo, 1996). Internal organizational features or decisions, rather than the external environment, motivate change. As was noted earlier, these models reflect intentionality. Key aspects of the change process include planning, assessment, incentives and rewards, stakeholder analysis and engagement, leadership, scanning, strategy, restructuring, and reengineering (Brill & Worth, 1997; Carnall, 1995; Huber & Glick, 1993; Keller, 1983, 1997; Peterson, Dill, & Mets, 1997). At the center of the process is the leader who aligns goals, sets expectation, models, communicates, engages, and rewards. Strategic choices and human creativity are highlighted (Brill & Worth, 1997). Goal formation, implementation, evaluation, and modification based on experience are an ongoing process. The metaphor for this model would be the changemaster, to use Rosabeth Kanter's (1983) image. The leader is the focus; this is a human model with the change agent at the center using rational, scientific management tools. This is, by far, the area with the most research and models (Kezar, 2001).

Perhaps the best-known model or theory within the teleological tradition is organizational development (Golembiewski, 1989; Goodman, 1982). Organizational development starts by diagnosing the problems within the organization (on an ongoing basis—so it is generative) and searching for solutions—change initiatives. Goals are set for addressing the change; yet there is a heavy cultural emphasis on values, attitudes, and organizational norms. Many group meetings are conducted to help the change initiative develop momentum and to overcome resistance (Carr et al., 1996). Organizations proceed through distinct stages, and it is the role of leaders to effectively manage the transition from one stable state to another (Golembiewski, 1989). Transition is a homogeneous, structured, step-by step process. Reengineering, another popular scientific management approach, focuses on modifying aspects of the organizational structure as the key to creating change (Guskin, 1996). The leader's role is to inventory and assess the organizational structures and to think about ways to structure differently. Mapping processes is a key management technique for helping to reengineer, which entails cross-functional teams meeting for extended periods of time to describe and chart a process from beginning to end with all divisions involved hearing the processes of other functional areas and identifying ways that processes can be altered collectively. Technological advancements, new products, retrained employees, cost cutting, and other changes are facilitated by leaders who create a technology office, provide a new human resources office, or reduce the number of offices in charge of a particular function.

The benefits of these models are significant, including the key role of leadership and change agents in the change process, the role of collaboration, staff development, the ability to forecast or identify the need for change, and helping organizations to survive and prosper in what otherwise would have been difficult times.

INTERPRETIVE AND POSTMODERN PARADIGMS: SOCIAL COGNITION SCHOOL OF THOUGHT

Social cognition models and theories have gained popularity in the past twenty years. A variety of models emphasize cognition, from sensemaking to institutionalism to imaginization (Morgan, 1986; Scott, 1995; Weick, 1995). These models tend to come from an interpretive view of organizations, but many social cognition theories are also conducted with goals of control and serving managers' or elites' interest.

Cognitive models highlight the role of learning and development with regard to change (Kezar, 2005). Studies of resistance to change illustrated the need for people to learn new approaches and examined how this might occur. New phenomena related to cognition/change were discovered, such as knowledge structures, paradigms, schemata, cybernetics, sensemaking, cognitive dissonance, cause maps, and interpretation, which are all key concepts in these theories (Albert & Whetten, 1985; Bushe & Shani, 1991; March, 1991; Morgan, 1986). Research on how the brain works discovered that knowledge is usually developed by building on past information called knowledge structures or schemata; theorists contemplated how proposals for institutional change could build on prior organizational knowledge (Hedberg, 1981). Learning also occurs as two pieces of conflictual information are brought together, often labeled as cognitive dissonance (Argyris, 1994).

Social cognition models examine how leaders shape the change process— through framing and interpretation—and how individuals within the organization interpret and make sense of change (Chaffee, 1983; Harris, 1996; Kenny, 2006). Change can be understood and enacted only through individuals (Harris, 1996; Martin, 1992). Part of the difficulty of creating change is realizing that people are interpreting their environment so differently (Cameron & Quinn, 1988). Also, facilitating change is sometimes explored as the process of allowing people to let go of the identity attached to past strategies and successes (Morgan, 1986). The reason for change in organizations is linked more to appropriateness and a reaction to cognitive dissonance (Collins, 1998). There is not necessarily an environmental necessity, developmental challenge, leader's vision, or dialectical or ideological tensions. Instead, people simply reach a point of cognitive dissonance when values and actions clash or something seems out of fashion and they decide to change. The outcome of change is a new frame of mind or worldview. The metaphor for this approach to change is usually the brain: complex, interrelated systems, mental models, and interpretation.

Argyris's (1982, 1994) and Schon's (1983) single and double loop learning theory reflects the social cognitive perspective and is a key concept in organizational learning and change. Single loop learning refers to retaining existing norms, goals, and structures and doing better the things currently done (Argyris, 1982, 1994). This is often associated with first-order change and an internal standard of performance (e.g., employees' views of quality). Double loop learning refers to the process in which existing norms, goals, and structures are reformulated to embark on innovative solutions. It is usually associated with second-order change and employs external standards of performance (e.g., state mandated regulations of quality). In double loop learning, people (or organizations) come to terms with problems or mismatches in the governing variables (beliefs) that guide their action (Hedberg, 1981). The common assumption that people are driven to fix inconsistencies between their thoughts and actions or between their actions and consequences was shown to be invalid in Argyris's and Schon's work. To acknowledge inconsistencies is seen as finding fault or mistakes in our actions, which people resist, particularly in hierarchical environments where blame is often assigned and people held accountable for mistakes. Argyris's and Schon's research identified how an environment of trust must be created in order to have double loop learning occur, since people are reluctant to examine inconsistencies for fear of blame or reprisal (Argyris, 1982).

The emphasis on different ways of viewing the organization spawned work by researchers such as Cohen and March (1974, 1991a, 1991b), Bolman and Deal (1991), Morgan (1986), and Weick (1995). Such research began examining organizations through an interpretive perspective, in which it is acknowledged that there are multiple views of organizational reality. These theorists suggest that leaders who view the organization through different lenses can accomplish change by examining issues through the logic of perspectives. Bolman and Deal (1991) suggest that leaders need to see change as a structural issue though the bureaucratic lens; as a training issue through the human resource lens; as a power issue through the political lens; and, lastly, as an issue of identity and meaning through the symbolic lens. Leaders create change by helping employees to view the organization through different lenses and by reframing issues so that different people can understand and enact the needed change.

One of the major contributions of these theories is a more phenomenological approach to the study of change, expanding vastly the interpersonal and human aspects of change. Individual meaning construction was mostly left out of theories that focused on systems, organizational dialectical tension, environment, life cycle of organizations, or scientific management structures (Magala, 2000). These other schools of thought discount the human element of individuals that make up the system; social cognition theories focus on how change is about individual learning and sensemaking. The realization that change often fails because individuals simply do not understand or comprehend the change at hand has been helpful.

INTERPRETIVE: CULTURAL THEORY

The cultural school of thought suggests that change occurs naturally as a response to alterations in the human environment; cultures are always changing

(Morgan, 1986; Peterson, 1997). The change process tends to be long term and slow. Change within an organization entails alteration of values, beliefs, myths, and rituals (Schein, 1985; Shaw & Lee, 1997). There is an emphasis on the symbolic nature of organizations, rather than the structural, human, or cognitive aspects emphasized within earlier theories (Simsek, 1997). History and traditions are important to understand, as they represent the collection of change processes over time. Cultural approaches share many assumptions with social cognition theories; change can be planned or unplanned, regressive or progressive, and can contain intended or unintended outcomes and actions (Smircich, 1983). Change tends to be nonlinear, irrational, nonpredictable, ongoing, and dynamic (Simsek & Louis, 1994; Smircich, 1983). Some cultural models focus on the leaders' ability to translate the change to individuals throughout the organizations through the use of symbolic actions, language, or metaphors as the key to creating change (Feldman, 1991; Gioia, Thomas, Clark, & Chittipeddi, 1996). If there is an external motivator, it tends to be legitimacy, which is the primary motivator within the cultural model, rather than profit or productivity, which exemplify the teleological and environmental models.

Cultural approaches tend to emphasize phenomenological and social constructivist approaches to the study of organizations. They also suggest the difficulty of deep change, realizing that radical change involves core modifications that are unlikely to occur without alterations to fundamental beliefs. One only needs to look at the research on cultural change within history, anthropology, or political science to realize it is often long term and nonsequential and appears to be unmanageable (Chermak, 1990).

Schein (1985) is perhaps one of the best-known theorists of cultural change. Culture is a collective and shared phenomenon; it is reflected at different levels through the organizational mission, through individual beliefs, and at a subconscious level. Change occurs as various aspects of the organizational culture are altered. For example, if the mission is realigned or new rituals or myths are developed, this can help move a particular change initiative forward. Schein's perspective on culture is reflected in the symbolic action approach in which managers create change by modifying organizational members' shared meaning— leaders re-create aspects of the symbolic system and culture. For example, leaders interpret events and history for people, creating ceremonies and events that alter culture, therefore creating change (Cameron, 1991).

The major contribution of cultural models to the change literature is the emphasis on context, values and beliefs, irrationality, the spirit or unconscious, and fluidity and complexity of organizations (Collins, 1998; Neumann, 1993). This set of theories reemphasizes the temporal dimension of change, especially the extremely lengthy process related to second-order change, that is not emphasized in social cognition and teleological models that had gained popularity over evolutionary and dialectical models in recent years (Collins, 1998). Making the relationship between institutional culture and change apparent is also a major contribution.

CRITICAL THEORY: POLITICAL OR DIALECTICAL THEORY

Dialectical models (Van de Ven and Poole, 1995) and the political metaphor of change (Morgan, 1986) are similar in their assumptions. The name dialectical refers directly to the Hegelian-Marxian perspective in which a pattern, value, ideal, or norm in an organization is always present with its polar opposite. Organizations pass through long periods of evolutionary change (as the dialectical interaction between the polar opposites occurs) and short periods of second-order or revolutionary change, when there is an impasse between the two perspectives (Gersick, 1991; Morgan, 1986). Organizations' polar opposite belief systems eventually clash, resulting in radical change and eventual synthesis or reconciliation of the competing belief systems. Conflict is seen as an inherent attribute of human interaction. The outcome of change is a modified organizational ideology or identity.

Change processes are seen as predominantly bargaining, consciousness raising, persuasion, influence and power, and social movements (Bolman & Deal, 1991; Childers, 1981; Gumport, 1993; Rhoades, 1995). Leaders are key within any social movement and are a central part of these models. Yet collective action is usually the focus. Progress and rationality are not necessarily part of this theory of change; dialectical conflict does not necessarily produce a better organization. Organizations are perceived as political entities in which dominant coalitions manipulate their power in order to preserve the status quo and maintain their privilege (Baldridge, 1971; Hearn, 1996).

Dialectical models do not assume that everyone is involved; instead, they emphasize that inactivity is quite prevalent (Baldridge, Curtis, Ecker, & Riley, 1977; Conrad, 1978). Similar to the fact that few people vote, few people participate in governance and are interested in change. People who create change can become involved in interest groups, flowing in and out. When resources are plentiful, few people worry about changes or come into conflict. It is when resource constraints and pending changes might impact people (or an inability to create changes because of lack of resources) that people mobilize. These models focus on human motivation and needs; intuition is just as important to change as facts and figures that are emphasized within other models (Berquist, 1992; Lindquist, 1978). Social interaction is more critical than environmental scanning, planning, or assessing the life cycle of the organization. The metaphor for understanding the dialectical school of thought is a social movement (Carlson-Dakes & Sanders, 1998).

Kotter (1985) provides an analysis of the skills needed to create political change: (1) agenda setting; (2) networking and forming coalitions; and (3) bargaining and negotiation. Setting an agenda is different than establishing a vision, a typical process within teleological models that is usually leader derived. Instead, setting an agenda involves listening to people throughout the organization and including their interests; agendas are responsive to stakeholder concerns (Bolman & Deal, 1991). Networking is the next step for creating change. In order to build coalitions, change agents need to identify key people to facilitate change as well as individuals who will resist the change. One of the primary purposes of networking is developing relationships with key people who can overcome resistance so that they can be used to influence people when necessary (Hearn, 1996). Change agents must also develop a power base by succeeding at certain efforts and become aligned with other powerful individuals. Once the leader has an agenda, network, coalitions, and power base, the change agent is ready to bargain and negotiate in order to create change. Empowerment approaches to change represent an even more positive spin on the political approach to creating change. In these approaches, change agents are encouraged to examine whether the change has mutually beneficial consequences for all involved parties, whether the change is moral, and whether it demonstrates caring for employees (Bolman & Deal, 1991). A few studies have illustrated that empowerment models are instrumental in facilitating change (Astin & Leland, 1991; Bensimon & Neumann, 1993).

A major benefit of these models is their departure from the focus on rationality and linearity (Gimport, 1993; Gumport, & Pusser, 1995). Evolutionary and teleological models emphasize that change is rational and progressive, leading toward something better. Many theorists could point to changes that were not for the good of organizations and often noted the erratic, political nature of organizational change (Morgan, 1986). This school of thought also shows the value-laden aspect of change and highlights interests at play. This model provides explanation for regressive change and highlights irrationality. The more popular dialectical models are those that emphasize social movements and leaders' role because they provide a strong and hopeful analogy for change.

Using Multiple Theories to Understand
Higher Education Change

Each paradigm, theory, or school of thought can help build a more complex picture of change. What you should take away from this chapter is that a complex understanding of change takes into account the external environment, adaptation, people, planning, rewards, learning, development and training, mental models, image, politics, power, agenda setting, history, values, and culture. Furthermore, change is not always intentional, rational, or progressive; nor is change always random, regressive, and uncontrollable. Change is difficult to achieve because people tend to analyze organizational situations from a single perspective, even though we know that complex social and organizational phenomena like change typically involve various organizational subsystems including human relations, organizational structures, politics, and resources. Change involves altering organizational culture, and the process of change is also shaped by organizational culture. Cultural elements of organizations include mission, tradition, and history (Birnbaum, 1991; Kezar, 2001). Multiframe thinking (which helps people approach analysis using all these dimensions) is well summarized in a book by Bolman and Deal (1991). Studies continuously demonstrate that organizational participants tend to focus on or approach change from a single vantage point such as mapping systems of power and navigating politics or setting up new organizational structures and restructuring. One of the limitations to enacting and understanding change tends to be the mind-set from which people approach change.

In this section, I want to highlight some concepts that have been identified as important to change in the higher education setting from these schools of thought. I will use an example from higher education—service learning—that was successful. Service learning is a pedagogical innovation that incorporates experiential learning and reflection into teaching and learning practices. It emerged from the work of John Dewey in the 1930s and reemerged in the 1970s briefly and then became a successful innovation in the 1990s. Service learning leaders took a multifaceted and complex approach to change.[12] In the early 1990s, approximately 200 campuses in the country offered service learning courses, and service learning was mostly unknown. By 2008, close to 2,500 campuses across the country offered service learning courses, and currently it is one of the best-known pedagogical strategies. It is offered across every institutional type and discipline.

I propose that the service learning movement leaders approached the change process understanding the dynamics of system/institutional change processes. Service learning leaders used multiframe thinking, developed sensemaking, adopted politics, created a clear vision, and used external pressures and other strategies that are often not utilized by postsecondary leaders who take a more rational, simplistic, and linear approach to change. While there is not space to review all the various strategies and techniques they used to move the service learning movement forward, a few are showcased that cut across the various schools of thought and paradigms.

EVOLUTIONARY CONCEPTS: EXTERNAL LEVERS WITHIN THE SECTOR/SYSTEM

The evolutionary school of thought suggests that external pressure can deeply affect change within a system. In particular, government, funders such as foundations, disciplinary societies, and existing intermediary organizations that influence the system (such as accreditors, federal and state agencies, community organizations) are important facilitators of change. External levers also contribute to sustainability of change by making the change a part of the larger system. The service learning leaders worked from the outside in creating pressure to make service learning part of campus activities. For example, service learning is now part of government legislation and funding (Americorps legislation), foundation priorities, accreditation standards, disciplinary societies dialogue, a new Carnegie classification—the engaged campus, and state and community funding systems. Each part of the system was capitalized on to enable and support change.

TELEOLOGICAL CONCEPTS: VISION AND RATIONALE

One of the reasons for the success of the service learning movement is that the leaders made a clear case for the importance of academic service learning to democratic understanding, citizenship, and experiential learning—all priorities on most campuses. They demonstrated the academic rationale and emphasized how it helped meet the institutional learning goals. Movement leaders defined the difference between service learning and volunteer opportunities. They addressed the feedback that it was a better fit for certain disciplines and described, through a series of handbooks, how service learning could be incorporated into any discipline from chemistry and humanities to social sciences. The clear vision of how service learning fit into institutional goals and mission, the solid academic rationale, and the tangibility of the concept through the handbooks made the possibility for change more real. Movement leaders were aware of the need for a clear vision with simple and exacting rationale.

SOCIAL COGNITION CONCEPTS: SENSEMAKING AND SYSTEMS FOR LEARNING

A variety of studies (Eckel & Kezar, 2003a, 2003b; Kezar & Eckel, 2002b; Gioia & Thomas, 1996; Schon, 1983; Weick, 1995) demonstrate that one of the main reasons for changes not to occur is that people fundamentally do not understand the proposed change and need to undergo a learning process in order to successfully enact the change. Service learning leaders made sure to create concept papers about the nature of and value of service learning at the national level that could be shared locally. They organized dialogues and national forums that could inform on-campuses dialogues. They encouraged service learning centers to host camps, retreats, and workshops and have "converted" faculty talk about the value of service learning in relation to specific disciplinary norms—in a language more understandable to faculty from varying disciplines. Some workshops would be hosted for faculty in the humanities or sciences—separately. National speakers went around to campuses across the country to help spread the word about service learning helping people truly understand this pedagogy by explaining it philosophically, underscoring the rationale, value, and potential.

CULTURAL CONCEPTS: CULTURALLY RESPONSIVE PRINCIPLES

Understanding the institution's history is part of developing an effective change strategy, which is cognizant of previous change initiatives, campus politics, and past leadership (Kezar & Eckel, 2002b). Developed strategies that take into account current campus climate and culture are much more likely to resonate with existing faculty and staff and to be embraced more readily with fewer barriers and resistance. Sensemaking is further facilitated when the change is contextualized. Service learning leaders were aware of the differences by institutional type and developed unique strategies for research universities and community colleges, appealing to different values, reward systems, and goals. They enlisted a national association that worked with different sectors to create guidelines and principles for service learning that served the mission and goals of these institutions. They also challenged the underlying values of the academy that work against service learning such as scholars should be separate from society, the value of abstract and pure research over engaged research, and the importance of a value-neutral scholar offering other perspectives for understanding academic work.

DIALECTICAL CONCEPTS: POLITICS AND USING POLITICAL SKILLS

Postsecondary institutions are extremely political environments, and ignoring politics is likely to lead to an unsuccessful change process. Service learning leaders used political strategies to forward their goals. For example, leaders within Campus Compact were aware that if college presidents, especially of elite institutions like University of Michigan, made a statement about the importance of service learning and campus-community partnerships this would help to create buy-in. Leaders also argued that service learning centers should be housed in academic affairs rather than student affairs, in order to underscore the essential role of faculty, curriculum, and pedagogy. This change would also signal service learning work as academically credible. They established state and regional networks through Campus Compact to support and provide legitimacy for individual leaders on college campuses.

While service learning is a successful example of change, many others changes have not succeeded or been institutionalized. As demonstrated in the section on paradigms, sometimes changes are not integrated because they challenge the existing order. However, service learning does disrupt the status quo (passive teaching techniques such as lecture), power structures (student affairs staff often involved with service learning and traditionally faculty lay claim for the curriculum), and certain interests on campus (supports interdisciplinary work). I argue that change can occur if the right levers, strategies, and approaches are used, even if it is against the status quo.

Conclusion

Change, is indeed, an ever constant part of human experience, one that has proven hard to understand, predict, or navigate. Change within colleges and universities, as has been alluded to throughout the chapter, is complex and much more difficult to understand than most of the individual theories or schools of thought that exist. Only by becoming familiar with various paradigms, schools of thought, and theories can we come close to capturing a glimpse of this elusive process. Functionalist theories, the most common perspective, offer ways to view organizations as predictable entities and focus on improving the efficiency and effectiveness of the change process by carefully documenting successful change processes and including an increasing number of factors that may impact the process. This chapter has demonstrated the importance of the interpretive paradigm because it helps identify the role of perspectives, beliefs, culture, language, and meaning to the change process. Critical theory examines the role of power, interests, and conflict in change processes, often overlooked and essential concepts. And lastly, postmodernism scholars reframe change as ongoing and see the episodic view of change as a way to control and maintain institutional norms. The newer change theories (e.g., cultural, political) that have emerged reflect these new paradigms, highlighting the importance of new phenomena to understand change such as learning, culture, sensemaking, empowerment/agency, cognitive dissonance, ideology, self-organizing, and strategic choice.

But change will likely remain a difficult area of study for researchers and of practice for higher education professionals. Researchers and practitioners are best ready for the challenge if they open themselves up to a broad assortment of assumptions and theories. The more paradigms and perspectives brought to bear, the richer the analysis.

NOTES

1. In this chapter, I do not provide detailed explanations of these paradigms but focus specifically on how they frame studies of organizational change. For general discussions of research paradigms, please see Crotty 1998.

2. See the following texts for summaries or examples of the functionalist paradigm of change: Collins 1998, Kotter 1985, 1996.

3. While many studies of change conducted within a functionalist paradigm reflect a managerial bias, this is not inherent in the paradigm. However, the researchers conducting studies using this perspective tended to study organizations from the perspective of advancing managerial interests. There is often an overlap between functionalism and a managerial perspective.

4. Phenomenology is an interviewing methodological tradition that emphasizes capturing the lived experience of people and essences of experience through in-depth interviewing and researcher reflection.

5. One set of literature (epoch postmodernism) describes how in a globalized and postmodern environment that is volatile and competitive change is much more pressing and necessary (Kenny, 2006). Within this literature base the only reference to postmodernism is how the world is more interconnected, technology more prevalent, and the organizational environment more complex (Clegg, 1989). However, these studies tend to utilize functionalist approaches to developing strategic and planned processes for managing this complexity within the postmodern environment.

6. This book actually combines critical and postmodern paradigms. Here I emphasize the postmodern elements of the study.

7. Some researchers suggest that paradigms are generally commensurable but that some assumptions do conflict and contradict each other (Denzin & Lincoln, 2000). Other researchers tend to see paradigms as incompatible (see Crotty, 1998.)

8. While I recognize this is a debatable view, for the purposes of this section, I am implying that interviews with people might identify this trend—not that this is an empirical truth or fact.

9. Schools of thought are constellations of related theories and models. Van de Ven

and Poole (1995) identified four schools of thought to organize the vast amount of literature on change. Kezar (2001) built on their schools of thought, creating six broad areas, and applied these schools of thought in higher education.

10. Even these schools of thought have stark contrasts in assumptions, although they are within the same paradigm. These two schools of thought tend to represent an opposition of materialism and idealism and dichotomies including social/technical, intentional/ deterministic, and subjective/ objective, with planned change reflecting the first set of characteristics in these series of dichotomies and adaptive change reflecting the second set of aspects of the dichotomies. Two authors note that there is "a comfort in the fact that the two schools criticize each other leading to improvements and achieving a kind of balance" (Czarniawska & Sevon, 1996, p. 14).

11. This section draws largely on Kezar 2001.

12. Although I cannot prove that this change process was successful because movement leaders used a multifaceted and complex approach (which am recommending to readers) rather than following one narrow school of thought. Causation is not possible to isolate.

REFERENCES

Albert, S., & Whetten, D. (1985). Organizational identity. *Research in Organizational Behavior, 7,* 263–295.

Andrews, J., Cameron, H., & Harris, M. (2008). All change? Managers' experience of organizational change in theory and practice. *Journal of Organizational Change Management, 21*(3), 300–314.

Antonacopoulou, E. P., & Gabriel, Y. (2001). Emotion, learning and organizational change: Towards and integration of psychoanalytic and other perspectives. *Journal of Organizational Change Management, 14*(5), 435–451.

Argyris, C. (1982). How learning and reasoning processes affect organizational change. In P. S. Goodman (Ed.), *Change in organizations.* San Francisco: Jossey-Bass.

Argyris, C. (1994) *On organizational learning.* Oxford: Blackwell.

Astin, H. S., & Leland, C. (1991). *Women of influence, women of vision: A cross generational study of leaders and social change.* San Francisco: Jossey-Bass.

Atkinson, E. (2002). The responsible anarchist: Postmodernism and social change. *British Journal of Sociology of Education, 23*(1), 73–87.

Aune, B. P. (1995). The human dimension of organizational change. *Review of Higher Education, 18*(2), 149–173.

Baldridge, J. V. (1971). *Power and conflict in the university.* New York: Wiley.

Baldridge, J. V., Curtis, D. V., Ecker, G. P., & Riley, G. L. (1977). Alternative models of governance in higher education. In G. L. Riley & J. V. Baldridge (Eds.), *Governing academic organizations* (pp. 2–25). Berkley, CA: McCutchan.

Baldridge, J. V., & Deal, T. E. (1983). The basics of change in educational organizations. In J. V. Baldridge, T. E. Deal, & C. Ingols (Eds.), *The dynamics of organizational change in education* (pp. 191–210). Berkley, CA: McCutchan.

Beeson, I., & Davis, C. (2000). Emergence and accomplishment in organizational change. *Journal of Organizational Change Management, 13*(2), 178–189.

Benjamin, M. (1996). *Cultural diversity, educational equity and the transformation of higher education.* Westport, CT: Greenwood.

Bensimon, E., & Neumann, A. (1993). *Redesigning collegiate leadership: Teams and teamwork in higher education.* Baltimore: Johns Hopkins University Press.

Berdahl, R. O. (1991). Shared governance and external constraints. In M. W. Peterson, E. E. Chaffee, & T. H. White (Eds.), *Organization and governance in higher education* (4th ed.). Needham Heights, MA: Ginn Press.

Berquist, W. (1992). *The four cultures of the academy: Insights and strategies for improving leadership in collegiate organizations.* San Francisco: Jossey-Bass.

Berquist, W. (1993). *The postmodern organization: Mastering the arts of irreversible change.* Dubuque, IA: Kendall/Hunt.

Berquist, W. (1998). The postmodern challenge: Changing our community colleges. In J. S. Levine (Ed.), *Organizational change in the community college: A ripple or a sea of change.* San Francisco: Jossey-Bass.

Berman, H., Ford-Gilboe, M., & Campell, J. (1998). Combining stories and numbers: A methodologic approach for a critical nursing science. *Advances in Nursing Science, 21*(1), 1–15.

Berquist, W. (2007). *The six cultures of the academy.* San Francisco: Jossey-Bass.

Birnbaum, R. (1991). *How colleges work: The cybernetics of academic organization and leadership.* San Francisco: Jossey-Bass.

Boje, D., & Dennehym, R. (1993). *Managing in the postmodern world: America's revolution against exploitation.* Dubuque, IA: Kendall/Hunt.

Boje, D., Gephart, R., & Thatchenkery, T. (Eds.). (1996). *Postmodern management and organization theory.* Thousand Oaks, CA: Sage.

Bolman, L. G., & Deal, T. E. (1991). *Reframing organizations: Artistry, choice, and leadership.* San Francisco: Jossey-Bass.

Boyce, M. E. (1996). Organizational story and storytelling: A critical review. *Journal of Organizational Change Management, 9*(5), 5–26.

Boyce, M. E. (2003). Organizational learning is essential to achieving and sustaining change in higher education. *Innovative Higher Education, 28*(2), 119–135.

Brill, P. L., & Worth, R. (1997). *The four levers of corporate change.* New York: American Management Association.

Brown, T. H. (2006). Beyond constructivism: Navigationism in the knowledge era. *On the Horizon, 14*(3), 108–120.

Burke, W. (1995). Organizational change: What we know, what we need to know. *Journal of Management Inquiry, 4*(2),158–171.

Burnes, B. (1996). *Managing change: A strategic approach to organizational dynamics.* London: Pitman Publishing.

Bushe, G., & Shani, A. (1991). Parallel learning structure: Increasing innovation in bureaucracies. Reading, MA: Addison-Wesley.

Cameron, K. S. (1991). Organizational adaptation and higher education. In M. W. Peterson, E. E. Chaffee, & T. H. White (Eds.), *Organization and governance in higher education* (4th ed., pp. 284–299). Needham Heights, MA: Ginn Press.

Cameron, K., & Quinn, R. (1988). Organizational paradox and transformation. In K. Cameron & R. Quinn (Eds.), *Paradox and transformation*. New York: Bellinger.

Cameron, K. S., & Smart, J. (1998). Maintaining effectiveness amid downsizing and decline in institutions of higher education. *Research in Higher Education, 39*(1), 65–86.

Carlson-Dakes, C., & Sanders, K. (1998). *A movement approach to organizational change: Understanding the influences of a collaborative faculty development program*. Paper presented at the annual meeting of the Association for the Study of Higher Education, Miami, Florida. ED427591.

Carnall, C. A. (1995). *Managing change in organizations* (2nd ed.). London: Prentice Hall.

Carnoy, M., & Rhoten, D. (2002). What does globalization mean for educational change? A comparative approach. *Comparative Education Review, 46*(1), 1–6.

Caroli, E., & Van Reenen, J. (2001). Skill-biased organizational change? Evidence from a panel of British and French establishments. *Quarterly Journal of Economics, 116*, 1449–1492.

Carr, D., Hard, K., & Trahant, W. (1996). *Managing the change process: A field book for change agents, consultants, team leaders, and reengineering managers*. New York: McGraw-Hill.

Chaffee, E. (1983). Three models of strategy. *Academy of Management Review, 10*(1), 89–98.

Chermak, G. L. D. (1990). Cultural dynamics: Principles to guide change in higher education. *CUPA Journal, 41*(3), 25–27.

Childers, M. E. (1981). What is political about bureaucratic-collegial decision-making? *Review of Higher Education, 5*(1), 25–45.

Clark, B. R. (1998). *Creating entrepreneurial universities: Organizational pathways of transformation*. Oxford: Pergamon Press.

Clegg, S. (1989). *Frameworks of power*. London: Sage.

Cohen, M. D., & March, J. G. (1974). *Leadership and ambiguity: The American college president*. Boston: Harvard Business School Press.

Cohen, M. D., & March, J. G. (1991a). Leadership in an organized anarchy. In M. W. Peterson, E. E. Chaffee, & T. H. White (Eds.), *Organization and governance in higher education* (4th ed., pp. 195–207). Needham Heights, MA: Ginn Press.

Cohen, M. D., & March, J. G. (1991b). The processes of choice. In M. W. Peterson, E. E. Chaffee, & T. H. White (Eds.), *Organization and governance in higher education* (4th ed.). Needham Heights, MA: Ginn Press.

Collins, D. (1998). *Organizational change: Sociological perspectives*. London: Routledge.

Conrad, C. F. (1978). A grounded theory of academic change. *Sociology of Education, 51*, 101–112.

Crossan, M., Lane, H., White, R. E., & Klus, L. (1996). The improvising organization: Where planning meets opportunity. *Organizational Dynamics, 24*, 20–35.

Crotty, M. (1998). *The foundations of social science research*. Thousand Oaks, CA: Sage.

Curry, Barbara K. (1992). *Instituting enduring innovations: Achieving continuity of change in higher education*. ASHE-ERIC Higher Education Report No. 7. Washington, DC: George Washington University, School of Education and Human Development.

Czarniawska, B., & Sevon, G. (1996). *Translating organizational change*. Berlin: Walter de Gruyter & Co.

Dawson, P. (1994). *Organizational change: A procedural approach*. London: Paul Chapman Publishing.

Dehler, G. E., Welsh, M. A., & Lewis, M. W. (2001). Critical pedagogy in the "new paradigm." *Management Learning, 32*(4), 493–511.

Denzin, N. K., & Lincoln, Y.S. (2000). Paradigmatic controversies, contradictions, and emerging confluences. In N. K. Denzin & Y. S. Lincoln (eds.), *Handbook of qualitative research* (pp. 163–189). Thousand Oaks, CA: Sage.

DePaula, R. (2004). Lost in translation: A critical analysis of actors, artifacts, agendas, and arenas in participatory design. In *Artful integration: Interweaving media, materials and practices*, Vol. 1. New York: ACM.

Derrida, J. (1976). *Of grammatology* (Gayatri Chakravorty Spivak, Trans.). Baltimore: Johns Hopkins University Press.

Dill, D. D. (1982). The management of academic culture: Notes on the management of meaning and social integration. *Higher Education, 11*, 303–320.

Eckel, P., Hill, B., Green, M., & Mallon, B. (1999). *Taking charge of change: A primer for colleges and universities*. On Change Occasional Paper, No. 3. Washington, DC: American Council on Education.

Eckel, P., & Kezar, A. (2003a). Strategies for making new institutional sense: Key ingredients to higher education transformation. *Higher Education Policy, 16*(1), 39–53.

Eckel, P., & Kezar, A. (2003b). *Taking the reins: Institutional transformation in higher education*. Phoenix, AZ: ACE-ORYX Press.

El-Khawas, E. (2000). The impetus for organisational change: An exploration. *Tertiary Education and Management, 6*, 37–46.

Feldman, M. S. (1991). The meanings of ambiguity: Learning from stories and metaphors. In P. J. Frost, L. F. Moore, M. R. Louis, C. C. Lundberg, & J. Martin (Eds.), *Reframing organizational culture* (pp. 145–156). Newbury Park, CA: Sage.

Ferlie, E. (1997). Large-scale organizational and managerial change in healthcare: A review of the literature. *Journal of Health Services Research and Policy, 2*(3), 180–189.

Finstad, N. (1998). The rhetoric of organizational change. *Human Relations, 51*(6), 717–739.

Foucault, M. (1975). *Discipline and punish: The birth of the prison*. New York: Random House.

Gergen, K. J., & Thatchenkery, T. J. (2004). Organization science as social construction: Postmodern potentials. *Journal of Applied Behavioral Science, 40*(2), 228–249.

Gersick, C. J. G. (1991). Revolutionary change theories: A multilevel exploration of the punctuated equilibrium paradigm. *Academy of Management Review, 16*(1), 10–36.

Gioia, D. A., Schultz, M., & Corley, K. G. (2000). Organizational identity, image, and adaptive instability. *Academy of Management Journal, 25*(1), 63–81.

Gioia, D. A., & Thomas, J. B. (1996). Identity, image, and issue interpretation: Sensemaking during strategic change in academia. *Administrative Science Quarterly, 41*, 370–403.

Gioia, D. A., Thomas, J. B., Clark, S. M., & Chittipeddi, K. (1996). Symbolism and strategic change in academia: The dynamics of sensemaking and influence. In J. R. Meindl, C. Stubbart, & J. F. Poroc (Eds.), *Cognition in groups and organizations*. London: Sage.

Golembiewski, R. T. (1989). *Ironies in organizational development*. London: Transaction Publishers.

Goodman, P. S. (1982). *Change in organizations: New perspectives on theory, research and practice*. San Francisco: Jossey-Bass.

Grubbs, J. A. (2000). Cultural imperialism: A critical theory of interorganizational change. *Journal of Organizational Change Management, 13*(3), 221–234.

Gumport, P. (1993). Contested terrain of academic program reduction. *Journal of Higher Education, 64*(3), 283–311.

Gumport, P. J., & Pusser, B. (1995). A case of bureaucratic accretion: Context and consequences. *Journal of Higher Education, 66*(5), 493–520.

Gumport, P. J., & Pusser, B. (1999). University restructuring: The role of economic and political contexts. In J. C. Smart (Ed.), *Higher education: Handbook of theory and research,* Vol. 14 (pp. 146–200). New York: Agathon Press.

Gumport, P. J., & Sporn, B. (1999). Institutional adaptation: Demands for management reform and university administration. In J. C. Smart (Ed.), *Higher education: Handbook of theory and research,* Vol. 14 (pp. 103–145). New York: Agathon Press.

Guskin, A. (1996). Facing the future: The change process in restructuring universities. *Change, 28*(4), 27–37.

Hancock, P., & Tyler, M. (2001). *Work, postmodernism, and organization.* Thousand Oaks, CA: Sage.

Harris, S. G. (1996). Organizational culture and individual sensemaking: A schema-based perspective. In J. R. Meindl, C. Stubbart, & J. F. Poroc (Eds.), *Cognition in groups and organizations.* London: Sage.

Hassard, J., & Parker, M. (Eds.) (1993). *Postmodernism and organizations.* London: Sage.

Hearn, J. C. (1996). Transforming U.S. higher education: An organizational perspective. *Innovative Higher Education, 21*(2), 141–54. EJ534330.

Hedberg, B. (1981). How organizations learn and unlearn. In P. C. Nystrom & W. H. Starbuck (Eds.), *Handbook of organizational design* (pp. 3–27). New York: Oxford University Press.

Heracleous, L. (2002). The contribution of a discursive view to understanding and managing organizational change. *Strategic Change, 11*(5), 253–261.

Heracleous, L., & Barrett, M. (2001). Organizational change as discourse: Communicative actions and deep structures in the context of its implementation. *Academy of Management Journal, 44*(4), 755–778.

Hrebiniak, L. G., & Joyce, W. F. (1985). Organizational adaptation: Strategic choice and environmental determinism. *Administrative Science Quarterly, 30,* 336–349.

Huber, G. P., & Glick, W. H. (1993). *Organizational change and redesign: Ideas and insights for improving performance.* New York: Oxford University Press.

Kanter. R. (1983). *The change masters.* New York: Simon and Schuster.

Keller, G. (1983) Shaping an academic strategy. In G. Keller (Ed.), *Academic strategy: The management revolution in American higher education* (pp. 40–55). Baltimore: Johns Hopkins University Press.

Keller, G. (1997). Examining what works in strategic planning. In M. Peterson, D. Dill, & L. Mets (Eds.), *Planning and management for a changing environment.* San Francisco: Jossey-Bass.

Kelly, M. (1998). Enabling metaphors of innovation and change. In J. Meyerson (Ed.), *New thinking on higher education* (pp. 63–80). Bolton, MA: Anker.

Kenny, J. (2006). Strategy and the learning organization: A maturity model for the formation of strategy. *Learning Organization, 13*(4), 353–368.

Kezar, A. (2001). *Understanding and facilitating organizational change in the 21st Century: Recent research and conceptualizations.* ASHE-ERIC Higher Education Report. Washington, DC: George Washington University, School of Education and Human Development.

Kezar, A. (Ed.). (2005). *Higher education as a learning organization: Promising concepts and approaches.* New Directions for Higher Education, No. 131/Fall. San Francisco: Jossey-Bass.

Kezar, A. (2007). Tools for a time and place: Phased leadership strategies for advancing campus diversity. *Review of Higher Education, 30*(4), 413–439.

Kezar, A., Carducci, R., & Contreras-McGavin, M. (2006). *Rethinking the "l" word in leadership: The revolution of research on leadership.* San Francisco: Jossey-Bass.

Kezar, A., & Eckel, P. (2002a). The effect of institutional culture on change strategies in higher education: Universal principles or culturally responsive concepts? *Journal of Higher Education, 73*(4), 435–460.

Kezar, A., & Eckel, P. (2002b). Examining the institutional transformation process: The importance of sensemaking, inter-related strategies and balance. *Research in Higher Education, 43*(4), 295–328.

Kezar, A., Eckel, P., Contreras-McGavin, M., & Quaye, S. (2008). Creating a web of support: An important leadership strategy for advancing campus diversity. *Higher Education, 55*(1), 69–92.

Kezar, A., & Lester, J. (2009). Supporting faculty grassroots leadership. *Research in Higher Education, 50*(7), 715 740.

Kezar, A., & Lester, J. (2011). *Enhancing campus capacity for leadership: An examination of grassroots leaders.* Stanford, CA: Stanford University Press.

Kondakci, Y. (1998). *Continuous change in higher education: A case study on the structuredness of change.* Unpublished manuscript.

Kotter, J. (1985). *Power and influence: Beyond formal authority.* New York: Free Press.

Kotter, J. (1996). *Leading change.* Boston: Harvard Business School Press.

Levin, J. S. (1998). Organizational change and the community college. In J. S. Levine (Ed.), *Organizational change in the community college: A ripple or a sea of change* (pp. 1–15). San Francisco: Jossey-Bass.

Levy, A., & Merry, U. (1986). *Organizational transformation: Approaches, strategies, theories.* New York: Praeger.

Lindquist, J. (1978). *Strategies of change.* Washington, DC: Council for Independent Colleges.

Linstead, S., Brewis, J., & Linstead, A. (2005). Gender in change: Gendering change. *Journal of Organizational Change Management, 18*(6), 542–560.

Lueddeke, G. R. (1999). Toward a constructivist framework for guiding change and innovation in higher education. *Journal of Higher Education, 70*(3), 235–260.

Luscher, L. S., Lewis, M. W., & Ingram, A. (2006). The social construction of organizational change paradoxes. *Journal of Organizational Change Management, 19*(4), 491–502.

Macdonald, J. (1997). *Calling a halt to mindless change: A plea for commonsense management.* New York: American Management Association.

Magala, S. (2000). Critical complexities (from marginal paradigms to learning networks). *Journal of Organizational Change Management, 13*(4), 312–333.

March, J. G. (1991) Exploration and exploitation in organizational learning. *Organizational Science, 2*(1), 71–87.

March, J. G. (1994) The evolution of evolution. In J. A. C. Baum & J. V. Singh (Eds.), *Evolutionary dynamics of organizations* (pp. 110–127). New York: Cambridge University Press.

Martin, J. (1992). *Cultures in organizations: Three perspectives.* New York: Oxford University Press.

McWilliam, C. L., & Ward-Griffin, C. (2006). Implementing organizational change in health and social services. *Journal of Organizational Change Management, 19*(2), 119–135.

Meyerson, D. (2003). *Tempered radicals.* Cambridge, MA: Harvard Business School Press.

Morely, L. (1997). Change and equity in higher education. *British Journal of Sociology of Eduation, 18*(2), 321–242.

Morgan, G. (1986). *Images of organization.* Newbury Park, CA: Sage.

Morgan, G. (1997). *Imaginization.* San Francisco: Berrett-Koehler.

Neumann, A. (1993). College planning: A cultural perspective. *Journal of Higher Education Management, 8*(2), 31–41.

Neumann, A. (1995). On the making of hard and good times: The social construction of resource stress. *Journal of Higher Education, 66,* 3–31.

Nevis, E. C., Lancourt, J., & Vassallo, H. G. (1996) *Intentional revolutions: A seven-point strategy for transforming organizations.* San Francisco: Jossey-Bass.

Palmer, I., & Dunford, R. (1996). Conflicting uses of metaphors: Reconceptualizing their use in the field of organizational change. *Academy of Management Review, 21*(3), 691–717.

Pearce, C., & Conger, J. (2003). *Shared leadership.* Thousand Oaks, CA: Sage.

Peterson, M. (1995). Images of university structure, governance, and leadership: Adaptive strategies for the new environment. In D. Dill & B. Sporn (Eds.), *Emerging patterns of social demand and university reform: Through a glass darkly* (pp. 142–161). Oxford: Pergamon Press.

Peterson, M. (1997). Using contextual planning to transform institutions. In M. Peterson, D. Dill, & L. Mets (Eds.), *Planning and management for a changing environment* (pp. 127–157). San Francisco: Jossey-Bass.

Peterson, M. W., Dill, D. D., & Mets, L. A. (1997). *Planning and management for a changing environment: A handbook on redesigning postsecondary institutions.* San Francisco: Jossey-Bass.

Pettigrew, A. (1987). Context and action in the transformation of the firm. *Journal of Management Studies, 24*(6), 649–670.

Phillips, R., & Duran, C. (1992). Effecting strategic change: Biological analogues and emerging organizational structures. In R. L. Phillips & J. G. Hunt (Eds.), *Strategic leadership: A multiorganizational-level perspective* (pp. 195–216). Westport, CT: Quorum Books.

Quattrone, P., & Hopper, T. (2001). What does organizational change mean? Speculations on a taken for granted category. *Management Accounting Research, 12,* 403–435.

Rhoades, G. (1995) Rethinking and restructuring universities. *Journal of Higher Education Management, 10*(2), 17–23.

Rhoades, G. (1996). Reorganizing the workforce for flexibility: Part-time professional labor. *Journal of Higher Education, 67*(6), 626–659.

Rhoads, R. (1998). *Freedom's web.* Baltimore: Johns Hopkins University Press.

Rhodes, C. (1996). Researching organisational change and learning: A narrative approach. *Qualitative Report, 2*(4).

Rhodes, C. (1997). The legitimation of learning in organizational change. *Journal of Organizational Change Management, 10*(1), 10–20.

Schein, E. (1985). *Organizational culture and leadership: A dynamic view.* San Francisco: Jossey-Bass.

Schon, D. (1983). *The reflective practitioner.* New York. Basic Books.

Scott, R. (1995). *Institutions and organizations.* London: Sage.

Shaw, K. A., & Lee, K. E. (1997). Effecting change at Syracuse University: The importance of values, missions, and vision. *Metropolitan Universities: An International Forum, 7*(4), 23–30.

Simsek, H. (1997). Metaphorical images of an organization: The power of symbolic constructs in reading change in higher education organizations. *Higher Education, 33*(3), 283–307.

Simsek, H., & Louis, K. S. (1994) Organizational change as paradigm shift: Analysis of the change process in a large, public university. *Journal of Higher Education, 65*(6), 670–695.

Smircich, L. (1983). Organizations as shared meanings. In L. R. Pondy, P. J. Frost, G. Morgan, & T. C. Dandridge (Eds.), *Organizational symbolism.* Greenwich, CT: JAI Press.

Smircich, L., & Calás, M. (1982). Organizational Culture: A critical assessment. In M. Peterson (Ed.), *ASHE reader on organization and governance* (pp. 159–171). Needham Heights, MA: Ginn Press.

Sporn, B. (1999). *Adaptive university structures: An analysis of adaptation to socioeconomic environments of US and European universities.* London: Jessica Kingsley Publishers.

Tierney, W. (1993). *Building communities of difference: Higher education in the twenty-first century.* Westport, CT: JF Bergen and Garvey.

Tierney, W. (1999) *The responsive university: Restructuring for high performance.* Baltimore: Johns Hopkins University Press.

Trowler, P. R. (1998). *Academics responding to change: New higher education frameworks and academic cultures.* Philadelphia: Open University.

Van de Ven, A. H., & Poole, M. S. (1995). Explaining development and change in organizations. *Academy of Management Review, 20*(3), 510–540.

Weick, K. E. (1989). Theory construction as disciplined imagination. *Academy of Management Review, 14*(4), 516–531.

Weick, K. E. (1995). *Sensemaking in organizations.* Thousand Oaks, CA: Sage.

Weick, K. E., & Quinn, R. E. (1999). Organizational change and development. *Annual Review of Psychology, 50*, 361–386.

Wheatley, M. J. (1999) *Leadership and the new science: Discovering order in a chaotic world* (2nd ed.). San Francisco: Berrett- Koehler.

White, R. F., & Jacques, R. (1995). Operationalizing the postmodernity construct for efficient organizational change management. *Journal of Organizational Change Management, 8*(2), 45–71.

PART THREE

NEW LINES OF INQUIRY

CHAPTER EIGHT

Diversity

A Bridge to the Future?

DARYL G. SMITH

Diversity in higher education, like technology, is a major reality in society and institutions. Indeed, the study of diversity in higher education now includes a large and ever expanding literature, focusing not only on how race/ethnicity, gender, sexual orientation, class, and other salient identities impact faculty, staff and students but also on questions about institutions and their capacity to engage diversity within and without. Less has been done on how issues of diversity impact the study of organizations, especially, in the context of higher education. Moreover, where diversity and organization theory and practice are linked, the research and theory are often located in a body of literature connected to diversity rather than to the study of higher education organizations. This chapter suggests that the next generation of research on organizational studies in higher education must bring these literatures together.

A review of the core literature on the study of organizations in higher education will reveal that organizational research on diversity as used in this chapter is largely missing. Kezar, Carducci, and Contreras-McGavin (2006) note that while literatures exist that study, for example, leadership in cross-cultural contexts, little of that has impacted the core study of leadership in higher education. Though there is considerable research on institutional change, Antonio and Muñiz (2007) suggest that work on the intersection of diversity and transformation has only begun. Further, many scholars of color have observed that how institutions are racialized or gendered is largely absent from the study of organizations within or outside higher education (Chin & Sanchez-Hucles, 2007; Gumport, 2002; Nkomo & Cox, 1996). Calás and Smircich (1992) describe it this way: "The organizational literature that supposedly considers gender has been labeled women-in-management literature. The . . . label reveals that gender is important to organization theorizing only because the biological entities—women—suddenly arrived in management, changing the nature of the situation. Prior to the entrance of women, there was (apparently) no 'gender' in management" (p. 229).

The significance of this quotation is that diversity and the identities associated with diversity are not only about individuals and groups. Rather, they are embedded in institutions and, indeed, in the study of institutions in ways that are more often ignored than addressed. This chapter, then, addresses diversity at the organizational level by asking a series of research-relevant questions: How should we think about diversity in an institutional context? How is the presence or absence of diversity in the study of higher education as organizations influencing how issues are framed, what is studied, and the conclusions that are drawn? What do we know about the experience of individuals in the context of higher education as a workplace? Finally, what are the implications for the next generation of work on diversity and organizational studies in higher education at the institutional rather than group or individual level?

Diversity and Identity

Any study of diversity in higher education inevitably begins with the fundamental question about definition. What do we mean? In the study of organizations this is particularly relevant because diversity in that context often means diversity of institutional types (Birnbaum, 1983; Morphew, 2009; Palfreyman, 2001). In this chapter, however, I am looking at diversity in terms of its role in institutions related to identities that have emerged as salient in a given social, political, historical, and cultural context. To do this adequately, it is important first to look at the newer research on identity. While that work naturally frames identity and the emerging understanding of identity in relation to individuals and groups, it is foundational to our understanding of how to think about diversity *institutionally*.

As the Calás and Smircich (1992) quotation above suggests, diversity identities are not just a function of individuals and groups. In the context of identity in institutions, questions of where the characteristic should be attributed (to the group or the institution) are critical. As I shall emphasize, ignoring or marginalizing diversity (and by implication identity) in the study of higher education institutions will become more and more problematic.

In the context of U.S. higher education, race and gender have been central to the scholarship on diversity as reflecting individuals and groups who have been excluded or marginalized in society and institutions. The legacy of race and racism in society and continued evidence of inequity leaves race a highly salient part of identity. Even as women—particularly white women—have made progress, there are many contexts in which gender remains extremely salient for women (Blau, Brinton, & Grusky, 2006). At the same time, more identities have emerged as salient and include issues of class, ethnicity, disability, sexual orientation, gender identity, and culture. After 9/11, religion, and in particular the experience of Muslims on campus, emerged as very salient.

Because of the dynamic quality of diversity, it is important to understand that while a growing list of identities salient to diversity can be developed, an understanding of diversity cannot just be a list. The default practices of either focusing on a single identity or creating a "laundry list" of identities are no longer adequate—theoretically or conceptually (Smith, 2009). In each case of identity, the particulars of the salience differ, and the implications for institutions and individuals will vary. As examples, domestic partner benefits may be a key issue for gay and lesbian faculty, accessibility or accommodation for persons with disabilities, faculty hiring and retention for African American, Latino, and American Indian faculty. Conceptually, diversity must be inclusive, but it also must differentiate issues.

Fortunately, some of the emerging developments in research and theory about identity are helpful in engaging the complexity of diversity and will provide a foundation for the chapter. While that literature cannot be fully developed here, the following summary and the reflection of the complexity of identity will facilitate thinking about diversity in institutional contexts. There are three important themes in the literature on identity: context and salience, multiplicity and intersectionality, and comprehensiveness.

CONTEXT AND SALIENCE

Many kinds of identities have been identified. *Personal* identity distinguishes individuals from others, and *social* identity contrast characteristics that connect the individual with the group (e.g., Beatty & Kirby, 2006; Carter, 2008; Gutman, 2003; Monroe, Hankin, & Van Vechten, 2000; Parekh, 2008).

The literature reflects a growing understanding that identity and the degree to which it is salient, instead of being static qualities, are influenced and even defined by context—social, political, historical, and even local (e.g., Crisp & Hewstone, 2007; Friedkin, 2004). Indeed, the kinds of identities that have emerged as salient for diversity conversations have done so in large part because of their broad social context—historical, political, social, and economic. Identities that form socially and culturally may add to the vitality of a community and engender solidarity in a group. These forms of salience underlie the language of multiculturalism, phrases like the "celebration of diversity," and the ways in which identity contributes to self and society.

These same contexts, however, may increase the salience of a particular identity because of inequities and stratification in which some identity groups experience positions of power and dominance while others are in subordinate positions. How and why group identification emerges in ways to exclude and even to escalate into discrimination and violence is the source of decades of research. However, as Inzlicht and Good (2006) comment, "Social Psychological research shows us that our environments can be threatening. They can remind us of our social identities, activate negative stereotypes, and otherwise communicate that our groups are marginalized, devalued, and not accepted" (146). While often a source of discomfort in institutional engagement with diversity, the existence of stratification requires that power, structural inequity, and discrimination be addressed in any discussion of diversity and identity. The use of critical theory and critical race theory provides important resources for institutional analysis (e.g., Solórzano, Ceja, & Yosso, 2000; Villalpondo & Delgado Bernal, 2002).

As a result of the connection of identity to social context and structural inequities, the concept of asymmetry emerges as important. When identity intersects with power, privilege, or inequity in institutional contexts, the experience of identity is likely to be *asymmetrical* depending on where one is positioned socially. Holland, Lachicotte, Skinner, and Cain (1998) describe this positionality from the following perspective: "Social position has to do with entitlement to social and material resources and so to the higher deference, respect, and legitimacy accorded to those genders, races, ethnic groups, castes, and sexualities privileged by society" (p. 271). Thus discussions of diversity that don't consider asymmetry will almost inevitably be flawed (e.g., Cole, 2009).

At the same time, this can lead to simultaneous and sometimes contradictory behaviors in society—something commonly observed when positions of both power and subordination are present. Frankenberg (1993), for example, points to the ways in which white women experience gender and then do or do not address race, suggesting that gender can be an important factor in racial dynamics and that race can influence gender dynamics.

Thus, the individual and institutional experience of identity is not static and can be triggered or downplayed given a particular context. For institutions this can be very significant.

MULTIPLICITY AND INTERSECTIONALITY

The concepts of multiplicity and intersectionality are critical in the emerging work on identity. There is growing recognition that any given individual has *multiple* identities and that these identities must be seen as they *intersect* one another.

The development of identity as a single and coherent concept was core to early literature on development (Erikson, 1997). The literature in ethnic and women's studies, and other fields, began to make explicit the multiplicity of identities for any given individual and their complexity (Ali, 2003; Anzaldúa, 2002; Cole, 2009; Dill & Zambrana, 2009; Espiritu, 1997; Frable, 1997; Hull, Scott, & Smith, 1982; Omi, 2001; Renn, 2000; Torres, Howard-Hamilton, & Cooper, 2003).

When multiplicity is acknowledged, identities can be seen as competing with one another for significance in a social context. However, early scholars, especially women of color, critiqued the binary approach to identity, underscoring the need to address its intersections. Higginbotham (1993) complained that "race only comes up when we talk about African Americans and other people of color. Gender only comes up when we talk about women, and class only comes up when we talk about the poor and working class" (p. 14). One of the classic book titles in the early literature on ethnic studies underscores the intersection of race and gender: *All the Women Are White, All the Blacks Are Men, But Some of Us Are Brave: Black Women's Studies* (Hull et al., 1982).

Williams (1994) emphasized the concept of *intersectionality* and the importance of understanding the interrelationships of (for example) gender, race, and class in her work on the status of women globally. More recently, the concept of intersectionality and its significance for theory and research has been gaining in prominence (e.g., Cole, 2009; Dill & Zambrana, 2009; hooks, 2000). As Hall (1996) has noted, "The essential issues of race always appear historically in articulation, in a formation, with other categories and divisions and are constantly crossed and re-crossed by categories of class, of gender, and ethnicity" (p. 444). It is in the dynamic interplay of context, multiplicity, intersectionality, and inequity that a more adequate understanding of identity develops. As Symington (2004) suggests, "People live multiple, layered identities derived from social relations, history, and the operation of structures of power. People are members of more than one community at the same time, and can simultaneously experience oppression and privilege" (p. 2).

COMPREHENSIVENESS

In addition to context and salience, multiplicity and intersectionality, the literature on identity recognizes (though practice often does not) that for any given individual, single—or multiple—sets of identities are not comprehensive descriptors for the person.

From a research point of view, it is still quite rare for scholars to investigate the intersections of identity in context even though we are now seeing profoundly significant findings suggesting that the intersections of race, class, and gender matter in many domains of research in higher education. Indeed, it is clear that conclusions drawn through a study of only one category may be false or misleading. Being more intentional about studying and reframing the complexity of identity as core to institutional functioning is critical for the next phases of transformation in the study of institutions.

To be sure, the complexity that results reflects a paradox. By considering intersectionality and multiplicity, for example, the meaning of any single dimension of identity becomes less clear. Yet, even so, a single identity has powerful meaning because of its social salience. Fried (1995) expresses this paradox with respect to race: "Biologically race is an illusion. Sociologically it is a pervasive phenomenon" (p. 6).

Moreover, because of the association of identity with political movements, institutions interested in creating community often think of diversity as potentially divisive. Current research, however, suggests the opposite. Paradoxically, instead of downplaying identity, a more powerful strategy for society and institutions would be to build on the multiplicities and intersections of identities and look at the similarities and differences across them as well as the social context in which identities emerge (Brewer, 2000; Crisp & Hewstone, 2007; Pettigrew, 1998; Smith, 2009; Tropp, 2006). The recent developments in the conceptualization of identity, including multiplicity, intersectionality, and asymmetry, actually facilitate intergroup work.

The next sections show how the research on higher education institutions might evolve to incorporate diversity more fully first by describing other fields and their transformation with respect to incorporating diversity.

Transformation of Scholarship

How the field of organizational behavior, and in particular the study of organizations in higher education, might be informed by diversity is not unique to this field. It is instructive to review, even if only briefly, how scholarship in other fields has been transformed by the inclusion of perspectives introduced by diversity.

Race and gender emerged as salient in higher education in the 1960s as a result of social activism. It led not only to a focus on issues of access to higher education for underrepresented minorities and for white women in fields like science and math but also to an explosion in academic scholarship that identified how these perspectives were missing from traditional scholarship. Fields like ethnic studies and women's studies emerged to place these identities at the center of scholarship. Over the past decades, these fields have substantially influenced and in many cases transformed the disciplines.

Invisibility was an important theme noting that the absence of the treatment of diversity was as, if not more, significant than its presence in terms of what it symbolized. Takaki (1993) asked: "What happens when historians leave out many of America's people?" (p. 16). Adrienne Rich (1986) captures the significance of invisibility in the academy in the following statement: "But invisibility is a dangerous and painful condition. . . . When those who have power to name and socially construct reality choose not to see you and hear you, whether you are dark-skinned, old, disabled, female, or speak with a different accent . . . , when someone with the authority of a teacher, say, describes the world and you are not in it, there is a moment of psychic disequilibrium, as if you looked into a mirror or saw nothing" (p. 199). The efforts to transform the curriculum were in part compensatory in nature, but at their core they were also trying to show how generic approaches to knowledge were not sufficient and how knowledge itself reflects existing power and social structures (e.g., Butler & Walter, 1991; Espiritu, 1997; Hu-DeHart, 1995; Hune, 2003; Minnich, 2005; Nardi & Schneider, 1998).

McIntosh's (1983) curriculum transformation scheme provides a heuristic and conceptual framework for the intellectual shifts that have occurred in many disciplines. Looking at the current stages of organizational work in higher education through this framework is, I believe, informative. The first stage is the *generic discipline* without regard to diversity. In this stage, grand conclusions and great generalizations provide knowledge as if it applies to all and locates other approaches to the discipline as peripheral. Studies of college presidents, without regard to who the presidents are and their institutional context, would be an example. The second stage focuses on *the discipline with exceptions* so that diversity can be addressed. For example, a book on college presidents might include the requisite leader of color, and a book on organization theory might have a chapter on diversity with few, if any, of the remaining chapters acknowledging how race, gender, or diversity in general is present in the more "generic" literature.

The next stage involves studying why it is that groups are not present usually in terms of *deficit* characteristics. In this period, one attributes absence to characteristics of the group—background characteristics or pipeline to explain the absence of diversity in the faculty; women's brains for math and science; or the family in the study of college students. One sees considerable research on why many diverse groups are not well represented in the disciplines, or why certain characteristics associated with a group's identity may weaken opportunities for leadership.

As ethnic studies, women's studies, and other focused studies grew, they gave voice to a large body of literature focused not on deficits but rather on the study of groups *in their own right*. This period also gave rise to the early work concerning the intersections of race and gender and increasingly to work on class, sexuality, abilities, and so on. This phase of research, which continues today, has allowed for the knowledge base that has informed much current scholarly work and which continues to push for the final stage in McIntosh's model—*intellectual and curricular transformation*. Significantly, those responsible for adding transformative scholarship most often came from the groups most marginalized in the academy.

By opening up fields of scholarship to new ways of understanding and thinking, many disciplines have changed. The study of race, class, gender, sexuality, and culture has transformed fields not only because of what is learned about those who are "different" but also because of what emerges about the validity of knowledge, the development of adequate theories, the methodologies employed, and the connections to practice (Gergen, 2001; Minnich, 2005).

In some fields, leading scholars have suggested that the viability of a field is threatened and risks being anachronistic if the complexity introduced by diversity is not engaged at its center (e.g., Gergen, 2001). In reframing organizational studies in higher education, the work on diversity in higher education will be significant, not simply to serve diverse populations but also to rethink and reorient what this research and theory imply for building diverse institutions that work in a very pluralistic society.

Diversity in the Study of Organizations

Indeed, the emerging research on diversity in higher education, the research on diversity in the workplace, and the social psychological study of identity in institutional contexts have significant implications for the next generation of organizational studies in higher education. Peterson's (2007) notion of contextual models that locate institutions at the intersection of their environment and their interior processes sets the stage for significant breakthroughs.

In other fields within the study of higher education, diversity has begun to assume a more central rather than marginal place. Yet in many studies of leadership, leadership is still studied without regard to the diversity of the leaders, the institutional context, and the dynamics between the two. The ability to generalize to all leadership based on white male samples is exemplified by the titles of articles and books. We would not accept a study of black women college presidents titled "a study of college presidents"; yet we continue to assume that a study of white male college presidents can be a study of "college presidents" in general and that we can generalize about leadership from this population. Similarly, white women can stand for leadership research on women when articles are titled "women in leadership" whether or not any diversity among women has been included. Until we incorporate research that engages perspectives of diversity in a variety of contexts, we will need to be very cautious about when and how generalized theories can be made.

There are many domains that are included in the study of organizations and which exist in both the generic literatures and diversity literatures within and outside higher education. For example, Chesler, Lewis, and Crowfoot (2005) provide a framework for the institutional elements that play a critical role in thinking about diversity institutionally. They look at the mission, culture, power, membership, technology, resources, and boundary management as places to be studied. For this chapter, the literatures on institutional culture, notions of power and privilege, leadership, change, and workplace concerns provide a good starting point for looking at how diversity is or might be incorporated into the academic study of higher education institutions and how the scholarship in the field can be strengthened by that effort.

INSTITUTIONAL CULTURE

The study of institutional culture has grown enormously in recent years in the broad organizational literature, as well as in the higher education literature. It is the study of norms, values, and practices and the historical and social circumstances in which the institutions were developed and in which they exist. And it represents an important framework for understanding how institutions function; what decisions are made; how they admit, value, and reward people; and how change is understood. While the literature on organizational culture often includes some reference to diversity, it is the literature on diversity that highlights the ways in which culture reflects the stratification and values of higher education and society (Chesler et al., 2005; Ibarra, 2000; Ramirez & Castañeda, 1991). It is in that literature that what is often described generically as institutional culture is uncovered to show the ways in which culture is racialized, gendered, classed, and so on.

Identity and culture in the study of institutions are as complex as they are in work on individuals and groups, though the literature today rarely reflects this complexity. As with individuals and groups, identity in institutions has a variety of origins, can be the source of immense pride, takes multiple forms, is not comprehensive in capturing all characteristics of the institution, and is very much shaped by context. Institutional patterns in particular can be shaped by history, location, and mission. Research on special-purpose institutions such as tribal colleges, historically black colleges and universities (HBCUs), and women's colleges illuminates how institutions formed from different missions reflect cultures more attuned to those they were designed to serve (at least in terms of that particular identity).

Studies of institutional culture suggest that when an individual's identities align significantly with the cultural identity of an institution, there is usually a sense of comfort and a lack of awareness of certain salient features. Institutional and societal norms are taken for granted. The institution can appear to be a neutral, cultureless place whose values and practices are, simply, the way "one does business" and where "individuals are treated as individuals." As a result, many institutional elements related to identity can be rendered *invisible*. What is more, the degree of alignment between an individual or group and the institution can translate into definitions of excellence that reward some groups and not others. The same is true for research on institutions where diversity is rendered invisible to research questions, methods, and conclusions. However, the "normal" questions an institution or study might ask necessarily reflect deeply held values embedded in its culture and history (of the institution and the academic disciplines): How is excellence defined? What does leadership look like? What defines "merit"? Who defines "merit"? How should selection be practiced? What defines a family for purposes of benefits? What kind of knowledge is important? What do different forms of expression mean and what is appropriate?

Acceptable ways of talking and wearing one's hair, as well as patterns of work, can be translated from cultural norms to acceptable work norms quite easily. For example, Bertrand and Mullainathan's (2004) study on the significance of names suggests that a name on a résumé that is "too black" or "too ethnic" can impact search decisions. Even today, the association of science with maleness continues to be an impediment to opening science up for women at all levels (e.g., Valian, 2005).

As Ragins (1995) suggests: "Organizational culture is shaped and supported by the power-holders of the organization. These individuals influence the values, assumptions, and ideologies of the organizations culture" (p. 97). It is no surprise, then, that most people in an institution tend to hire people like themselves and perceive that those most like themselves are the most qualified (Elliott & Smith, 2004). However, as society is changing, institutions are beginning to elevate the importance of diversity in hiring. A number of scholars now note that diversity in leadership is coming to symbolize change. For example, Eagly and Carli (2003), pointing to Shirley Tilghman's appointment as president of Princeton, suggest that "appointments of women signal an organization's departure from past practices and help it to capture signals of innovation and progressive change" (p. 827).

POWER AND PRIVILEGE

The higher education literature on power rarely addresses how power manifests itself when diversity is present (as it always is), though many theorists suggest it would be beneficial to do so (e.g., Gergen, 1992; Hardy, 1990: Pfeffer, 1981). Terms like "privilege" and "power" carry both political and emotional weight. They are often difficult to engage and may be thought to have relevance only in a political arena. Yet it becomes increasingly clear that how institutional dynamics are viewed and studied is influenced by power dynamics both in the research and in the institutional context (Chesler et al., 2005; Johnson, 2001; Maher & Tetrault, 2007; Thompson & Louque, 2005; Tierney, 1997).

Maher and Tetrault (2007), in their study of three universities in transition, found that an important element in institutional transformation, and therefore the study of institutions, was to take into account forms of privilege that are embedded in institutional norms and practices—forms of privilege that may be invisible to some but are very visible to those on the margins of that experience. White privilege. Class privilege. Gender privilege. Heterosexual privilege. While it often takes scholars who are on the outside of the privilege of a given identity to point this out, the history of transformation suggests that at some point the field itself must be open to seeing how knowledge is enhanced by these perspectives.

There are several examples of how the invisibility of privilege and power and the structural and knowledge inequities that result influence institutions and the study of institutions. Today more architecture programs are intentionally raising the issue of physical access with students who take it for granted. Persons without disabilities are often unaware that they are enjoying a privilege that is denied to others: the right of access. To be sure, no woman who attends a big event and finds herself standing at the end of an interminably long line to the ladies' room doubts that the design of public restroom facilities is gendered. It is only when environments diversify that such patterns of privilege become obvious.

If we doubt how deeply embedded the power to frame and define is, we can look at several examples in engineering and medicine. Early airbags were dangerous for many women and children. Why? The assumption built into the design was that the average passenger was the height and weight of an average *man*—an assumption that led to airbags being a danger, rather than a safeguard, for people who did not fit the design specifications.

The Matthew effect was described by Merton in studies of science as the process of "cumulative advantage," a process in which advantage accrues further to people in already advantaged positions. Merton (1988) says that "the concept of cumulative advantage directs our attention to the ways initial comparative advantage of trained capacity, structural location, and available resources make for successive increments of advantage such that the gaps between the haves and have-nots in science (as in other domains of social life) widen until dampened by countervailing processes" (p. 606). The concept of cumulative advantage certainly can be applied to the study of higher education in understanding how privilege accrues. Indeed, each of these examples show how diversity can enhance the adequacy of both knowledge and practice related to higher education institutions.

As described earlier, embedded in the notions of power, privilege, and advantage is the concept of *asymmetry*. That is, the dynamics among individuals and groups will not be symmetrical because of inequities in power. Asymmetry in intergroup relations is a consistent theme in the literature on diversity in groups and intergroup dynamics, particularly in organizational and societal contexts.

At the same time, research indicates that those in power positions tend to view group efforts in terms of individual competence and to assume neutrality or symmetry with respect to context and power. This pattern connects at both the practice and research level in which individuals are the focus of investigation, rather than a study of institutions or individuals in an institutional context (e.g., Levin & van Laar, 2006). As Dale (2004) notes: "Identity and the experience of the parties [in conflict] is constructed differently given their relative high or low power position" (p. 189).

LEADERSHIP

Virtually every study of change in higher education has identified the importance of having senior leadership that is committed and knowledgeable (e.g., Eckel, Green, & Hill, 2001; Heifetz, 1994; Kaiser, Hogan, & Craig, 2008). In a new era, what do we mean by leadership and how should it be studied? What forms of intelligence and what kinds of talents and capacities will be required? Explicit in so much of the organizational behavior literature, the diversity literature, the literature on epistemology, is the recognition that excellence, intelligence, and leadership are not unidimensional phenomena nor are they fixed across different contexts. Rather, they are multidimensional and are very much framed by context. Still, these literatures rarely intersect in considering the theory and research on leadership.

So much of the newer literature in leadership emphasizes the need for creative thinking, recognizing new patterns, interpersonal skills for working on teams, building connections, listening, and tolerating the kind of complexity and ambiguity so present in organizations and in society (Kezar, 2000, 2009; Lipman-Blumen, 1998; Pink, 2006). Nonaka (2005), writing in the context of the knowledge organization, adds that successful leaders draw people to them and have the ability to energize their emotional and spiritual resources. The association of the concept of the knowledge organization (all too often understood as solely rational) with emotionality and spirituality, while somewhat paradoxical, is very important. In addition, Blackwell, Kwoh, and Pastor (2002) suggest that leadership for diverse contexts, in particular, requires competencies in crossing borders and boundaries across sectors; building one's own ability to see multiple perspectives, especially multiracial and multiethnic perspectives; a commitment to justice for all; and a commitment to keep learning.

Creating a multidimensional understanding of talent and leadership and developing capacity for identifying talent have implications for research on leadership, hiring, definitions of merit, institutional change, and understanding how to build organizational capacity for diversity. This will require diversity in those who do research, as well as having enough diversity around decision-making tables to make those judgments and to develop those processes (Aguirre & Martinez, 2007; Blackwell et al., 2002; Eagly & Carli, 2003; Goleman, 2006; Kezar et al., 2006; Lipman-Blumen, 1998; Sternberg & Grigorenko, 2004; Wheatley, 2006).

With all the calls for diversifying leadership, more work is needed on what happens when leadership changes. What happens when the identity of the president or provost (or researcher) places them in a token position? As described in the next section, tokenism is a critically important area for study, and there is emerging work on the response of the institution and the response of communities (e.g., Aguirre & Martinez, 2007). The recent research on followership is quite relevant here because it begins to reframe leadership more concretely as a dynamic between the community and those in leadership positions (Bligh, Pillai, & Uhl-Bien, 2007; Cavalieri & Seivert, 2005).

Another emerging approach to leadership suggests that studies of leadership might be reframed to locate leaders in the middle rather than at the top of a pyramid (Gilmore, 1997; Eckel, Green, & Hill, 2001). This model emphasizes the ways in which leaders are negotiating on behalf of the institution among many constituencies and between those stakeholders above, such as boards, or those outside in the community, in government, in foundations, and those within the institution. It is so easy to imagine, for those committed to diversity, that when a leader representing diversity is chosen the path to change will be easy. However, though a deep commitment to diversity may be clear, his or her path to success may be more challenging. While being in the middle is true of all leaders, people in token positions must negotiate many challenges of being visible as a representative and invisible as an individual.

Diversity research also suggests the importance of leadership distributed throughout the campus (Clayton-Pederson, Parker, Smith, Moreno, & Teraguchi, 2007; Rendón, 2005; Smith, 2009). If so, we need much more research on leadership in faculty, staff, and administration beyond the research on college presidents (Smerek & Peterson, 2007). Sturm (2007) describes the critical role for campus catalysts who mobilize knowledge and people for change.

The next generation of leadership studies might reflect questions concerning not only how diversity in leadership contributes to institutional capacity, and the conditions under which institutions can build capacity to embrace diverse leaders, but also whether theories of leadership are sufficiently complex with respect to diversity.

CHANGE

Studies of change emerge in much of the organizational, leadership, and diversity literatures, though often in parallel. One consistent theme is the need for transformation. Several insights from the organizational literature suggest that negotiating transformation through institutional culture needs greater exploration. The Kellogg project on leadership and change noted that "to make progress on a change initiative, an institution develops ways to operate paradoxically: changing its culture in ways congruent with its culture" (Eckel, Hill, Green, & Mallon, 1999, p. 7).

The notion of connecting change to something that can coalesce many of the disparate efforts of a campus is common to much of the literature on change (Eckel et al., 1999). In this work, culture can be a source of strength as well as an impediment to change, to impart "a strong sense of what is enduring across discontinuity so people can cope with change by having some sense of stability" (Gilmore, Hirschhorn, & Kelly, 1999, p. 12.) In Hirschhorn and May's (2000) discussion of strategic change in higher education, they invoke the notion of a campaign strategy (as in capital campaign) to mobilize scarce resources to implement deep change.

Moreover, the broader literature on change and organizational learning underscores the importance of *sensemaking* (e.g., Weick, 1995), implying a *process* that "allows people to craft, understand, and accept new conceptualizations of the organization (Kezar & Eckel, 2002, p. 314). It also suggests that the best vision is one in which different segments of the campus can see themselves and the relevant work they are doing rather than the vision being something entirely new (Collins, 2000; Gardner, Csikszentmihaly, & Damon, 2001; Hirschhorn & May, 2000; Sturm, 2007; Wheatley, 2006). The work in these areas would seem to provide important models for work on institutional transformation related to diversity.

Because culture, leadership, and change represent such important domains of the organizational and higher education literatures, there is urgency in engaging how these areas can be transformed through the lens of diversity, as has happened in so many other academic areas within and outside higher education.

WORKPLACE ISSUES

Topics concerning diversity are now more visible in the research on organizations that deals with the workplace, partly as a result of the increasing centrality of diversity issues at work and the need to build institutional competence (Jayne & Dipboye, 2004; Judy & D'Amico, 1999; Miller & Katz, 2002; Pfeffer, 1985). The workplace literature also includes research on organizational justice and the conditions under which people perceive that an organization treats them equitably (e.g., Colquitt, Greenberg, & Scott, 2005). The following sections address, in particular, the literature on the benefits of diversity and issues of hiring and retention.

The Benefits of Diversity for the Institution. Both in higher education and in the management literature there is an increasing body of research on the benefits of diversity. While the research has led to some important conclusions about creating pluralistic environments that work, most of this literature emerged defensively to defend why diversity should be important. The "business case" for diversity, as it is called, rests almost entirely on what is perceived as the relationship between changing demographics, credibility with diverse markets, and profit. It often includes the claim, supported by some evidence, that diversity directly benefits the organization vis-à-vis creativity and productivity (Adkins, 2003; Cox, 2001; Hartenian & Gudmundson, 2000).

Other research, however, has suggested that while diversity needs to be engaged by organizations, the simple presence of diversity is not sufficient to manifest the benefits so often suggested and indeed might produce negative results in the form of conflict, lack of trust, and less productivity (Kochan et al., 2003;

Skerry, 2002). A growing number of studies suggest that it is essential to understand *under what conditions* diversity will enhance or detract from the effectiveness of the organization (e.g., Cox, 2001; Ely & Thomas, 2001; Friedkin, 2004; Gardenswartz & Rowe, 2003; McMillan-Capehart, 2006; O'Reilly, Williams, & Barsade, 1997; Page, 2007; Pettigrew, 1998; Smith et al., 1994). Ely and Thomas (2001), in a study of the factors that influence outcomes of diversity, found that when diversity is seen by the leadership as essential to the organization for the variety of perspectives and contributions that can be made, the outcomes are much more positive than when diversity exists simply to increase representation or to gain legitimacy in outside communities. For example, a study by Herring (2006), looking at the relationship between racial diversity and performance, showed a consistent and positive relationship in environments in which racial minorities were *not* confined to token positions. The context in which individuals interact and work matters, and the issue of diversity is salient for those in dominant and subordinate positions.

One of the methodological and conceptual limitations of much of the research that looks at the impact of the diversity of the group (e.g., race, gender, age, tenure) on productivity is that diversity is most often understood to be a characteristic of the individuals in the group. Despite years of research suggesting that women are more collaborative, for example, it is not clear that collaboration is a product of being a woman but rather may be a reflection of the fact that women may be in an environment where they are less likely to hold power, making collaborative strategies necessary. When a group is seen as angry, is it because the *individuals* are angry people or because anger emerges from disempowerment and experiences with racism, sexism, or heterosexism?

A number of researchers are trying to reframe the research paradigm from a study of the individual or group to a study of the institutional conditions for the group. Page (2007), in his provocative and empirically based book on diversity, stresses that identity concerns are not necessarily about the characteristics associated with the individuals but rather about the collective experiences and perspectives that emerge. Konrad (2003) concludes that many of the diversity issues facing institutions are associated with power and equity related to the groups for whom access and inclusion are lacking. Similarly Baugh and Graen (1997) point to the difficulty in studying one unit of analysis (the team) in the context of another unit of analysis (the institution). Without attending to structure and situation, the results of studies on group process may inaccurately be associated with the diversity of people, rather than the conditions of institutions (Baugh & Graen,

1997; Ely & Thomas, 2001; Konrad, 2003; Polzer, Milton, & Swann, 2002; van der Vegt, Bunderson, & Oosterhof, 2006).

In addition, while there is a reasonable body of research in the management literature that looks at how and in what context diversity benefits institutions, rarely is this question studied from the reverse point of view: What is the price of *not* creating these conditions? What can be said about *not* engaging diversity at the institutional level? Not much is written about this aspect, though some studies in management look at the cost of discrimination suits, boycotts, and racism (e.g., Feagin, 2006). Studies of turnover, dissatisfaction, conflict, team-building work, and institutional productivity require deep understanding of the institutional context and organizational strategies (American Bar Assoc., 2006; Cox, Lobel, & McLeod, 1991; Dobbin & Kalev, 2007; Forman, 2003; Friday, Moss, & Friday, 2004). Again, all this literature has relevance for the study of higher education.

Hiring and Retention. Many approaches related to diversity in the workplace hinge on hiring and retaining diverse workers. The literature on hiring describes how institutional cultures reinforce the hiring of people like those already in power, how to hold managers and leaders accountable for hiring and retaining diverse talent pools, and the challenges of creating more pluralistic and inclusive environments. Power, climate, institutional culture, privilege, and discrimination remain a fundamental part of the literature on this topic (Bertrand & Mullainathan, 2004; Committee on National Statistics, 2004; Cummings, 2004; Elliott & Smith, 2004; Feagin, 2006; Kilian, Hukai, & McCarty, 2005; Kirkman, Tesluk, & Rosen, 2004). Leadership development, removing sources of inequity such as experience and education, and mentoring each constitute a separate literature addressing the need and means to increase diversity (Ensher & Murphy, 2005; Thomas, 2001).

In higher education, there is significant research on hiring and retaining a diverse faculty in the diversity literature. A parallel universe exists in the general writings on faculty in higher education that only sometimes engage diversity, and most often as a demographic issue. Indeed, in that literature limited pipelines are described as explanations for failure to diversify the faculty; in contrast, the dominant themes in the diversity literature have been the lack of effort on the part of campuses to seriously recruit, the existence of bias in how candidates are selected, and the lack of serious hiring efforts in spite of a great deal of rhetoric. To those outside, institutional practices and campus culture reflect continuing structural inequities, bias, and lack of commitment (e.g., Allen, Epps, Suh, &

Stassen, 2002; Misra, Kennelly, & Karides, 1999; Smith, 2005; 2009; Smith, Wolf, Busenberg, & Assoc., 1996; Tippeconic, 2002; Turner, 2002; Valian, 2005; Villalpondo & Delgado Bernal, 2002). Other empirical studies have documented the slow pace of progress in diversifying the faculty, issues of faculty turnover, the lack of any significant growth in the level of senior professors despite the efforts at hiring assistant professors years ago, and the growth in diversity among PhDs (e.g., Beutel & Neslon, 2006; Moreno, Smith, Clayton-Pedersen, Parker, & Teraguchi, 2006; Turner, 2002).

Bias has been documented in a number of studies. Studies looking at letters of reference for women candidates and evaluations of résumés document bias favoring male candidates even when the records are identical, how institutional affiliation and where one has published are surrogates for excellence, and attitudes toward scholarship on diversity (e.g., Busenberg & Smith, 1997; Merritt & Resken, 1997; Moody, 2004; Trix & Psenka, 2003; Valian, 2005). Research is now needed to study what has been observed as the overscrutiny of women and minority candidates, including scrutiny of their tenurability, their degrees, and their research (Kulis, Chong, & Shaw, 1999; Misra et al., 1999). Moreover, the classroom as contested terrain emerges regularly as a theme in which students challenge the competence, position, and role of faculty of color and women faculty (Harlow, 2003; McGowan, 2000; Pope & Joseph, 1997).

This body of research also points to the role of institutional culture, climate, and mission in both hiring and retention. What is required is that what individuals bring in terms of culture, perspective, language, and values are appreciated and are seen as being important for the department or institution (Antonio, 2002; Lawler, 1999; Moody, 2004; Rendón, 2005; Thompson & Louque, 2005; Turner, 2002, 2003). The challenge now is to connect this body of research with the more generic literatures on the faculty, job satisfaction, and hiring.

Individual Experiences in Institutional Contexts

There is also a substantial body of knowledge related to how individuals experience institutions that has relevance for the next generation of research in the study of organizations in higher education. This research is significant in terms of how diverse individuals, often in token positions, experience the campus. Four interrelated topics highlight the impact of structural inequity for individuals and groups—stigma, microaggressions, tokenism, and critical mass. The research that has emerged underscores the role of institutional context and dynamics in the experience of individuals and groups as well as the interrelationships among individuals and groups. The following, because of space limitations, provides only a brief summary of each of these areas.

There are many examples, large and small, where, even in spite of inclusive rhetoric, people experience their identity as not welcomed or valued and where efforts to participate may be invalidated. A robust body of literature addresses the experience of *stigma*, often associated with exclusion, harassment, and denial of resources (Konrad, 2003). Being stigmatized can have powerful implications for identity, for relationships with others, and for feelings of competence and even for performance (Inzlicht & Good, 2006; Levin & van Laar, 2006). As Crocker and Garcia (2006) note, "The stigmatized often feel caught between two alternatives—confront or overlook prejudice—each of which has undesirable consequences" (p. 288).

The growing literature on *microaggressions* describes how many of the experiences associated with discrimination do not take the form of major affronts. Rather, they often take the form of smaller incidents that occur, perhaps unconsciously on the part of the other person but which are experienced by minorities as insulting, degrading, or potentially threatening. Any one incident can be seen as minor, but the accumulation over time becomes significant. A 2007 review of the literature in the *American Psychologist* reflects the growing importance and patterns of interaction related to microaggressions (Sue et al., 2007). To the individual experiencing the microaggression, there is the time and effort spent questioning whether the event occurred, whether it had to do with his or her identity, and then whether to say anything for fear of being called oversensitive or paranoid (Crocker & Garcia, 2006; Inzlicht & Good, 2006; Levin & van Laar, 2006; Solórzano et al., 2000; Sue et al., 2007).

The intersection of an individual's identity with institutions and societies is particularly relevant when an individual is a token, one of a few in an organization sharing a salient identity. The dynamics associated with tokenism can occur at any level of the institution—committee, department, school, and institution. Some important themes resonate through the literature on tokenism (Kanter, 1977; Yoder, 2002). For one, a person may be *visible* as a representative of the group but invisible as an individual. Studies also document the cost to individuals in terms of stress, overload, and visibility that would make working at such a place less desirable (Kanter, 1977; Smith, Yosso, & Solórzano, 2006; Thompson & Louque, 2005; Turner, 2002; Yoder, 2002). For the institution, the results can also be damaging if the dynamics on campus or in a department increase the likelihood of turnover, lawsuits, or decreases in satisfaction.

Some emerging evidence suggests that communities from which the leader has come can add to the tension. Aguirre and Martinez (2007) suggest that "diverse communities in higher education often expect more from diverse leadership in higher education than it can deliver" (p. 83). Leaders can hope that they are trusted and seen as committed to their own history even as they have to show that they are not *just* committed to that community.

While the research on tokenism is still limited, it is apparent from numerous studies that context matters. Research has consistently shown that the more one is outnumbered, the greater the likelihood that the environment will trigger awareness of one's marginal position or negative stereotypes (Kramer, Konrad, & Erkut, 2006; Thomson & Sekaquaptewa, 2002). Although being the token can occur for anyone—a white man in nursing, for example—Yoder (2002) reports that the impact on the individual and the dynamics in the organization vary considerably with gender role violations and are asymmetrical. A man's experience in a woman's field is asymmetrical to a woman in a man's field. Here the status of the field and gender interact.

Rosabeth Moss Kanter's (1977) early work suggested that when a group constitutes 20% of the organization, the impact of tokenism is decreased. More recent research suggests that to limit the impact of skewed environments, 35% would be a better percentage for any group (a percentage that few underrepresented racial or ethnic groups can achieve singly in predominantly white institutions) (e.g., Kramer et al., 2006). With such representation, individuals are more likely to be seen as individuals without the visibility and stress of being a token. Paradoxically, it also helps to dispel stereotyping. The larger the membership in an identity group, the greater likelihood that there will be individual variation that will facilitate the breakdown of stereotypes. Greater proportionality can also create more positive views of the organization and more optimism about the possibilities for success (Ely, 1994).

Though it may be clear that achieving a critical mass for a salient identity group is critical for the individual and for the institution, the concept itself is not well understood. It may be that the complexity of critical mass reflects the complexity of identity itself. How and when can we aggregate critical mass so that we look at the numbers and percentages of persons of color? Is the unit of analysis the institution, or does critical mass have to be achieved in the location where individuals work or study? The research on HBCUs, women's colleges, and tribal colleges (and perhaps one day Hispanic Serving Institutions (HSIs) certainly provides a lens on how dynamics might change when a particularly salient identity is no longer a token.

This not only has implications for students and their exposure to diversity, but it also has huge implications for faculty and their ability to thrive and focus energy on teaching, scholarship, and service (Allen et al., 2002; Cooper & Stevens, 2002; Moody, 2004; Tierney & Bensimon, 1996; Weinberg, 2008).

Each of these topics could be placed in the context of human resource management or studies of institutional climate. But they are as well essential to an understanding of culture, leadership, change, and power discussed above. These are interrelated concepts and have conceptual and methodological significance for the study and practice of higher education.

Implications for the Next Generation of Research

All the issues identified in this chapter relate directly to building the research *capacity* of the field and the *capacity* of colleges and universities to function in an increasingly pluralistic society and to do so in contexts that are too often characterized by inequities. Capacity building concerns the creation of structures that serve institutional purposes and that connect the institution's core purposes and society. It involves the allocation of financial and other resources, as well as strengthening human capital, expertise, and culture. Capacity building is particularly reflected in the way decisions are made, what knowledge and expertise are valued, how power is distributed, and the characteristics of institutional culture. The understanding of diversity as related to institutional capacity building might, as Peterson (2007) suggests, "provide the impetus for new organizational models to help explain or understand the institutional changes and their new dynamics" (p. 180).

The challenge for the field is to ask, How might research take diversity into account? All these bodies of knowledge must intersect and not operate in parallel forms. If this is a study of leadership, how might research questions, methodology, and theories of leadership engage diversity? The study of diversity inevitably requires looking at systems that blur the boundaries between institutions and their surrounding communities, at equity, and at asymmetry. This invites, indeed mandates, notions of interdependence and is consistent with systems approaches to the study of organizations (Baez, 2000; Gergen, 2001; Peterson, 2007).

Who does the research of building bridges between diversity and organizational studies? It is abundantly clear that as scholars themselves become more diverse, diversity is more likely introduced into their research and into the field. This has been true of every stage of the transformation of knowledge in almost every academic area. The implications for organizational studies are clear. Making sure diversity is engaged will require intentional efforts at critique by diverse teams and individual scholars and the development of more scholars with diverse perspectives. It is also clear that it will require the recognition of all those in the field that the viability and legitimacy of the field will rest in part on the degree to which questions about diversity are engaged.

The research presented in this chapter suggests that there is a long way to go to building equitable institutions that can maximize the opportunities presented by diversity. Diverse perspectives and cultural values can benefit institutions on structural as well as individual levels and can make the difference between effectiveness and failure, equity and stratification (Blackwell et al., 2002; Chin & Sanchez-Hucles, 2007).

Finally, embedding diversity frameworks in the study of organizational dynamics in higher education can in fact shed light on the field itself. Instead of being a separate domain, such frameworks can provide an opportunity to better understand key elements of the study of organizations related to such topics as culture, leadership, change, and governance. Just as the scholarship in ethnic studies and women's studies has ultimately informed the work in many of the disciplines, organizational studies is now positioned to benefit from decades of conceptual, theoretical, and practical work on diversity in higher education.

ACKNOWLEDGMENT

Some of the material from this chapter was adapted from Daryl G. Smith's *Diversity's Promise for Higher Education: Making It Work*, published in 2009 by Johns Hopkins University Press.

REFERENCES

Adkins, G. Y. (2003). *Diversity beyond the numbers: Business vitality, ethics and identity, in the 21st century.* Long Beach, CA: GDI Press.

Aguirre, A., Jr., & Martinez, R. O. (2007). *Diversity leadership in higher education.* ASHE-ERIC Higher Education Reports No. 32(3). San Francisco: Jossey-Bass.

Ali, S. (2003). *Mixed-race, post-race: Gender, new ethnicities and cultural practices*. Oxford: Berg Publishers.

Allen, W., Epps, E., Suh, S., & Stassen, M. (2002). Outsiders within: Race, gender and faculty status in U.S. higher education. In W. A. Smith, P.G. Altbach, & K. Lomotey (Eds), *The racial crisis in American higher education: Continuing challenges for the twenty first century* (revised ed., pp. 189–220). Albany: State University of New York Press.

American Bar Association. (2006). *Visible invisibility: Women of color in law firms*. Retrieved September 21, 2006, from www.abanet.org

Antonio, A. L. (2002). Faculty of color reconsidered. *Journal of Higher Education, 73*(5), 582–602.

Antonio, A. L., & Muñiz, M. M. (2007). The sociology of diversity. In P. Gumport (Ed.), *Sociology of higher education: Contributions and their context* (pp. 266–294). Baltimore: Johns Hopkins University Press.

Anzaldúa, G. E. (2002). Beyond traditional notions of identity. *Chronicle of Higher Education, 49*(7), B11.

Baez, B. (2000). Race-related service and faculty of color: Critical agency in academe. *Higher Education, 39*(3), 363–391.

Baugh, S. G., & Graen, G. B. (1997). Effects of team gender and racial composition on perceptions of team performance in cross-functional teams. *Group and Organizational Studies, 22*(3), 366–383.

Beatty, J. E., & Kirby, S. L. (2006). Beyond the legal environment: How stigma influences invisible identity groups in the workplace. *Employee Responsibilities and Rights Journal, 18*(1), 29–44.

Bertrand, M., & Mullainathan, S. (2004). Are Emily and Greg more employable than Lakisha and Jamal? A field experiment on labor market discrimination. *American Economic Review, 94*(4), 991–1014.

Beutel, A. M., & Nelson, D. J. (2006). Gender and race-ethnicity of faculty in top social science research departments. *Social Science Journal, 43*, 111–125.

Birnbaum, R. (1983). *Maintaining diversity in higher education*. San Francisco: Jossey-Bass.

Blackwell, A. G., Kwoh, S., & Pastor, M. (2002). *Searching for the uncommon common ground: New dimensions on race in America*. New York: Norton.

Blau, F. D., Brinton, M. C., & Grusky, D. B. (Eds.). (2006). *The declining significance of gender?* New York: Russell Sage Foundation.

Bligh, M., Pillai, R., & Uhl-Bien, M. (2007). The social construction of a legacy: Summarizing and extending follower-centered perspectives on leadership. In B. Shamir, R. Pillai, M. Bligh, & M. Uhl-Bien (Eds.), *Follower-centered perspectives on leadership* (pp. 265–278). Greenwich, CT: Information Age.

Brewer, M. B. (2000). Reducing prejudice through cross categorization: Effects of multiple social identities. In Oskamp, S. (Ed.), *Reducing prejudice and discrimination* (pp. 165–184). Mahlwah, NJ: Erlbaum.

Busenberg, B. E., & Smith. D. G. (1997). Affirmative action and beyond: The woman's perspective. In M. García (Ed.), *Affirmative action's testament of hope: Strategies for a new era in higher education* (pp. 149–180). Albany: State University of New York.

Butler, J. E., & Walter, J. C. (1991). *Transforming the curriculum: Ethnic studies and women's studies.* Albany: State University of New York Press.

Calás, M. B., & Smircich, L. (1992). Re-writing gender into organizational theorizing: Directions from feminist perspectives. In M. Reed & M. Hughes (Eds.), *Rethinking organization: New directions in organization theory and analysis* (pp. 227–253). London: Sage.

Cavalieri, S., & Seivert, S. (2005). *Knowledge leadership.* Burlington, MA: Elsevier.

Carter, R. (2008). Multiplicity: The new science of personality, identity, and the self. New York.: Little, Brown.

Chesler, M., Lewis, A., & Crowfoot, J. (2005). *Challenging racism in higher education: Promoting justice.* Oxford: Rowman and Littlefield.

Chin, J. L., & Sanchez-Hucles, J. V. (2007). Diversity and leadership. *American Psychologist, 62*(6), 608–609.

Clayton-Pedersen, A. R., Parker, S., Smith, D. G., Moreno, J. F., & Teraguchi, D. H. (2007). *Making a real difference with diversity: A guide to institutional change.* Washington, DC: Association of American Colleges and Universities.

Cole, E. R. (2009). Intersectionality and research in psychology. *American Psychologist, 64*(3), 170–180.

Collins, P. H. (2000). Toward a new vision: Race, class and gender as categories of analysis and connection. In M. Adams et al. (Eds.), *Readings for diversity and social justice* (pp. 457–462). New York: Routledge.

Colquitt, J. A., Greenberg, J., & Scott, B. (2005). Organizational justice: Where do we stand? In J. Greenberg & J. A. Colquitt (Eds.), *Handbook of organizational justice* (pp. 589–619). Mahwah, NJ: Erlbaum.

Committee on National Statistics. (2004). *Measuring racial discrimination.* Report brief, Division of Behavioral and Social Sciences and Education. Washington, DC: National Academies Press.

Cooper, J. E., & Stevens, D. D. (Eds.). (2002). *Tenure in the sacred grove: Issues and strategies for women and minority faculty.* Albany: State University of New York Press.

Cox, T. H., Jr. (2001). *Creating the multicultural organization: A strategy for capturing the power of diversity.* San Francisco: Jossey-Bass.

Cox, T. H., Jr., Lobel, S. A., & McLeod, P. L. (1991). Effects of ethnic group cultural differences on cooperative and competitive behavior on a group task. *Academy of Management Journal, 34,* 827–847.

Crisp, R. J., & Hewstone, M. (2007). Multiple social categorization. In M. P. Sanna (Ed.), *Advances in experimental social psychology,* Vol. 39 (pp. 163–254). Orlando, FL: Academic Press.

Crocker, J., & Garcia, J. A. (2006). Stigma and the social basis of the self: A synthesis. In S. Levin & C. Van Laar (Eds.), *Stigma and group inequality* (pp. 287–308). Mahwah, NJ: Erlbaum.

Cummings, J. N. (2004). Work groups, structural diversity and knowledge sharing in a global organization. *Management Science, 50*(3), 352–364.

Dale, R. (2004). Comments on chapters 9 and 10. In A. H. Eagly, R. M. Baron, & V. L. Hamilton (Eds.), *The social psychology of group identity and social conflict: Theory, application, and practice* (pp. 189–192). Washington, DC: American Psychological Association.

Dill, B. T., & Zambrana, R. E. (Eds). (2009). *Emerging intersections: Race, class, and gender in theory, research and practice.* New Brunswick, NJ: Routledge.

Dobbin, F., & Kalev, A. (2007). The architecture of inclusion: Evidence from corporate diversity programs. *Harvard Journal of Law and Gender, 30,* 279–301.

Eagly, A. H., & Carly, L. L. (2003). The female leadership advantage. *Leadership Quarterly, 14,* 807–834.

Eckel, P., Green, M., & Hill, B. (2001). *On change V: Riding the waves of change: Insights from transforming institutions.* Washington, DC: American Council on Education.

Eckel, P., Hill, B., Green, M., & Mallon, B. (1999). *On change: Reports from the road: Insights on institutional change.* Washington, DC: American Council on Education.

Elliott, J. R., & Smith, R. A. (2004). Race, gender and workplace power. *American Sociological Review, 69*(3), 365–386.

Ely, R. (1994). The effects of organizational demographics and social identity on relationships among professional women. *Administrative Science Quarterly, 39,* 203–238.

Ely, R. J., & Thomas, D. A. (2001). Cultural diversity at work: The effects of diversity perspectives on work group processes and outcomes. *Administrative Science Quarterly, 46*(2), 229–273.

Ensher, E. A., & Murphy, S. E. (2005). *Power mentoring: How successful mentors and proteges get the most out of their relationships.* San Francisco: Jossey-Bass.

Erikson, E. H. (1997). *The life cycle completed.* New York: Norton.

Espiritu, Y. L. (1997). *Asian American women and men.* Thousand Oaks, CA: Sage.

Feagin, J. R. (2006). *Systemic racism: A theory of oppression.* New York: Routledge.

Forman, T. (2003). The social-psychological costs of racial segmentation in the workplace: A study of African Americans' well-being. *Journal of Health and Social Behavior, 44*(3), 332–352.

Frable, D. E. S. (1997). Gender, racial, ethnic, sexual, and class identities. *Annual Review of Psychology, 48,* 139–162.

Frankenberg, R. (1993). *White women, race matters: The social construction of whiteness.* Minneapolis: University of Minnesota Press.

Friday, S. S., Moss, S. E., & Friday, E. (2004). Socioethnic explanations for racial and ethnic differences in job satisfaction. *Journal of Management Development, 23*(2), 152–168.

Fried, J. (1995). *Shifting paradigms for student affairs: Culture, context, teaching, and learning.* Alexandria, VA: American College Personnel Association.

Friedkin, N. E. (2004). Social cohesion. *Annual Review of Sociology, 30,* 409–425.

Gardenswartz, L., & Rowe, A. (2003). *Diverse teams at work: Capitalizing on the power of diversity.* Alexandria, VA: Society for Human Resource Management.

Gardner, H., Csikszentmihalyi, M., & Damon, W. (2001). *Good work: When excellence and ethics meet.* New York: Basic Books.

Gergen, K. J. (1992). Organization theory in the postmodern era. In M. Reed & M. Hughes (Eds.), *Rethinking organization: New directions in organization theory and analysis* (pp. 207–226). London: Sage.

Gergen, K. J. (2001). Psychological science in a postmodern context, *American Psychologist, 56*(10), 803–813.

Gilmore, T. N. (1997). *Leaders as middles.* Philadelphia: Center for Applied Research.

Gilmore, T. N., Hirschhorn, L., & Kelly, M. (1999). *Challenges of leading and planning in higher education.* Philadelphia: Center for Applied Research.

Goleman, D. (2006). *Social intelligence: The new science of human relationships.* New York: Bantam.

Gumport, P. J. (2002). *Academic pathfinders: Knowledge creation and feminist scholarship.* Westport, CT: Greenwood.

Gutman, A. (2003). *Identity in democracy.* Princeton, NJ: Princeton University Press.

Hall, S. (1996). New ethnicities. In S. Hall, D. Morely, & K. Chen (Eds.), *Stuart Hall: Critical dialogues in cultural studies* (pp. 441–450). New York: Routledge.

Hardy, C. (1990). Putting power into university governance. In J. C. Smart (Ed.), *Higher education: Handbook of theory and practice,* Vol. 4 (pp. 393–426). New York: Agathon Press.

Harlow, R. (2003). Race doesn't matter, but: The effect of race on professors' experiences and emotion management in the undergraduate classroom. *Social Psychology Quarterly, 66*(4), 348–363.

Hartenian, L. S., & Gudmundson, D. E. (2000). Cultural diversity in small business: Implications for firm performance. *Journal of Developmental Entrepreneurship, 5*(3), 209–219.

Heifetz, R. (1994). *Leadership without easy answers.* Cambridge, MA: Harvard University Press.

Herring, C. (2006). *Does diversity pay? Racial composition of firms and the business case for diversity.* Unpublished manuscript. University of Illinois at Chicago and Institute of Government and Public Affairs, University of Illinois.

Higginbotham, E. (1993). Sociology and the multicultural curriculum: The challenges of the 1990s and beyond. *Race, Sex, and Class, 1,* 13–24.

Hirschhorn, L., & May, L. (2000). The campaign approach to change: Targeting the university's scarcest resources. *Change, 32*(3), 30–37.

Holland, D., Lachicotte, Q., Jr., Skinner, D., & Cain, C. (1998). *Identity and agency in cultural worlds.* Cambridge, MA: Harvard University Press.

hooks, b. (2000). *Where we stand: Class matters.* New York: Routledge.

Hu-DeHart, E. (1995). Ethnic studies in U.S. higher education: History, development and goals. In J. A. Banks (Ed.), *Handbook of research on multicultural education* (pp. 696–707). New York: Macmillan.

Hull, G. T., Scott, P. B., & Smith, B. (Eds.). (1982). *All the women are white, all the blacks are men but some of us are brave: Black women's studies.* New York: Feminist Press.

Hune, S. (2003). Through «our eyes»: Asian Pacific Islander American women›s history. In S. Hune & G. M. Nomura (Eds.), *Asian Pacific Islander American Women* (pp. 1–12). New York: New York University Press.

Ibarra, R. (2000). *Beyond affirmative action: Reframing the context of higher education.* Madison: University of Wisconsin Press.

Inzlicht, M., & Good, C. (2006). How environments can threaten academic performance, self knowledge, and sense of belonging. In S. Levin & C. V. Laar (Eds.), *Stigma and group inequality* (pp. 129–150). Mahwah, NJ: Erlbaum.

Jayne, M. E. A., & Dipboye, R. L. (2004). Leveraging diversity to improve business performance: Research findings and recommendation for organizations. *Human Resource Management, 43*(4), 409–424.

Johnson, A. G. (2001). *Privilege, power, and difference*. Boston: McGraw-Hill.

Judy, R. W., & D'Amico, C. (1999). *Workforce 2020: Work and workers in the 21st century*. Indianapolis, IN: Hudson Institute.

Kaiser, R. B., Hogan, R., & Craig, S. B. (2008). Leadership and the fate of organizations. *American Psychologist, 63*(2), 96–100.

Kanter, R. M. (1977). Some effects of proportions on group life: Skewed sex ratios and responses to token women. *American Journal of Sociology, 5*, 965–990.

Kezar, A. J. (2000). Pluralistic leadership: Incorporating diverse voices. *Journal of Higher Education, 71*(6), 722–743.

Kezar, A. J. (2009). *Rethinking leadership in a complex, multicultural, and global environment*. Sterling, VA: Stylus Press.

Kezar, A., & Eckel, P. D. (2002). Examining the institutional transformation process: The importance of sensemaking, interrelated strategies, and balance. *Research in Higher Education, 43*(3), 295–328.

Kezar, A. J., Carducci, R., & Contreras-McGavin, M. (2006). *Rethinking the "l" word in higher education*. ASHE Higher Education Report No. 31(6). San Francisco: Jossey-Bass

Kilian, C. M., Hukai, D., & McCarty, C. E. (2005). Building diversity in the pipeline to corporate leadership. *Journal of Management Development, 24*(2), 155–168.

Kirkman, B. L., Tesluk, P. E., & Rosen, B. (2004).The impact of demographic heterogeneity and team leader-team member demographic fit on team empowerment and effectiveness. *Group and Organization Management, 29*(3), 334–368.

Kochan,T., Bezruka, K., Ely, R., Jackson, S., Joshi, A., & Jehn, K. (2003). The effects of diversity on business performance: Report of the Diversity Research Network. *Human Resources Management, 42*(1), 3–21.

Konrad, A. (2003). Defining the domain of workplace diversity scholarship. *Group and Organizational Management, 28*(1), 4–17.

Kramer, V., Konrad, A., & Erkut, S. (2006). *Critical mass on corporate boards: Why three or more women enhance governance* (Report no. 781 283<H>2510). Wellesley, MA: Wellesley Centers for Women.

Kulis, S., Chong, Y., & Shaw, H. (1999). Discriminatory organizational contexts and black scientists on postsecondary faculties. *Research in Higher Education, 40*(2), 115–148.

Lawler, A. (1999). Scientific community: Tenured women battle to make it less lonely at the top. *Science, 286*(5443), 1272–1278.

Levin, S., & van Laar, C. (Eds.). (2006). *Stigma and group inequality*. Mahwah, NJ: Erlbaum.

Lipman-Blumen, J. (1998). Connective leadership: What business needs to learn from academe. *Change, 30*(1), 49–53.

Maher, F. A., & Tetrault, M. K. T. (2007). *Privilege and diversity in the Academy*. New York: Routledge.

McGowan, J. M. (2000). African American faculty classroom teaching experiences in predominantly white colleges and universities. *Multicultural Education, 8*(2), 11–22.

McIntosh, P. (1983). *Interactive phases of curriculum re-vision: A feminist perspective*. Working paper series, no. 124. Wellesley, MA: Wellesley College, Center for Research on Women.

McMillan-Capehart, A. (2006). Heterogeneity or homogeneity: Socialization makes the difference in firm performance. *Performance Improvement Quarterly, 19*(1), 83–98.

Merritt, D. J., & Resken, B. F. (1997). Sex, race and credentials: The truth about affirmative action in law faculty hiring. *Columbia Law Review, 97(199)*, 206–230.

Merton, R. K. (1988). The Matthew effect in science, II. *ISIS, 79*, 606–623.

Miller, F. A., & Katz, J. H. (2002). *The inclusion breakthrough: Unleashing the real power of diversity.* San Francisco: Berrett-Koehler.

Minnich, E. K. (2005). *Transforming knowledge* (2nd ed.). Philadelphia: Temple University Press.

Misra, J., Kennelly, I., & Karides, M. (1999). Employment chances in the academic job market in Sociology: Do race and gender matter? *Sociological Perspectives, 42(2)*, 215–247.

Monroe, K. R., Hankin, J., & Van Vechten, R. B. (2000). The psychological foundations of identity politics. *Annual Review of Political Science, 3*, 419–447.

Moody, J. (2004). *Faculty diversity: Problems and solutions.* New York: Routledge Falmer.

Moreno, J., Smith, D. G., Clayton-Pedersen, A. R., Parker, S., & Teraguchi, D. (2006) *The revolving door for underrepresented minority faculty in higher education.* San Francisco: James Irvine Foundation, www.irvine.org/assets/pdf/pubs/education/insight_Revolving_Door.pdf

Morphew, C. C. (2009). Conceptualizing change in the institutional diversity of U.S. colleges and universities. *Journal of Higher Education, 80(3)*, 243–270.

Nardi, P., & Schneider, B. E. (Eds.). (1998). *Social perspectives in gay and lesbian studies.* New York: Routledge.

Nkomo, S. M., & Cox, T. (1996). Diverse identities in organizations. In S. Clegg, C. Hardy, & W. Nord (Eds.), *Handbook of organization studies* (pp. 338–356). Thousand Oaks, CA: Sage.

Nonaka, I. (2005). Managing organizational knowledge: Theoretical and methodological foundations. In K. G. Smith & M. A. Hitt (Eds.), *Great minds in management: The process of theory development* (pp. 373–394). Oxford: Oxford University Press.

Omi, M. A. (2001). The changing meaning of race. In N. J. Smelser, W. J. Wilson, & F. Mitchell (Eds.), *America becoming: Racial trends and their consequences,* Vol. 1 (pp. 243–263). National Research Council, New Jersey Commission on Behavioral and Social Sciences and Education. Washington, DC: National Academy Press.

O'Reilly, C., Williams, K., & Barsade, S. (1997). Group demography and innovation: Does diversity help? In E. Mannix & M. Neale (Eds.), *Research in the management of groups and teams,* Vol. 1 (pp. 77–140). Greenwich, CT: JAI Press.

Page, S. E. (2007). *The difference: How the power of diversity creates better groups, firms, schools and societies.* Princeton, NJ: Princeton University Press.

Palfreyman, D. (2001). *The state of UK higher education: Managing change and diversity.* Philadelphia: Open University Press.

Parekh, B. (2008). *A new politics of identity: Political principles for an interdependent world.* New York: Palgrave Macmillan.

Peterson, M. W. (2007). The study of colleges and universities as organizations. In P. Gumport (Ed.), *Sociology of higher education: Contributions and their context* (pp. 147–186). Baltimore: Johns Hopkins University Press.

Pettigrew, T. F. (1998). Intergroup contact theory. *Annual Review of Psychology, 49*, 65–85.

Pfeffer, J. (1981). *Power in organizations.* Boston: Pitman.

Pfeffer, J. (1985). Organizational demography: Implications for management. *California Management Review, 28,* 67–81.

Pink, D. H. (2006). *A whole new mind: Why right brainers will rule the future.* New York: Riverhead Books.

Polzer, J. T., Milton, L. T., & Swann, W. B. (2002). Capitalizing on diversity: Interpersonal congruence in small work groups. *Administrative Science Quarterly, 47,* 296–324.

Pope, J., & Joseph, J. (1997). Student harassment of female faculty of African descent in the academy. In L. Benjamin (Ed.), *Black women in academe: Promises and perils* (pp. 252–260). Gainesville: University Press of Florida.

Ragins, B. R. (1995). Diversity, power, and mentorship in organizations: A cultural, structual, and behavioral perspective. In M. Chemers, S. Oskamp, & M. Costanza (Eds.), *Diversity in organizations* (pp. 91–132). Newbury Park, CA: Sage.

Ramirez, M., & Castañeda, A. (1991). Toward a cultural democracy. In B. Murchand (Ed.), *Higher education and the practice of democratic politics* (pp. 115–121). Dayton, OH : Kettering Foundation.

Rendón, L. I. (2005). Recasting agreements that govern teaching and learning: An intellectual and spiritual framework for transformation. *Religion and Education, 32*(1), 79–108.

Renn, K. A. (2000). Patterns of situational identity among biracial and multiracial students. *Review of Higher Education, 23*(4), 399–420.

Rich, A. (1986). *Blood, bread, and poetry.* New York: Norton.

Skerry, P. (2002). Beyond sushiology: Does diversity work? *Brookings Review, 20,* 2023.

Smerek, R. E., & Peterson, M. (2007). Examining Herzberg's theory: Improving job satisfaction among non-academic employees at a university. *Research in Higher Education, 48*(2), 229–250.

Smith, D. G. (2005). *The challenge of diversity: Involvement or alienation in the academy* (reprinted with an introduction by D. G. Smith and L. Wolf-Wendel). ASHE Higher Education Report No. 31(1). San Francisco Jossey-Bass.

Smith, D. G. (2009). *Achieving diversity's promise for higher education: Making it work.* Baltimore: Johns Hopkins University Press.

Smith, D. G., Wolf, L. E., Busenberg, B., & Associates. (1996). *Achieving faculty diversity: Debunking the myths.* Washington, DC: Association of American Colleges and Universities.

Smith, K. G., Smith, K. A., Olian, J., Sims, H., O'Bannon, D., & Scully, J. (1994). Top management team demography and process: The role of social integration and communication. *Administrative Science Quarterly, 39,* 412–438.

Smith, W. A., Yosso, T. J., & Solórzano, D. G. (2006). Challenging racial battle fatigue on historically white campuses: A critical race examination of race-related stress. In C. A. Stanley (Ed.), *Faculty of color: Teaching in predominantly white colleges and universities* (pp. 299–328). Boston: Anker.

Solórzano, D. G., Ceja, M., & Yosso, T. (2000). Critical race theory, racial microaggressions, and campus racial climate. *Journal of Negro Education, 69*(1), 60–73.

Sternberg, R. J., & Grigorenko, E. L. (Eds.). (2004). *Culture and competence: Contexts of life success.* Washington, DC: American Psychological Association.

Sturm, S. (2007). Gender equity as institutional transformation. In A. J. Stewart, J. E. Malley, & D. La Veque-Manty, *Tranforming science and engineering: Advancing academic women* (pp. 262–279). Ann Arbor: University of Michigan Press.

Sue, D. W., Capodilupo, C. M., Torino, G. C., Bucceri, J. M., Holder, A. M. B., Nadal, K. L., & Eaquilin, M. (2007). Racial microaggressions in everyday life. *American Psychologist, 62*(4), 271–286.

Symington, A. (2004, August). Intersectionality: A tool for gender and economic justice. *Women's rights and economic change* (Association for Women in Development, No. 9). Toronto: AWD.

Takaki, R. (1993). *A different mirror: A history of multicultural America.* New York: Little, Brown.

Thomas, D. A. (2001). The truth about mentoring minorities: Race matters. *Harvard Business ness Review, 79*(4), 99–107.

Thompson, G. L., & Louque, A. C. (2005). *Exposing the culture of arrogance.* Sterling, VA: Stylus Publishing.

Thompson, M., & Sekaquaptewa, P. (2002). When being different is detrimental: Solo status and the performance of women and racial minorities. *Analysis of Social Issues and Public Policy, 2,* 183–203.

Tierney, W. G. (1997). *Academic outlaws: Queer theory and cultural studies in the academy.* Thousand Oaks, CA: Sage.

Tierney, W. G., & Bensimon, E. M. (1996). *Promotion and tenure: Community and socialization in academe.* Albany: State University of New York Press.

Tippeconnic, J. W., III. (2002, April 21–23). American Indians and Alaska Native faculty in academe: The good, the bad and the ugly. In *Conference proceedings from the Keeping Our Faculties conference* (pp. 53–59). St. Paul: University of Minnesota.

Torres, V., Howard-Hamilton, M. F., & Cooper, D. L. (2003). *Identity development of diverse populations: Implications for teaching and administration in higher education.* ASHE-ERIC Higher Education Report, No. 29(6). San Francisco: Jossey-Bass.

Trix, F., & Psenka, P. (2003). Exploring the color of glass: Letters of recommendation for female and male medical faculty. *Discourse and Society, 14*(2), 191–220.

Tropp, L. R. (2006). Stigma and intergroup contact among members of minority and majority status groups. In S. Levin & C. van Laar (Eds.), *Stigma and group inequality* (pp. 171–192). Mahwah, NJ: Erlbaum.

Turner, C. S. V. (2002). Women of color in academe: Living with multiple marginality. *Journal of Higher Education, 73*(1), 74–93.

Turner, C. S. V. (2003). Incorporation and marginalization in the academy: From border towards center for faculty of color? *Journal of Black Studies, 34*(1), 112–125.

Valian, V. (2005). Beyond gender schemas: Improving the advancement of women in academia. *Hypatia, 20*(3), 198–213.

van der Vegt, G. S., Bunderson, J. S., & Oosterhof, A. (2006). Expertness diversity and interpersonal helping in teams: Why those who need the most help end up getting it least. *Academy of Management Journal, 49*(5), 877–893.

Villalpondo, O., & Delgado Bernal, D. (2002). A critical race theory analysis of barriers that impede the success of faculty of color. In W. A. Smith, P. G. Altbach, & K. Lomotey,

(Eds.), *The racial crisis in American higher education: Continuing challenges for the twenty-first century* (revised ed., pp. 243–269). Albany: State University of New York Press.

Weick, K. E. (1995). *Sensemaking in organizations.* London: Sage.

Weinberg, S. L. (2008). Monitoring faculty diversity. *Journal of Higher Education, 79*(4), 365–387.

Wheatley, M. J. (2006). *Leadership and the new science: Discovering order in a chaotic world* (3rd ed.). San Francisco: Berrett-Koehler.

Williams, K. C. (1994). Mapping the margins: Intersectionality, identity politics, and violence against women of color. In M. A. Fineman & R. Mylitiuk (Eds.), *The public nature of private violence* (pp. 93–118). New York: Routledge.

Yoder, J. D. (2002). Context matters: Understanding tokenism processes and their impact on women's work. *Psychology of Women Quarterly, 26,* 1–8.

CHAPTER NINE

Social Movements
and the University

FABIO ROJAS

Social movements go hand in hand with universities. Nearly every significant movement in the past century has had a significant relationship with the university system. The civil rights movement, which transformed America, included highly influential student groups. The Student Non-Violent Coordinating Committee began with North Carolina students who supported a lunch counter sit-in (Carson, 1981). Internationally, university students in Asia and Africa participated in decolonization and antiauthoritarian politics, such as the movement against the apartheid system in South Africa (Altbach, 1984; Aspinall & Berger, 2001; Federici, Caffentzis, & Alidou, 2000). The May 1968 uprising in France stemmed from radical student committees at Nanterre and the Sorbonne (e.g., Gregoire & Perlman, 1970; Touraine, 1971). Later, the American conservative movement of the 1980s had roots in college Republican clubs of the 1960s and 1970s (Andrew, 1997). In 1989, the Chinese democracy movement had strong roots in Beijing University (Zhao, 2001).

The academic system itself is often changed by movements. The campus revolts of the 1960s led to ethnic studies, women's studies, and other new areas of inquiry (Boxer, 1998; Cole, 2006; Olzak & Kangas, 2008; Rojas, 2006, 2007). Later, student movements would rise around issues such as gay rights (Van Dyke, 1998), recycling (Lounsbury, 2001), antiapartheid actions (Soule, 1999), and sweatshop activism (e.g., Featherstone & United Students, 2002; Mandle, 2000). Each movement demanded that the university change its policies. Gay rights activism resulted in "LGBT" centers on campus. Environmentalists instituted campus recycling, while antiapartheid and sweatshop activists succeeded in having universities divest from nongreen enterprises.

How can one systematically understand this multitude of movements and their outcomes? What variation exists among movements and the universities they are connected with? How might this variation lead to a theory of movements in the university? The purpose of this chapter is to sketch an answer to these questions. This chapter describes the panoply of movements in universities with a typology relying on two distinctions: insider/outsider status and relation to the academic mission. The typology captures much of the basic terrain of social movements in the higher education context. Movements are defined by the students and scholars who lead them (Frickel & Gross, 2005; Frickel & Moore, 2005; Rhoads, 1998; Yamane, 2001). Other movements are organized by people other than students and faculty, such as modern conservatism, which targeted universities in an effort to combat policies such as affirmative action (Meyer & Staggenborg, 1996).

Another argument is that movements can affect the university itself or "spill out" into nonacademic realms. In considering how movements affect universities, I rely on a model developed by W. Richard Scott (2008). Organizations have multiple levels such as individual practices, routines, subunits, policies, and entire multiorganization systems. It may also be the case that movements in universities affect the state, public opinion, or other institutions. Thus, movements should be understood in terms of how they affect educational institutions as well as other social organizations, which may even lead to "push back" and repression of movements (Meyer & Staggenborg, 1996).

The subsequent sections explore these issues in detail. The next section starts by formulating a typology of movement-university interactions. The chapter then discusses examples of movements that represent the ideal types. Later sections discuss examples of movements that affect the different elements of institutions of higher education and the issue of "push back" against movements. The concluding discussion presents hypotheses about social movements and universities that might inform future research.

A Typology of Movement-University Interactions

Movements and universities vary in at least two key dimensions: the activists' relationship to the university and the movement's goals. In other words, there is the issue of who is mobilized and the separate issue of what they want. Within academic settings, a movement may be staged by students and professors or by activists from beyond the academy. Similarly, a movement may have academic or nonacademic goals. This typology surely simplifies things. Some movements, such as the labor movement, may include significant numbers of students and nonstudents and may mix academic and nonacademic goals. However, as a heuristic device, this typology assists in identifying themes and trends.

Table 9.1 illustrates this classification and provides examples. The first two columns indicate activist identities and movement goals. Each row represents a particular combination of actors and goals, illustrated with examples. The first row shows examples of movements that are associated with academic insiders and that promote academic goals. One such example is the 1990s student movement for multicultural curricula (e.g., Rhoades, 1998; Yamane, 2001). Conversely, the last row shows examples of movements with a tangential relationship to the university. These movements, such as the campus recycling movement, were often associated with broader political trends that went beyond the university (e.g., environmentalism) and brought policies that had no obvious academic content (e.g., recycling—Lounsboury, 2001).

A related but equally important issue is movement outcomes. What do activists get for their trouble? How can movement outcomes be described? This is a vast topic that has attracted the attention of many scholars (e.g., Giugni, 1998), but in this chapter I provide a simplified description. First, a movement outcome may be described in terms of how much it changes the organizational and institutional dimensions of the university. Some movements may ask only for a few very specific policy changes, such as a single course, or a pay raise for graduate student instructors. In contrast, other movements may demand whole-scale reconstruction of the higher education system and its values. Second, a movement's outcome may be described as a spillover into domains outside higher education. A movement may create ideas and practices that affect the public at large.

Table 9.2 provides examples of different outcomes associated with movements in universities. Each row lists a different type of outcome. The top row indicates movement outcomes that affect the routines and practices within universities. The aforementioned campus recycling movement, for example, focused on one specific procedure within the university: waste disposal. There are broader organizational outcomes of movements, such as structural change in universities. The ethnic studies movement of the 1960s promoted entirely new academic programs. The broadest academic change is that which affects an entire university system. In the 1960s, the civil rights movement successfully ended segregation, which had been a regular feature of college admissions in predominantly white colleges.

The bottom half of Table 9.2 describes movements that spill out into the

TABLE 9.I.
Typology of movement-university relations

Activists	Goals	Examples	Characterization
Academic	Academic	Multiculturalists demanding new courses (Bryson, 2005; Rhoads, 1998; Yamane, 2001)	Insiders challenging legitimacy of curriculum
		Heterodox philosophers (Gross, 2002)	Intellectuals challenging disciplinary or professional system
		Scientists against nuclear weapons (Moore, 2008)	Using the university as symbolic and social resource in politics
Academic	Nonacademic	Chinese democratization 1989 (Zhao, 2001)	Using the university as a launching pad for anti–Communist Party activism
Nonacademic	Academic	Nineteenth-century Christian progressives demanding early social science programs (Haskell, 1977)	Outsiders demand representation in the academy
		Conservative legal activists challenging university affirmative action policies (Teles, 2008)	Making the university a symbolic example
Nonacademic	Nonacademic	Vietnam War activists (Gitlin, 2003)	University as a source of rank-and-file student activists
		Environmentalists demanding campus recycling (Lounsbury, 2001)	Movement encourages universities to adopt ideologically favored policies

broader society from the academic sector. In rough terms, movements may affect culture or formal institutions, such as the state. This list is not meant to be exhaustive, but it is intended to draw attention to the complexity of movements in universities. Not only do they affect what happens in the higher education system, but they also ripple out into other domains. One example is the conservative legal movement. Forming within various law schools and economics programs, the conservative law and economics movement provided the intellectual resources that conservative elected officials needed to successfully defend policies and statutes from court challenges (Teles, 2008). Thus, this intellectual movement within the university system was a vital element of the wave of policies associated with the Reagan-Bush administrations.

TABLE 9.2.
Dimensions of university-based movement outcomes

Movement Changes	Examples
Inside higher education	
Practices	Recycling movement, multiculturalism
Organizational structure	Ethnic studies, disciplinary mobilizations, feminism/ women's centers
Field of higher education	Civil rights movement/college desegregation, affirmative action
Outside higher education	
Culture	Conservative legal activism, gay rights
State	Student pro-democracy groups, decolonization politics

Surveying the Terrain: Student Movements

It is difficult to make broad generalizations about student movements before the twentieth century because of sparse historical documentation of early universities (Cobban, 1971). There are, however, a number of scholars who have documented student activism in nineteenth- and twentieth-century Europe. For example, European historians note that college students participated in nationalist politics in the interwar period (e.g., Altbach, 1997; Judt, 2005). In Germany, university students founded organizations to discuss and promote liberal ideas in the nineteenth century. As revolutionary socialism became more prominent in nineteenth-century Europe, it was not uncommon for intellectuals and student groups to participate in various socialist causes (Gouldner, 1983).

Student activism in America appeared in the twentieth century. By the 1930s, American student activism emerged in a form that is recognizable today (Altbach, 1997; Brax, 1981). College students frequently participated in movements of the Left, such as labor, civil rights or ethnic rights, feminism, antiauthoritarianism, democracy, and peace. The American Youth Congress, an early twentieth-century student group, opposed racism and met in Washington, D.C., with officials from the Roosevelt administration. Cohen (1993) also points out that the Left of the FDR era had its roots at various colleges. The "Old Left" organizations of the 1930s drew their leadership from students who ran leftist campus clubs.

After World War II, student activism continued to grow. In the 1950s, it was common to find political groups on American campuses. Later, in the 1960s, student groups became key actors in American politics because they led movements that defined the era. One such group was the Students for a Democratic Society (SDS), which opposed the Vietnam War. SDS was important not only because it spearheaded the peace movement; its leaders became prominent in American politics (Adelson, 1972; Gitlin, 2003). Similarly, the Student Non-Violent Coordinating Committee emerged from student politics to lead the fight against segregation (Carson, 1981). Its leaders became prominent activists and elected officials, usually associated with the Democratic Party.

The rise of powerful student groups was not limited to the United States. Student groups established themselves in nearly every university system, often around similar issues. Notable examples include student groups that initiated the "May 1968" uprisings that nearly toppled the de Gaulle government in France (Gregoire & Perlman, 1970; Touraine, 1971), the anti-PRI student activists in Mexico (Poniatowska, 1975; Rhoads & Mina, 2001), and the 1968 student uprisings in Tokyo (Tsurumi, 1975).

Student movement groups often reflect the issues of the day and mirror broader social trends, such as college-based civil rights groups (Carson, 1981). However, in a few cases, movements within universities may develop a hostile stance toward society and use unorthodox, and occasionally violent, tactics to enact radical social transformation. For this reason, universities can act as incubators for movements that trigger substantial unrest, rather than just mirror social trends. Perhaps the most infamous example is Peru's Sendero Luminoso ("The Shining Path"). Started by philosophy professor Abimael Guzmán in the 1960s, the Sendero Luminoso was a Maoist group that formed within the San Cristobal of Huamanga University. Convinced that Peru was a corrupt and decadent capitalist state, Guzmán and his student followers waged class war within Peru. In the 1980s and 1990s, the group violently tried to topple the Peruvian state (Gorritti, 1999; Rochlin, 2003). Other examples of extremist student groups that formed in universities include the Weather Underground, which split from SDS in 1969 (Varon, 2004); the Black Panthers and the US Organization, which partially sprang from Oakland and Los Angeles college student politics (Brown, 2003; Ogbar, 2004); the notorious student gangs at the University of Havana in the 1930s, which included a young Fidel Castro (Thomas, 1998); anti-Western student groups in Iran (Mirsepassi-Ashtiani, 1994); and recently formed anti-Chavez student groups in Venezuela (Suggett, 2008).

There have been two recent developments that distinguish contemporary student activism from movements that formed before the 1960s. First, conservative movements have asserted themselves on college campuses, and they are not ephemeral anti-Left groups. The most notable conservative movement organization is probably Young Americans for Freedom (YAF) (Andrew, 1997). Started in 1960, the group's explicit goals are to defend the Constitution, individual choice, free markets, and the sovereignty of the United States. This organization is exceptionally important because it was the most prominent American alternative to left student politics and provided the conservative movement of the 1980s with the skills and infrastructure needed for electoral success (Andrew, 1997). Former YAF members became lawyers, business leaders, and political activists. The rise of conservatives in the 1980s depended, in part, on the networks developed in colleges during the 1960s and 1970s.

A second change that merits attention is that students began organizing around academic reform (Rhoads, 1998). It has always been the case that students have fought with faculty within colleges, but, as noted by historians, it was rare for students to demand control over the content of the curriculum (e.g., Cobban, 1971). Before the twentieth century student-faculty conflict often focused on whether faculty could control the daily life of students (Altbach, 1997; Veysey, 1965). Students also wanted control over the quality and content of instruction (Cobban, 1971). However, before the 1960s it was somewhat rare for students to make the university itself a target for sustained political action. In other words, students rarely demanded that universities change their mission. That began to change with the 1960s, and such demands intensified throughout the 1990s. Students in the 1960s, for example, demanded new academic programs such as ethnic studies and women's studies (Boxer, 1998; Rojas, 2007). Later, activists demanded multicultural courses in various universities (Bryson, 2005; Yamane, 2001).

Surveying the Terrain: Intellectual Movements and Academic Disciplines

Movements are not only the domain of students. Intellectuals and scholars may create their own movements. New disciplines and academic programs may emerge from contention among intellectuals and the attempt to gain control over the curriculum and research agenda of the university. For these reasons, there has been a renewed sociological interest in framing disciplinary change as a sort of social movement housed within the university system (Frickel & Gross, 2005). Using the typology of Table 9.1, intellectual movements are mobilizations of insiders for the purpose of internal reform. The creation of new disciplines and academic specialties is now seen as highly analogous to a social movement. An aggrieved group of scholars work together because they view the existing disciplinary system as unjust or constrained. They appropriate the resources needed to institutionalize new ideas.

The history of the academic disciplines lends support for this view. An early study by Ben-David and Collins (1966) framed the rise of psychology in such terms. Frustrated by limited career opportunities and the belief that philosophy was ill suited for the study of the human mind, the first generation of psychologists broke off from the philosophical profession. Similarly, Gross (2002) has characterized the split within contemporary philosophy, between analytical and heterodox philosophers, in the same way. Philosophers associated with the dominant analytical tradition viewed the mainstream as uncompromising and hostile to their ideas. In response, philosophers who specialized in other schools of philosophy, such as pragmatism, Continental philosophy, and feminism, organized breakaway groups, which even included protest during professional conventions. In reviewing this literature, Frickel and Gross (2005) postulate that certain conditions facilitate mobilization within disciplines. For example, if intellectuals begin to view the academic mainstream as illegitimate, they are more likely to mobilize. Intellectual movements that can acquire financial and symbolic resources are more likely to succeed in attracting adherents and possibly starting a new academic community. In summary, Frickel and Gross present intellectual movements as social movements highly similar to those outside the intellectual world.

Intellectual change may be due to outsiders. Social movements with few connections to universities or colleges may demand academic concessions. One notable example is the Christian progressive movement of the late nineteenth century. Haskell (1977) discusses how Christian progressives imagined a social science promoting virtue and decency in American society. They formed a professional association with its own journals and conferences. By the late 1880s, the Social Science Association lobbied research universities for academic programs. Though it failed, it created the environment for future disciplines in the university. The American Economic Association and the American Historical Association both broke off from the Social Science Association to become the main professional organization of each discipline in America.

Scholars have also examined the political organizations of scientists who mobilize on behalf of issues outside the university. In this case, the university is used as a resource in a larger political campaign. The university may give activists legitimacy, or it may provide physical resources (e.g., a place to meet) and financial resources. A key study on this topic is Moore's *Disrupting Science: Social Movements, American Scientists, and the Politics of the Military, 1945–1975* (2008). Based on case studies of scientist-run public interest groups, Moore shows how scientists negotiated the tenuous relationships between the academy, the state, and the public. Moore's study focuses on how scientists operated in the boundary between the state and the university and how each generation of scientists built on previous generations of campus activism. The university provided not only authority for that movement but also a link to the state via government contracts and consultation. These two resources, authority and state contacts, became a valuable resource for scientists mobilizing against nuclear weapons, the Vietnam War, and other issues.

Surveying the Terrain: Outsiders Target the University

Universities can be homes for student-based activism or sites of worker-driven organizational change. However, universities can also be the target of social movements that are not primarily identified with education. Social movements can choose higher education as a battleground on which they can make a symbolic point. For example, in the United States, conservative political groups have often targeted colleges and entire university systems in an attempt to promote preferred social policies (Andrew, 1997). Teles's (2008) recent work on legal conservative activism documents how lawyers strategically litigated against various universities to overturn affirmative action policies and campus speech codes. The goal, in many cases, was to use one student's grievance to set a precedent for further legal activism outside the academy. A decision against affirmative action in law school admissions, for example, could be used to justify litigation against race-based awards of government contracts. Similarly, conservative activists successfully promoted a 1998 California referendum that banned the use of race as a criterion in public university admissions decisions. It was hoped that this tactic could then be used to prohibit the use of race in other public policy, though there is little evidence that this has happened (Pusser, 2000).

Outsiders also use the university as a stage and launching pad for activism. For example, it is common for movements to recruit college students. Nearly every major social movement has, at one time, attempted to recruit students into its ranks. Numerous examples abound. The civil rights movements had important student groups, as do the labor movement, feminist organizations, and peace groups. Teles (2008) provides a recent informative example, the Federalist Society, the conservative legal association. Created by law students, the Federalist Society provides opportunities for outsiders to visit law schools and gather support for their own causes. Law students often get their first organized exposure to conservative legal activism through this organization. Activists litigating political "hot button" cases often rely on their contacts within the Federalist Society to acquire the expertise needed to press the case.

Change inside the University: Organizational Change

Organizations can be described as having multiple levels (Scott, 2008). Perhaps the most basic elements are practices and daily routines of the organization. An intermediate level is the organization itself. An organization can be described in terms of its units, policies, goals, and overall structure. The organization itself may be embedded in a larger environment, which includes other similar organizations. This larger environment has often been called the "organizational field." These multiple social systems are governed by institutions, which are the stable rules, formal and informal, that reflect the social consensus behind an organization. Social movements transform the university by changing any of these different elements of the organization (Davis, McAdam, Scott, & Zald, 2005).

The social movements of the 1960s are responsible for much change in the organizational structure in American higher education. At that time, there were many movements for new courses and departments, such as ethnic studies, black studies, and women's studies (Boxer, 1998; Brint, Turk-Bicakci, Proctor, & Murphy, 2009; Olzak & Kangas, 2008; Rojas, 2007). In some cases, the effects were obvious and direct. Universities adopted new courses in response to activist students and faculty. The establishment of these academic programs is the stamp that the 1960s left on university organization.

In other cases, movement outcomes are more indirect and can be seen at the level of practice. Once again, curricular reform movements of the 1960s provide an instructive example. Without new courses or departments, faculty members in a wide range of fields introduced ethnic- or gender-focused material into their courses. For example, the 1970s and 1980s witnessed a large growth in the application of feminist theory to issues in literary criticism, history, and the rest of the humanities. This was often couched in terms of the feminist mobilization of the late 1960s and early 1970s. Similarly, the rise of the ethnic studies movements of the late 1960s was soon followed by a wave of courses in traditional departments on the topic of African Americans, Asian Americans, Native Americans, and other American minorities (Cole 2006; Brint et al., 2009).

It is worth mentioning how professors interpreted these curricular changes. Multiple commentators have noted that later generations of students and faculty did not approach multicultural or feminist courses and departments with the same fervor as the generation of the 1960s (Bryson, 2005; Rojas, 2007; Yamane, 2001). At the height of these curricular reform movements, new courses were often seen as part of a larger effort at wholesale social change. For example, black studies activists often claimed that black studies departments could train students to work in poor inner-city areas. However, these motivations were soon amended, or even replaced, by academic professionalism. Students and professors in the 1990s and later were much more likely to see black studies as another academic specialty, much like Russian studies or chemistry (Rojas, 2007).

An important question is which universities are most likely to respond to movement activism. Which universities will create new programs or institute new courses? A number of recent studies have addressed this question with systematic data on universities. Rojas's (2006, 2007) analysis of the black studies movement shows that adoption of black studies in one university is strongly linked with student protest and the creation of similar programs in other universities. Cole (2006) shows that ethnic colleges (e.g., tribal colleges) are ten times as likely to adopt "ethnocentric" courses as mainstream colleges. Olzak and Kangas's (2008) joint analysis of ethnic studies and women's studies courses shows that the demographic profile of colleges is highly correlated with creation of these programs. Interestingly, Olzak and Kangas show that there is an asymmetric effect at work. Institutions with women's studies programs are likely to have ethnic studies, while the converse is not true. These findings suggest that a movement will be successful if its proposals resonate with the identity and mission of the college.

What happens when the movement and university have differing goals? One possibility is that faculty and staff will reformulate new policies and structures so that they have more traditional goals. This might be called the "cooling out" effect of institutions. In general, it is very difficult for a movement to resist this tendency. Administrators control budgets and may reward students and faculty when they propose or enact changes that are consistent with traditional academic standards. Another possibility—and one that involves a more subtle course of action—is that administrators may approve the hiring of faculty or the admission of students into new programs only if they eschew a movement's more radical tendencies. There are also external pressures. Even if administrators completely endorse a movement's goals, faculty may have trouble getting published, attracting research grants, and building a profile as a legitimate researcher.

For these reasons, the emergence of ethnic studies, and other disciplines arising from movements, merits continued attention from researchers. Despite the pressures to adopt a mainstream stance, these movement-inspired disciplines retain an important element of radicalism and have institutionalized it to a great degree. Academic programs and other formalized spaces, such as research centers, that exist within them mainstream yet retain strong identifications with the movements that spawned them; they have been called "counter-centers," to indicate their tenuous position (Rojas, 2007).

Change Spanning the University System: Reforms, Exits, and Start-Ups

It is often the case that a movement's goals and impact will not be confined to specific organizations. Political mobilization may target the broader environment in ways that go beyond structural change in a single college or university. The higher education environment itself may be the thing that is thought to be in need of change. Such efforts may be classified, broadly, as changing the "institutional environment." A movement may change the higher education system by altering or amending the rules that govern organizations. Another possibility is that movement activists find the traditional academic field completely inflexible, which may lead to their exit. I call these two options "institutional reform" and "exit."

This chapter has already addressed numerous examples of institutional reform. The civil rights movement is perhaps the best-known example. Over a period of thirty years, civil rights activists worked to change a very basic feature of American education: racial segregation. Through a complex series of court battles, legislative pushes, and protests, students, lawyers, and scholars managed to open up American colleges to students of all backgrounds. Affirmative action may be an example of fieldwide reform (Rhoads, Saenz, & Carducci, 2005). Countermovements may also attempt to reverse changes in the moral framework for higher education. As noted earlier, conservative legal activists have tried to reverse or ban affirmative action policies in universities through court actions and state referenda (Teles, 2008). These efforts have resulted in substantial policy changes in Texas, California, Michigan, and elsewhere. At the present, however, it is not evident that mobilization around these issues has resulted in wholesale reversal of the college admissions practices created in the 1970s and 1980s.

Intellectual movements may also engender institutional reform. Academics may change what is viewed as legitimate to teach and research across the higher education system. Much disciplinary change can be viewed in this way. When scholars and academics view existing disciplines as limited or inadequate, they may resort to political mobilization within the university system. The result can be a new discipline, which affects what is viewed as a proper domain of study in many universities.

This is not to say that all disciplinary change occurs in the same way. Intellectual movements may have an entire discipline in mind as they mobilize. For example, the rise of American studies might be viewed in such a light (Wise, 1979). Early on, intellectuals were specifically searching for a discipline that would draw on historical and humanistic approaches to American history. At other times, disciplinary change may emerge piecemeal, as programs at individual universities start and then form an entire academic field. An example of such change was the early movement for computer science (e.g., Aspray, 1999). Administrators often tried to place computer science in traditional engineering, mathematics, and library science programs. As computing become more commonplace and more universities housed mainframe computers and computer science research groups, computer science coalesced as a discipline in the 1960s and 1970s after mobilization by emergent computer scientists.

Institutional exit is the most radical alternative for social movement. It may the case that activists believe that their intellectual or educational goal simply can't be accomplished within the existing academic system. They may try to create organizations, student groups, and professional associations that exist independently of the traditional university system. One example can be drawn from the history of ethnic studies. For a few years in the late 1960s, activists attempted to establish all-black colleges such as Nairobi College and Malcolm X Liberation University (Belvin, 2004; Fergus, 2009; Van Deburg, 1992). The justification was that traditional academia could not accept a complete realignment toward Africa or African Americans. The colleges, which existed only briefly, were designed to channel students toward social work in inner cities and Africa. Conservative universities are another informative example. Feeling that mainstream academia did not pay enough attention to Christian values, Liberty University and Patrick Henry College were created to promote conservative viewpoints. Unfortunately, there is relatively little research on these institutions. Though documentation of such efforts is sporadic, there is evidence to suggest that many movements consider, and occasionally enact, higher education outside the traditional system.

Spill Out and Unintended Consequences

Movements in higher education settings may have important effects outside the academy. One important effect stems from how movements use universities as launching grounds for broader actions. Perhaps the two most sensational cases were the May 1968 protests that nearly toppled the de Gaulle government (Gregoire & Perlman, 1970; Touraine, 1971) and the 1989 Tiananmen Square movement (Zhao, 2001). In each case, universities acted as an incubator for a movement that strongly questioned the legitimacy of the state. Following a period of cultural and political liberalization, student groups emerged in the hothouse environment of the university. Then, students used the distinctive physical landscape of the university campus to stage demonstrations that could be hard for the state to control. The May 1968 students used the narrow streets of Paris to block police access, and the Tiananmen protesters coordinated without hassle because Beijing campuses tended to be demarcated from the rest of the city with high walls. In time, the growing student movement joined other groups, such as workers and intellectuals. Similar processes have been documented in the civil rights case where campus groups exploited the environment of black colleges in the 1950s and 1960s (Lowe, 2007; Polleta, 1999). In each of these three cases, the university-based mobilization resulted in massive confrontations with the state. These studies suggest that there are distinctive features of university organization and physical layout that are conducive, in certain circumstances, to mass movement mobilization.

Another important consequence is the effect that movements have on the wider political culture. Here, it is difficult to measure how university-based movements generate broad change, but particular cases are suggestive. For example, the civil rights movement fought many battles over school segregation, which became a model for demanding equality in other circumstances. Antiwar scientists are another useful example (Moore, 2008). It is plausible to think that the actions of scientists, especially in Europe, were contributing factors to the public's desire to limit the proliferation of nuclear weapons in Europe. These examples show the need for systematic study. When do university-based movements spill out into the public consciousness? How durable are these cultural changes? Does the fact that ideas emerge from academic contexts give them more or less legitimacy for the public?

The unintended consequences of university movements are another unexplored area. At least two are worth mentioning. First, university movements may change the lives of those who participate in them (McAdam, 1988). Research on activists often shows that they continue to participate in politics and that student activism is often the first stage in a political career. This suggests that, for certain students, campus activism is a gateway into a longer political career. This is a prominent theme in biographical accounts of civil rights activists. College students were recruited into activism through campus organizations, which then helped these individuals begin a lifelong habit of political activism.

Second, successful political mobilization may undermine educational organizations by altering the reason for their existence. For example, the civil rights and women's movements may have inadvertently accelerated the contraction of historically black colleges and women's colleges (Miller-Bernal & Poulson, 2007; Thomas & McPartland, 1984). A major reason for the existence of these institutions was race and gender-based segregation. With the end of legal segregation, these higher education sectors have often faced debilitating declines in enrollments. Successful mobilization may change the institutional environment that justifies particular organizations.

Shutting Down Movements and Regulatory Buildup

Social movements in higher education may trigger repression by the state, university leaders, and other actors (Meyer & Staggenborg, 1996). Repression itself may change institutions of higher education and society at large. The "push back" against movements may include changes in popular opinion, new regulations of campus life, and changes in the state itself. For these reasons, any account of movements in universities must also include a description of movement-countermovement dynamics.

Perhaps the most notable recent example of repression is the Chinese state's actions during the 1989 movement. After weeks of open challenge, movement sympathizers within the Chinese Politburo were overruled, leading to violent repression (Zhao, 2001). The catastrophic end of the democracy movement is not the only outcome of the repression. The Chinese state tightened its grip over the universities to prevent another challenge. Zhao reports that a number of countermovement reforms were instituted by the Chinese state. Students were more closely monitored by party representatives, the Chinese state reintroduced mandatory military service, and students were no longer allowed unrestricted access to foreign academic materials. In short, the repression of the student democracy movement resulted in a redefinition of the relationship between the state and the university.

Movement repression by authorities within the university system is an important but unexplored topic, though there are a few early studies (e.g., Lammers, 1977). Accounts of student strikes provide some evidence about the ways administrators target movements. A common theme is that administrators rely on the disciplinary system of the university to undermine or control movements. *The Time of the Furnaces* (Anthony, 1971), written by a former student activist, recounts how California State College administrators suppressed black student demonstrators by employing harsh sanctions. Even when disciplinary rules are lax, administrators will try to introduce stronger rules before confronting a movement (Rojas, 2010). It is also the case that administrators will try to defuse movements through less sensational means such as giving partial, or complete, concessions in the hope that disruption will stop. Furthermore, administrators may view the university as a place for students to explore ideas and exercise free speech. These views may create additional variation in the response to activism. Because this area of research is undeveloped, there is no current theory about the conditions under which administrators will resort to repression or concession or join with activists.

Interestingly, more can be said about the repression of intellectual movements because disputes among scholars are well documented. A key insight is that the rewards of the academic system go to those who publish in well-regarded journals and university presses. Thus much conflict revolves around the production, dissemination, and recognition of research (e.g., Gross, 2002; Harris, 1993). For these reasons, administrators rarely respond to intellectual movements by directly manipulating or controlling them. Instead, conflict centers on aggrieved intellectuals and the discipline's mainstream. Incumbent intellectuals can exercise numerous strategies for controlling or otherwise affecting insurgents within their discipline. One simple strategy is exclusion. Mobilized intellectuals may have their research ignored or rejected by the editors of journals and university presses (e.g., Gross, 2002). This tactic, framed as adherence to quality or an enforcement of intellectual boundaries, has the effect of suppressing the careers of intellectuals not aligned with the mainstream. Another tactic is delegitimization. Prominent intellectuals may provide a discourse that frames insurgents as anti-intellectual or incoherent. For example, a number of mainstream scientists have taken great efforts to delegitimize creationists who seek college credit for their courses or publication of their writings (Binder, 2002; Numbers, 2006).

When Do Movements in Universities Succeed or Fail?

This review shows the wide range of movements in universities and their impact. This chapter expended much effort in simply describing the nature of social movements and their relation to higher education. However, one may develop hypotheses about the efficacy of movements. The first hypothesis is that social movements are no more or less successful than their allies or counterparts in the nonacademic realm. This might be called the "correlation hypothesis." The success of a movement is correlated with the success of their nonacademic analogues. Perhaps the most prominent example is the civil rights movement. Black student activism in the 1950s and 1960s was enabled by the broader success of civil rights politics in American society. As the civil rights movement matured, there were more opportunities for students to learn from activists off campus.

In contrast, there may be a decoupling between academic movements and their off-campus allies. The higher education environment is distinct, and there might be no direct link between success within and outside the higher education system. For example, social conservatism has had remarkably little success within contemporary mainstream academia. As mentioned earlier, creationists, and others, have had a very difficult time in getting universities to accept their ideas as legitimate science (Binder, 2002; Numbers, 2006). Even though that movement has substantial resources, there is little evidence showing that these resources—money, robust movement networks, and organizations—have any currency within the academy. Perhaps the networks and ideas that permitted social conservatism to be successful in the American electoral politics have no validity among the constituencies of the university.

Then there are movements that do not have any counterpart outside the academy. The intellectual movements discussed in a previous section fit this description. For example, the movement of psychologists breaking away from professional philosophy in the nineteenth century has no counterpart outside the academy. There are other hypotheses that can be developed for such movements. One might be called the "Kuhnian" hypothesis: intellectual movements are most likely to succeed at times of perceived intellectual or academic crisis (Kuhn, 1962). These crises might be the intellectual analogues of "political opportunities" (e.g., elections, wars) that shape other movements. This hypothesis suggests that Kuhn's account of intellectual change might be a somewhat routine aspect of academic disciplines. Academic communities will occasionally have moments when old ideas and institutions come into question. Departing from Kuhn, there is no reason to believe that such crises are linked to theory falsification. Instead, crises may be political (e.g., disputes over authority within a discipline) or organizational (e.g., there are not enough resources for all groups within a profession). The result is a movement that modifies or secedes from a discipline.

Finally, it is worth drawing attention to an issue that may affect the success of all types of movements in universities—resource dependence (Pfeffer & Salancick, 1978). As noted multiple times, the university itself has resources that facilitate movements. There are meeting spaces, funds for student clubs, and a captive audience of potential converts. Therefore, success may be linked to the movement's integration and exploitation of the universities' resources. These hypotheses do not exhaust all possibilities but are presented to convey the need to develop a comprehensive theory of how academic movements achieve their outcomes.

Implications for Higher Education Research

The study of movements in university settings has implications for higher education research and organizational analysis. First, research in this area draws attention to the fact that student movements and intellectual politics have important effects. Instead of being disorganized and ephemeral happenings, movements can be sustained actions that introduce, intentionally or unintentionally, policies, ideas, and curricula into the academic system. Second, movements may be a natural source of change in academic settings. Students, or outsiders, will likely find some aspect of the university to be illegitimate and mobilize around the issue. Similarly, disputes among intellectuals may be translated into collective action, leading to change in academic programs and disciplines. In either case, contentious politics appears to be a constant force for change in universities. A third issue is that movements define how the university system relates to the broader polity. As discussed in the section on "spill out," movements can have important effects on states and popular opinion. Conversely, states, and the public, may move to censure or regulate the university because of student movements. Movement politics affect the tone of the relationship between universities and the state.

A different question for education researchers is how movements affect the basic structure of the higher education system. Though movements have been an important presence in the academic system since the 1800s, possibly earlier, there appears to be little evidence that the fundamental structure of academia has changed because of them. Movements may add disciplines, or occasionally create a new college, or alter access to higher education, but the system of colleges, departments, and disciplines remains the same. This is consistent with Burton Clark's (1986) observation that academia is a loosely coupled and highly adaptable system. Since universities are interchangeable bundles of programs and departments, it is easy to add another without disrupting the entire system. Education researchers can ask whether this is indeed a correct characterization, or whether there is substantial structural change due to movements. If not, then researchers should specify the mechanisms that allow the higher education system to remain unaltered in the face of repeated challenges.

Conclusion

Social movements are important because they change universities and society. For this reason, it is very important for higher education researchers to develop a well-supported theory of movements in the university. Such a theory, I suggest, must address the diversity of movements stemming from universities and the many ways that they change educational institutions and the larger culture. This chapter has presented an initial step in this path of inquiry. A taxonomy of movements and their outcomes is useful because it presents a list of "variables" to be examined through research. It is not the final stage of research; a successful research program will explain how these variables are related. Explaining how universities, movements, and social change are related will establish a strong, and much needed, link between research in higher education and related fields such as sociology, political science, and history.

REFERENCES

Adelson, A. (1972). *SDS*. New York: Charles Scribner's Sons.

Altbach, P. (1984). Student politics in the third world. *Higher Education, 13*, 635–655.

Altbach, P. (1997). *Student politics in America*. New Brunswick, NJ: Transaction Publishers.

Andrew, J. (1997). *The other side of the sixties: Young Americans for Freedom and the rise of conservative politics*. New Brunswick, NJ: Rutgers University Press.

Anthony, E. (1971). *The time of the furnaces: A case study of black student revolt*. New York: Dial Press.

Aspinall, E., & Berger, M. T. (2001). The break-up of Indonesia? Nationalism after decolonisation and the limits of the nation-state in post-cold war Southeast Asia. *Third World Quarterly, 22*, 1003–1024.

Aspray, W. (1999). Command and control, documentation, and library science: The origins of information sciences at the University of Pittsburgh. *IEE Annals of the History of Computing, 21*, 4–20.

Belvin, B. (2004). *Malcolm X Liberation University: An experiment in independent education*. Unpublished master's thesis, Department of History, North Carolina State University, Raleigh.

Ben-David, J., & Collins, R. (1966). Social factors in the origins of a new science: The case of psychology. *American Sociological Review, 31*(4), 451–465.

Binder, A. (2002). *Contentious curricula: Afrocentrism and creationism in American public schools*. Princeton, NJ: Princeton University Press.

Boxer, M. (1998). *When women ask the questions: Creating women's studies in America*. Baltimore: Johns Hopkins University Press.

Brax, R. (1981). *The first student movement: Student activism in the United States during the 1930s*. Port Washington, NY: Kennikat Press.

Brint, S. G., Turk-Bicakci, L., Proctor, K., & Murphy, S. P. (2009). Expanding the social frame of knowledge: Interdisciplinary, degree-granting fields in American colleges and universities, 1975–2000. *Review of Higher Education, 32,* 155–183.

Brown, S. (2003). *Fighting for US: Maulana Karenga, the US organization, and black cultural nationalism.* New York: New York University Press.

Bryson, B. (2005). *Making multiculturalism: Boundaries and meaning in US English departments.* Stanford, CA: Stanford University Press.

Carson, C. (1981). *In struggle: SNCC and the black awakening of the 1960s.* Cambridge, MA: Harvard University Press.

Clark, B. (1986). *The higher education system: Academic organization in cross-national perspective.* Berkeley: University of California Press.

Cobban, A. (1971). Medieval student power. *Past & Present, 53,* 28–66.

Cohen, R. (1993). *When the old left was young.* New York : Oxford University Press.

Cole, W. (2006). Accrediting culture: An analysis of tribal and historically black college curricula. *Sociology of Education, 79,* 355–387.

Davis, G., McAdam, D., Scott, W. R., & Zald, M. N. (2005). *Social movements and organization theory.* Cambridge: Cambridge University Press.

Featherstone, L., & United Students Against Sweatshops. (2002). *Students against sweatshops.* London: Verso.

Federeci, S., Caffentzis, G., & Alidou, O. (2000). *A thousand flowers: Social struggles against structural adjustment in African universities.* Trenton, NJ: Africa World Press.

Fergus, D. (2009). *Liberalism, black power, and the making of American politics, 1965–1980.* Athens: University of Georgia Press.

Frickel, S., & Gross, N. (2005). A general theory of scientific and intellectual movements. *American Sociological Review, 70,* 204–232.

Frickel, S., & Moore, K. (2005). *The new political sociology of science.* Madison: University of Wisconsin Press.

Gitlin, T. (2003). *The whole world is watching: Mass media in the making and unmaking of the New Left.* Berkeley: University of California Press.

Giugni, M. G. (1998). Was it worth the effort? The outcomes and consequences of social movements. *Annual Review of Sociology, 24,* 371–393.

Gorriti, G. (1999). *The Shining Path: A history of the millenarian war in Peru.* (Robin Kirk, Trans.) Chapel Hill: University of North Carolina Press.

Gouldner, A. W. (1983). Artisans and intellectuals in the German Revolution of 1848. *Theory and Society, 12,* 521–532.

Gregoire, R., & Perlman, F. (1970). *Worker-student action committees, France, May '68.* Detroit: Red and Black Press.

Gross, N. (2002). Becoming a pragmatist philosopher: Status, self-concept, and intellectual choice. *American Sociological Review, 67,* 52–76.

Harris, R. (1993). *The linguistics wars.* New York: Oxford University Press.

Haskell, T. (1977). *The emergence of professional social science.* Urbana: University of Illinois Press.

Judt, T. (2005). *Postwar: A history of Europe since 1945.* New York: Penguin Press.

Kuhn, T. (1962). *The structure of scientific revolutions.* Chicago: University of Chicago Press.

Lammers, C. (1977). Tactics and strategies adopted by university authorities to counter student opposition. In D. W. Light, (Ed.), *The dynamics of university protest* (pp. 171–198). Chicago: Nelson Hall.

Lounsbury, M. (2001). Institutional sources of practice variation: Staffing college and university recycling programs. *Administrative Science Quarterly, 46,* 29–56.

Lowe, M. (2007). An "oasis of freedom" in a "closed society": The development of Tougaloo College as a free space in Mississippi's civil rights movement, 1960 to 1964. *Journal of Historical Sociology, 20,* 486–519.

Mandle, J. R. (2000). The student anti-sweatshop movement: Limits and potential. *Annals of the American Academy of Political and Social Science, 570,* 92–103.

McAdam, C. (1988). *Freedom summer.* New York: Oxford University Press.

Meyer, D., & Staggenborg, S. (1996). Movements, countermovements, and the structure of political opportunity. *American Journal of Sociology, 101*(6), 1628–1660.

Mirsepassi-Ashtiani, A. (1994). The crisis of secular politics and the rise of political Islam in Iran. *Social Text, 38,* 51–84.

Miller-Bernal, L., & Poulson, S. (2007). *Challenged by coeducation: Women's colleges since the 1960s.* Nashville, TN: Vanderbilt University Press.

Moore, K. (2008). *Disrupting science: Social movements, American scientists, and the politics of the military, 1945–1975.* Princeton, NJ: Princeton University Press.

Numbers, R. (2006). *The Creationists: From scientific creationism to intelligent design.* Cambridge, MA: Harvard University Press.

Ogbar, J. O. G. (2004). *Black power: Radical politics and African American identity.* Baltimore: Johns Hopkins University Press.

Olzak, S., & Kangas, N. (2008). Ethnic, women's, and African American studies majors in US institutions of higher education. *Sociology of Education, 81,* 163–188.

Pfeffer, J., & Salancik, G. R. (1978). The external control of organizations: A resource dependence perspective. New York: Harper and Row.

Polletta, F. (1999). Free spaces in collective action. *Theory and Society, 28,* 1–38.

Poniatowska, E. (1975). *Massacre in Mexico.* New York: Viking.

Pusser, B. (2000). The contemporary politics of access policy: California after proposition 209. In D. E. Heller (Ed.), *The states and public higher education: Affordability, access, and accountability* (pp. 121–152). Baltimore: Johns Hopkins University Press.

Rhoads, R. A. (1998). *Freedom's web: Student activism in an age of cultural diversity.* Baltimore: Johns Hopkins University Press.

Rhoads, R. A., & Mina, L. (2001). The student strike at the National Autonomous University of Mexico: A political analysis. *Comparative Education Review, 45,* 334–353.

Rhoads, R. A., Saenz, V., & Carducci, R. (2005). Higher education reform as a social movement: The case of affirmative action. *Review of Higher Education, 28,* 191–220.

Rochlin, J. F. (2003). *Vanguard revolutionaries in Latin America: Peru, Colombia, Mexico.* Boulder, CO: Lynne Rienner Publishers.

Rojas, F. (2006). Social movement tactics, organizational change and the spread of African-American Studies. *Social Forces, 84,* 2139–2158.

Rojas, F. (2007). *From black power to black studies: How a radical social movement became an academic discipline.* Baltimore: Johns Hopkins University Press.

Rojas, F. (2010). Power as institutional work: Academic authority in the third world strike. *Academy of Management Journal, 53,* 1263–1280.

Scott, W. R. (2008). *Institutions and organizations.* Thousand Oaks, CA: Sage.

Soule, S. (1999). The diffusion of an unsuccessful innovation. *Annals of the American Academy of Political and Social Science, 566,* 120–131.

Suggett, J. (2008). Anti-Chávez student group attacks police, creates chaos in Mérida, Venezuela. *Venezuela Analysis.* Retrieved February 16, 2009, from www.venezuelanalysis.com/news/3640

Teles, S. (2008). *The rise of the conservative legal movement: The battle for control of the law.* Princeton, NJ: Princeton University Press.

Thomas, G., & McPartland, J. (1984). Have college desegregation policies threatened black student enrollment and black colleges? *Journal of Negro Education, 53,* 389–399.

Thomas, H. (1998). *Cuba, or the pursuit of freedom.* Cambridge, MA: Da Capo Press.

Touraine, A. (1971). *The May revolt: Revolt and reform—the student rebellion and workers' strikes.* New York: Random House.

Tsurumi, K. (1975). *Student movements in 1960 and 1969: Continuity and change.* Tokyo: Tokyo Press.

Van Deburg, W. (1992). *New day in Babylon: The black power movement and American culture, 1965–1975.* Chicago: University of Chicago Press.

Van Dyke, N. (1998). Hotbeds of activism: Locations of student protest. *Social Problems, 45,* 205–220.

Varon, J. (2004). *Bringing the war home: The Weather Underground, the Red Army Faction, and revolutionary violence in the sixties and seventies.* Berkeley: University of California Press.

Veysey, L. (1965). *The emergence of the American university.* Chicago: University of Chicago Press.

Wise, G. (1979). "Paradigm dramas" in American studies: A cultural and institutional history of the movement. *American Quarterly, 31,* 293–337.

Yamane, D. (2001). Student movements *for multiculturalism: Challenging the curricular color line in higher education.* Baltimore: Johns Hopkins University Press.

Zhao, D. (2001). *The power of Tiananmen: State-society relations and the 1989 Beijing student movement.* Chicago: University of Chicago Press.

CHAPTER TEN

Agency Theory
in Higher Education Organizations

JASON E. LANE

No institution in the United States puts more constraints on its
administration than a university. The administration cannot hire or
fire a faculty member on its own initiative. It cannot initiate a new
course offering, or modify or abandon an old one. It cannot
determine the requirements for completion of a course of study, or
decide whether or not a student has met those requirements. And in
most cases, it can neither admit nor dismiss a student.

> *Adam Yarmolinski (1923–2000)*
> *Professor of Public Policy*
> *University of Maryland, Baltimore County*

Colleges and universities are complex organizations with complicated relationships
between a variety of stakeholders, including administrators, faculty, governing
boards, and students. Several explicit and implicit contracts set the operational
parameters of the relationships. Contracts and their underlying assumptions are
the domain of principal-agent theory (PAT). At its most basic level, agency theory
assumes that social life is governed by a series of contracts. The "principal" enters
into a contractual relationship with an "agent" to provide goods or services. Contracts specify the responsibilities of both the agent and principal (Perrow, 1986).
By understanding and investigating the agency assumptions and the contractual
aspects of social life, scholars and administrators can better understand a wide
variety of governance and administrative arrangements and how to make them
more equitable and effective.

The use of PAT in higher education research over the past two decades has
been largely idiosyncratic, although there has been increasing recognition among

scholars of its utility for understanding higher education governance, policymaking, and administration.[1] The purpose of this chapter is not to provide an exhaustive literature review of the theory's existing use in higher education scholarship, nor is it to investigate the mathematical modeling some theorists use to predict principal-agent behaviors.[2] Rather, the chapter serves to introduce higher education scholars and practitioners to PAT, particularly its potential use in understanding administrative practice. The following provides an overview of the theory and its core concepts and discusses potential applications to the field of higher education administration.

Origins and Core Concepts of PAT

Many well-known observers of human behavior have noted the problem at the heart of the agency relationship: how to compel the agent to act in the best interest of the principal. The economist Adam Smith is generally recognized for providing one of the first descriptions of the principal-agent problem. In *The Wealth of Nations*, Smith (1776/1991) describes a corporate structure in which owners (principals) hire managers (agents) to run a corporation on behalf of the owners. Because managers are paid a salary and do not receive direct benefit from increased profit, Smith believed that the managers would shirk their duties and make wasteful spending decisions. Max Weber, an early scholar of organizations, noted a similar relationship in public bureaucracies. "The 'political master' finds himself in the position of the 'dilettante' who stands opposite the 'expert,' facing the trained official who stands within the management of administration" (Weber, 1958/1991, p. 232). Smith's observation focused on the fact that agents often have different motivations than their principals, and Weber's contribution identified the reality that agents often have specialized knowledge, making it difficult for the principal to monitor or assess the work of the agent. These two behavioral observations form the foundational assumptions of PAT.

More formal investigation of the agency relationship began in the 1970s with several articles investigating how concepts such as information asymmetry, self-interest, and incentives affected the relationship between two parties. Spence and Zeckhauser (1971) used an insurance policy to examine how trade-offs between risks and incentives affect individual behavior in relationships with asymmetrical information. In their article, the authors demonstrated that a driver is much more likely to engage in dangerous behavior if he or she has little to lose (i.e., being fully insured against loss) than if he or she had a financial incentive to act more prudently. Deductibles were found to reduce the likelihood that a driver would purposefully engage in risky behavior because the driver assumes some financial responsibility in case of accident.

Extending Spence and Zeckhauser's (1971) conclusions about incentives and risk taking, other theorists developed agency theory.[3] Miller (2005) identified six core assumptions of the canonical PAT model. First, the actions of the agent affect a payoff to the principal. Second, there exists an information asymmetry in that the outcome produced by the agent is observable by the principal but the agent's actions and abilities are not. Third, the agent has different preferences than the principal and has an interest in pursuing those interests in lieu of the principal's. Fourth, the agent reports to a single principal and that principal has a coherent set of preferences. Fifth, principal and agent share common information about the "structure of the game, effort costs, probability distribution of outcomes, . . . other parameters, . . . and agent's rationality" (p. 206). Therefore, the principal will try to construct an incentive package that provides the agent with only slightly more benefits than the agent's opportunity costs. Sixth, the principal can engage in ultimatum bargaining in that the principal can cancel the contract should the agent not accept the bargain.

Since the 1970s, agency theory has been applied to a number of different settings and situations, often relaxing one or more of the assumptions of the canonical model to allow it to better fit different types of organization such as public bureaucracies (e.g., Moe, 1984, 1990, 2005) and nonprofit organizations (e.g., Hansmann, 1987).[4] For example, Miller (2005) noted in his review of the use of PAT in political science that the theory has "been modified in ways that are inconsistent with the original formulations, but often in ways that are distinctly advantageous for progress in political science" (p. 206). Nonetheless, foundational aspects such as the existence of a principal, agent, and contract remain constant among all approaches. It is important, though, for those wanting to use PAT to study higher education to understand both the canonical model and how it may be adapted to fit with the characteristics of higher education institutions. The following concepts are central to understanding how the canonical model has evolved to study public bureaucracies and nonprofit organizations and may be applied to higher education.

Contract

The relationship between the principal and the agent is governed by either an explicit or implicit contract in which the principal delegates authority to the agent to act on the principal's behalf. While early theorists believed the existence of a

PAT relationship required an explicit contract (Tosi, Katz, & Gomez-Mejia, 1997), scholars such as Eisenhardt (1989) and Bergen, Dutta, and Walker (1992) interpreted the contract more as a metaphor than as a detailed legal proscription. Explicit and implicit contractual relationships are ubiquitous in higher education (Lane & Kivisto, 2008). Employment is governed by contracts. Students contract with the institution to provide educational opportunities. Governments and foundations contract with the institution to provide education, research, service, and economic development. Universities create colleges and schools, which in turn create departments. The relationship between these subunits is typically governed by implicit contractual expectations.[5]

Economists have identified two basic contractual models: behavior-based contracts and outcome-based contracts (Eisenhardt, 1989), although not all contracts fit neatly into one or the other. Behavior-based contracts reward the agent based on behavior—for example, rewarding faculty for sitting in their office during posted office hours, using approved teaching techniques, and spending a certain number of hours per week engaging in research and/or writing. Outcome-based contracts measure an output or indicator of performance. In contrast to rewarding faculty for a particular behavior, outcome-based contracts would reward research productivity or student learning outcomes.

Furthermore, under the canonical model, the principal and the agent are assumed to have the ability to freely enter and exit the contract.[6] While higher education institutions have many contracts in which parties can freely enter and exit (e.g., some employment contracts), there are also contracts with which there is no clear exit strategy, leading to bilateral negotiations. The governing board has the freedom to hire and fire the president. The president has the freedom to accept, reject, or end his or her contract with the institution. The same is true for all employees. Even tenured faculty, with whom it is often difficult for the institution to end a contract, can be terminated, and the faculty member has the freedom to accept, reject, or end his or her contract, although tenured faculty tend to have more negotiating leverage than nontenured faculty. However, most public universities are agents of the state government that charters and funds them, and it is reasonable to assume that leaving or ending the contract is not a feasible option for either entity (Lane & Kivisto, 2008). Similarly, because universities are loosely coupled systems (Weick, 1976), most organizational units (particularly within academic affairs) are semiautonomous, self-governing entities. A unit such as a college of education is an agent of the university created and funded to engage in teaching, research, and service related to education. While not impossible, it is very improbable that the university would end its relationship with the college; similarly, the college cannot detach itself from one university and move to another.[7] Not being able to freely exit the contract changes how the actors interact; so too does the difficulty in how a contract may be ended (e.g., adjunct faculty may act differently than tenured faculty owing to the job protections provided in the contract). Similarly, a faculty member with multiple job offers has more power in a principal-agent relationship than one with limited alternative career opportunities.

Shirking and Slippage

A primary concern of the agency relationship is how to align the actions of the agent with the preferences of the principal. It is assumed that the principal and the agent are self-motivated utility maximizers that will engage in behaviors that increase their own individual utility (Davis, Schoorman, & Donaldson, 1997; Frey, 1993; Kiewiet & McCubbins, 1991). While it may be possible for the agent and principal to share goals, it is unlikely. In fact, some theorists suggest that it is impossible for full agreement between the agent and principal to ever exist (e.g., Bednar, 2006). Further, Ostrom (1999) notes that decades of empirical evidence suggest that "the temptation to cheat always exists. No amount of monitoring and sanctioning reduces the temptation to zero" (p. 508). This dynamic leads to the heart of the agency dilemma, implementing mechanisms to reduce shirking to a point tolerable by the principal.

Shirking refers to the misalignment between the actions of the agent and preferences of the principal and has historically been assumed to be due to the self-interested pursuit of different preferences. A predominance of the PAT literature continues to be based on this assumption. However, in recent years, a few scholars, particularly those studying international organizations, have used the term "slippage" to describe the disconnect between agent actions and principal preferences. Slippage can occur as a result of shirking or of structural issues. Long chains of principals and agents can create communication breakdowns wherein the ultimate agent does not know or is misinformed about the preferences of the ultimate principal (Goodin, 2003; Waterman & Meier, 1998). Consider the multiple layers of administration that often exist between university presidents and faculty, as well as the fact that decision-making processes are often unclear and participation in those processes often fluid (Cohen, March, & Olsen, 1972). Moreover, the existence of multiple principals can send mixed signals or contribute to information loss or overload (Nielson & Tierney, 2003). As a result, the agent may engage in activity that it believed was aligned with the preference of the principal but which, in actuality, was not.

Moreover, incentive mechanisms in contracts used by colleges and universities may not align with the stated goals. Such a disconnect between goals and incentives could lead to apparent shirking on behalf of employees, who are actually responding to incentives rather than stated goals. For example, even though an administrator may complain about faculty shirking their teaching responsibilities, the reality of the situation may be that the incentives put in place by the institution/professional environment reward faculty for their research and scholarly activities and not teaching or service responsibilities. PAT may be useful for further understanding such perceived shirking of faculty as well as other situations in which incentives and goals are misaligned.

One way to overcome some shirking is for the principal to actively monitor the activities of the agent. This oversight can increase efficiency by limiting activities not of benefit to the principal. Yet such monitoring can be costly, time consuming, and sometimes impossible when the principal does not have the knowledge to discern between value-added and non-value-added behaviors, as is often the case when dealing with professional bureaucracies like educational organizations (Mintzberg, 1979).[8] Transaction costs include the costs of contract negotiations, execution, and enforcement. Thus, once an agency relationship is created, the principal must weigh the costs of monitoring against the potential costs of allowing the agent to shirk. The principal may realize that allowing a small amount of shirking to occur is an acceptable loss if the cost of preventing that shirking is more than merely allowing it to happen. In addition to the costs involved, performance monitoring has been shown to have unintended social consequences, such as decreased knowledge sharing; inhibited work effort; resistance behaviors, such as cheating; and the corrosion of organizational trust (Knox, 2010). Paradoxically, monitoring may actually encourage or reinforce the very behaviors it is designed to prevent.

Information Asymmetry

A major contributor to shirking is information asymmetry, which exists when one actor has more information about a situation than another. Information asymmetry is a common aspect of agency relationships and usually occurs for two reasons. First, the principal cannot oversee the activities of the agent and therefore does not know the extent to which shirking may be occurring. Second, some agents possess specialized knowledge about the process and the output, making it difficult for the principal to assess the effectiveness of the process used or the quality of the product. For example, faculty are contracted to provide a course for a student. Because faculty possess specialized knowledge about their field of study, it makes it difficult for nonexperts to assess their work.[9]

The existence of information asymmetry leads to two potential dilemmas for the principal: moral hazard and adverse selection (Eisenhardt, 1989). Moral hazard refers to the possibility that the agent may engage in behaviors that detract from the goals or payout of the principal. These behaviors are discussed above in the section on shirking. Adverse selection refers to the agent misrepresenting its abilities. In some situations, it is not possible for the principal to verify the skill or knowledge of the agent. This may lead to the principal contracting with an agent that does not have the ability to complete the contract. Eisenhardt (1989) uses the example of hiring a research scientist who claims to possess a certain scientific specialty, which the employer is unable to judge either during the hiring process or, sometimes, while the person is working. To deal with the possibility of adverse selection in employment decisions, Spence (1973) suggested that potential employees use higher education credentials as a way to signal their worth to potential employers. Employers may also use other measures such as passing a certification exam and employment references, though it is impossible to eliminate all risk that a potential hire will not perform to the level expected.

Principals: Single, Multiple, and Collective

While the canonical model assumes one principal contracts with one agent, many scholars have since recognized more complex types of principal-agent relationships.[10] The single principal acts alone in its relationship with the agent. Ideally, the principal has a clear set of preferences and expects the agent to engage in activities based on those preferences. As only two actors are involved in the model, it is also the simplest to understand and study. However, higher education institutions are replete with more complex principal-agent relationships. Some relationships include an agent reporting to multiple principles. In other instances, a principal, such as a governing board, may be comprised of a collective of individuals that must agree on the contract; and, thus, form a collective principal.

Multiple Principals

Multiple principals exist when two or more principals have separate contracts with an agent (Lyne & Tierney, 2003). Such relationships contain systemic dilemmas for the agent, as the multiple agents could potentially desire the agent to pursue contrary goals (although they could also seek pursuit of complementary goals). Moe (1984) noted that "competitive, multiple principals" are an inherent component of democratic designs and that "bureaus are 'partial agents' of various governmental principals, without being under the complete authority of any one in particular, and without any common understanding of how authority is legitimately divided among the competing principals. The net result is that politicians in general have a more difficult time controlling the bureaucracy" (pp. 768–769). Thus agents in public bureaucracies are pulled in multiple directions. Similar sets of relationships exist in higher education institutions. Even though legal responsibility for an institution may lie in a single entity such as a governing board, multiple actors such as the legislature, the governor, higher education commissioner, and coordinating board all could compete for some controlling interest in the decision-making processes of public colleges and universities. Within the institution, faculty sometimes have joint appointments reporting to different departments. Departments sometimes report to different divisions— for example, an academic department with graduate programs could be subject to the authority of its disciplinary home (e.g., College of Arts and Sciences) and also the School of Graduate Studies. This puts the agent in a difficult situation when fulfillment of one principal's request may mean defying the request of a another principal. The dean of Arts and Sciences may be pushing to increase the number of full-time faculty teaching undergraduate courses, while the dean of Graduate Studies may have a goal of increasing the number of graduate courses being offered. In such a case, the department has to decide which request to follow, particularly if no new resources are available.

When multiple principals operate as part of a governance structure, a number of potential problems arise, two of which I will highlight here. First, assuming all principals agree on the nature of the contract, the major agency problem becomes one of enforcement. Someone should be responsible for the monitoring of the contract. Ideally, this responsibility would be discussed and shared by the agents. Often, though, an issue of free ridership occurs when one principal assumes responsibility for oversight and the other principal(s) benefit from free-riding. Essentially, those not engaged in the enforcement process benefit from having the contract enforced without having the costs associated with enforcement.

Second, suppose the agent possesses separate and competing contracts with two or more principals. In such a case, the agent must decide which contract to fulfill, sometimes flip-flopping between contracts based on factors such as convenience for the agent or shifts in power among the principals. The result of such flip-flopping is potential incoherence in policy outcomes and agent behavior, particularly given shifts in political or administrative power over time (Hammond &

Knott, 1996). For example, consider the role of a state commissioner of higher education, who is a member of the governor's cabinet and an employee of a state coordinating board. In this example, the commissioner has separate contracts with both the governor and the coordinating board. If competing demands arrive from the governor and the board, the commissioner has two alternatives: flip-flop based on the most recent contract change or make a choice based on the relative power between the two principals (Lyne & Tierney, 2003). In the latter option, the agent must in some way reconcile the difference in demands with the contractual terms with each principal. In another example, a faculty member might have dual contracts with two departments. Some faculty have joint appointments, such as with both the Department of History and Department of Political Science. Conflict may arise if the faculty member is required to attend concurrent faculty meetings. Or one department may emphasize good teaching as the primary evaluative mechanism while the other department focuses on research productivity. In this case, the faculty member must decide which contract to fulfill, realizing the fulfillment of one may lead to not fulfilling the other.

When competing contractual demands exist, agent behavior may seem erratic or incoherent to individual principals. Further, a variety of factors involved in the political and administrative dynamics may complicate outcomes. Governors, legislators, presidents, board members, deans, department chairs, and other decision makers change. The contractual expectations of the principal(s) may be unclear as actors or policy preferences change. The agent may not fully understand the power dynamics between/among the principals. In sum, there is no simple solution to the problem of multiple principals with competing expectations, but further research is necessary to determine how agents reconcile such situations.

Collective Principals

Collective principals exist when more than one individual must agree on the nature of the contract with the agent (Kiewit & McCubbins, 1991; Lynn & Tierney, 2003). Collective principals are common in higher education: governing board, faculty senates, departmental faculty, and so forth. Multiple members constitute each of these principals, and either a plurality or majority of the members must agree on the nature of a contract and methods of enforcement. A key theoretical question thus arises: Should these entities be viewed in the same way as a single principal such as a president or dean? Or does their composition as a collective change the nature of the principal-agent relationship?

Take the example of an institutional governing board. Ideally, governing boards operate as unitary actors, legally endowed with corporate status and, thus, recognition as an individual in the eyes of the law. However, each individual member of the governing board has her individual preferences and expectations. Thus, in assessing the relationship between a president and her board, one cannot simply assume that the board is a unitary actor. The relationship between the principal and the agent may differ based on who constitutes the membership of the board and how that membership interacts. Figure 10.1 uses potential voting patterns of a governing board of five members to illustrate how different voting patterns can affect the relationship between the principal and the agent. In the diagram on the far left, all members share the same preference, with Policy 1 being the optimal choice. In this case, there is a unanimous vote. The board acts essentially as a single principal. In the central diagram, the vote is split, with members A, B, and C voting for Policy 1, while members, D and E vote for Policy 3. In this case, it may be worth considering who constitutes the principal. Does one consider the action of the majority vote as a decision of a unitary principal? Or is the principal composed of only the majority voters in this case, with members D and E not considered part of the contractual principal? Or is the principal the swing vote that tipped the balance in favor of Policy 1? How does a split vote affect the relationship between a member of the board and the president? Will compliance with a unanimous decision of a collective principal differ from that of a divided collective principal? Are only the winning members responsible for monitoring compliance with the decision? Do power dynamics on the board influence the action of the president who is seeking a particular policy outcome? Will she solely lobby a key power broker, such as the board president, because of his ability to influence the voting?

In the diagram on the right in Figure 10.1, the relationship becomes more complex because of differing levels of power associated with the collective. In this diagram, member C is the board chair and has a strong preference for Policy 2. Policy 2 is not the preferred choice of the other members of the board; however, the members feel obliged to vote along with the board chair and therefore vote unanimously in favor of Policy 2. The power of the board chair essentially creates a unitary principal, as the other members of the collective become subordinates to the board chair. When such a case is applied to a governing board of a single institution, the critical relationship worthy of study is that between the board chair and the institution's president. Even though there is the appearance of a collective agent, in reality the relationship may operate as that between a single principal and single agent.

The research in this area has been primarily theoretical in nature, though its

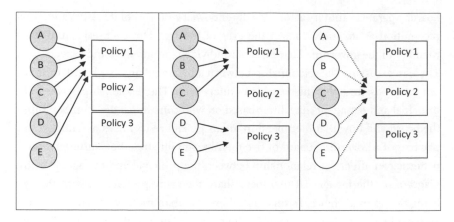

Figure 10.1. Collective Principal Decision Making. Adapted from Lynn & Tierney 2003

applicability to higher education seems readily apparent. The higher education sector is filled with multiple and collective principals, and yet there is very little scholarship about how principal composition affects the relationship with the principal. Still, the theoretical considerations being put forth could be of benefit to both scholars and practitioners interested in understanding the dynamics of such relationships.

Nondistribution Constraint of Nonprofits

Unlike its for-profit counterpart, a "nonprofit organization is . . . barred from distributing its net earnings, if any, to individuals who exercise control over it, such as members, officers, directors, or trustees" (Hansmann, 1980, p. 835). This nondistribution constraint results in the organization having less incentive to produce cheaper (and lower-quality) goods or services, as the excess profits are not returned to the owners (Hansmann, 1980), although, as most workers (either in the for-profit or nonprofit sector) do not directly benefit from increased profits, it does not necessarily reduce the incentive for employees to be less productive. Hansmann (1980) extrapolates that in markets like education and health care where it is difficult to assess the quality of the service rendered, the nondistribution constraint may entice consumers to do business with a nonprofit rather than a for-profit entity.

Following Nelson and Krashinsky (1973), Hansmann (1980) posited that nonprofit organizations generally thrive in markets where there is a high degree of information asymmetry and it is difficult for the principal to effectively monitor or evaluate the work of the agent. Agency theory would suggest that in such an environment the agent would pursue its own goals in lieu of the principal's, resulting in the delivery of an inferior product or service. Because the nondistribution constraint reduces the amount of personal financial benefit the managers receive from providing low-quality services, Hansmann (1987, p. 29) suggests that they thus "have less incentive to take advantage of their customers than do the managers of a for-profit firm."

Not all scholars agree that there is less likely to be shirking in nonprofits than in for-profits, however. Economists focusing on property rights suggest that nonprofit managers tend to have greater autonomy in the performance of their job duties than their for-profit colleagues. This heightened level of autonomy, particularly when combined with the nondistribution constraint, could lead to increased levels of shirking. However, this shirking is in the form of on-the-job consumption rather than providing an inferior good or service. Because nonprofit managers do not receive benefit from increased profits, they could be less likely to consume goods or time while on the job (Alchian, 1977; Alchian & Demsetz, 1972). One concern with this line of inquiry is that it assumes, possibly incorrectly, that increased managerial discretion leads to more shirking (Valentinov, 2006). Another potentially fruitful application of PAT to higher education is studying whether such a link between increased freedom and shirking exists; existing studies of the academic ratchet (discussed below) suggest that increased autonomy leads to shirking among faculty, although these studies simply assume connection without comparing different types of faculty contracts based on levels of autonomy.

PAT in Higher Education Administration

Application of the theory has mostly come from scholars studying the governance and politics of higher education who focus on the relationship between government and higher education institutions.[11] Within the area of higher education administration, PAT has been used in higher education research to study such topics as students' institutional choice (Dill & Soo, 2004), resource allocation (Massy, 1996), faculty shirking (i.e., academic ratchet) (Massy & Wilger, 1992), impact of government policy (Kivisto, 2007; Knott & Payne, 2004; Lane, 2003, 2005), and bureaucratic accretion (i.e., academic lattice) (Clotfelter, 1996; James, 1990; Ortmann & Squire, 2000), as well as the development of science policy (e.g., Braun, 1993; Meulen, 1998) and research and development initiatives (e.g., von Zedtwitz & Gassman, 2002). Indeed, for those interested in studying PAT, higher education institutions provide a favorable social laboratory for exploring the theoretical robustness and versatility of the principal-agent concept.

In each of the following sections, different groups of actors are used to explore various past and potential applications of PAT to higher education. Many of these scenarios are meant to challenge readers to explore new ways in which PAT may be used to study higher education organizations. Readers should note that the following discussions are not exhaustive and there are many other potential applications of PAT to higher education. In some cases, the ideas presented may be applicable to other agency relationships in the higher education environment. For example, while the goal of prestige maximization is discussed within the context of the student-institution relationship, it could also be used to understand the actions of governing board members, administrators, and faculty.

Academic Ratchet and the Administrative Lattice

The employment of faculty creates an example of the classic principal-agent relationship in that faculty jobs are mostly not task driven—the manager cannot preprogram faculty activities and then evaluate the faculty as to the extent to which they engage in those activities (Gomez-Mejia & Balkin, 1992). Indeed, it is often improbable, if not impossible, for administrators to fully evaluate the quality of the outcomes (e.g., student learning or journal articles) delivered by faculty. In the past twenty years, PAT has been used sporadically to explain the determinants of faculty pay (e.g., Gomez-Mejia & Balkin, 1992) and how reward structures affect faculty behavior (Massy, 1996; Ortmann & Squire, 2000).

Two concepts that have become better understood through the application of PAT to higher education are the academic ratchet and the administrative lattice. Academic ratchet is the tendency of faculty over time to shift effort away from tasks such as teaching, student advising, and committee work in order to spend more time on research and other endeavors that are more personally or financially rewarding (James, 1990; Massy & Wilger, 1992; Massy & Zemsky, 1994). The administrative lattice describes the growing administrative structures, usually with the number of administrative posts growing faster than the number of faculty (Ortmann & Squire, 2000).

To illustrate how the academic ratchet directly affects the administrative lattice, Ortmann and Squire (2000) engaged in one of the most thorough applications of PAT to higher education. Drawing upon their earlier work (Ortmann & Squire, 1996), in which they identified four cascading levels of principal-agent games (i.e., students and alumni, the overseers, the administrators, and the professors), the authors created a model principal-agent game. In the model, "the prototypical professor has three related objectives: job security, freedom to spend his time on activities he prefers, and maximization of professional reputation and prestige" (Ortmann & Squire, 2000, p. 380). The administrator has similar goals in that she pursues job security, an enhanced reputation, and freedom to pursue additional income opportunities.

As predicted by many authors, faculty are assumed to shirk on duties that are difficult to measure (e.g., teaching) or could be performed by others (e.g., shared management duties such as advising and committee work), thus creating a set of administrative tasks for which the administrator is held responsible. The administrator, who also wants additional free time, could complete the administrative tasks, force the faculty member to do those duties, or hire additional administrative staff to carry out those duties. Since the administrator does not want to perform those tasks not performed by the faculty member and usually does not have sufficient leverage to force the faculty member to do those duties (particularly if the faculty member is tenured), the administrator will hire additional administrators, growing the administrative lattice.

Nonprofit Status

Most academic institutions operate as nonprofit organizations. According to the 2005 Carnegie Classification of Higher Education Institutions, 79% of the 4,391 academic institutions operating in the United States are nonprofit organizations. Most nonprofits operate by receiving charitable donations (donative) or charging for their services (commercial). Most nonprofit colleges and universities in the United States act as both donative and commercial nonprofits.[12] Even in the 1600s, Harvard College charged tuition, received government subsidy, and benefited from a large number of donations (Morrison, 1936). Today, colleges and universities provide a number of commercial services: governments and foundations purchase research, various agencies purchase services, and students purchase an education.

Education is a sector in which there is a great deal of information asymmetry between the producer (agent) and consumer (principal). Students who purchase the opportunity to pursue advanced learning at a higher education institution have little ability to truly assess the value of that degree until long after the fact, a troubling fact when one considers the high stakes associated with the choice. Historically, college has been a singular purchase. If a student completes a degree at Harvard and realizes that it was not a good purchase, it is unlikely that student would pursue another degree from Penn State (although it is increasingly likely for students to transfer among institutions or return to school for retraining). Based on the assumptions put forth by Hansmann (1980, 1987), students would prefer to enter into a contract from a nonprofit educational entity rather than a for-profit because the nonprofit entity may be less likely to shirk on the quality of the product—although the increasing number of students enrolling in for-profit educational institutions may challenge this assumption and scholars may seek to investigate the applicability of Hansmann's theories to the higher education sector.

Academic institutions also tend to be donative organizations. Many people donate money and goods to nonprofit academic institutions and, hereto, contractual relationships are created. Most donations go to support operational or programmatic costs, including scholarships for students. As Hansmann (1987) observes,

> A donor is, in an important sense, a purchaser of services, differing from the customers of commercial nonprofits (and of for-profit firms) only in that the services he or she is purchasing are either (1) delivery of goods to a third party . . . [as in the case of an alumni endowing a scholarship to support the education of future students]; or (2) collective consumption goods produced in such aggregate magnitude that the increment purchase by a single individual cannot be easily discerned [as in the case of multiple donors contributing to the annual fund, used to support the general operations of the university]. In either case, the purchaser is in a poor position to determine whether the seller has actually performed the services promised; hence the purchaser has an incentive to patronize nonprofit firm. (p. 30)

A third type of donation is the transference of stewardship over works of arts and other items of cultural significance. While it is possible for the donor to monitor the use and care of the works of art, most donations occur with the intent that the preservation of the item will continue after the death of the donor.

Such donations create a contractual relationship wherein the donor provides the donation with the expectation of some service being provided by the organization. Some of these contracts are more explicit than others. A donation to the annual fund may be tied to a general desire to improve the institution, hardly a measurable objective, and most people who donate to the annual fund do not have very explicit goals for the use of their money. Other donors tie explicit expectations to their donations, such as using their money to provide certain programs or scholarships to certain students. In recent years, critics have begun to question some universities' commitment to donative contracts. Two recent examples include Fisk University's attempts to sell artwork donated by the artist Georgia

O'Keeffe[13] and the family of a donor challenging how Princeton University was using the donated funds.[14]

The effects of an educational institution's nonprofit status have received scant scholarly attention. Yet it seems that the nondistribution constraint of such organizations could impact their relationship with students and other actors, and much could be gained from a comparative perspective with for-profit institutions. Moreover, the contracts that exist between donors and higher education institution have not been of scholarly interest but may be a ripe area for research particularly given the increased concerns of donors about how their donations have been used by the institutions.

Prestige Maximization

The relationship between students (and alumni) and their college or university is very complicated. First, students do not simply purchase an education or a credential; they purchase the opportunity to pursue an education, often with the hope of being awarded a degree.[15] Second, the institution often selects who has the opportunity to purchase its product. Third, the institution has a vested interest in how well the student performs both while in school and after he or she leaves the institution because the value of the institution's product is, in part, based on the performance of those who purchased the product previously.

Substituting a prestige (or utility) motivation (Garvin, 1980; James, 1986, 1990) for a profit motivation in a principal-agent contract raises interesting propositions for the study of higher education. In such cases, students can no longer be viewed simply as a principal contracting with the university (agent) for an education. By selecting who has the opportunity to pursue an education, the institutions (as principal) are contracting with the student (the agent) to engage in behaviors that increase the institution's prestige. If one accepts this assumption about the institution-student relationship, then institutions would be expected to develop mechanisms that reward the student for behavior that garners prestige for the institution, create mechanisms to assist students to be successful, and/or punish the student for engaging in activities that reduce or threaten institutional prestige.

Some may dismiss the application of PAT to such situations because it is believed to be viewed as overly cynical or failing to acknowledge the altruistic motivations of some individuals and institutions. However, accepting an institution's contract with students to provide prestige maximization presents a set of explanations for activities and behaviors that may not have been previously consid-

ered. Universities provide a range of incentives for students to engage in prestige-maximizing behaviors. The ultimate is the awarding of a degree if students
successfully complete enough educational units. The more successful (measured
in a number of different ways) students are when they leave college, the more prestige is garnered for the institution. To improve the likelihood of a student being
successful after leaving the institution, the institution has an interest in ensuring
that the student completes a course of study designed to maximize its success
and will not award a degree until that course of study is completed. Beyond the
awarding of degrees, there are other awards ranging from the outstanding Greek
freshman to academic fellowships to membership in honor societies. All these
activities reward and encourage prestige-maximizing behaviors. Moreover, institutions create contracts, such as a student code of conduct or honor code, that
outline the types of behaviors that are not permissible (and often punished) because they tarnish institutional prestige.

In fact, unlike the student's contract with the university to purchase an education which ends upon separation from the institution, a prestige-maximization
contract could be interpreted as extending beyond the tenure of the individual as
a student. Even for alumni, institutions maintain a schema of incentives designed
to encourage the prestige-building activities of alumni. Institutions provide an
array of alumni merit awards to recognize contributions of the alumni. Many
institutions also provide alumni networking opportunities and lifelong career
counseling services to help students even after they graduate. True, some may
argue that such awards are motivated by profit maximization motives and are
designed to encourage donative activities; however, as Winston (2000) observes,
the purpose of maximizing donative behaviors is to support prestige-pursuing
activities such as scholarships and endowed professorships.

Contract Enforcement

The university is a social institution, and students engage in wide range of contractual relationships, some of which they willingly comply with and others they
do not (e.g., athletic teams, scholarships, student organizations, student-worker
positions). Therefore the relationship between the student and the institution is
regulated not by a single contract but by multiple contracts, enforced in a variety
of ways, with differing levels of oversight, and by principals who are not always
evident to the student. For example, some coaches require athletes to sign contracts that they will not engage in certain behaviors. By accepting admission to
the university, the student agrees to abide by a student code of conduct or an

honor code. Students also accept various roles such as student-worker positions, campus tour guides, student organization leadership, graduate assistantships, and so forth. Yet application of PAT to the relationship between students and institution is essentially nonexistent.

An excerpt from an article in *About Campus* helps illustrate the complex contractual obligations of students and how those contracts may affect student behavior. In this example, an underage student discusses in a class why he seemingly has no problem drinking on campus any time except for two days prior to an athletic competition. The student stated that he chose not to drink because his coach forbids all athletes from drinking during the forty-eight hours before an athletic competition: "[The instructor] asked [the student] why he chose to follow the forty-eight-hour rule, while he seemingly disregarded the laws of . . . state and the policy of . . . campus. . . . He answered [the] question candidly: 'If I'm caught with a beer in the dorm, I just get a fine, but if my coach hears that I drank before a game, he'll make me run until I puke'" (Mueller, 2009). In this example, there are two "contracts" with a similar goal: to prevent the student from drinking. The student willingly complies with one while willfully disregarding the other. Clearly, by the student's own acknowledgment, the contract with the coach is more effective than the broader contract with the institution (student code of conduct). Both of these contracts are an extension of the prestige maximization contract the institutions holds with the student. Coaches do not want their athletes to engage in behavior that could threaten the chances of the team winning (and thus threatening the prestige of the institution). Therefore they enact a contract with the student to reduce behaviors that would have a negative effect on the team's performance. Similarly, the institution wants students to not engage in activities that may reduce institutional prestige (e.g., underage drinking), and it, too, has a contract: if the student violates the contract, he or she is punished.[16]

Critiques of Agency Theory

While the fields such as economics, political science, and sociology have largely accepted agency theory, it has not been without critique. Some critics (e.g., Jones, 1983; Perrow, 1986) suggest that the foundational assumptions derived from economic theory overemphasize the motivations of self-interest and efficiency and fail to account for more intrinsic motivations such as altruism and morality. However, some economists (Williamson, 1981, 1985) would argue that in the case of altruism the utility of the agent is based on the utility of others and optimizes behavior accordingly. For example, a student affairs administrator may engage in student development because of the reasons listed above or because of the personal gratification associated with seeing a student develop over time. Both motivations could be construed as a form of self-interest. While readers may disagree with or dislike the explanation, they should keep in mind that this is merely an attempt to apply one theory in a way to explain certain aspects of human behavior within the university. Issues of morality, though, are not so easily dealt with. And a potential area of study may be to examine how personal development, such as that explored by Chickering (1969), Gilligan (1982), or Kohlberg (1971), affects the behavior of either the principal or the agent. Extant work has not incorporated such psychological dynamics into actor behavior in the model.

Also, application of the theory often focuses on the existence of a simple contract usually with one general goal without accounting for how principal and agent may have different optimization strategies for the same goal. A department chair and junior faculty member may both have the goal of the junior faculty member achieving tenure. However, while earning tenure may be the highest priority for the junior faculty member, the department chair needs to balance that priority against a whole host of other departmental priorities, such as having classes taught and students advised. Thus while the junior faculty member may want to maximize time spent on research (assuming that is the primary measure for determining whether a faculty member receives tenure) by minimizing student contact hours or committee work, the department chair (who also wants the faculty member to achieve tenure) may have to require the faculty member to teach large classes or participate in multiple committees so that the work of the department is carried out. Further, the treatment of the junior faculty member may differ if he or she is hired into an understaffed department rather than one that is fully staffed. These types of environmental concerns are not often accounted for in the agency framework.

In fact, this leads to another criticism in that PAT has not accounted for the role and effect of teamwork (Nilakant & Rao, 1994). Even in the relationship between two organizational units (e.g., a college and a department), research examines the unit as a unitary entity (not examining how the collective actors worked together to produce a certain product or service). Alchian and Demsetz (1972) suggest that in teamwork-based environments there are two types of effort exerted by members of a team: operational effort and facilitative effort. Operational effort involves the tasks associated with transforming an input into an output—such as an instructor transforming knowledge into a consumable output for students. Facilitative effort involves "acquisition of inputs, coordination of inputs, intermediate outputs and transformation processes, and the selection of conversion technologies" (Nilakant & Rao, 1994, p. 660). For example, a department chair engages in much facilitative effort in providing the collective educational opportunities students need to attain a degree. In complex production environments, such as universities, a great deal of facilitative and operational effort is often required to produce the output, possibily making it difficult to create an efficient contract with some actors. All faculty in a department usually have the same written employment contract, yet some exert more effort on teaching and others exert more on research. It is the role of the department chair, through her or his facilitative efforts, to ensure the faculty collectively contribute to the delivery of the curriculum and produce scholarship. However, PAT research does not easily account for facilitative efforts or other contributions of the faculty to collectively produce the outputs of the department.

Conclusion

PAT holds great potential for the study of higher education administration and is becoming more widely used by organization theorists and political scientists who study higher education. The assumptions associated with self-interest, information asymmetry, and incentives provide scholars with an opportunity to deconstruct and identify alternative explanations for actor and subsystem behavior. The core of the theory is relatively simple. A principal contracts with an agent to carry out the needs of the principal. Assuming that the agent and principal have different interests, the principal establishes a set of rewards and punishments (carrots and sticks) to entice the agent to act in the best interest of the principal. Then the principal monitors compliance through observing the agent's behavior or outputs or both. Whether there is a written piece of paper or not, PAT considers this a contractual relationship. PAT provides the framework to analyze the nature of this relationship and understand why actors (or organizations) act in the way that they do.

Over the course of the past forty years, PAT has been used to explain actor and organizational behavior in a variety of organizational types (e.g., for-profit firms, government bureaucracies, the court system, and nonprofit organizations). More recently, scholars have begun to apply PAT to examine contractual relationships in higher education. While most scholars have focused on governance-related issues, this article discusses the potential for using PAT to examine more internal aspects of colleges and universities. It does not provide an exhaustive review of all potential uses but does highlight some potentially interesting ways to reconceptualize institutional motivations and, thus, actor behavior.

Indeed, higher education proves an excellent social laboratory for investigating interesting twists on both canonical and modified principal-agent relationships. For example, when considering student workers on campus, how does a work-study student compare with a regularly employed student? Do staff expect more of the non-work-study student than the work-study student because more of the departmental budget is being used to pay the non-work-study student? Are contractual expectations clearer for non-work-study students? This raises questions about whether how an employee is paid affects the relationship between the principal and the agent.

Already, there is evidence of the ability to use PAT to explore complex relationships. Studies using agency theory to explore the effect of tenure on the academic ratchet and administrative lattice provide an interesting explanation for how tenure can lead to an increase in the number of administrative staff at an university. In an environment in which faculty often complain about the bloating of administrative structures, the work of Ortmann and Squire (2000) suggests that it may be the behavior of faculty that leads to the very administrative bloating that they complain about. While Ortmann and Squire's (2000) work is conceptually based, it provides opportunity for future scholars to engage in empirical research to determine the accuracy of these claims and whether they hold true in different institutional settings.

In conclusion, the flexibility of the principal-agent theory has resulted in it being widely accepted by economists, political scientists, and sociologists to study a wide range of contractual relationships. While the theory has already been applied in limited ways to higher education, there remains much fertile ground for future scholars to use the theory to investigate the myriad of contractual relationships that exist in academe, including that between the student and institution, institution and government, faculty and deans, and so forth. Readers are encouraged to think creatively about how the theory may be used to advance knowledge about the administration of higher education institutions.

NOTES

1. See Lane & Kivisto 2007 for an extensive review of the use of PAT scholarship in studying higher education governance.

2. Readers are directed to Laffont & Martimort 2002 for an overview of the formal principal-agent modeling techniques.

3. Early writings in this area include Alchian & Demsetz 1972, Holstrom 1979, Jensen & Meckling 1976, and Shavell 1979.

4. The canonical model was based on assumptions derived from employment contracts and the activities of for-profit firms.

5. Because these units often operate as semiautonomous entities similar to public bureaucracies, it is possible to examine the intraorganizational relationships through the lens of PAT. For example, one might examine how a college's resource allocation model affects the actions of an academic department.

6. In this case, the ability to "freely" enter and exit the contract does not imply that such decisions are made without costs. For example, a contract will often include penalties if one party chooses to end the contract prematurely. However, the entities party to the contract have the freedom to choose to enter or exit the contract.

7. The superstructure has the option to dismantle a unit or merge it with another; however, the likelihood of this happening tends to be minimal. Thus bargaining between the two organizational units is usually engaged in without either being threatened by a termination of the contract but both also knowing that their relationship will continue after the immediate round of negations is completed.

8. For example, because faculty possess specialized knowledge about their field of study, it is difficult for nonexpert administrators to assess the quality of curricula, content delivered during class, degree requirements, and so forth.

9. The assessments such as student evaluations of teaching, standardized tests, and certification exams are attempts to overcome information asymmetry by assessing how well faculty teach and how much students learn.

10. This section is adapted from a paper presented at the annual meeting of the Association for the Study of Higher Education in 2005.

11. For example, Kivisto 2007, Lane 2007, Lowery 2001, McLendon 2003, Toma 1986, 1990.

12. Sometimes the donative function is handled by a separate entity such as a foundation, particularly if the institution is considered public and subject to government regulations; however, the funds raised by the foundations are usually used to support the activities of the institution.

13. Approximately sixty years ago, Georgia O'Keeffe donated 101 pieces of artwork, including works by Picasso and Renoir, for the purposes of assisting in art education, and it is believed the intent of O'Keeffe was not to have the collection broken up. In the midst of financial struggles, the university attempted to sell two pieces from the collections for several million dollars. After the court disallowed the sale of the paintings, the university attempted to sell a share of the ownership of the collection to a planned Tennessee museum. The court ruled against that option as well, determining that the collection must remain complete and be displayed.

14. The essence of a very complicated case is that heirs of Charles and Marie Roberston, who donated $35 million in 1961 to Princeton University, sued the university for mismanagement of funds, including uses not in line with the intent of the gift.

15. In this case, credentials such as those provided by many diploma mills are not considered.

16. How underage drinking affects institutional prestige could be interpreted in many ways. For example, if law enforcement catches an underage student drinking, negative publicity could harm the institution's image. A different explanation could be that underage drink-

ing could have negative consequences on the health and well-being of the student which could reduce the student's likelihood of being academically or professionally successful.

REFERENCES

Alchian, A. A. (1977). Economic forces at work. Indianapolis: Liberty Press.

Alchian, A. A., & Demsetz, H. (1972). Production, information costs, and economic organization. *American Economic Review, 62*(5), 777–795.

Bednar, J. (2006). Is full compliance possible? Conditions for shirking with imperfect monitoring and continuous action space. *Journal of Theoretical Politics,18*(3), 347–375.

Bergen, M., Dutta, S., & Walker, O. C., Jr. (1992). Agency relationships in marketing: A review of the implications and applications of agency and related theories. *Journal of Marketing, 56,* 1–24.

Braun, D. (1993). Who governs intermediary agencies? Principal-agent relations in research policy-making. *Journal of Public Policy, 13*(2), 135–162.

Chickering, A. W. (1969). *Education and identity.* San Francisco: Jossey-Bass.

Clotfelter, C. T. (1996). *Buying the best: Cost escalation in elite higher education.* Princeton, NJ: Princeton University Press.

Cohen, M. D., March, J. G., & Olsen, J. P. (1972). A garbage can model of organizational choice. *Administrative Science Quarterly, 17*(1): 1–25.

Davis, J. H., Schoorman, F. D., & Donaldson, L. (1997). Toward a stewardship theory of management. *Academy of Management Review, 15*(3), 369–381.

Dill, D. D., & Soo, M. (2004). Transparency and quality in higher education. In P. Teixeira, B. Jongbloed, D. Dill, & A. Amaral (Eds.), *Markets in higher education: Rhetoric or reality* (pp. 61–85). Dordrecht, Netherlands: Kluwer.

Eisenhardt, K. (1989). Agency theory: An assessment and review. *Academy of Management Review, 14*(1), 57–74.

Frey, B. S. (1993). Does monitoring increase work effort? The rivalry with trust and loyalty. *Economic Inquiry, 31*(4), 663–670.

Garvin, D. A. (1980). *The economics of university behavior.* New York: Academic Press.

Gilligan, C. (1982). *In a different voice.* Cambridge, MA: Harvard University Press.

Gomez-Mejia, L. R., & Balkin, D. B. (1992). Determinants of faculty pay: An agency theory perspective. *Academy of Management Journal, 35*(5), 921–955.

Goodin, R. E. (2003). Democratic accountability: The distinctiveness of the third sector. *European Journal of Sociology, 44*(3), 359–397.

Hammond, T. H., & Knott, J. H. (1996). Who controls the bureaucracy? Presidential power, congressional dominance, legal constraints and bureaucratic autonomy in a model of multiinstitutional policy-making. *Journal of Law, Economics and Organization, 12*(1), 119–166.

Hansmann, H. (1980). The role of nonprofit enterprise. *Yale Law Journal, 89*(5), 835–902.

Hansmann, H. (1987). Economic theories of nonprofit organizations. In W. W. Powell (Ed.), *The nonprofit sector* (pp. 27–42). New Haven, CT: Yale University Press.

Holstrom, B. (1979). Moral hazard and observability. *Bell Journal of Economics, 10,* 74–91.

James, E. (1986). Cross-subsidization in higher education: Does it pervert private choice and public policy? In D. C. Levy (Ed.), *Private education: Studies in choice and public policy* (pp. 237–257). New York: Oxford University Press.

James, E. (1990). Decision processes and priorities in higher education. In S. A. Hoenack & E. L. Collins (Eds.), *The economics of American universities: Management, operations, and fiscal environment* (pp. 77–106). Albany: State University of New York Press.

Jensen, M. C., & Meckling, W. H. (1976). Theory of the firm: Managerial behavior, agency costs and ownership structure. *Journal of Financial Economics, 3*(4), 305–360.

Jones, G. R. (1983). Transaction costs, property rights and organizational culture: An exchange perspective. *Administrative Science Quarterly, 28* (September), 454–467.

Kiewiet, D. R., & McCubbins, M. (1991). *The logic of delegation: Congressional parties and the appropriations process.* Chicago: University of Chicago Press.

Kivisto, J. A. (2005). The government-higher education institution relationship: Theoretical considerations from the perspective of agency theory. *Tertiary Education and Management, 11*(1), 1–17.

Kivisto, J. A. (2007). *Agency theory as a framework for the government-university relationship.* Tampere, Finland: Higher Education Group/Tampere University Press.

Knott, J. H., & Payne, A. A. (2004). The impact of state governance structures on management and performance of public organizations: A study of higher education institutions. *Journal of Policy Analysis and Management, 23*(1), 13–30.

Knox, D. (2010). A good horse runs at the shadow of the whip: Surveillance and organizational trust in online learning environments. *Canadian Journal of Media Studies, 7* (Special Congress Issue), 1–34.

Kohlberg, L. (1971). *From is to ought: How to commit the naturalistic fallacy and get away with it in the study of moral development.* New York: Academic Press.

Laffont, J. J., & Martimort, D. (2002). *The theory of incentives: The principal-agent model.* Princeton, NJ: Princeton University Press.

Lane, J. E. (2003). *State government oversight of public higher education: Police patrols and fire alarms.* Paper presented at the annual meeting of the Association for the Study of Higher Education, Portland, Oregon.

Lane, J. E. (2005). *State oversight of higher education: A theoretical review of agency problems with complex principals.* Paper presented at 2005 Annual Conference of the Association for the Study of Higher Education, Philadelphia.

Lane, J. E. (2007). Spider web of oversight: Latent and manifest regulatory controls in higher education. *Journal of Higher Education, 78*(6), 1–30.

Lane, J. E., & Kivisto, J. A. (2008). Interests, information, and incentives in higher education: A review of principal-agent theory in higher education governance. In J. C. Smart (Ed.), *Higher education: Handbook of theory and research,* Vol. 23 (pp. 141–180). New York: Springer.

Lowry, R. C. (2001). Governmental structure, trustee selection, and public university prices and spending. *American Journal of Political Science, 45*(4), 845–861.

Lyne, M., & Tierney, M. (2003) *The politics of common agency: Unitary, multiple and collective principals.* Paper presented at the annual meeting of the American Political Science Association, Philadelphia.

Massy, W. F. (1996). *Resource allocation in higher education.* Ann Arbor: University of Michigan Press.

Massy, W. F., & Wilger, A. K. (1992). Productivity in postsecondary education: A new approach. *Educational Evaluation and Policy Analysis, 14,* 361–376.

Massy, W. F., & Zemsky, R. (1994). Faculty discretionary time: Departments and the "academic ratchet." *Journal of Higher Education, 65*(1), 1–22.

McLendon, M. K., Hearn, J. C., & Deaton, R. (2006). Called to account: Analyzing the origins and spread of state performance-accountability policies for higher education. *Educational Evaluation and Policy Analysis, 28*(1), 1–24.

Meulen, B. V. (1998). Science policies as principal-agent games: Institutionalization and path dependency in the relation between government and science. *Research Policy, 7,* 397–414.

Miller, G. J. (2005). The political evolution of principal-agent models. *Annual Review of Political Science, 8,* 203–225.

Mintzberg, H. (1979). *The structuring of organizations: A synthesis of the research.* Englewood Cliffs, NJ: Prentice Hall.

Moe, T. M. (1984). The new economics of organization. *American Journal of Political Science, 28*(4), 739–777.

Moe, T. M. (1990). Political institutions: The neglected side of the story. *Journal of Law, Economics and Organization, 6,* 213–253.

Moe, T. M. (2005). Power and political institutions. *Perspectives on Politics, 3*(2), 215–234.

Morrison, S. E. (1936). *Three centuries of Harvard.* Cambridge, MA: Harvard University Press.

Mueller, A. C. R. (2009). The forty-eight-hour rule: Emotional engagement and the student athlete. *About Campus, 13,* 6.

Nelson, R., & Krashinsky, M. (1973). Two major issues of public policy: Public policy and organization of supply. In R. Nelson & D. Young (Eds.), *Public subsidy for day care of young children* (pp. 47–69). Lexington, MA: D. C. Heath and Co.

Nielson, D. L., & Tierney, M. J. (2003). Delegation to international organizations: Agency theory and world bank environmental reform. *International Organization, 57,* 241–276.

Nilakant, V., & Rao, H. (1994). Agency theory and uncertainty in organizations: An evaluation. *Organization Studies, 15*(5), 649–672.

Ortmann, A., & Squire, R. C. (1996). *The internal organization of colleges and universities: A game-theoretic approach.* Discussion paper #232. Program on Nonprofit Organizations, Yale University.

Ortmann, A., & Squire, R. (2000). A game-theoretic explanation of the administrative lattice in institutions of higher learning. *Journal of Economic Behavior and Organization, 43,* 377–391.

Ostrom, E. (1999). Coping with tragedies of the commons. *Annual Review of Political Science, 2,* 493–535.

Perrow, C. (1986). *Complex organizations: A critical essay* (3rd ed.). New York: McGraw-Hill:

Shavel, S. (1979). Risk sharing and incentives in the principal and agent relationship. *Bell Journal of Economics, 10,* 55–73.

Smith, A. (1776/1991). *A wealth of nations.* Amherst, NY: Prometheus Books.

Spence, M. (1973). Job market signalling. *Quarterly Journal of Economics, 87,* 355–374.

Spence, M., & Zeckhauser, R. (1971). Insurance, information, and individual action. *American Economic Review, 61,* 380–87.

Toma, E. F. (1986). State university boards of trustees: A principal-agent perspective. *Public Choice, 49,* 155–163.

Toma, E. F. (1990). Boards of trustees, agency problems, and university output. *Public Choice, 67,* 1–9.

Tosi, H. L., Jr., Katz, J. P., & Gomez-Mejia, L. R. (1997). Disaggregating the agency contract: The effects of monitoring, incentive alignment, and term in office on agent decision making. *Academy of Management Journal, 40*(3), 584–602.

Valentinov, V. (2006). Nondistribution constraint and managerial discretion: Disentangling the relationship. *Public Organization Review, 6*(4), 305–316.

von Zedtwitz, M., & Gassman, O. (2002). Market versus technology drive in R&D internationalization: Four different patterns of managing research and development. *Research Policy, 31,* 569–581.

Waterman, R.W, & Meier, K. J. (1998). Principal-agent models: An expansion? *Journal of Public Administration Research and Theory, 8*(2), 173–202.

Weber, M. (1958/1991). *From Max Weber: Essay in sociology.* New York: Routledge.

Weick, K. (1976). Educational organizations as loosely coupled systems. *Administrative Sciences Quarterly, 21,* 1–19.

Williamson, O. (1981). The economics of organization: The transaction cost approach. *American Journal of Sociology, 87,* 548–77.

Williamson, O. E. (1985). *The economic institutions of capitalism: Firms, markets, relational contracting.* New York: Free Press.

Winston, G. C. (2000). *The positional arms race in higher education.* Williams Project on the Economics of Higher Education, Discussion Paper.

CHAPTER ELEVEN

Organizational Cognition in Higher Education

ANNA NEUMANN

A chapter on cognition seems out of place in a book section about new ideas in the study of college and university organization. Cognition is not a new topic in the organizational study of higher education. We have grappled with it since the field's beginning but with other words. If cognition is already part of our field's established understanding, representing what cognitive scientists call our "prior knowledge" (Bransford, Brown, & Cocking, 1999), then according to those scientists, we are unlikely to change it conceptually—unless we make our own cognition, indeed of higher education organizational cognition, itself a subject of study: we need to take the full measure of our established knowledge about how people think in organizations and critique that as part of any larger knowledge development effort. Bearing this in mind, I provide an analytical review of the higher education field's extant understandings of cognition—our salient "prior knowledge" of it.[1] I then introduce several recent ideas and perspectives from the cognitive sciences, feminist studies of knowledge, and sociology that in conjunction with our growing self-awareness could reshape how we understand cognition in higher education organizations.

I define cognition as the work of the human mind—literally as "mindwork"—thus as encompassing multiple modes of knowing and of learning as coming to know *and* as striving (even struggling) to know (Neumann, 2009). Learning, as a central feature of cognition, includes coming to awareness, taking into consciousness, questioning or doubting what one thinks one knows, struggling to master or simply to comprehend, struggling to understand or make sense—all with regard to an aspect of substantive knowledge: an idea, belief, or thought. This view of human cognition, of knowing and learning, frames the following discussion.

Cognition in Prior Studies of Higher Education Organization

Regardless of how attentive they are to behavior, events, and other observable phenomena, many higher education organizational texts can be "reread" from a cognitive (internal to the viewer) perspective by asking (1) What were organizational actors assuming, perceiving, or otherwise thinking—what did they know or strive to know—as they took the actions that authors/researchers describe? (2) What were the authors/researchers assuming about human thought as they wrote about their study participants' words and actions? I used these questions, especially the second, to guide a cognitively interested historical rereading of the higher educational organizational literature.

To foreshadow what I learned: although higher education organization theories and perspectives have changed over time, one core concept—a foundational schema—has remained constant: the open system. I conclude that the persistence of this schema has been both good and bad for the field's learning—good because its foundation-like properties have allowed it to support multiple organizational images and forms (see Birnbaum, 1988; Bolman & Deal, 1984; Morgan, 1986) while anchoring the field's attention on the topic at issue: organization. Bad because like all foundational schemata that direct attention to things in particular, the open system filters out potentially useful alternatives to it. The higher education organization, assumed to exist as an "open system," cannot become anything other than that. If alternatives exist, open systems ideation obscures them from researchers who, by virtue of their socialization in the field's ways of knowing, have learned them deeply and well. We must wonder: What could researchers possibly see if the foundational schema of the open system slipped away? What new images of organization might arise?

Before addressing these questions, we must consider first the images of organization that the open system has led us to see even as it has obscured others. I suggest that historically the open system has let us see college/university organizations as (1) structuring survival and persistence in a largely tumultuous world, (2) engaged in sensemaking, (3) facilitating strategy making, and (4) opening up spaces for knowing, thinking, and learning. Despite their differences, these themes reflect two commonalities: they emphasize top administrator standpoints; they attend to observable behavior.

STRUCTURING SURVIVAL AND PERSISTENCE

Though images of higher education organization have changed over time (Birnbaum, 1988), their most basic outlines have persisted over the history of the field of higher education. For example, Marvin Peterson (1985) characterized studies of college and university organization carried out prior to and during the mid-1980s as attentive to human behavior in collective settings, tensions between process and structure, the power of external environments to mediate organizational action and control, tensions between externalist viewpoints (emphasizing "social facts"), and subjective experience for framing organization theory. Peterson's expansive review of the organization theory, epistemology, and method of the field's earliest organizational research echoes, in nascent form, strains we still hear today: emphasis on college and university performance tuned to productivity (process/structure), concerns about public accountability and campus and professional autonomy (environment/agency), and tensions between evidence-based and experience-oriented research (externalist/subjective) (see, e.g., Altbach, 1999).

Like the researchers of the 1970s and 1980s whose work he reviews, Peterson construed colleges and universities as open systems searching for "inputs" critical to their survival (dollars, students, social support) in resource-limited, tumultuous social environments (Katz & Kahn, 1978). On locating usable resources, the organizational open system takes them in and then processes them through the specialized functioning of the "academic core" into academic end products assuming "value added" (Katz & Kahn, 1978). Such products—referred to as "system outputs"—are returned to the surrounding environment for use by others in it (businesses, government, schools) capable of sending new resources ("inputs") to the system or otherwise supporting it. The cycle repeats unless disrupted by threat or breakdown.

For example, an open systems view, as an ideal model, portrays matriculating undergraduates as the key "inputs" to a college or university (the system). Once "in" the system, entering students are processed (educated) within the system's "academic core" (the central "throughput" unit that processes college entrants, originally the "inputs," into graduates or "outputs"). The quality of outputs determines the future of the cycle and thus of the system overall: it may continue, be revised, or come apart. The model generalizes to numerous resources and products: for example, viewing research grants as system "inputs" and publications and inventions as "outputs" (the "throughput" in this example is intellectual endeavor), or viewing community interests as "inputs" and community/public service programs as "outputs." Open systems thinking offers a broadly spanning logic of how higher education organizations function.

Open systems thinking invites the assumption that in a society of limited resources multiple organizations, competing for existence, vie for scarce resources—

students, research dollars, status, political support, intellectual "star power," and so on. In this view, an organization's coming to understand the larger world on which it believes it depends for core resources involves scanning, tracking, identifying, and strategizing. Since organizations as open systems are, by definition, environmentally dependent (Pfeffer & Salancik, 1978), the organization's key actors struggle to understand the nature of organizational/environmental dependence and to get around it. In this view, college and university leaders frame their organizing efforts—and higher education researchers frame their research on those efforts—in response to a basic interest: protection, support, and strengthening of the environmentally dependent college or university.

What kind of sensibility does an open systems orientation create? Certainly it creates organizational leaders attuned to campus persistence in a world of scarce resources. It also views college administrators as striving to buffer their organization's "academic core" ("technical core") from environmental invasion, granting its inhabitants (the faculty) as much professional autonomy—protection from external disruption—as possible or shielding the public from a view of how the system really works (Meyer & Rowan, 1977, 1978). This image assumes that the academic core's (and thereby the larger organization's) ability to persist is tied to leaders' abilities to ward off threat to their campuses' inner workings. It further creates organizational researchers attuned to this view of the world and of options for action.

Many of the field's ideas about academic organization and leadership have been developed from within an imagery of the college or university as (1) resource dependent, (2) resource seeking, and (3) resource preserving. To survive—and hopefully thrive—in scarce, tumultuous, and unpredictable environments, an organization must be all three. This view has long guided the thinking and actions of college presidents and other chief administrators, as well as the researchers who study them.

SENSEMAKING

Writing at about the same time as Peterson, Robert Birnbaum (1988) likewise explored higher education organizations as open systems but with explicit attention to their leadership. Defining the input-output scheme of the "open system" as incomplete in its representation of "organizational realities," Birnbaum sought to enter more fully *into* what he called the "black boxes" of college and university organizations to examine how administrative leaders conceptualize ("make sense of") what they and their organizations are up to (Birnbaum, 1988, 1992). He also sought to articulate how administrators think as they strive to achieve organizational aims and especially to establish organizational credibility in a re-source-strained world (Birnbaum, 1988). In light of these interests, Birnbaum explored "how colleges work" from the standpoint of presidents and other top administrators; he viewed leadership as concerned with "sensemaking" (Weick, 1979)—of leaders and of those they led.

Like the theorists who guided his work (Cohen & March, 1974; Meyer & Rowan, 1977, 1978; Weick, 1979), Birnbaum conceived of leaders as possessing power to define organizational realities—purposefully or without realizing it, often ret-rospectively. In *How Colleges Work* (1988), Birnbaum portrayed the American college as able to assume various forms (bureaucracy, collegium, political body, culture, cybernetic system), serially or simultaneously, across all its parts or se-lectively in some but not others. Then—whether intentionally or inadvertently—Birnbaum turned this multipart view of academic organization (emphasis on form) into a multipart conceptual lens that presidents and other top college lead-ers might don, mindfully, to make sense of the organization they lead, both to themselves and others within and outside the organization. What was initially a treatise about "organization out there" (beyond its leader) suddenly became an organizational image inside the leader's head—her or his way of seeing and de-fining, thereby creating campus realities.

Publications emanating from the Institutional Leadership Project that Birn-baum directed in the late 1980s and early 1990s alternated between "views of *organization*" (organizational forms) and "analyses of the *viewers' frames of mind at work*" as they (with others) created the diverse forms. Despite the force of this shift—from a focus on organization (in multiple forms) to a focus on the varied and nuanced "mindwork" that creates organization—no texts have explicitly commented on Birnbaum's epistemic transition through these years: from em-phasis on organizational form to emphasis on leaders' sensemaking of it. It is unclear at what point the bureaucratic, collegial, political, and symbolic forms that Birnbaum wrote about initially converted into leadership lenses or procliv-ities of mind ("frames" as he often referred to them). I suggest that this shift, though unarticulated, represented a major turning point in the study of higher education organization. It turned scholars' attention from concerns about how organizations persist (which organizational forms work best, when, and why) to questions of how leaders make sense of and create "organization" as they know it, and as others, participating in their leadership, know it too. *Form* and *frame* (or *lens*) represent two analytically distinct (though not unrelated) targets of study. Movement from one to the other signaled an openness to the study of cognition in higher education organization, but with attention primarily to the mindwork of top leaders.

Though Peterson and Birnbaum differed in many ways, their views cohered. Whereas Peterson saw academic organizations (and those guiding them) as reaching for a broad and internally diverse analytical rationality attuned to survival in a tumultuous world (i.e., a capacity to scan environments for dangers and resources, assess possibilities and implications, and plan strategically for uncertain futures), Birnbaum assumed that to persist organizations required multiple and diverse rationalities (e.g., capacities to think collegially, politically, symbolically, culturally) as supports for sensemaking attuned to survival. Despite their differing substantive interests, Peterson and Birnbaum converged on an assumptional "why": each viewed his own distinctive take on organizations as serving goals of campus persistence in a changing and often unruly, hard-to-predict surround. Thus both were products of their scholarly times: the "open system" anchored each of their otherwise differing ideas.

STRATEGY MAKING

Though evident in Birnbaum's writings and signaled in Peterson's, the "cognitive turn"—from a view of organization as "out there," separate from the person thinking about it, to one of people (i.e., college/university leaders) as creating it—occurred also in the research of another of their contemporaries. Ellen Earle Chaffee, a researcher at the National Center for Higher Education Management Systems (NCHEMS), struggled too with conceptions of organizational persistence and also effectiveness; like Peterson and Birnbaum, she wondered what it takes for a higher education organization to make it in a resource-limited world. But she added something: she puzzled over what it takes for a higher education organization to hold firm to its central values and identities while struggling to survive and function in a turbulent world—how to avert loss of important shared meanings, how to amplify sustaining values under stress. Drawing on advancing work in the social sciences (see Daft & Weick, 1984), Chaffee used the term "interpretive" to capture this organizational outlook. She then searched for convergences and divergences between interpretivism and open systems thought (see Chaffee, 1984, 1985).

Chaffee's contributions were unique in another way. Unlike Birnbaum, who, probably unknowingly, tacked back and forth between attention to organizational forms and leaders' cognitive frames (lenses) for understanding organization, Chaffee integrated these foci by adopting a conceptual mechanism that scholars in business and organizational studies were then elaborating. That mechanism was *strategy* (Mintzberg, 1973, 1987; Mintzberg & Waters, 1983) powered by an elaborated resource dependence theory (e.g., Pfeffer & Salancik, 1978) within the continuing—and now strengthened—open systems tradition in higher educa-tion organizational studies.

The study of strategy was not new to higher education researchers at the point that Chaffee picked it up. In the early 1980s, Peterson used it to advance data-based, analytical thought amid environmental complexity and turbulence (Jeda-mus & Peterson, 1980). Though not explicitly in Birnbaum's work, 1980s strat-egy concepts align nicely with bureaucratic leadership, a theme that Birnbaum did take up. Like Peterson, Chaffee relied heavily on a logic of broad analytical rationality as a guide to organizational survival. Like him, too, she portrayed strat-egy as forward moving and action oriented, targeted at previously contemplated change, directed thoughtfully into the future (Chaffee, 1984, 1985). Whereas Birnbaum defined strategy largely as a product of a bureaucratic mind-set (though it also might reflect bureaucracy's symbolic-political potential), Chaffee positioned strategy as encompassing fully all the mind-sets (frames/lenses) that Birnbaum wrote about: bureaucratic, collegial, political, symbolic. Though she did not write about it, her views are consistent also with Birnbaum's fifth frame, the cybernetic. Further, in positioning strategy as a *vehicle* for driving forward the emerging syn-thetic view (rather than positioning it as among the stuff to be synthesized), she added agency, analysis, and empirical thought (the strengths of Peterson's view) to the expanding array of organizational images for which Birnbaum was striving at about the same time.

What, then, is the conceptual vehicle that, in Chaffee's view, strategy repre-sents? And what is the nature of the content that that vehicle can carry? In Chaffee's presentation, the strategic vehicle represents action—intentional and therefore conscious, empirically grounded and thus substantiated, synthetic, and thereby integrated. Strategy, as a conceptual vehicle, also is analytical—defining options for action, asking whether particular actions are likely to yield particular results, choosing action on the basis of forecast results. It thereby represents targeted and studied organizational activity. The strategy of the times assumed causal linkages and sought to articulate likelihood. The strategic vehicle is, how-ever, more than a tool for organizational protection and advancement; it is indeed a vehicle—one that carries varied content: it has the capacity to carry social, in-deed human meaning quite apart from administrative/technical knowledge keyed to organizational survival and persistence (in the open systems view), though it does carry that too. Chaffee conceptualized strategy's content as simultaneously linear (reflecting Peterson's data-driven, analytically powered rationality), adaptive (driven by an open-systems-anchored attentiveness to external environmental change), and interpretive (considering the sensemaking of leaders and those with whom they work à la Birnbaum but adding in appreciation of human beings' strivings for meaning in their work). Echoing Birnbaum, Chaffee asserted that a fair amount can be learned "in action"—that is, within the very process of organizational work, including that of a campus leader—as well as in hindsight on it. In this view, strategy is correctible. It can be thought about and learned. While Chaffee never explicitly said this, her work implied it, and others who followed picked up on it.

Though clearly unique, Chaffee's work resonated with that of Peterson and Birnbaum in two ways: first, her work was macroscopic in its attentional focus, steering away from particularistic person-centered and interpersonal issues. Second, her work conceptualized the college or university as an open system attentive and responsive to changing and hard-to-predict external realities, thereby needing to adapt. But Chaffee's academic organization could also be refreshingly (strategically) proactive, striving to shape and reshape, meaningfully, the collective self. It had the capacity to reinterpret itself, externally and internally. Given these strategic interpretive capacities, that organization could respond adaptively to shifting needs in shifting times (in the spirit of the open system)—but within the constraints of its long-standing and meaning-laden identity (thereby reaching beyond the open systems model while remaining in it). Resource dependence, also a feature of open systems thought, was a byword of Chaffee's work, but now researchers might enact it in different (strategic) ways: linearly in the spirit of rational data-driven and analytical thought, adaptively through attentiveness to changing patterns of external resource availability, and interpretively given growing desires to bridge gaps between an organization's self-understanding and the understandings (and increasingly, expectations) of its key external stakeholders. In Chaffee's view, as in Birnbaum's and Peterson's, organizational leaders had much to think about, and indeed, to learn—as did the higher education researchers who wrote about leaders' efforts.

OPENING UP SPACES FOR KNOWING, THINKING, AND LEARNING

Often research progresses as scholars layer new thoughts upon older thoughts. Yet many new ideas link back to prior ideas. Setting aside analytical models of how higher education organizations (as designed processes and structures) respond to environmental scarcity and tumult (see Peterson, 1985), we encounter images of diverse organizational forms and frames for leaders' sensemaking (see

Birnbaum, 1988)—some as instrumentally concerned as the earlier "processes and structures" and others as attuned to human meaning (Dandridge, Mitroff, & Joyce, 1980; Morgan, Frost, & Pondy, 1983). Setting aside the forms and frames, we encounter strategy as planful and self-conscious pursuit of meaningful campus goals but as concerned nonetheless with survival and persistence as continuing themes. What, we might ask, came next?

By the early 1990s, organizational cognition—thinking, knowing, learning, believing, understanding, rethinking—was already a topic of researcher concern. Writing alongside Peterson, Birnbaum, and Chaffee, Estela M. Bensimon and I, early in our careers, tackled the topic of cognition as central to two sound-alike but differing perspectives: existence *of* organization (the theme of Peterson's, Birnbaum's, and Chaffee's work) and existence *in* organization. The latter (*in*) brought *people* centrally into the organizational discourse in ways that the earlier view (*of*) had obscured: initially "organizational people" included mostly formal leaders; later they included individuals working with or influenced by leaders.

Together and often with Robert Birnbaum, Estela Bensimon and I offered these research-based claims: people in formal campus leadership positions learn on the job. They make mistakes, and sometimes they strive to correct them. At times (usually early career), leaders reflect on the sources of their error, rethinking significant features of their leadership (Neumann, 1990). Over time, leaders typically increase in the frames or lenses (Bensimon, 1989), leadership theories (Birnbaum, 1989), and strategies (Neumann, 1989) at their disposal, and they learn to orchestrate their internal and external interpretive efforts, defining what their organization is up to to audiences on and beyond the campus (Neumann & Bensimon, 1990). Thus leaders become cognitively, strategically, and tactically complex in their thought and possibly in their action. Their interpretive capacities expand as they learn to help others understand what they are up to and why (Bensimon, 1991b)—for example, during financial "hard times" when meaning and value are contested (Neumann, 1995).

Until the early 1990s, research on college and university organization largely portrayed leadership as enacted by a single individual, usually a top-level administrator. Bensimon and I (1993) provided evidence that organizationally facile (and cognitively versatile) college presidents came to view their leadership, and use it, instead as a team. Team members orchestrate, among themselves, the "playing out" of their own and each others' unique insights and cognitive talents. Ideally, they coalesce into a "social mind"—diverse, flexible, and expansive in its thinking capabilities (Neumann 1991). How team members' "mindwork" converges and what team members commit to focusing on (or what they systemati-

cally do not address) can powerfully influence what the team accomplishes. Thus, the work of a "thinking team" can be real and substantive, creating new knowledge and meaningful action. Or it can be illusory, of purely emblematic value, inattentive to meaning (Bensimon, 1991a). Since individuals bring unique modes of thinking to the "leadership table," the full team's cognitive interplay will be complex yet never as varied as the larger social surround (the organization, its environment) that the team strives to understand (Ashby, 1956; Birnbaum, 1988).

Through this period of higher education research, the overriding model of the college and university as an open system that cognitively complex leaders steer strategically through a competitive, resource-limited, often harsh environment made room for an accompanying image: the campus as a place where people know, think, create, learn, and feel in both "good times and hard times." Rather than a vessel to be steered, a college, in this view, is the people in it. Their understandings, and their personal and interpersonal responses to—and feelings about—those understandings, contribute to the making of both organization and leadership. This statement is not a platitude. As conscious beings, people know and think. Indeed, they feel, a largely ignored point up to this time (see Boler, 1999). As these persons think, they draw from the past and present to assert what they know, defining themselves and their worlds; this is a leadership act that *any person* can carry out. Thus, both those "in" and "not in" formal organizational leadership positions have powers to construct some portion of their own and others' day-to-day realities. In observing their formal leaders' actions and in hearing their words—understanding or misunderstanding them—persons not in formal leadership roles may go so far as to construct, among themselves, beliefs about how well their formal leaders are doing, or simply, about *what* they are doing.

Cognition has long been a theme of higher education organizational inquiry, showing up initially—often unworded—in studies of organizational structure and process, then more openly in research on leadership and strategy, and finally, in studies of human mind as creating organization, its leadership, and strategy. Despite the extensive array of organization theories and perspectives at play in this unfolding literature, the content, from beginning to end, reflects a consistent theme: concern with survival, persistence, and existence itself. Whether as a consequence of this existential outlook or creating it, all these theories and perspectives presuppose *the power of the open system as a foundational schema for conceptualizing organization*. Two additional themes come through: the *primacy of administrators'* (vs. faculty members' or others') sensemaking, and the *privileg-*

ing of behavior (external enactment) in the design and write-up of research. I suggest that we must take account of the fullness of our conceptual legacy—in effect, our prior learning—if in the future we are to get past what we know (perhaps too well), for this is the layered stuff on which the "new stuff" will grow.

Future Directions: Cognition in Higher Education Organizational Research

As researchers of human cognition have noted, to develop deep understanding of an idea, an individual must unearth his or her current knowledge of it (Bransford et al., 1999), compare the existent knowledge with the new, and engage with differences and connections between them (Shulman, 2004b). What's more, individuals do not enter a learning situation tabula rasa—knowing nothing at all about "what's to be learned." They bring previously formed knowledge—beliefs, ideas, hunches, values, assumptions, suppositions, ways of thinking and knowing—to their interactions with new knowledge. Some may bring even more basic, hard-to-articulate sensibilities of what is existentially possible or not. I count all this as "prior knowledge." Two of its features are pertinent: prior knowledge is pervasive, touching on things that learners may not know they know. Prior knowledge can act like a sponge, soaking "new ideas" into itself, preserving established content and form. Without surfacing and examining their prior knowledge, learners add to but do not change what they know foundationally (see Bransford et al., 1999).

I hypothesize that this dynamic applies to the learning not only of individuals (including researchers) but also of groups including disciplinary and professional communities: collectivities of scholars, professors, administrators, or policymakers working in intellectual proximity to one another on/with shared knowledge (Pallas, 2001). At their best, disciplinary or professional communities, as expert knowledge groups, do surface and assess ideas absorbed in the past—occasionally reframing them but preserving traces of past knowing. This bears on my point: though typically scrupulous about reviewing their past knowledge, disciplines, fields, and other scholarly communities rarely fully let go of their deepest prior understandings. These collectivities' deepest assumptional outlines may remain. The remnants of a group's past knowing can influence, lightly or boldly, the group's attempts to engage with "new ideas" or, simply, new realities. It is hard to set aside, much less forget, that which we have come to know deeply in our lives (Bransford et al., 1999) and, I suggest, in the histories of our communities.

I suggest that within academe individuals, groups, and communities, including organizations, struggle to let go of what they already know even as their
members create new knowledge that often they layer atop their older assumptional knowledge. The "underlayer" will continue to influence newer conceptualizations (layered on top), often absorbing them. This is what I worry the open
system as a key "underlayer" of our thought today may do to future research on
academic organization if we do not treat it differently than we have in the past.

I do think it likely that the open system will persist in our field. We have
learned it deeply and well. That is not bad: the open system accommodates multiple organizational forms, albeit selectively; it has been useful. That said, I do
believe that we need to learn to hold and use it far more lightly than we have in
the past. A lighter hold on open systems thought—acknowledging its presence
while searching beyond it—may allow new vistas to come into view, possibly useful knowledge that exceeds the open systems view, maybe hints of schemata beyond those we know too well.

Acknowledging the power of our prior knowledge, we next turn to the question of what ideas about organizational cognition might shape the horizon of
higher education research should we succeed in relaxing our shared cognitive
grip on open systems thought. I offer three responses: standpoint theory, social-
institutional conceptualization, and mindwork.

STANDPOINT

Whose cognition merits the attention of higher education organizational research? Higher education researchers' privileging of chief administrators' organizational sensemaking has shaped the field's understandings of higher education organization and leadership, much as have the sensemaking proclivities of
dominant males in a world where "thinking from women's lives" is rarely represented as legitimate (Harding, 1986, 1991; Smith, 1987; for earlier standpoint
logic, see Merton, 1973). How so research-wise? Higher education research has
taken as its theoretical point of departure the prior knowledge, and knowledge
needs, of top administrators given *where they stand* within structures of organizational knowledge and power, while positioning the distinctive views of others as
responses to administrator understandings. What this positioned view cannot access is the knowledge of organization that might develop if, alternatively, the
standpoints of others (e.g., faculty) served as points of departure for research
questions. The world looks and feels different depending on where, in a structure
of power, one begins one's thought, thereby establishing a standpoint (Harding,
1986, 1991).

The limitations of my own past research on organizational responses to financial stress illustrate how the extant (administratively privileged) epistemic dynamic plays out. I structured my analysis of two financially distressed colleges by assessing, first, the president's representation of the college's financial state, then the faculty's understanding of what they heard the president say about their financial state, and finally, the sense that I (as an independent analyst of the college's records) made of the campus' financial state in comparison with the president's interpretation.

At one college—financially solid in my analysis—the president communicated forthcoming financial difficulty, probably unknowingly. His vague financial message infused feelings of uncertainty and fear among faculty; they grew out images of loss as they spoke privately to each other. At the other college, the president communicated possibility even as she spoke to the faculty about a foreboding financial future (I concurred). There the faculty faced the "hard facts" but responded with hope, energy, and will. Although my conclusion—underlining the influence of the president's constructed financial picture on faculty members' outlooks—was interesting in and of itself, I wondered months after publication: What more might I have been able to say—indeed about faculty members' outlooks—had I anchored my narrative (and before that, research questions and data collection) less in the president's communication and faculty members' reading of it than in those instructors' and professors' career and life narratives: What did academic work mean and feels like to them? How did they feel about themselves as teachers and learners? With this basic layer of thought established, I could have later examined what these faculty heard their president say and consider what that meant to them in light of the values and meanings they had, earlier, narrated to me. A shift like this, in my research plan, would have required different research questions, research design, and analytical strategy formulated up front. I would then have written a different story, still organizational but told from a faculty (not so much administrator) standpoint. What would have resulted and why might that matter? Using the faculty's experience as the starting point of a study of organizational experiences of financial stress would have given me access to the "inside world" of the faculty who struggle to make happen the "higher learning" that higher education claims to provide to society. We have little by way of bottom-up academic organization theory that we can appreciate in and of itself or contrast with top-down theory.

If higher education researchers wish to expand beyond the extant understanding of organizational cognition, exploring its varied vistas from multiple knowledge standpoints, those researchers must understand that *where* they *begin* their inquiries bears on where they will go substantively in their learning. Although researchers cannot take all organizational members' standpoints into account (researchers are not omniscient), they must be conscious of whose cognitions they attend to and whose they do not. They also must ask the more illusive question: Cognition of what?

SOCIAL INSTITUTIONS

Because the open system, as a foundational schema, supports multiple conceptualizations of academic organization—for example, as bureaucracy, collegium, political amalgam, and so on (Birnbaum, 1988; Morgan, 1986)—it appeals to researchers: it provides both a stable base and opportunity for development from it. As I note early in this chapter, the open system's pervasive hold on the field's prior knowledge is a sign of higher education researchers' deep attachment to it. That devotion may, however, blind researchers to gleaning possible alternatives to it. Such is the nature of prior knowledge.

One way, possibly, to loosen these epistemic bounds is to conceptualize modern organizations (e.g., colleges and universities, schools, corporations, hospitals, and so on) as constituents of still larger collectivities resembling constellations and defining of key social institutions: the economy (a constellation of corporations and other businesses), law and polity (government and its multiple agencies, governing bodies, networks, community organizations), medicine (hospitals, public health systems and organizations, health networks), education broadly (colleges, universities, schools, and other educating groups and activities), among others—the family, religion, the military, to name but a few. A social institution encompasses formal organizations (e.g., hospitals in medicine) and much more as well—for example, semiorganized activity that supports the larger institution's aims and interests (e.g., fund-raising for breast cancer research, public education about HIV-AIDS, medical publications and public health conferences). As a constellation, a social institution is composed of multiple phenomena (see Meyer & Rowan, 2006, especially Rowan, 2006).

Social institutions are territories of diffuse interest, energy, and activity that, collectively, articulate a socially acceptable rationale for society's support of a defined set of valued social functions (Rowan, 2006) that are, in a sense, talked and believed into being—normatively, cognitively, and regulatively (Scott, 1995). Although these social institutions may be cast as responding to constructed social needs (by virtue of their offerings, e.g., providing higher education, medicine, government) or cultural sensibilities (Baker, Eslinger, & Thorne, 2007), their very existence may stimulate such sensibilities and needs (e.g., for medical care, safety and social order, work and citizenship preparation). What may result are cycles of realization–rationalization–extended realization that, over time, create social phenomena that are distinct from the minds of their creators (Scott, 1995), thereby talked and thought about as "real" (Berger & Luckmann, 1967).

I view higher education broadly as just such a large-scale phenomenon, ratio-nalized and institutionalized mimetically and repetitively into being. Whereas much prior higher education research portrayed social constructivism in the con-text of particularistic leadership and organizational cultures, activities, or organi-zations (Bensimon, 1991b; Neumann, 1995; Tierney, 1988), I discuss it here on a far larger societal scale. In the expanded view, college and university organiza-tions are but partial expressions of a larger, encompassing constellation of con-temporary higher-education-interested activities: the social institution of higher education. That "constellation" is composed of *organizations* like colleges and universities but also philanthropies, academic software or other product develop-ment firms, professional associations like the American Association of University Professors, unions, legislative committees, and so on—and more diffusely, of *more fluid activities* (not so clearly organized) like raising funds for a cause, lobbying, grassroots organizing, and so on. In this view, researchers can ask (1) how colle-giate organization, discipline or field, or profession/occupation influence work on a campus, and (2) how the larger social institution (constellation) of higher educa-tion influences faculty members', administrators', and students' understandings of and engagement in the particularities of their campus work—including their knowing of what they are up to, and their learning to enact the social roles at issue: How does higher education, as a social institution, create the faculty member, the college president, the department chair, the college student, the college parent, the educational policymaker? (See DiMaggio & Powell, 1991, for a complete overview.)

Social institutions—here higher education—may be more readily conceptual-ized in longitudinal (historical) perspective than cross-sectionally (mapped out at one point in time). Looking at higher education as a social institution histori-cally, one notes that its membership, social positioning and power, and content vary over time—for example, as new populations (women, racial minorities, people of diverse ages and economic backgrounds) enter it in varying roles (as students, professors, support staff, administrators, policymakers, public spokes-persons, etc.), no doubt reshaping it from within. One also may consider how the larger social institution's social status and public meaningfulness wax and wan over historical time, or how its relationships to *other* social institutions change (e.g., shifts in connections between higher education and business, or between higher education and federal or state government), as well as how such change touches on local, day-to-day work. Institutional factors such as these may influence what goes on in a particular college or university more profoundly than classic open systems thinking can account for (see DiMaggio & Powell, 1991).

This perspective on higher education—as subject to social-institutional theorization, encompassing of organization theory but exceeding it—opens up the following questions: Is higher education, indeed, a social institution in and of itself? Does it have the kind of social standing and knowledge resources that would put it on an equal footing with other social institutions (the economy, polity and the law, the military) with whom, these days, it must regularly interact? Or is higher education less than a social institution, existing perhaps as a thematic construction that partially constitutes other social institutions, possibly being "used" by them? For example, these days does higher education exist largely as an arm of the economy (a powerful social institution)—producing new ideas and technologies toward industrial and corporate development and preparing future workers? Or alternatively, is higher education a socialization arm of the government, preparing future citizens and adults to act and think in line with socially or culturally dominant views of what it means to be a person, an adult, and a citizen? Regardless of its status—as a social institution in itself or as an outgrowth of other more powerful social institutions—to what extent does higher education share any of these activities with the K–12 schooling sector, and to what extent are these two seemingly distinct educating constellations really part of one?

From this expanded perspective, higher education's political standing among other social institutions—including what discrete colleges and universities do to enhance it toward their own good or that of the larger whole—overshadows more instrumental concerns ("making the organization run") but without invalidating these or the open systems model that defines modern colleges and universities as distinct from other higher education institutional components. Using a social-institutional and organizational perspective together broaches complex questions: Campus strategy for what or toward what? Organizational design that features connection with or openness to what, and why? Leadership of or toward what? In the larger social-institutional view, to survive and thrive—to achieve and be valued—is about far more than college leaders working on their own campus "making it" (i.e., as a competitive and struggling open system). Rather, to survive and thrive is about college leaders and others, in and outside traditional college and university organizations, working together to advance higher education as a valued social activity worthy of the "reality" that the larger social world grants to it.

MINDWORK

That the workings of the human mind matter in higher education organizational research is not "news." We see glimmers of it in the field's extant research on college leadership (Bensimon & Neumann, 1993; Birnbaum, 1988; Cohen & March, 1974; Kezar, Contreras-McGavin, & Carducci, 2006), organizational-environmental relationships (Peterson, Dill, & Mets, 1997), strategy (Chaffee, 1984), and campus cultures (Kuh & Whitt, 1988; Tierney, 1988). But these writings mostly speak to the cognitive organizing of organization itself. It rarely addresses the higher education substances being organized: subject matter or disciplinary knowledge, academic identities, teaching, among others. There is more to be organized, cognitively, in higher education than organization itself. All such matters could be subject to the study of organizing.

Consider this analogy: because learning differs depending on "what's learned" and who learns it (Shulman, 2004a, 2004b), so does organizing differ depending on what's organized and who does it. Like learning, organizing assumes a doing to, with, or in *certain thing(s)*; the unique "thingness" of whatever is organized (or learned) will direct and color its *organizational (learned) form*. Because a particular content constrains certain organizing moves while inviting others—while other content constrains and invites such moves differently—organizing varies by the stuff organized. Acts of organizing different things, just like acts of learning different things, are not commensurate; generalizing across discrete acts of organizing, (or learning) when what's being organized (or learned) differs, is risky. A particular organizing move will not apply in quite the same way to the varying "stuffs" constituting modern-day campuses.

Because *what gets organized* matters to how the organizing proceeds and what it yields, it will be useful to name classes of higher education "things" that are likely to get organized. In this view, organizing, typically cast as instrumental, is also cognitive (Weick, 1979). Campuses are composed of *multiple content domains* (classes of things to be known) to which campus members apply their minds in acts of organizing: (1) administrative, organizational, and governance knowledge, (2) social-institutional strategic knowledge (knowledge of higher education as a social institution), (3) occupational cultural knowledge, and (4) substantive academic knowledge.

Administrative, Organizational, and Governance Knowledge. As members of organizations, higher education administrators, faculty, and staff—and the researchers who study them—become conversant with normative views of academic leadership and organization, most of which reflect the open system. Some researchers openly discuss the open systems bases of their work (e.g., virtually all writers discussed in first section of this chapter), usually without questioning them; others seem not to see the open systems view that, to readers understanding the open system, drives their work (e.g., Keller, 1983). Still others (e.g., Ferguson, 1984) openly disavow the open system although their words of disavowal draw others' attention to the object being disavowed. Regardless of whether contemporary researchers support or discuss open systems views underlying their work, the schema pervades much writing on the topic; even writing that resists it draws attention to it.

Social-Institutional Strategic Knowledge. This knowledge domain addresses the regulative (instrumental, expedient, bounding), normative (morally persuasive), and cognitive (meaning-making, representational, symbolic) features of higher education as a broad social sector (Scott, 1995); as a social institution higher education includes colleges, more diffused activities, practices and public beliefs about college, and the like. Viewing a college as a member of a larger social institution (higher education) that, at some point in time, develops a meaningful relationship with another social institution (e.g., government, the economy) helps explain why college leaders believe "it's okay" or possibly desirable to align a college activity with the larger national economy, the military, or other social institutions at certain historical times while at other times not. A social-institutional view suggests that a college takes certain actions because, given what it means to be a college at a certain time, a college can do that kind of thing, or it's desirable for college to do it—it's normative. In contrast, an open systems view interprets a college as acting in response, primarily, to environmental pressure, concern, or opportunity irrespective of the ethos of the times. The open system does not clearly communicate socially pervasive views of what is possible, desirable, or called for by a college striving to act like a "good college" of its unique times. In this sense, a social-institutional view widens the lens on social and organizational reality that the open system views more narrowly.

Further, social-institutional strategic knowledge may express higher education leaders' efforts to associate their campus strategically with other intrainstitutional entities—for example, advancing a shared cause through coalition building ("partnership building") or striving to raise a college's status in the public eye by aligning it with respected peers ("benchmarking"). Alliance-building and status-improvement efforts merit particular attention: just as social institutions are stratified within society (the public esteems and privileges some over others, e.g., medicine over education), so are they internally stratified. Therefore, where, in a social-institutional stratification scheme, a constituent member, like a college, "sits" matters. A college on the high end of a stratification scheme (e.g., looks and acts like the larger culture wants a college to, or sets a standard for that) garners privileges—access to valued resources—that another college, on the low end, does not. The well-placed college may even be able to forge relationships with members of other (valued) social institutions (economy, medicine, government, etc.) in self-benefiting ways. But doing so requires concerted actions. Administrators may attempt to align their campus with a peer group that collectively attracts the support of other high-status social institutions (e.g., economy, government). Thus in forging intrainstitutional alliances, college leaders can advance the aims or status of their own college, the peer collegiate group, and possibly the larger social institution of which all are parts. Elevating one's campus involves elevating a collectivity of campuses, even as simultaneously, within the collectivity, members may compete with one another.

Researchers contributing to social-institutional views of higher education include Bastedo (2009), Levy (2006), Morphew (2009), Pusser (2003), and Pusser, Slaughter, and Thomas (2006). Drawing on Birnbaum (1983), Levy and Morphew extend conceptions of higher education organizational diversity and isomorphism. Bastedo's (2005, 2009) analyses of translation—between individuals' sensemaking (cognitive and normative institutional "pillars," Scott, 1995) and larger interorganizational policymaking dynamics (regulative)—are useful examples. Most higher education social-institutional writings focus on the national level, but some suggest that a global system may exist (e.g., Ramirez, 2006).

Occupational Cultural Knowledge. Occupational culture refers to webs of intertwined local and general knowledge associated with specialized academic work roles and practices for faculty members, administrators, and support staff. Typically, organizational entrants bring unique expertise gained elsewhere (e.g., professional/occupational training) to the local work site. Higher education occupational cultures have been conceptualized as *academic workplaces* (Austin & Gamson, 1984) and *communities of practice* (Wenger, 1998). Because campus life is created through highly diverse work, I consider here only that of the faculty.

Besides the local employing campus, the faculty's key home is the discipline or field that in early career (graduate school) scaffolded their disciplinary or interdisciplinary expertise. Although some scholars may "change fields" in early or midcareer, the majority stay with their original choices for life, though engaging in cross-disciplinary endeavor from time to time. A discipline or field, or subpart of either, includes the *people* in it (members) and the particular *knowledge* and *knowledge practices* in which they share (Becher & Trowler, 2001).

For faculty, occupational cultural knowledge includes knowledge practices of one's disciplinary/interdisciplinary (or professional) communities, and local work-place knowledge (of the employing campus). A new faculty member usually is not a complete stranger to her new academic program even on her first day on the job given colleagues' involvement, alongside her, in unique disciplinary knowledge practices. The newcomer may, however, find that she is unfamiliar with how the shared mores of her discipline come to life locally—how they convert into workday practices. Thus the new faculty member learns at the confluence of a cosmopolitan disciplinary culture (beyond campus) and a local campus-based culture. Amid this local-cosmopolitan mix, the organizational entrant learns what it means to be a disciplinary scholar in the faculty role she occupies "here." Some contributors to this content domain include Austin and Gamson (1984); Becher and Trowler (2001); Gappa, Austin, and Trice (2007); O'Meara, Terosky, and Neumann (2008); and Tierney (1988).

Substantive Academic Knowledge. This content domain focuses on the specialized substantive knowledge and ways of knowing of the academic organization's "core" actors: the faculty whose subject matter expertise (disciplinary knowledge), and efforts to expand and share it, constitute a college as a college, as opposed to as a business, government agency, counseling center, or something other than what a college is by virtue of its distinctive social charter: to advance substantive knowledge, knowledge creation, and learning. This content domain speaks to the *disciplinary and interdisciplinary subject matters and ways of knowing* expressed through academic research or creative endeavor, teaching, and substantive service. In emphasizing disciplinary subject matter, this knowledge domain deemphasizes organizational/professional vehicles for delivering content (e.g., curricula, academic programs, roles, policies, procedures) though recognizing their real existence and impact on "what's known" (see Gumport & Snydman, 2002).

With few exceptions (e.g., Shulman, 2004a, 2004b), higher education researchers have not plumbed well this knowledge domain. As field-based specialists themselves, higher education researchers appreciate that their own knowledge of others' substantive knowledge can but be a shadow of it (given their minimal immersion in it). Yet recent studies of K–12 teaching and learning suggest that educational researchers do have much to gain, for their own fields, from consideration of the epistemic properties of topics in fields with which they have but a passing acquaintance (Shulman, 2004b). Yet some higher education researchers have edged that way (see Lattuca 2001, 2002; Neumann, 2009). Although it can be challenging to distinguish subject matters from academic-organizational matters (see Veysey, 1973), doing so may help researchers improve understanding of college teaching, research, and service (e.g., see Lamont, 2009).

Developing Knowledge among the Four Domains. The four content domains described above are central to the collective mindwork of an organization's people. Each assumes "stuff to know"—"stuff to be learned." But some higher education knowledge may involve crossing them.

For example, Spillane and Burch's (2006) analysis of contemporary K–12 curricular/pedagogical pressures reflects both social-institutional strategic and substantive academic knowledge. Given that powerful accountability measures (standard setting, the testing movement) are now entering and actively reshaping the teaching-learning "technical core" of K–12 schools, Spillane and Burch offer a strong critique of prior organization theory: that in light of "loose coupling" between the "technical core" of teaching and learning in schools and external regulators, teachers (as professionals engaged in specialized professional practices with specialized knowledge) enjoy pervasive and continuous autonomy (Meyer & Rowan, 1978; Weick, 1979). Concluding that the new realities of schooling lead to very different conclusions ("loose coupling" is no longer as useful a characterization of schools), Spillane and Burch show how teaching and school leadership are changing. Given higher education's historical efforts to preserve the faculty's academic freedom and signs that intrusions now prominent in K–12 education may soon land in the postsecondary sector (see Arum & Roksa, 2011), researchers would do well to develop cross-domain frameworks and tools allowing them to track postsecondary phenomena like those that Spillane and Burch describe.

Though it is not prevalent in higher education study, some researchers have engaged in related cross-domain work. Bastedo's (2005, 2009) identification of "mechanisms"—concepts, issues, or problems that, by virtue of their translatability, can conceptualize college administration, organization, and governance, on the one hand, and features of the larger social institution of higher education, on the other—is one such example. Gumport and Snydman's (2002) study of the "co-evolution of [academic knowledge] and academic structure" traces relationships between bureaucratic and academic knowledge change that may influence what does and does not count as knowledge; this work reflects the authors' attention simultaneously to knowledge of administration-organization-governance and academic substance. Finally, Anderson's (2002) identification of a continuing but unarticulated "knowledge apartheid" within the legislated (hence, public) postapartheid South African nation required integration of social-institutional strategic perspectives and substantive academic knowledge: Anderson shows how a much publicized policy of expanded higher education access (signaled by new buildings, "open doors," government messages) veiled a substantively and demographically zoned postsecondary curriculum in South Africa, a pattern that later he discerned too in New York City. But how might a researcher conceptualize research that, like these studies, considers local organization while reaching well beyond it? For possible approaches, see Vavrus and Bartlett (2009).

Understanding Mindwork. Administrative, organization, and governance knowledge; social-institutional strategic knowledge; occupational cultural knowledge; and substantive academic knowledge are four content domains—subjects to which higher educators, and higher education researchers, can put their minds to—that align somewhat with traditional higher education areas of study: administration, state and campus policy, faculty and other specialist work roles, and teaching and learning. I referred to several of these topic areas in the overview of prior higher education organizational research early in this chapter. What's so noteworthy about the content domains as I rerepresent them above?

What's noteworthy is their framing less as things, people, or activities "out there" than as knowledge, of any and all, "in here"—in minds that are, indeed, shaped in a larger world of knowledge and knowing, yet a world to which those minds can contribute even while being influenced back. This is what I mean by mindwork. Mindwork assumes organizational actors as actively knowing and negotiating what they know—striving to grasp, understand and question, reframe, and help others reframe. Thus they learn; they also may teach: all organizational members (and not just "leaders") have the power to shape the knowing and learning of others. How, and importantly what, higher education faculty, students, administrators, and others put their minds to—and how, when, and why they change their own and each other's minds (or try to)—is worthy of higher education researchers' attention. Importantly, *what* it is that higher education faculty, students, academic administrators, and others know, and have access to knowing, *can* be orchestrated by others—central administrators, policymakers, government leaders—but also by themselves, willingly and agentically (Pallas, 2007). Much the same applies to the researchers who study all this. At this stage in our field's thinking we have yet to understand how to build higher education organizations that support agentic learning across the full organizational curriculum of what can be learned, and especially with regard to what organizational members and researchers can contribute.

Conclusion

I have made the following points:

First, the study of cognition in organization is not new; it has gone on for a long time, probably because organization requires interaction among diverse people's thoughts about what they and others are up to, what they would like to be up to, and why. Organization creates time and space, and means, for such interaction. Historically, research on higher education organization has attended to cognition but under different names (leadership, culture, planning).

Second, to advance understandings of cognition in higher education organizations we must examine extant knowledge of it. This involves (1) selecting, studying, adapting, and using ideas about cognition formulated in other fields but relevant to our interests, (2) surfacing our field's "prior knowledge," and (3) considering how the former (new ideas) may induce critical questioning of the latter (our prior knowledge), as well as how the latter is bound to shape our views and use of the former.

Third, whereas it matters that we surface what we know already (our field's core assumptions), it matters too that we flex (stretch, critique, reframe) that prior knowledge, assessing how (1) people who think and talk from differing social-epistemic standpoints may enrich their own long-held ideas, (2) individual campuses' connections to the larger social institutions they compose (e.g., education) or relate to (e.g., government, business) expand prior knowledge of higher education, and (3) traditional higher education knowledge classifications—the very words that academic actors, policymakers, and researchers use—avail and constrain meanings.

I close with a quandary: whereas I view organizational cognition as a promising lens, I do not believe it can address all we need to know about the human mind. There is yet the humanity of it all to grapple with: Who among our students and faculty will truly get to bring their learning to life—authentically—and who will not? Why? Who among them will have the space and privilege to reflect on personal meaning—pursuits born of burning curiosity and desire, of intellectual or social commitment, of needs to engage with beauty and goodness? Who will not, and why? Who among them will be relegated to partial or distorted learning, or to learning that is of little consequence to themselves, their families, their communities? How so? Not least, who among them will have the opportunity to create and designate that which others, beyond them, will learn? My last question broaches a tougher one: Who will be—who can be—tomorrow's creators of the knowledge that others, after them, will use as points of departure for their own creations? How might the possibilities of "who can be" be opened up so as to strengthen the utmost of humanistic pursuit? Questions such as these should be of concern—now and continuously—to students, faculty, higher education leaders, policymakers, and all who care about this. All are learners who, in effect, struggle for access to it.

NOTE

1. I discuss here only leading or representative ideas. Since this discussion is partly historical, I cite texts aligned with the thinking of the times in which higher education researchers would have been formatively influenced by them, emphasizing key meanings then in use.

REFERENCES

Altbach, P. G. (1999). Harsh realities: The professoriate faces a new century. In P. G. Altbach, R. O. Berdahl, & P. J. Gumport (Eds.), *American higher education in the twenty-first century* (pp. 271–98). Baltimore: Johns Hopkins University Press.

Anderson, G. (2002). *Building a people's university in South Africa: Race, compensatory education, and the limits of democratic reform.* New York: Lang.

Arum, R., & Roksa, J. (2011). *Academically adrift: Limited learning on college campuses.* Chicago: University of Chicago Press.

Ashby, W. R. (1956). *An introduction to cybernetics.* London: Chapman and Hall/University Paperbacks.

Austin, A. E., & Gamson, Z. F. (1984). *Academic workplace: New demands, heightened tensions.* Washington, DC: Association for the Study of Higher Education.

Baker, D. P., Eslinger, P., & Thorne, S. L. (2007). *Cognition, culture, and institutions: Affinities within the social construction of reality.* Unpublished paper. University Park: Pennsylvania State University.

Bastedo, M. N. (2005). The making of an activist governing board. *Review of Higher Education, 28*(4), 551–570.

Bastedo, M. N. (2009). Conflicts, commitments, and cliques in the university: Moral seduction as a threat to trustee independence. *American Educational Research Journal, 46*(2), 354–386.

Becher, T., & Trowler, P. R. (2001). *Academic tribes and territories: Intellectual enquiry and the culture of disciplines* (2nd ed.). Buckingham, UK: Society for Research into Higher Education and Open University Press.

Bensimon, E. M. (1989). The meaning of good presidential leadership: A frame analysis. *Review of Higher Education, 12,* 107–123.

Bensimon, E. M. (1991a). How college presidents use their administrative groups: "Real" and "illusory" teams. *Journal for Higher Education Management, 7,* 35–51.

Bensimon, E. M. (1991b). The social processes through which faculty shape the image of a new president. *Journal of Higher Education, 62*(6), 637–660.

Bensimon, E. M., & Neumann, A. (1993). *Redesigning collegiate leadership: Teams and teamwork in higher education.* Baltimore: Johns Hopkins University Press.

Berger, P. L., & Luckmann, T. (1967). *The social construction of reality.* New York: Doubleday Anchor.

Birnbaum, R. (1983). *Maintaining diversity in higher education.* San Francisco: Jossey-Bass.

Birnbaum, R. (1988). *How colleges work: The cybernetics of academic organization and leadership*. San Francisco: Jossey-Bass.

Birnbaum, R. (1989). The implicit leadership theories of college and university presidents. *Review of Higher Education, 12*(2), 125–136.

Birnbaum, R. (1992). *How academic leadership works: Understanding success and failure in the college presidency*. San Francisco: Jossey-Bass.

Boler, M. (1999). *Feeling power: Emotions and education*. New York: Routledge.

Bolman, L. G., & Deal, T. E. (1984). *Modern approaches to understanding and managing organizations*. San Francisco: Jossey-Bass.

Bransford, J. D., Brown, A. L., & Cocking, R. R. (Eds.). (1999). *How people learn: Brain, mind, experience, and school.* Committee on Developments in the Science of Learning, Commission on Behavioral and Social Sciences and Education, National Research Council. Washington, DC: National Academy Press.

Chaffee, E. E. (1984). Successful strategic management in small private colleges. *Journal of Higher Education, 55*(2), 212–241.

Chaffee, E. E. (1985). Three models of strategy. *Academy of Management Review, 10,* 89–98.

Cohen, M. D., & March, J. G. (1974). *Leadership and ambiguity: The American college presidency.* New York: McGraw-Hill.

Daft, R. L., & Weick, K. E. (1984). Toward a model of organizations as interpretive systems. *Academy of Management Review, 9*(2), 284–295.

Dandridge, T. C., Mitroff, I., & Joyce, W. F. (1980). Organizational symbolism: A topic to expand organizational analysis. *Academy of Management Review, 5*(1), 77–82.

DiMaggio, P. J., & Powell, W. W. (1991). Introduction. In W. W. Powell & P. J. DiMaggio (Eds.), *The new institutionalism in organizational analysis* (pp. 1–38). Chicago: University of Chicago Press.

Ferguson, K. E. (1984). *The feminist case against bureaucracy.* Philadelphia: Temple University Press.

Gappa, J. M., Austin, A. E., & Trice, A. G. (2007). *Rethinking faculty work: Higher education's strategic imperative.* San Francisco: John Wiley and Sons.

Gumport, P. J., & Snydman, S. K. (2002). The formal organization of knowledge. *Journal of Higher Education, 73*(3), 375–408.

Harding, S. (1986). *The science question in feminism.* Ithaca, NY: Cornell University Press.

Harding, S. (1991). *Whose science? Whose knowledge? Thinking from women's lives.* Ithaca, NY: Cornell University Press.

Jedamus, P., & Peterson, M. W. (Eds.). (1980). *Improving academic management: A handbook of planning and institutional research.* San Francisco: Jossey-Bass.

Katz, D., & Kahn, R. L. (1978). *The social psychology of organizations* (2nd ed.). New York: Wiley.

Keller, G. (1983). *Academic strategy: The management revolution in American higher education.* Baltimore: Johns Hopkins University Press.

Kezar, A., Contreras-McGavin, M., & Carducci, R. (2006). *Rethinking the "l" word in higher education: The revolution of research on leadership.* ASHE Higher Education Reports, Vol. 31, No. 6. San Francisco: Jossey-Bass.

Kuh, G. D., & Whitt, E. J. (1988). The invisible tapestry: Culture in American colleges and universities. ASHE Higher Education Reports, Vol. 17, No. 1. San Francisco: Jossey-Bass.

Lamont, M. (2009). *How professors think: Inside the curious world of academic judgment.* Cambridge, MA: Harvard University Press.

Lattuca, L. R. (2001). *Creating interdisciplinarity: Interdisciplinary research and teaching among college and university faculty.* Nashville, TN: Vanderbilt University Press.

Lattuca, L. R. (2002). Learning interdisciplinarity. *Journal of Higher Education, 73*(6), 711–739.

Levy, D. C. (2006). How private higher education's growth challenges the new institutionalism. In H. D. Meyer & B. Rowan (Eds.), *The new institutionalism in education* (pp. 143–161). Albany: State University of New York Press.

Merton, R. K. (1973). The perspectives of insiders and outsiders. In R. K. Merton, *The sociology of science: Theoretical and empirical investigations* (pp. 99–136). Chicago: University of Chicago Press.

Meyer, H. D., & Rowan, B. (Eds.). (2006). *The new institutionalism in education.* Albany: State University of New York.

Meyer, J. W., & Rowan, B. (1977). Institutionalized organizations: Formal structure as myth and ceremony. *American Journal of Sociology, 83*(2), 340–363.

Meyer, J. W., & Rowan, B. (1978) The structure of educational organizations. In M. W. Meyer & Associates (Eds.), *Environments and organizations* (pp. 71–97). San Francisco: Jossey-Bass.

Mintzberg, H. (1973). Strategy-making in three modes. *California Management Review, 16*(2), 44–53.

Mintzberg, H. (1987). Crafting strategy. *Harvard Business Review, 65*(4), 66–75.

Mintzberg, H., & Waters, J. A. (1983). The mind of the strategist(s). In S. Srivasta (Ed.), *The executive mind* (pp. 58–83). San Francisco: Jossey-Bass.

Morgan, G. (1986). *Images of organization.* Newbury Park, CA: Sage.

Morgan, G., Frost, P. J., & Pondy, L. R. (1983). Organization symbolism. In L. R. Pondy, G. Morgan, P. J. Frost, & Dandridge (Eds.), *Organizational symbolism* (pp. 3–35). Greenwich, CT: JAI Press.

Morphew, C. (2009). Conceptualizing change in the institutional diversity of U.S. colleges and universities. *Journal of Higher Education, 80*(3), 243–269.

Neumann, A. (1989). Strategic leadership: The changing orientations of college presidents. *Review of Higher Education, 12*(2), 137–151.

Neumann, A. (1990). Making mistakes: Error and learning in the college presidency. *Journal of Higher Education, 61*(4), 386–407.

Neumann, A. (1991). The thinking team: Toward a cognitive model of administrative teamwork in higher education. *Journal of Higher Education, 62*(5), 485–513.

Neumann, A. (1995). On the making of hard times and good times: The social construction of resource stress. *Journal of Higher Education, 66*(1), 3–31.

Neumann, A. (2009). *Professing to learn: Creating tenured lives and careers in the American Research University.* Baltimore: Johns Hopkins University Press.

Neumann, A., & Bensimon, E. M. (1990). Constructing the presidency: College presidents' images of their leadership roles, a comparative study. *Journal of Higher Education, 61*(6), 678–701.

O'Meara, K., Terosky, A. L., & Neumann, A. (2008). *Faculty careers and work lives: A professional growth perspective*. ASHE Higher Education Reports, Vol. 34, No. 3. San Francisco: Jossey-Bass.

Pallas, A. M. (2001). Preparing education doctoral students for epistemological diversity. *Educational Researcher, 30*(5), 6–11.

Pallas, A. M. (2007). A subjective approach to schooling and the transition to adulthood. In R. Macmillan (Ed.), *Constructing adulthood: Agency and subjectivity in adolescence and adulthood* (pp. 173–198). Amsterdam: Elsevier, JAI Press.

Peterson, M. W. (1985). Emerging developments in postsecondary organization theory and research: fragmentation or integration. *Educational Researcher, 14*(3), 5–12.

Peterson, M. W., Dill, D. D., & Mets, L. (Eds.). (1997). *Planning and management for a changing environment: A handbook on redesigning postsecondary institutions*. San Francisco: Jossey-Bass.

Pfeffer, J., & Salancik, G. R. (1978). *The external control of organizations: A resource dependence perspective*. New York: Harper and Row.

Pusser, B. (2003). Beyond Baldridge: Extending the political model of higher education organization and governance. *Educational Policy, 17*(1), 121–140.

Pusser, B., Slaughter, S., & Thomas, S. L. (2006). Playing the board game: An empirical analysis of university trustee and corporate board interlocks. *Journal of Higher Education, 77*(5), 747–775.

Ramirez, F. O. (2006). Growing commonalities and persistent differences in higher education: Universities between global models and national legacies. In H. D. Meyer & B. Rowan (Eds.), *The new institutionalism in education* (pp. 123–142). Albany: State University of New York.

Rowan, B. (2006). Then new institutionalism and the study of educational organizations: Changing ideas for changing times. In H. D. Meyer & B. Rowan (Eds.), *The new institutionalism in education* (pp. 15–33). Albany: State University of New York.

Scott, W. R. (1995). *Institutions and organizations*. Thousand Oaks, CA: Sage.

Shulman, L. S. (2004a). *Teaching as community property: Essays on higher education*. San Francisco: Jossey-Bass/Wiley.

Shulman, L. S. (2004b). *The wisdom of practice: Essays on teaching, learning, and learning to teach*. San Francisco: Jossey-Bass.

Smith, D. E. (1987). *The everyday world as problematic: A feminist sociology*. Boston: Northeastern University Press.

Spillane, J., & Burch, P. (2006). The institutional environment and instructional practice: Changing patterns of guidance and control in public education. In H. D. Meyer & B. Rowan (Eds.), *The new institutionalism in education* (pp. 87–102). Albany: State University of New York.

Tierney, W. G. (1988). Organizational culture in higher education: Defining the essentials. *Journal of Higher Education, 59*(1), 2–21.

Vavrus, F., & Bartlett, L. (Eds.). (2009). *Critical approaches to comparative education: Vertical case studies from Africa, Europe, the Middle East, and the Americas*. New York: Palgrave Macmillan.

Veysey, L. (1973). Stability and experiment in the American undergraduate curriculum. In C. Kaysen (Ed.), *Content and context* (pp. 1–63). New York: McGraw-Hill, 1973.

Weick, K. E. (1979). *The social psychology of organizing* (2nd ed.). New York: Random House.

Wenger, E. (1998). *Communities of practice: Learning, meaning, and identity.* Cambridge: Cambridge University Press.

PART FOUR

RECONSTRUCTING THEORY

CHAPTER TWELVE

Building Theories

Using Sticky Social Mechanisms to Understand and Improve Educational Work

MICHAEL N. BASTEDO

In the first chapter, I argued that organization theorists need to return to the study of educational work and practice specifically connected to issues of contemporary concern in higher education. This chapter seeks to explain how studies of higher education can more effectively build organization theory based on empirical studies of these major issues. To effectively serve the needs of both researchers and practitioners, organization theories in higher education need to have greater precision and theoretical weight to contribute to our understanding of contemporary practice.

In this chapter, I describe how defining and elaborating social mechanisms—intermediary processes that explain how one event influences another event—can increase the precision and power of organizational theories and improve our ability to engage issues of contemporary concern in higher education. This, I argue, is the conceptual key to making organization theory more central and relevant in higher education and to diffusing "sticky" organizational ideas among higher education educators and managers that are useful, memorable, and persuasive.

What Are Organizational Theories?

There are three primary ways to think of organizational theories (DiMaggio, 1995). First, we can think of organizational theories as a set of covering laws, a series of general but not universal causal statements, derived from empirical knowledge. The statements are general in that they apply across a defined set of cases other than just the ones under empirical study, but they are not universal in that they do not necessarily apply to all cases in all times. Thus one of the major goals of a covering law approach is to specify the conditions under which a causal claim does and does not apply. If you argue that "states are a major influence on higher education," for example, you need to specify the differences in influence among public and private institutions, the differences in buffering between research universities and community colleges, and many other conditions. This is the functionalist approach that is most common in the literature.

We can also look at theory in a completely different way: as a "surprise machine" that is complex, defamiliarizing, and rich in paradox (Gouldner, 1970). In this view, theory is primarily useful when it undermines our conventional wisdom about organizing, takes us to new places or new dimensions, and highlights the nuances and paradoxes of our organized world. This is "theory as enlightenment," which inspires us to understand instead of seeking to make generalizable statements across cases. This type of theorizing is fairly rare in higher education, particularly in organizational studies that are so often grounded in postpositivist paradigms (Kezar & Dee, forthcoming). One of the most prominent examples of this approach is Weick's concept of loose coupling, which is grounded in pure observation but which as a metaphor for organizing has proved to be illuminating for decades of students (Weick, 1976). This is consistent with Weick's (1989) famous description of theory construction as "disciplined imagination."

Finally, we can think of organization theory as narrative, as rich descriptions of a social process that are demonstrably plausible and tested empirically. Hypotheses are made within cases that are rigorously testable and which are then connected to descriptions of human behavior that could plausibly generate the revealed patterns in social processes. The expectation within this approach is that a nuanced and empirical approach to cases will, by nature, lead to knowledge that generalizes to similarly situated cases. However, a narrative approach should always generate more precise descriptions of social action than a covering law approach that simply seeks to identify patterns of behavior.

To fully understand what is theory, it is very useful to also point out what is *not* theory, which is discussed brilliantly in a piece by Sutton and Staw (1995). They argue convincingly that scholars often convey the impression of theory, without producing theory itself, which in turn confuses readers about what theory actually is. This makes it difficult for people to use and understand theory and makes theory less useful and relevant to people outside academia. Yet we must "build theory" because it is the sine qua non of original contributions to the literature, particularly in the disciplines or for those seeking disciplinary legitimacy.

Theory must, at its heart, convey the causal logic of social explanation. This is why long lists of *references*—empirical findings with literature citations—do not themselves constitute theory. Prior empirical findings might justify the inclusion of concepts in the theory, but theories at their heart are plausible descriptions of the logic among those concepts. Citing prior theories also does not constitute theory without describing the argument of the theory, the causal logic employed to describe social processes. Similarly, *data* are also not theory because consistent patterns are not causal explanations. It is also common to see *lists of variables or constructs* used as substitutes for theory—in quantitative studies in particular—but theories must explain the origins and connections related to these variables and constructs. The same applies for the themes used to organize findings in qualitative research.

Theories must also convey the *why* of social action, providing a plausible explanation of the reasons underlying human behavior. As a result, it is not adequate to make predictions about the future. (This is contrary to Milton Friedman's famous assertion that he did not care if his models accurately conveyed reality as long as they accurately predicted future behavior.) This is why *diagrams, figures, and conceptual frameworks* are not theory. Although these diagrams often do a wonderful job of conveying the concepts important to a study and relationships between them, they cannot explain why the concepts are important or why the relationships occur. This can be done only with textual argument. Similarly, *hypotheses* cannot be theory. Although they are precise predictions about the future, they describe only what is expected to occur, not why.

This discussion leads us to some conclusions about theory. First, many different forms of theory can be valuable, from a formal covering law approach that makes causal assertions and specifies scope conditions to an enlightenment approach that seeks to surprise readers and undermine conventional wisdom. Consistent with the argument of this chapter, the narrative approach is particularly valuable. Narrative theory generates the rich descriptions of social process needed to understand educational work and practice. The narrative approach requires rigorous empirical work but allows for many kinds of qualitative and quantitative work to establish the foundation for theorizing. Ultimately, the narrative approach provides the strongest conceptual foundation for theorizing that leverages the strengths of professional fields, yielding systematic and testable propositions without an overly restrictive or functionalist approach.

The narrative approach is particularly powerful when it seeks to develop social mechanisms. In the next section, I describe how social mechanisms form a conceptual anchor that helps generate precise theory. Social mechanisms also serve our other purposes: to help focus organizational theory on educational work, and to help organizational theorists make compelling contributions to educational practice and contemporary concerns. I then discuss some prominent examples of mechanism-based theorizing in the organizational literature on higher education.

What Are Mechanisms?

At the most basic level, mechanisms describe a generalizable social process by which one event influences the state of another event (Hedström & Swedberg, 1998). While most covering law theory would treat that social process as a black box, mechanisms seek to explain the causal logic of the social process itself (Elster, 2007). To describe this causal logic, one needs to describe individual behavior at a micro level, with the goal of explaining the macro processes that result from patterns in micro behavior (Schelling, 1978). The social processes that are identified are primarily judged by their explanatory utility but also by their realism, even if the mechanism cannot be directly observed.

Gross (2009) lays out a common set of characteristics that all mechanisms should have. First, mechanisms must identify the linkages that *mediate between cause and effect*. It is not enough merely to say that one event causes another event. If you think of X →Y, the mechanism is not X or Y, it is the arrow. And it's not merely that there *is* an arrow but *how* the arrow occurs in a social dynamic that plausibly demonstrates the connection between X and Y. Social mechanisms also *unfold over time*. There is a temporal sequence of events that causes X to influence Y, and effective mechanisms must specify both the events and their order.

Mechanisms are not universal, but they are *generalizable to similarly situated events*. There are many reasons why individuals behave in certain ways, but a mechanism-based approach is interested only in those events that recur in a particular order across individuals facing similar conditions. Each person "need not be subject to the mechanism, or affected by it in the same way, but a social mechanism is a causal process with some minimum level of generality" (Gross, 2009, p. 363).

Explaining the causal process underlying these mechanism thus requires a great deal of detail about specific events—in fact, far more detail than could be used to explain an entire sociological phenomenon. Indeed, it is the interaction of mechanisms that helps to yield broader sociological phenomena (Stinchcombe, 1991). Mechanisms are thus intermediary processes *that are necessarily less complex than the phenomenon they help to explain*.

To reconnect to our earlier discussion of theory, we can see that mechanisms share some things in common with covering laws: in particular, the requirement to identify social causes that are generalizable to new, similar situations (Steel,

2004). However, a mechanism-based approach rejects the most purely positivist claim of the covering law approach: the claim to universality, which requires assumptions about the ability of theory to model social life that most find to be, at best, overstated. The idea that all social life can be conceptualized, operationalized, empirically tested, and theorized strikes many as the height of disciplinary hubris. Thus mechanisms have a conceptual humility about our ability to model the social world.

While the rejection of positivism has led many to postmodern assumptions about reality and truth, and in particular a deep skepticism about patterns of causality, a mechanisms approach is more accurately described as postpositivist. Postpositivists believe that a social world is not merely perceptual but is real and can be observed. However, postpositivists believe that their perception of the social world is necessarily partial, owing to the cognitive limitations of the human mind and the inescapable biases we have toward our own perceptions. Postpositivist approaches are thus deeply pragmatic, seeing individual behavior as the result of cognitive-affective habits that are patterned and rooted in experience (Camic, 1986; Gross, 2009; Phillips, 1983).

What Are Some Prominent Examples of Mechanisms?

The salutary example of social mechanisms is undoubtedly the self-fulfilling prophecy (Merton, 1948, 1968). A self-fulfilling prophecy is an individual's false belief about the future that is made true through the subsequent actions of that individual based on the false belief. Merton famously uses the example of bank failures to explain how self-fulfilling prophecies work. Our entire banking system relies on our faith "in the validity of the interlocking system of economic promises men live by" (Merton, 1948, p. 195). However, if people come to believe through rumors or panic that the banks are going to collapse, the banks *will* collapse at some future point as customers remove deposits in excess of the bank's holdings.

It is helpful to point out exactly how self-fulfilling prophecies function as mechanisms. The prophecy starts with a false belief, a prediction about the future that is demonstrably untrue given current conditions. (The false belief needs to be plausible to generate collective action; there is a reason bank panics occur during severe economic distress.) The false belief leads the person to decide to take a particular rational action based on that belief—in this case, removing his or her money from the bank. Individuals removing their money from the bank causes others to remove their money from the bank, fearing that the banks will run out of money. The result is a cascade that leads to bank panic and collapse despite no fundamental instability in the bank's finances. Thus the micro behavior of a few individuals withdrawing money leads to the macro behavior of bank panics.

The self-fulfilling prophecy is possibly the best-known concept in all of sociology and long ago moved out of academia and into popular culture. A recent Google search of the term yielded 596,000 uses, and Wikipedia identifies recent examples from *Star Wars, Harry Potter,* and *Lost.* In *The Matrix,* the Oracle tells Neo not to worry about a vase. As he turns to look at it, he breaks the vase. "What's really going to bake your noodle," she responds, "is would you still have broken it if I hadn't said anything?" Perhaps classier examples can be drawn from the Bible and Greek and Norse mythology.

The popularity of the self-fulfilling prophecy reflects important qualities about the concept: that its explanations are powerful, useful, and socially relevant. Yet its explanatory power is relatively *narrow.* It provides a plausible and compelling explanation of certain kinds of behavior but cannot constitute the whole of any outcomes we would seek to explain. Espeland and Sauder (2007) recently used the self-fulfilling prophecy to explain, in part, how law school administrators acted in response to rankings. They found it a powerful way to explain how administrators made predictions about the impact of rankings and then helped make those predictions come true. However, they needed other concepts, such as reactivity, to explain most of the administrators' behavior. And explaining rankings is merely part of a broader effort to understand how people are influenced by measurement, the quantification and commensuration of the vast amount of data presented in modern society. The self-fulfilling prophecy is thus part of a toolkit of mechanisms that theorists can use to provide partial explanations of broader organizational phenomena.

In higher education, Burton Clark is the undisputed king of the mechanism. (It may be no surprise, as he was the student of Philip Selznick, who was himself the student of Robert Merton.) In his early work on adult education, Clark (1956a, 1956b) identified precarious values as the mechanism by which organizations adapt to emerging problems in the tasks they face, which then diffuse to the field and then to society as those values become more secure. He described how an adult education school, with relatively undefined goals, responded by necessity to an "enrollment economy" that forced it to be sensitive to student demands. This enrollment economy changed the initial set of values held within the school but later became a source of authority and legitimacy when it sought public resources.

In later work, Clark (1970) identified the concept of an organizational saga whereby charismatic leaders create distinctive colleges that help build intense loyalty and commitment among stakeholders. Contrary to his earlier work on the enrollment-driven practices of adult education, the saga of distinctive colleges was dependent on indifference to external concerns and the construction of a unique narrative around a single heroic character that forms the basis of an integrative organizational culture (Clark, 1972).

Clark's best-known contribution, however, is undoubtedly the cooling-out function (Clark, 1960a, 1960b). In this work, Clark describes how community college guidance counselors advise students who they believe cannot handle the rigors of college-level academic work but who have aspirations to complete a college degree. The guidance counselors "cool out" the aspirations of the student in a process that follows a general pattern: they introduce students to transfer programs as substitutes or alternatives to the academic course, encourage gradual disengagement by having students sample vocational courses, and present the student with objective data from their grades and standardized tests. On an affective level, the counselors console students personally, stressing the value of many different kinds of occupations and talents.

The cooling-out function is a classic social mechanism. Clark describes the specific causal process by which students who entered community colleges with aspirations to achieve an academic degree instead willingly and even enthusiastically enter terminal programs for vocational certificates and degrees. He carefully describes how this process unfolds over time through multiple interactions with guidance counselors. He does not describe the cooling-out function as a universal process that applies to all educational situations, but he does assert that it is likely to generalize to community colleges that are juggling multiple and conflicting organizational goals and environmental demands. Finally, the cooling-out function is specific and powerful, but it cannot possibly explain the entirety of the process of educational attainment. Instead, it describes an organizational process that provides a partial explanation for the general phenomenon.

Clark's mechanism was intellectually compelling but highly disturbing to those concerned about student access and educational equity. Although Clark viewed the process as a kind and caring method by which guidance counselors gave students options where they could be successful, many others saw an invidious process by which community colleges reproduced stratification behind closed doors. Regardless of one's view, the cooling-out function has become one of the concepts in higher education that everyone, from the first-year master's student to the college president, is expected to know, comprehend, and, most likely, try to avoid.

Indeed, we can see changes in community colleges in response to Clark's work. Deil-Amen and Rosenbaum (2002) provide an excellent case study of how a community college develops an ideology of "stigma-free remediation" to maintain student aspirations but which results in students having no clue that they are not making progress toward academic degrees, often after years of study. They describe this as an unintended consequence, which itself is one of Merton's classic sociological mechanisms (Merton, 1936). Thus we have evidence that the cooling-out function has become performative, an abstract model of looking at the social world that has changed the nature of that world (e.g., Ferraro, Pfeffer, & Sutton, 2005; MacKenzie, 2006). There is now good empirical evidence that the cooling-out function is no longer generally operative in community colleges (Bahr, 2008).

There are other good examples of mechanisms in higher education. Claude Steele's work on stereotype threat is an excellent example from psychology (Steele & Aronson, 1995). Stereotype threat occurs when one is presented with situations that carry the risk of validating negative stereotypes connected to his or her group identity. The result is a self-fulfilling prophesy—a false belief about academic performance that becomes true (the false belief being that lower average group performance generalizes to each member of the group). Steele and Aronson specifically address a paradox throughout the literature on the black-white achievement gap: Why do standardized tests consistently overpredict the performance of minority students at all levels of achievement? Steele and Aronson argue that minority students have subconsciously internalized social stereotypes about the intellectual inferiority of minority groups and that these stereotypes are invoked when students are given standardized tests and other assessments of academic performance.

To test this mechanism, they conducted experiments on high-performing students and invoked stereotypes through varying experimental conditions. A long line of empirical work shows that minority performance suffers when stereotypes are invoked either implicitly or explicitly and, conversely, that whites and Asians show gains when positive stereotypes are invoked. This has led to educational work to find methods that reduce stereotype threat in schools. An intervention that addressed how students think about racial stereotypes, through a brief in-class writing assignment, reduced racial achievement gaps by 40% (Cohen, Garcia, Apfel, & Master, 2006).

I have recently sought to develop mechanisms more explicitly in my own work. In a study of ethical dilemmas among college trustees, I develop the concept of moral seduction to describe the process by which trustees are convinced to engage in ethically questionable behavior through their engagement in other social institutions, such as business firms, families, and political parties (Bastedo, 2009). I argue that cognitive biases in decision making convince trustees that conflicts of interest and other ethical violations are justifiable by serving more important external interests or creating "win-win" situations that benefit both the trustee and the university. Over time, the interaction between trustees and their political parties, financial interests, or other trustees creates cognitive changes in their conceptions of duty. Moral seduction is thus contrary to conventional wisdom that unethical trustees are Machiavellian agents who seek to control the university for nefarious ends, although there are undoubtedly times when this does occur. Thus moral seduction does not, by itself, explain all forms of unethical behavior by trustees.

To be clear about what mechanisms are, it is useful to highlight an example of a well-known organizational concept that is not a mechanism—loose coupling. Loose coupling refers to linkages between subunits of an organization that are responsive but allow each subunit to preserve its own identity and "its physical or logical separateness" (Weick, 1976, p. 3). These attachments are real but may be "circumscribed, infrequent, weak in . . . [their] mutual affects, unimportant, and/or slow to respond." Weick describes so accurately the autonomy of parts in modern schooling—both its joys and frustrations—that loose coupling remains an image of organizing that has become indelibly imprinted in education scholars for over three decades.

Loose coupling is not a mechanism, however, and it never claimed to be. It does identify a set of causes and effects and ironically shows the linkage between them. As a concept, it is certainly generalizable across similarly situated contexts, which is part of its popularity. The concept, however, remains largely a black box. It does not unfold over time but merely exists in varying degrees across certain organizational types. Furthermore, it does not describe the causal process by which units become more or less coupled. It is not like the self-fulfilling prophecy, where one can identify the false belief, the prediction about the future, and the behavior that makes the prediction true. As a result, further empirical study of loose coupling has proved to be nearly impossible, in universities or anywhere else, despite a major attempt to give the concept more precise form (Orton & Weick, 1990).

Garbage can theory is an interesting case. Garbage can theory describes organized anarchies characterized by ambiguous goals, fluid participation, and unclear technologies, with universities identified as the most typical case (Cohen & March, 1974; Cohen, March, & Olsen, 1972). The garbage cans are constituted by independent streams of problems, solutions, and participants interacting to create choice opportunities. The garbage cans seem mechanistic in that they describe a causal process, unfolding over time, that brings the independent streams together through choice opportunities characterized by resolution, flight, and oversight.

Although organized anarchies were originally justified, in part, through a decision simulation, the authors have always described both the ideas and the model as more illustrative and metaphorical than as a rigorous theory (Olsen, 2001). Like loose coupling, garbage cans may be more accurately described as "famously imagistic" (Meyer, 2009, p. 51). And on closer inspection, garbage cans lack the conceptual precision needed to serve as mechanisms. For example, the streams entering the garbage cans are unlikely to be independent, as problems and solutions are carried inevitably by the participants (Bendor, Moe, & Shotts, 2001). None of the criteria for a garbage can—unclear technologies, fluid participation, and ambiguous goals—provide a clear decision rule for researchers. (What is the tipping point that moves a technology from clear to unclear, participation from static to fluid, or a goal from broadly understood to ambiguous?) As a result, organized anarchies have proved to be very difficult to falsify or critique through empirical research (Heimer & Stinchcombe, 1998).

This is not a comment on the inherent value of loose coupling or organized anarchies as concepts. We should all be so lucky to provide such widely useful metaphors for understanding modern organizational life—loose coupling and garbage cans will likely outlive us all. These are ideas that have resonated with literally thousands of higher education practitioners and scholars. However, it is useful to have a clear idea about what mechanisms are so that we can understand their potential to help us accomplish important conceptual and practical tasks in understanding educational work.

What Can Mechanisms Help Us to Accomplish?

A mechanism-based approach to theorizing has a number of advantages. First, identifying mechanisms requires *increased precision around definitions and logics of causality*. To convince readers that you have a new social mechanism operating in organizations, you have to be specific about identifying the who, what, where, and why of your case. If the theorist fails to be precise about definitions, the reader will have little idea what the theorist is talking about. If theorists are unclear about logics of causality, they will fail to convince readers that they have identified anything truly new or insightful about organizations. By labeling something a new mechanism, readers are encouraged to be critical about the existence of a new and untested idea.

For all readers of organization theory, lack of clarity about concepts is a source of frustration and reduces the usefulness of the concepts being described (Suddaby, 2010). But for writers, nailing down precise definitions can be a difficult and unpleasant task, raising doubts and anxieties about the original contribution of the work. It is often easier for writers to finesse the issue by providing somewhat vague, alternative, or even competing definitions of concepts within the work. A mechanism-based approach makes this kind of obfuscation nearly impossible.

Because mechanisms force writers to provide clear definitions and logics of causality, this approach provides stronger leverage *to critique, elaborate, and reconstitute existing theory traditions*. Mechanisms ultimately provide a conceptual toolbox from which broader theories will be constructed. Mechanisms prevent the theorizing process from becoming overwhelming by breaking down the process to a manageable size, which is particularly important for younger scholars and others new to theory. These scholars then have the potential to contribute to creating new theory or to critique and elaborate theories in ways that make the original contribution obvious. The precision of mechanisms also help scholars avoid the "what theory is not" problems described by Sutton and Staw (1995) and the "construct clarity" problems described by Suddaby (2010).

Mechanisms help to address Peterson's (1985) call for higher education to have its own organizational theories. Given the richness and maturity of existing theory traditions in organizational studies, it is unlikely that higher education scholars will have to develop broad new theories from scratch. And as I noted in chapter 1, our major theory traditions were built upon studies of higher education organizations, so these theories have not been imported into higher education so much as applied by scholars with more practical interests. Mechanisms, however, provide leverage to refine existing organizational theories to accommodate the important differences between higher education and other organizational forms, without taking on the immense (and, I would argue, unnecessary) task of creating new theories from scratch.

The precision of mechanisms also has the benefit of creating new theory that is *empirically contestable*. Once definitions and logics of causality are precise, the elements of the mechanism can be operationalized by scholars to conduct empirical studies, either qualitative or quantitative. This opens up new opportunities for empirical scholarship, instead of creating "conceptual cul-de-sacs" that are intriguing and insightful but cannot generate strong empirical support or a coherent line of work that convinces policymakers, institutional leaders, and others outside academia. It also allows us to develop strong, coherent theoretical research programs that build and solidify the field of higher education and demonstrate clear and original contributions, both empirical and theoretical (Berger & Zelditch, 1993).

Conceptually, mechanisms often have the benefit of *connecting micro and macro levels of analysis*. Most conceptual thinking works at either the micro level, describing individual or group behavior, or the macro level, describing broad social processes. While focus is a crucial issue in theorizing, both of these approaches suffer from treating the other component as a "black box." Today, one of the major questions is how individual choices interact to generate social processes, which requires conceptualizing both events and linkages with precision. So we saw how Merton's example of a bank run results from choices by individuals to remove deposits that then spread virally through a community. Connecting micro and macro is particularly important in the organizational study of higher education, which lacks strong coordination and yet generates immense benefits for both individuals and society.

Finally, I would like to argue that mechanisms benefit the field by providing *stickiness without slogans*. "Sticky" concepts are memorable and widely understood,\ and have a lasting impact on an audience's opinions or behavior (Heath & Heath, 2007). In a later piece reflecting on the uses of the cooling-out function in higher education, Burton Clark (1980, pp. 16–17) described the process by which he decided to label his emerging concept.

> This effort to rechannel students could have been called "the counseling process" or "the redirection-of-aspirations process" or "the alternative-career process" or by some other similarly ambiguous term so heavily used in education and sociology. I played with the terms then readily available but all seemed to have the analytical bite of warmed-over potatoes. While I was stewing about how to point a concept, a friend called my attention to an article by Goffman (1952) in which, for various sectors of society, the need to let down the hopes of people was analyzed brilliantly. Goffman used terms from the confidence game in which the aspirations of the "mark" to get rich quick are out-of-line with the reality of what is happening to him or her, and someone on the confidence team is assigned the duty of helping the victim face the harsh reality without blowing his mind or calling the police. Now there was a concept with a cutting edge! So I adopted and adapted it, aware that it would not make many friends in community college administrative circles.

Note that for Clark, creating a concept that did not "have the analytical bite of warmed-over potatoes" was a high priority, causing him to stew "about how to point a concept." Clark consciously wanted to provide a concept that would be memorable for people in the field, and he was willing to adapt a concept developed for another purpose entirely in order to do it.

Clark's effort was certainly memorable, but it did have a downside: it subconsciously equated community college guidance counselors with con men, which was quite contrary to Clark's intentions. Clark wanted to argue that guidance counselors were faced with fundamentally inconsistent demands from the environment and the cooling-out process was a caring and kind means to guide students to more productive avenues. Thus the labeling of the concept was highly successful in producing discussion, debate, and action in the field, but it also generated a great deal of confusion and misunderstanding. Clark himself was mightily frustrated by the common misstatements of the meaning of his concept in the community college literature in the decades after he developed it (Clark, 1980, 2008).

What Are the Challenges of Developing Mechanisms?

This seems to be a common problem with mechanisms—they are routinely misconstrued and misinterpreted, and the problem gets progressively worse as the concept becomes more widely known. In some ways, this should be expected; ideas tend to diffuse like a game of telephone, and the underlying process becomes more vague as the idea moves from person to person. This has happened quite prominently with the concept of isomorphism in institutional theory, which even in the academic literature has often been simplified to "all organizations become more similar over time" (Beckert, 2010; DiMaggio, 1995; Mizruchi & Fein, 1999). Often entirely lost is the concept of fields, how interorganizational networks shape and diffuse ideas that ultimately lead to structural similarities through rational action, and potential for divergent organizational change.

Yet in other ways this confusion is unexpected. The whole point of mechanisms is conceptual precision, clearly identifying events and the order in which they proceed. One has to wonder: How hard is it to remember that isomorphism occurs through networks embedded in specific fields? The misinterpretations occur nonetheless. And in Clark's case, it is perfectly reasonable for readers to agree with his identification of the cooling-out process but to disagree vigorously that this is a process that is either kind or caring.

This is a widespread problem for mechanisms. Merton's self-fulfilling prophecy has become so widely used in popular culture that sometimes it no longer has any meaning at all. Stereotype threat is widely interpreted in the media as explaining the entire black-white achievement gap in academic performance, and standardized tests in particular. A few years ago, five introductory psychology textbooks were found to make this mistake, failing to note that the stereotype threat experiments adjust for SAT score (Sackett, Hardison, & Cullen, 2004). It is so common that this is likely a sign that your mechanism has reached the height of its power—I, for one, cannot wait for the day that "moral seduction" is widely misinterpreted. But without constant vigilance, this is also the day that a mechanism moves from useful explanatory concept to vaguely understood slogan.

Mechanisms also have the potential to add up to very little if they are not embedded in a coherent theoretical research program. You could imagine our theories merely consisting of a sea of disconnected mechanisms that ultimately do not provide a systematic understanding of important organizational phenomena. As the Baker's Wife sings in Sondheim's *Into the Woods,* "If life were only moments, would you ever know you'd had one?" It is crucial that mechanisms relate and complement each other, serving as a toolkit for a broader understanding. But ultimately, these broader understandings of complex organizational phenomena are built incrementally upon moments of enlightenment that occur to many scholars across multiple generations.

Mechanisms also have the potential to be excessively functionalist or positivist in approach (Abbott, 1988, 1992; Gross, 2009). It must be acknowledged that my own language here, describing mechanisms as causal logics of action that can be operationalized and empirically tested, is to some extent a positivist language. My own conceptual paradigm is explicitly pragmatic and postpositivist—I believe that a truth about reality exists but that our understanding of that reality is necessarily partial. Seeking out that truth is a regulative ideal that, while never fully achievable, serves to push knowledge generation forward in productive ways (Phillips, 1983). I am also somewhat neofunctionalist in a rejection of dichotomies of social action and social order and in explicitly seeking to theorize around micro-macro linkages (Alexander, 1988). It is quite common for mechanism-based approaches to fall within these paradigms (Hedström & Swedberg, 1998; van den Berg, 1998).

It is true that interpretive approaches that reject the existence of any systematic patterns in social behavior are not well suited to mechanism-based approaches to theorizing. Mechanisms explicitly seek to generalize to similarly situated cases. However, this does not require a positivist or even a postpositivist approach. From a pragmatic (but not functionalist) perspective, the habits that are common to humanity yield patterns of human behavior that do not require reifying existing social structures or having relatively naïve conceptions of the relationship between structure and action (Camic, 1986; Gross, 2009). It also does not require thinking about the world as a "general linear reality" as represented in basic quantitative models of social science (Abbott, 1988).

Indeed, many mechanism advocates (including myself) believe that traditional statistical explanations are often unreliable, at least in part, because they fail to account for differences in causation that occur *within* individual cases (Elster, 1998, 2007). That is to say, statistical explanations tend to treat all persons within an organization as acting monolithically if they are labeled by that organization or its type. A good example is the way that most social science research treats families as a monolithic unit, when there is often as much variation within families as there is from one family to another (Conley, 2005).

Mechanisms do present a number of methodological challenges. For qualitative researchers, the single-shot, retrospective interview studies common in higher education research are unlikely to allow them to discover mechanisms. Nearly all qualitative research that has generated useful mechanisms has been conducted through careful extended observation over time. This is not necessarily ethnography or grounded theory, but it does require ethnographic or grounded techniques of observation and theory building. In particular, it is difficult to discover mechanisms that unfold over time, across multiple interactions among participants, without careful observation.

More extensive use of participant observation and action research methodologies has a great deal to offer organization theorists. Consistent with the themes of this chapter, I believe the careful study of work would be greatly beneficial. This would require observation of how participants interact specifically with work-related tasks. We need to analyze what John Dewey and David Stark have called *indeterminate situations*—cases that are "disturbed, troubled, ambiguous, confused, full of conflicting tendencies, obscure, etc." (Dewey, 1938/1998, p. 171). Stark (2009) argues that our goal in the study of work should be to understand the reflexive cognition of our informants when faced with the indeterminate situations presented by complex tasks.

To come back to Clark, studying the cooling-out function was an enormous task, even when studying only a single community college—the then named San Jose Junior College. Clark first conducted a dozen exploratory interviews simply to select the case study topic and site. He conducted formal interviews with most of the administrators and nearly one-quarter of the teaching staff at San Jose Junior College. Those interviews were conducted repeatedly with individuals *"over a two-year period; in several cases, the reinterviewing took up to a dozen visits"* (Clark, 1960b, p. 180; emphasis added). None of this includes the informal interviewing, documents, and a number of surveys he conducted over the two years. His methodological approach was demanding but necessary to study the unfolding patterns in the indeterminate situations he sought to explain.

Quantitative researchers also face daunting challenges. As Brint (2002) points out, organizational studies in higher education have been inhibited for years by a lack of quality institutional data in our national datasets. (Can anyone imagine finding a mechanism in IPEDS?) Mechanisms are tough to develop through surveys in general, as it is difficult, if not impossible, to convey causal logics that unfold over time through a simple single-shot questionnaire.

To use a mechanism-based approach to quantitative research, I believe we need researchers to construct datasets that combine detailed inspection of educational work across (ideally) randomly selected institutions, combined with the broader survey data contained in national datasets. Detailed inspection of education work might include collecting data from course catalogs and syllabi, registrars and admissions offices, financial aid offices, technology transfer offices and other units. This is undoubtedly challenging data to collect and will at times be made impossible by FERPA or institutional reticence. But it can be done. Good recent examples include the construction of course catalog datasets (Brint, Turk-Bicakci, Proctor, Murphy, & Hanneman, 2009; Gumport & Snydman, 2002) and the multi-institutional dataset examining patterns of grade inflation (Rojstaczer & Healy, 2010).

There is also a great deal of potential in experimental methodologies, which have been underutilized. As Steele and Aronson (1995) demonstrated, mechanisms can be elucidated through the careful experimental designs. Much of our understanding of the mechanisms underlying organizational decision making and cognition has emerged from experimental designs, from anchoring effects (Tversky & Kahneman, 1974; applied in Bowman & Bastedo, 2011) to hedonic framing and other mechanisms in behavioral economics (Thaler & Johnson, 1990). Strong experimental designs allow researchers to test the causal logic underlying mechanisms under controlled conditions, with the unusual benefit (for organization theorists) of participants who are randomly assigned to conditions.

Conclusion

In chapter 1, I argued that we need organization theorizing that is relevant to major contemporary concerns in higher education. This requires, I believe, reorienting the concerns of organization theorists toward issues of educational work that have effects on these major outcomes in higher education. Mechanisms improve the study of educational work by specifying the connection between the micro-level behavior of students, faculty, and administrators with macro-level outcomes in student learning, academic knowledge, college costs, and student access and diversity. They are useful to practice by providing sticky ideas that are memorable and have the potential for lasting impact among practitioners.

This shift is equally important for those of us seeking to carry the banner of organizational knowledge in higher education as an intellectual field of study. Ball and Forzani (2007) distinguish between research *in education,* which they believe should be conducted by educational experts, and research *related to educa-tion,* which may be conducted both in education schools and in the disciplines and other professions. They ask, What is fundamentally educational about educational research? They argue that educational research must ultimately focus on the instructional dynamic in schools.

Similarly, organizational theorists must focus on the organizational dynamics within universities that will most benefit from deep and nuanced knowledge about higher education. This requires studying educational work that has *organizational centrality,* in that it has the potential to explain a substantial amount about how higher education organizations operate and demonstrates our *core competence* in discovering unique insights that are unlikely to be duplicated by disciplinary scholars (Heath & Sitkin, 2001). We might ask ourselves the degree to which our existing work on higher education organizations meets these two simple tests.

ACKNOWLEDGMENTS

I would like to thank Patti Gumport, Jim Hearn, Liudvika Leisyte, Anna Neumann, Marv Peterson, Julie Posselt, Ryan Smerek, and Bill Tierney for their incisive comments on an earlier draft of this chapter, as well as chapter 1. Molly Kleinman did a wonderful job preparing the index.

REFERENCES

Abbott, A. (1988). Transcending general linear reality. *Sociological Theory, 6,* 169–186.
Abbott, A. (1992). What is a case? In C. Ragin & H. S. Becker (Eds.), *What is a case? Exploring the foundations of social inquiry.* New York: Cambridge University Press.
Alexander, J. C. (1988). *Action and its environments.* New York: Columbia University Press.
Bahr, P. R. (2008). Cooling out in the community college: What is the effect of academic advising on students' chances of success? *Research in Higher Education, 49,* 704–732.

Ball, D. L., & Forzani, F. M. (2007). What makes education research "educational"? *Educational Researcher, 36,* 529–540.

Bastedo, M. N. (2009). Conflicts, commitments, and cliques in the university: Moral seduction as a threat to trustee independence. *American Educational Research Journal, 46,* 354–386.

Beckert, J. (2010). Institutional isomorphism revisited: Convergence and divergence in institutional change. *Sociological Theory, 28,* 150–166.

Bendor, J., Moe, T. M., & Shotts, K. W. (2001). Recycling the garbage can: An assessment of the research program. *American Political Science Review, 95,* 169–190.

Berger, J., & Zelditch, M. (1993). *Theoretical research programs: Studies in the growth of theory.* Stanford, CA: Stanford University Press.

Bowman, N. A., & Bastedo, M. N. (2011). Anchoring effects on world university rankings: Exploring biases in reputation scores. *Higher Education, 61,* 431–444.

Brint, S. (2002). Data for studies of higher education: Are the existing resources adequate? *American Behavioral Scientist, 45,* 1493–1522.

Brint, S., Turk-Bicakci, L., Proctor, K., Murphy, S. P., & Hanneman, R. A. (2009). *The market model and the growth and decline of academic fields in U.S. colleges and universities, 1975–2000.* Unpublished paper, University of California at Riverside.

Camic, C. (1986). The matter of habit. *American Journal of Sociology, 91,* 1039–1087.

Clark, B. R. (1956a). *Adult education in transition.* Berkeley: University of California Press.

Clark, B. R. (1956b). Organizational adaptation and precarious values: A case study. *American Sociological Review, 21,* 327–336.

Clark, B. R. (1960a). The cooling-out function in higher education. *American Journal of Sociology, 65,* 569–576.

Clark, B. R. (1960b). *The open-door college: A case study.* New York: McGraw-Hill.

Clark, B. R. (1970). *The distinctive college: Antioch, Reed, and Swarthmore.* Chicago: Aldine.

Clark, B. R. (1972). The organizational saga in higher education. *Administrative Science Quarterly, 17,* 178–184.

Clark, B. R. (1980). The "cooling out" function revisited. *New Directions for Community Colleges, 32,* 15–31.

Clark, B. R. (2008). *On higher education: Selected writings, 1956–2006.* Baltimore: Johns Hopkins University Press.

Cohen, G. L., Garcia, J., Apfel, N., & Master, A. (2006). Reducing the racial achievement gap: A social-psychological intervention. *Science, 313*(5791), 1307–1310

Cohen, M. D., & March, J. G. (1974). *Leadership and ambiguity: The American college president* (2nd ed.). Boston: Harvard Business School Press.

Cohen, M. D., March, J. G., & Olsen, J. (1972). A garbage can model of organizational choice. *Administrative Science Quarterly, 17,* 1–25.

Conley, D. (2005). *The pecking order.* New York: Vintage.

Deil-Amen, R., & Rosenbaum, J. E. (2002). The unintended consequences of stigma-free remediation. *Sociology of Education, 75,* 249–268.

Dewey, J. (1938/1998). *The pattern of inquiry.* In L. A. Hickman & T. M. Alexander (Eds.), *The essential Dewey: Ethics, logic, psychology,* Vol. 2 (pp. 169–179). Bloomington: Indiana University Press.

DiMaggio, P. J. (1995). Comments on "What theory is *not.*" *Administrative Science Quarterly, 40,* 391–397.

Elster, J. (1998). A plea for mechanisms. In P. Hedström & R. Swedberg, (Eds.), *Social mechanisms: An analytical approach to social theory* (pp. 45–73). New York: Cambridge University Press.

Elster, J. (2007). Mechanisms. In *Nuts and Bolts for the Social Sciences* (pp. 32–51). New York: Cambridge University Press.

Espeland, W. N., & Sauder, M. (2007). Rankings and reactivity: How public measures recreate social worlds. *American Journal of Sociology, 113,* 1–40.

Ferraro, F., Pfeffer, J., & Sutton, R. I. (2005). Economics language and assumptions: How theories can become self-fulfilling. *Academy of Management Review, 30,* 8–24.

Goffman, E. (1952). On cooling the mark out: Some aspects of adaptation to failure. *Psychiatry, 15,* 451–463.

Gouldner, A. (1970). *The coming crisis of Western sociology.* New York: Basic Books.

Gross, N. (2009). A pragmatist theory of social mechanisms. *American Sociological Review, 74,* 358–379.

Gumport, P. J., & Snydman, S. K. (2002). The formal organization of knowledge: An analysis of academic structure. *Journal of Higher Education, 73,* 375–408.

Heath, C., & Heath, D. (2007). *Made to stick: Why some ideas survive and others die.* New York: Random House.

Heath, C., & Sitkin, S. B. (2001). Big-B versus Big-O: What is organizational about organizational behavior? *Journal of Organizational Behavior, 22,* 43–58.

Hedström, P., & Swedberg, R. (1998). *Social mechanisms: An analytical approach to social theory.* New York: Cambridge University Press.

Heimer C. A., & Stinchcombe, A. L. (1998). Remodeling the garbage can: Implications of the origins of items in decision streams. In M. Egeberg & P. Lægreid (Eds.), *Organizing political institutions: Essays for Johan P. Olsen* (pp. 25–57). Oslo: Scandinavian University Press.

Kezar, A., & Dee, J. R. (forthcoming). Conducting multi-paradigm inquiry in the study of higher education organization and governance: Transforming research perspectives on colleges and universities. In *Higher education: Handbook of theory and research.*

MacKenzie, D. (2006). *An engine not a camera: How financial models shape markets.* Cambridge: MIT Press.

Merton, R. K. (1936). The unanticipated consequences of purposive social action. *American Sociological Review, 1*(6), 894–904.

Merton, R. K. (1948). The self-fulfilling prophecy. *Antioch Review, 8,* 193–210.

Merton, R. K. (1968). *Social theory and social structure.* New York: Free Press.

Meyer, J. W. (2009). Reflections: Institutional theory and world society. In *World Society: The Writings of John W. Meyer* (pp. 36–66). Oxford: Oxford University Press.

Mizruchi, M. S., & Fein, L. C. (1999). The social construction of organizational knowledge: A study of the uses of coercive, mimetic, and normative isomorphism. *Administrative Science Quarterly, 44,* 653–683.

Olsen, J. (2001). Garbage cans, new institutionalism, and the study of politics. *American Political Science Review, 95,* 191–198.

Orton, J. D., & Weick, K. E. (1990). Loosely coupled systems: A reconceptualization. *Academy of Management Review, 15,* 203–223.

Peterson, M. W. (1985). Emerging developments in postsecondary organization theory and research: Fragmentation or integration. *Educational Researcher, 14*(3), 5–12.

Phillips, D. C. (1983). After the wake: Postpositivistic educational thought. *Educational Researcher, 12*(5), 4–12.

Rojstaczer, S., & Healy, C. (2010). Grading in American colleges and universities. *Teachers College Record.* Retrieved June 15, 2011, from www.gradeinflation.com/tcr2010grading. pdf

Sackett, P. R., Hardison, C. M., & Cullen, M. J. (2004). On interpreting stereotype threat as accounting for African American-White differences on cognitive tests. *American Psychologist, 59,* 7–13.

Schelling, T. C. (1978). *Micromotives and macrobehavior.* New York: Norton.

Stark, D. (2009). *The sense of dissonance: Accounts of worth in economic life.* Princeton, NJ: Princeton University Press.

Steel, D. (2004). Social mechanisms and causal inference. *Philosophy of the Social Sciences, 34,* 55–78.

Steele, C. M., & Aronson, J. (1995). Stereotype threat and the intellectual test performance of African Americans. *Journal of Personality and Social Psychology, 69,* 797–811.

Stinchcombe, A. L. (1991). The conditions of fruitfulness of theorizing about mechanisms in social science. *Philosophy of the Social Sciences, 21,* 367–388.

Suddaby, R. (2010). Construct clarity in theories of management and organization. *Academy of Management Review, 35,* 346–57.

Sutton, R. I., & Staw, B. M. (1995). What theory is *not. Administrative Science Quarterly, 40,* 371–384.

Thaler, R., & Johnson, E. (1990). Gambling with the house money and trying to break even. *Management Science, 36,* 643–660.

Tversky, A., & Kahneman, D. (1974). Judgment under uncertainty: Heuristics and biases. *Science, 185,* 1124–1130.

van den Berg, A. (1998). Is sociological theory too grand for social mechanisms? In P. Hedström & R. Swedberg (Eds.), *Social Mechanisms* (pp. 204–237). New York: Cambridge University Press.

Weick, K. (1976). Educational organizations as loosely coupled systems. *Administrative Science Quarterly, 21,* 1–19.

Weick, K. (1989). Theory construction as disciplined imagination. *Academy of Management Review, 14,* 516–531.

Editor

MICHAEL N. BASTEDO is Associate Professor in the Center for the Study of Higher and Postsecondary Education at the University of Michigan. Professor Bastedo has been a Fulbright Scholar in the Netherlands, Research Director of the Institutes on Public University Governance, and a Ford Foundation Global Policy Fellow at the Institute for Higher Education Policy. He has also been a visiting scholar at the Bellagio Center, Stanford, and the Institut d'Études Politiques (SciencesPo) in Paris. His scholarly interests are in the governance, politics, and organization of public higher education in the United States and abroad. His work has been published in the *American Educational Research Journal, Review of Higher Education, Higher Education*, and *Research in Higher Education*. His most recent research, funded by the National Science Foundation and the National Center for Educational Statistics, has been reported by journalists at the *New York Times*, the *New Yorker*, the *Times* of London, *U.S. News & World Report*, and the *Chronicle of Higher Education*, among others.

Authors

PATRICIA J. GUMPORT is Vice Provost for Graduate Education, Professor of Education, and Director of the Stanford Institute for Higher Education Research (SIHER) at Stanford University. Dr. Gumport's research and teaching interests focus on key changes in the landscape of academic knowledge and the organizational character of American higher education. Her academic publications include six books and over sixty peer-reviewed articles and book chapters. Her 2007 edited volume *Sociology of Higher Education* (Johns Hopkins

University Press) identifies a wide range of foundational conceptual and empirical lines of inquiry in the field as well as the broader contexts that influenced those developments. Her forthcoming book, *Academic Legitimacy* (Johns Hopkins University Press) analyzes the ascendance of industry logic—expectations for public higher education to adopt corporate forms and to develop more and deeper ties with industry.

JAMES C. HEARN is Professor of Higher Education and Associate Director of the Institute of Higher Education at the University of Georgia. His research and teaching focus on postsecondary education organization and policy. In recent work, he has examined the emergence and impacts of state policies in higher education; states' leveraging of university research in the pursuit of economic development; the development of new models for higher education governance, organization, and management; and emerging faculty workforce issues. Professor Hearn's research has been published in sociology, economics, and education journals as well as in several books.

ADRIANNA KEZAR is Associate Professor for Higher Education, University of Southern California. Dr. Kezar has published over seventy-five journal articles, fifty book chapters, and twelve books. She has five new books: *Enhancing Leadership Capacity on Campus* (Stanford University Press, 2011), *Understanding the New Faculty Norm: Contingent Faculty in Higher Education* (Jossey-Bass, 2010), *Recognizing and Serving Low-Income Students in Higher Education* (Routledge, 2010), *Organizing for Collaboration* (Jossey-Bass, 2009), and *Rethinking Leadership Practices in a Complex, Multicultural and Global World* (Stylus Press, 2009). Other recent books include *Rethinking the "L" Word in Higher Education: The Revolution of Research on Leadership* (2006), *Higher Education for the Public Good* (2005), and *Creating Organizational Learning in Higher Education* (2005) all with Jossey-Bass.

JASON E. LANE is Assistant Professor of Educational Administration and Policy Studies at the State University of New York at Albany, where he is also a Senior Researcher with the Institute for Global Education Policy Studies, and a Senior Fellow at the Rockefeller Institute of Government. His research interests include educational issues pertaining to accountability, cross-border engagements, and globalization. As a Fulbright New Century Scholar, Lane spent several months in the United Arab Emirates and Qatar studying the development of American higher education in the Middle East. He has published four books and more than twenty articles and book chapters. His forthcoming books include the *Handbook for Academic Leadership* and the *Multi-National University: Leadership and Administration of International Branch Campuses*. Professor Lane has consulted and presented research in more than fifteen countries in Asia, Europe, the Middle East, North America, and South America. He is also the co-leader of the Cross-Border Education Research Team (C-BERT), a group of faculty and graduate students interested in the movement of academic programs and institutions across borders. Their research can be found at www.globalhighered.org.

SIMON MARGINSON is Professor of Higher Education at the University of Melbourne, where he works in the Centre for the Study of Higher Education. A PhD graduate from the University of Melbourne (1996), Simon focuses on higher education systems and policy and comparative and international higher education. He was designated an Honorary Fellow of the UK Society for Research in Higher Education in 2005, a member of the American Council on Education Panel on Global Engagement in 2010, and as one of the Coordinating Editors of the worldwide journal *Higher Education* in 2011. His current research is focused on the global strategies of research universities in the Asia-Pacific, intercultural education, the creation of public good in higher education, and higher education and creativity in the arts and sciences. Simon has published more than two hundred academic books, chapters, and articles. He is a regular public and media commentator in several countries and has completed policy-related research for the OECD, the European Commission, and the governments of Australia, Ireland, Japan, Hong Kong, Malaysia, and Vietnam.

MICHAEL K. MCLENDON is Associate Dean, Chief of Staff, and Associate Professor of Public Policy and Higher Education at Peabody College, Vanderbilt University. He studies state governance, finance, and politics of higher education. His work has appeared in the *Journal of Higher Education, Educational Evaluation and Policy Analysis, Teachers College Record, Review of Higher Education, Educational Policy, Research in Higher Education,* and *Higher Education: Handbook of Theory and Research* and as chapters in numerous books. Professor McLendon serves as an Associate Editor of *Higher Education: Handbook of Theory and Research* and on the editorial boards of *Research in Higher Education* and *Review of Higher Education.*

ANNA NEUMANN is Professor of Higher Education at Teachers College, Columbia University, where she directs the Program in Higher and Postsecondary Education. Her research considers professors', students', and administrators' thinking and learning in three key sites: the classroom, academic cultures, and college organization. Her most recent book, *Professing to Learn: Creating Tenured Lives and Careers in the American Research University* (Johns Hopkins

University Press, 2009), conceptualizes professors' scholarly learning in the early post-tenure career with attention to career strategies for advancing it on campuses that may both support and constrain it. Neumann is the 2010 recipient of the AERA Division J Exemplary Research Award and was recently named a Fellow of the American Education Research Association. She is President Elect of the Association for the Study of Higher Education.

BRIAN PUSSER is Associate Professor in the Center for the Study of Higher Education of the Curry School of Education at the University of Virginia. His research focuses on the politics of higher education, the organization and governance of postsecondary institutions, the role of the university as a public sphere, and the impact of international, national, and state policies on postsecondary education. He holds the PhD in Administration and Policy Analysis from Stanford University and is the author, coauthor, editor, or coeditor of numerous books, chapters, and refereed journal articles. His work on international and comparative higher education has appeared in English, Spanish, Chinese, and Korean editions. Most recently he has served as coeditor of *Universities and the Public Sphere: Knowledge Creation and State Building in the Era of Globalization*, forthcoming from Routledge.

FABIO ROJAS is Associate Professor of Sociology at Indiana University. His main research interest is organizational analysis and its intersections with political sociology. His book *From Black Power to Black Studies: How a Radical Social Movement Became an Academic Discipline* (Johns Hopkins University Press, 2007) uses data from the black studies movement to show how social movements generate lasting organizational change. He has also published in journals such as *Social Forces, Rationality and Society,* and the *Journal of Institutional Economics*. His new project examines how social movements adopt the role of formalized lobby with data on the current antiwar movement. In addition to his research on the black studies movement, Fabio has published papers and edited volume chapters on computer modeling, rational choice theory, and economic sociology. He received his PhD in sociology from the University of Chicago in 2003.

DARYL G. SMITH is Professor of Education and Psychology at the Claremont Graduate University. Prior to assuming her current faculty position at CGU in 1987, Smith served as a college administrator for twenty-one years in planning and evaluation, institutional research, and student affairs. Her current research, teaching, and publications have been in the areas of organizational implications of diversity, assessment and evaluation, leadership and change, governance, student affairs, and adult development. She is an author or coauthor of *Organizational Learning: A Tool for Diversity and Institutional Effectiveness, Strategic Evaluation: An Imperative for the Future of Campus Diversity, Diversity Works: The Emerging Picture of How Students Benefit*, and *Strategic Governance: Making Big Decisions Better.* Professor Smith also served as one of three Principals responsible for the evaluation of the Campus Diversity Initiative for the James Irvine Foundation in collaboration with the Association of American Colleges and Universities in Washington, DC. That project resulted in a monograph, *Making a Real Difference with Diversity: A Guide to Institutional Change.* She also served as part of two U.S. delegations to Ford Foundation–sponsored trinational conferences (India, South Africa, United States) on campus diversity in higher education.

WILLIAM G. TIERNEY is University Professor, Wilbur-Kieffer Professor of Higher Education, and Director of the Center for the Study of Higher Education at the University of Southern California. His work pertains to access, equity, and organizational behavior. He has recently published a book (with G. Hentschke) on for-profit higher education and a book on trust in organizations. His recent publications include *Preparing for College: Nine Elements of Effective Outreach* (edited with Julia Colyar and Zoë Blumberg Corwin; SUNY Press, 2005), *Competing Conceptions of Academic Governance: Negotiating the Perfect Storm* (editor; Johns Hopkins University Press, 2004), and *Building the Responsive Campus: Creating High Performance Colleges and Universities* (Sage Publications, 1999).

J. DOUGLAS TOMA was Professor at the Institute of Higher Education and Dean of the Franklin Residential College at the University of Georgia, where he directed the Atlanta-based executive EdD. He earned his PhD and JD from the University of Michigan. His most recent books are *Building Organizational Capacity: Strategic Management in Higher Education* (Johns Hopkins University Press, 2010) and *Managing the Entrepreneurial University: Legal Issues and Commercial Realities* (Routledge, 2011). He is also the author of *Football U.: Spectator Sports in the Life of the American University* (University of Michigan Press, 2003). Toma wrote and taught on legal issues, case study methods, and strategy and management in higher education. Professor Toma died in 2011, at the age of forty-seven, after a long battle with melanoma.